Learning Packaged to Go

Learning Packaged to Go:

A Directory and Guide to Staff Development and Training Packages

by Barbara Conroy

ORYX PRESS
1983

The rare Arabian Oryx is believed to have inspired the myth of the unicorn. This desert antelope became virtually extinct in the early 1960s. At that time several groups of international conservationists arranged to have 9 animals sent to the Phoenix Zoo to be the nucleus of a captive breeding herd. Today the Oryx population is over 400 and herds have been returned to reserves in Israel, Jordan, and Oman.

Copyright © 1983 by The Oryx Press
22 14 North Central at Encanto
Phoenix, AZ 85004

Published simultaneously in Canada

Printed and Bound in the United States of America

Library of Congress Cataloging in Publication Data

Conroy, Barbara.
  Learning packaged to go.

  Includes bibliographical references and index.
  1. Employees, Training of—Audio-visual aids.
2. Employees, Training of—Audio-visual aids—
Directories. I. Title.
HF5549.5.T7C5945   1983   658.3′124   82-42921
ISBN 0-89774-065-3

Table of Contents

Introduction

Today's organizations, public and private, issue persistent demands for skilled and productive personnel. Careful recruitment, selection, and placement are essential, but even more important is the need to train employees at all levels for improved performance. Why? Training is vital because of our mobile workforce, the pressures for increased productivity, the diminishing pool of literate workers, worker attitudes, deficiencies in basic schooling, and the changing nature of jobs due to structural employment shifts, automation, and robotics.

One-half the amount of money that all colleges and universities spend on education is now spent by corporations on employee training for executives and managers, first line supervisors, sales personnel, and clerical office staff. These expenditures represent seminars, conferences, and institutes held outside the organization and in-house produced sessions, courses, and programs. They include also printed, audio, and audiovisual materials together with equipment used to instruct, coach, and demonstrate. When training expenditures in public agencies and institutions and small and medium (noncorporate) businesses are added to the spending on corporate training, the figure is truly astounding.

Many managers and trainers view using commercially produced prepackaged training resources as a cost-effective approach to build new knowledge, improve basic skills, and demonstrate desired attitudes. Hundreds of these "off-the-shelf" packages, also known as "courseware," are now available. Technological advances bring increased quality both to the materials and to the equipment they require. And, the profit motive brings an even greater quantity than previously available. As these audio and audiovisual training resources become more available and better known, they can expand the internal capability of an organization to build and sustain its employees' abilities.

Audio and audiovisual packages can describe how work units function, demonstrate the use of specific equipment or processes, portray effective problem-solving approaches, or discuss new industry trends. They can be purchased for consistent use over time or rented for one-time use. Many are adaptable for either individual or group study. Most have printed guides for learners and instructors that increase their usefulness, but few can be successfully used without trainer intervention to help

individuals learn and then to transfer that to the job situation. A skilled trainer selects and integrates a relevant media package into the training program's sequence, tailoring it to fit particular needs and circumstances.

Just as these print and nonprint materials are developed and marketed, guides, directories, and other tools appear to aid managers and trainers to identify what they need. Even so, most trainers do not use all media extensively. Some have not found media resources that meet their training needs; others do not know what is available and whether or not it may fit their needs. Still others lack the skill of effectively integrating media into a training program or the tradition and ease of using such materials. Budget restraints or lack of adequate equipment and facilities curtail some. In short, the use of media training packages is limited in most organizations.

Part I of this volume will aid those responsible for employee training and development by opening up the possibility of using packaged audio and audiovisual learning resources to supplement print resources and their own skills. An introduction for some, a reminder for others, trainers wishing to instruct using media training packages can use this as a reference sourcebook. The emphasis throughout is pragmatic. Chapter One describes the rationale that supports the use of mediated training materials. Chapter Two explores how they are used and how to plan for their effective use. Chapter Three describes the sources and resources required to discover, select, and acquire such packages. Chapter Four offers a guide to resources for trainers and managers who are considering developing in-house media training materials. In sum, Part I is a helping hand for trainers who wish to expand their capabilities and improve their effectiveness as they design and deliver employee instruction with the use of media.

The directory in Part II includes nearly 1,700 entries which give essential information that a trainer needs to initially select the most suitable possibilities on a given topic. Each entry indicates the format, date, cost, producer or distributor, and content description. Arranged by subject, the topics included are those broadly applicable to business, nonpublic organizations, and public agencies. They range from basic job skills, such as dictation and delegation, to skills of working with people, such as customer relations and communication, to skills of managing organizations, such as planning and problem solving.

Knowing these entries exist enables trainers to consider integrating such media packages into their training programs, provide a quick backup for when original plans and schedules fall through, or furnish prepackaged review opportunities in response to requests from individual learners or work units. The directory is also well-suited to the independent self-directed learner who wishes to improve present skills or prepare for new responsibilities or to those who plan programing for organizations that offer public education opportunities. Together, Parts I and II provide a fingertip reference aid, enabling access to a genre of learning aids that add both depth and scope to the repertoire of the trainer, the independent learner, and the program planner.

Part I
Using Packaged Learning Materials

Chapter One
Why Use Media Packages in Training?

A number of reasons reinforce the choice of media packages for training. All of them are important for those who plan and deliver learning experiences to an organization's employees. Certainly, many managers and trainers recognize the importance of media training packages. *Training: The Magazine of Human Resources Development* reported in its extensive 1982 survey: "Well over half the respondents (63.8%) indicate their organizations buy or lease commercially produced films and videotapes; 51.3% report buying or leasing prepackaged programs."[1] Of the 991 respondents from a broad spectrum of American business (no governmental agencies or organizations of fewer than 50 employees were surveyed), the greatest proportion of organizations under 10,000 employees reported budgets for off-the-shelf packages as less than $2,000.[2] Obviously, media package use is less widespread than it might be.

This chapter describes the major reasons given by practitioners who advocate the use of such training methods. Reasons range from the theoretical to the pragmatic, and all are important for trainers to understand and examine.

1. Instruction through media is effective for learning. Edgar Dale's classic "cone of experience" pictures the broad range of audiovisual materials and devices and relates them to how people typically learn. (See Figure 1.) The range extends from pure abstraction, that is, verbal symbols, to direct experience. Direct experience, at the base, conveys learning immediately and effectively. Remember "learn by doing" and "trial and error"? Levels of pure abstraction, the upper end of the cone, pose difficult and tenuous learning challenges for those who have no base built from either direct or simulated experience. By selecting and using audiovisual packages with this cone in mind, a trainer's design can weave on-the-job experiences together with focused, relevant media to build the base for more abstract learning.

When presenting a case study, a demonstration, or a dramatization, for example, a film can trigger memories and relate to the learners' experiences in similar situations, pointing to the basic principles at work. Learners then can relate these concepts and principles to their own situations and understand new ways to communicate,

problem solve, or supervise more clearly than they could through a lecture or a diagram intended to convey the same information. Media, thus, offer a context short of direct experience but close enough to serve as a memorable connector for learners.

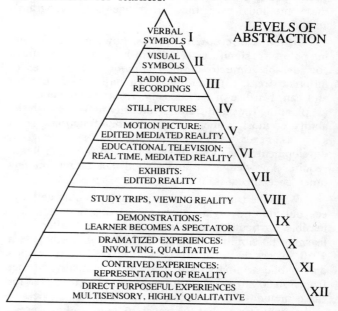

Figure 1. Dale's Cone of Experience.
From *Audiovisual Methods in Teaching*, 3rd Edition, by Edgar Dale. Copyright © 1969 by Holt, Rinehart and Winston. Reprinted by permission of Holt, Rinehart and Winston, CBS College Publishing.

With skilled guidance from a trainer, media's powerful ability to convey messages and create experiences has an impact at both cognitive and emotional levels. Media components can address well the essential conditions for adult learning: the need to perceive personal relevance in what is to be learned, respect for the learner's experience, the likelihood of addressing concrete and immediate needs to learn, and demonstration of the value of what is to be learned. Media are particularly useful because they can stimulate the active involvement and interaction that is the basis for most adult learning, offer a point of reference from which to work with others in discussion or action, and increase the degree of learning and retention, both of which are substantially improved by presenting visual and oral experiences. Media can illustrate the standard of performance sought and can serve both as role model and as a motivational factor. And, media can serve as a welcome change of pace, a variety in the training mode. In short, media, properly used, can respond to internal and implicit requirements of the learner as well as to the content of the training activity.

2. Instruction with media packages is cost effective. Given their significance in terms of learning, prepackaged media training programs are often more economical and as satisfactory as other approaches to training. In addition to using such training packages, 4 alternative methods are possible: using a stand-up trainer/instructor/presenter, sending learners to distant sites for training, bringing in consultants to do training in-house, or developing media training packages in-house. Each of these has its own advantages and disadvantages, and good training program planners will selectively use all of these methods over the full range of a program's activities.

In terms of cost-effectiveness, however, the following points are significant: (1) the in-house trainer requires considerable time to develop content in a number of different areas, (2) training is demanding and stressful and can, because of its intensity, result in burnout, and (3) planning time and training intensity may diminish the ability of most trainers to fulfill other functional roles such as needs assessment, evaluation, and program development. Use of media packages, on the other hand, requires knowledgeable and skilled facilitation but few other specialized skills.

With the travel costs skyrocketing, sending employees outside the organization to learn is less and less feasible, particularly in instances where viable alternative learning possibilities can exist in-house. According to a 1980 survey, between 30,000 and 40,000 short courses and public seminars, which are held annually, attract from 750,000 to 1,000,000 participants. The total cost for these includes $350 million in instructional services—and roughly twice that for travel, lodging, and expenses.[3] "Lost" employee worktime includes both learning time and travel time in addition to these amounts. Against these costs, training package costs are rising slowly, roughly in accord with inflation; training personnel salaries are increasing only moderately; and audiovisual equipment is generally dropping in price. Available packaged learning deserves strong consideration on the basis of such cost-effectiveness.

Media training packages can be rented or purchased in low-, moderate-, or high-priced ranges. No matter what the cost, however, such ready-made products cost less than creating, developing, and producing an equivalent quality in-house product. Media development requires specialized personnel, equipment, materials, and facilities, all of which are costly. Also, the time needed to develop such a package means it is not immediately available once the need for it is identified. In some instances, such a lag in time may be crucial. Where typical, rather than unique, training needs are addressed, "off-the-shelf" packages are usually preferable in terms of quality, timing, and development expense.

3. Use of media offers strong advantages. Most learners, familiar with radio and television, find media components used in training offer a clear message with a personal impact. They give a concrete image and content emphasis and provide on-tap expertise for minimal cost. Usually they can be easily adapted to various uses. For example, a single dramatization can be viewed as a portrayal of communication, customer service attitudes, or crisis decision making; it is easy to use and can be stopped or started to stimulate discussion or prompt written response. Media can be used effectively with an individual, a group of 20, or one of 200. Packages are convenient, promptly and consistently replicable, patient beyond belief, and run no risk of impairing their own ability by burnout caused by repetition.

An active trainer must confront the disadvantages of media, however, to create a viable learning experience. Learners may not have the skills to know how to learn effectively through media. Without orientation and a trainer's guidance, media presentations often appear prescriptive, implying results and solutions perhaps not applicable in other situations. Since the screen is a familiar medium, it may signal learners to expect passive entertainment rather than active listening and learning. A trainer can orient learners to prompt their critical thinking and the application of presented content. The trainer must become more than merely a package administrator by helping learners relate their personal meaning, learning needs, and work experiences.

4. Media training packages are abundant, available, and adaptable. The late 50s post-Sputnik effort brought scientific emphasis to education in the United States. This was followed in the 60s by Marshall McLuhan's emphasis on the medium being the message. Audio and audiovisual media became widely used in schools and military training. Producers sprang up to meet the emphasis, then they shifted gears to meet business and industry needs. First, media used presentations to promote business products or services directly to customers or to inform sales personnel about new products and services. Direct employee training was a later extension of that approach. Packages evolved as trainers and producers found the need for instructions and tips for making the most effective use of media.

Now, organizations that use media for training have 3 routes to consider. One is to develop and produce their own using the organizational personnel and either do or subcontract the technical production. Another is to contract for external individuals or firms to specifically develop materials to meet training needs inside the organization. The third is to purchase or rent packaged media programs available through commercial or educational channels. The basis for choice depends on the nature of the organization, its size, and the uniqueness and complexity of its training needs.

Those opting for the third choice will find a broad and rich selection of instructional possibilities available. Current materials, techniques, and equipment are of improved quality, produced by commercial firms, foundations, societies and professional associations, universities, and government agencies. In film/video alone, a 1980 study showed 289 producers and distributors with at least 5 titles for sale or lease, and an additional estimated 300 "one film" companies. The total of some 40,000 films and video includes educational titles in all areas with almost 4,000 in language arts (i.e., communication), 3,200 in health and safety, and 2,800 each in business and adult education.[4] Most of these are produced for school use and are closely tied to curricula, using school-oriented methods that relate content to age level. They are not relevant for most personnel training situations, but a substantial and growing number are intentionally aimed at general and specialized organizational training needs.

In addition to films and video, filmstrips and slides are popular, less expensive, and often as effective. Proportionally fewer of these, however, are produced for commercial marketing and distribution. They are often used for technical training and basic skill areas. Informational audiocassettes, produced with ease and in great variety, are being increasingly marketed. These often describe new trends, prompt motivational response, or inspire improved attitudes, frequently using professional presenters and a lecture format.

In a 1979 interview, Walt Carroll, a publisher, described the changes in the content areas available in prepackaged programs:

> Ten years ago you were seeing fairly hard-line how-to programs; subjects like time-and-motion studies, critical-path management, foreman training. By 1970, the field had taken off into management training. At that time, films were thought to cost a lot, so the elite managerial market was the first one to open up. Today, there is training software for all employee levels, even for entry-level and rank-and-file workers. Vocational and remedial materials also are selling well now.[5]

The adaptability of materials depends on a skilled trainer. A personal intermediary is essential to help ensure the relevance of content and approach, adapting them to the organization and its training needs. The elements to adapt are many: media brings key content experts, the voices and appearances of big names. New concepts—once "Management by Objectives," now "Quality Circles"—are introduced, described, and portrayed. Drama, analysis, and discussion reveal necessary skills and attitudes in supervision and interpersonal communication. A variety of approaches (animation, lecture and discussion, humor, dramatization, and train-

ing exercises) are shaped, supplemented, and directed by trainers to meet priority training needs.

5. Using media for instruction expands the trainer's capability. Even in a very large corporation with a substantial training and development function and skilled personnel, most organizations cannot meet all their needs for training within the organization. Use of media packages can offer a trainer high-quality content that is well-organized and presented but externally produced. Packages bring innovative ideas and outside alternatives to material otherwise presented from a trainer's single perspective. They can reduce preparation time and provide a valuable consistency when sessions must be frequently repeated with many employees. Media are especially helpful to the new trainer or to the trainer with peripheral subject knowledge or with little experience designing training exercises.

Trainers have a broad resource in media packages, but effectiveness depends upon selecting and using them in meaningful ways. It is the trainer's responsibility to fit media training resources into the sequence and design of the overall program, taking advantage of its quick response to need, strong impact, and flexibility. Here, in the overall program, is where the richness of media can be most fully exploited, expanding the capability of the trainer, the learner, and the training program itself.

The use of media does not replace the need for trainers, supervisors, and learners working together to identify and meet goals for personnel development. A instructor is essential to focus learning, to plan for it, to relate it to training needs, and to help the learner connect it with on-the-job application. Contrary to expectations raised by package producers and marketers, audio and audiovisual media (no matter how good their quality) are only minimally effective when used as the sole means of instruction. Consequently, to take advantage of the rationale for using media in instruction, knowing how to use them skillfully is essential.

References

1. "U. S. Training Census and Trends Report, 1982," *Training: The Magazine of Human Resources Development* 19 (10) (October 1982): 36.

2. "U.S. Training Census and Trends Report, 1982," p. 37.

3. Dominick M. Schrello, *The Seminar Market* (Long Beach, CA: Schrello Associates, Inc., 1981).

4. Salvatore J. Parlato, "40,000 Films Are Looking for a Home," *Instructional Innovator* 26 (5) (May 1981): 20–21.

5. "Meet the Man Who's 'Reviewed' More than 2,500 Training Flicks," *Training: The Magazine of Human Resources Development* 15 (9) (September 1978): 36.

Chapter 2
How to Plan for and Use Media Packages for Training

Developing training media in-house specifically to meet a single organization's needs requires extensive planning, considerable time, and substantial investment. Integrating commercially produced and generally available media packages into training activities, however, calls for consideration of them as an additional resource and modest expense. "Off-the-shelf" media training packages are intended to supplement and support an organization's training and development program, not to supplant its basic instructional approach or trainer responsibilities. Such packages offer trainers with little media experience opportunities to sample and experiment with these as they would with any resource to test the capabilities of the various formats and techniques.

This chapter offers the trainer who is inexperienced with instructional media brief guidance for planning and using media packages as a training resource. The first section offers an example, a systematic approach, and key questions to help focus important planning decisions. Special attention is given to planning for the necessary equipment and facilities when using media packages. The second section gives broad guidelines for using media packages, followed by a description of typical packages, and profiles of the various media formats most often used. Practical tips and techniques that enable a trainer to make effective use of media packages are included, as well as a list of selected resources for those seeking additional information.

PLANNING FOR THE USE OF MEDIA PACKAGES

Those responsible for training and development have their own approaches to planning and implementing an overall program with several specific training events and activities. They know the importance of a strong foundation that includes sound planning and evaluation processes. Nonetheless, a quick review of the essential components for a training and development program will establish a common context within which to relate decisions about if, how, when, and where to use media packages.

Planning for personnel training and development begins with assessing the needs of employees and those of the organization. Training that meets these needs enables employees to effectively and efficiently accomplish their responsibilities. An ongoing process rather than a one-time event, assessment is most helpful when built into regular functions such as performance appraisal or staff meetings as well as the more usual approach of special surveys and interviews. Needs of individuals relate to performance problems and reveal the gap between what is done now and what must be known and done to raise performance to the required level. Some needs do not call for training or learning. They may indicate instead a desire for different incentives or changed procedures or new equipment. Most organizational needs do not require a training response. Those that do, however, are usually in conjunction with organizational change—new equipment, policies, products, or services. To respond to these changes, personnel must learn and/or apply different practices. Thus, these needs do require a training response.

General training needs information, once collected and analyzed, forms the basis for establishing objectives for the overall program. Then, with more specific needs identified, objectives and designs take shape for activities within the program, such as a series of supervisory skills workshops or structured coaching for technical training or general orientation for new employees. Once program direction is determined from needs and objectives, overall program design is formulated as priority topics for learning are selected and key learner groups are identified.

At this point, the designer of training considers alternative learning methods and resources for the various activities within the program. Each alternative is then tested against the activity's objectives. Consideration must also include determining existing capabilities and constraints that exist, such as instructor skills, budget, facilities, and organizational policies. Media packages are considered as the salience of various methods and resources are calculated.

The following practical example will make this planning sequence concrete. An organization's supervisors have identified a high priority need as "how to effectively discipline employees." Their objectives for a training event state: "Supervisors will identify their own problems with discipline in their work units, will know the basic management principles relating to discipline, and will understand and be able to perform their responsibility to discipline employees." With this direction, the essential ingredients for 3 hours of training include (1) defining disciplinary responsibilities of supervisors, (2) showing the basics of why discipline is necessary (as well as how to do it appropriately), and (3) offering opportunities to discuss individual problems each supervisor has encountered with discipline.

At this stage, several designs would be developed. One possible design might include a presentation with handouts giving the organization's policy guidelines concerning discipline, followed either by training exercises involving simulation or role play or by one of 3 film/video training package possibilities. The latter choice includes *Discipline Interview, Discipline and Discharge,* or *Discipline—A Matter of Judgment.** When tested against the stated objectives, only one of the 3 films would be sufficiently relevant to warrant serious consideration.

As this example shows, decisions to use media packages occur during the planning process, but only after several prior decisions are made, including what message must be conveyed, who the learners should be, and what results are sought. The trainer weighs the advantages and limitations of the alternative methods and considers their feasibility. In this example, specific questions must be raised: Is the desired package, equipment, and space available? What is the cost? Does the time scheduled allow for all activities and discussion? How will each supervisor identify his/her problems with discipline? Who might present the organization's perspective of the supervisors' disciplinary role? Who can devise and manage the training exercises? What points would need to be drawn from a film/video discussion? Answers to questions such as these would be checked for each alternative method considered. The alternatives, tested against the objectives, then lead to a choice among methods and techniques for the activity's design.

Systematic Approach and Key Questions

What can assist trainers as they consider appropriate media possibilities for the training needed? Although no "magic" formula exists, trainers can use a systematic planning approach to obtain the essential information with which they then can make sound media choices.

* These titles are included in Part II of this volume.

Areas to consider include what learning results are sought, what media can be used, and what other resources are available. In each of these areas, key questions will assist trainers to systematically plan their use of media packages.

Before exploring these areas in some detail, certain assumptions must be made explicit. Understanding these assumptions is essential to approach media decision-making steps with clarity.
1. Media here refers to dynamic audio and audiovisual training packages, not to static instructional aids such as overhead visuals, flipcharts, or chalkboards.
2. Media packages are simply one available resource among many that may help accomplish a given training assignment.
3. Media packages include those generally available for purchase or rental from a producer or distributor, not those created specifically for a designated organization.
4. Before media possibilities are considered, a planning process must determine who the learners are, why they are to be trained, what they need to know or do, and the level of performance required.

In considering the selection and use of media packages, as with any other resource, determine first what results are sought from the training. The first question is whether behavioral change is to occur through use of training media. If the answer is "no," then the result sought is most likely that of information transfer. Then, the major requirements are that the media package includes the needed information in a comprehensible form. Addressing these subsequent questions will more specifically guide package selection:

- Is the information possible to transfer one-to-one? In a group? Either?
- Does the information require a visual component? An auditory component? Both?
- Does the message need to communicate information that is new to the learner? Information that is familiar?
- Must the information be presented in a particular sequence?

If, on the other hand, the answer is "yes" to the question of whether behavioral change is to occur through use of the training media, then selection and use of the appropriate media package would be guided by these questions:

- What must learners do differently?
- What must learners know in order to make the behavioral change sought?
- Is the desired behavior new to the learners? Familiar?
- What sequence must occur to be understood by learners?

- How specific must the knowledge be to enable learners to make behavioral change?
- How closely must portrayal replicate on-the-job performance for learners to understand its application?
- Is practice of the behavior during training desirable? Is it feasible?
- What attitudes are required to make the desired behavioral change?
- In what ways is the media package likely to guide learners to meet the required performance level sought?
- How does the impact of the media package relate to other design components being planned?

Keeping in mind the training objectives, the answers to the questions above will help the selection of the types and formats and titles of media packages.

The other area to systematically examine is that of the media package itself and other related resources. Useful questions to use for planning follow:

- What is known about the media package being considered?
- Has it been previewed? Can it be?
- Is the desired media package available at the time and place it is needed?
- What other resources (e.g., equipment and facilities) are required to make the media package effective?
- Is its cost feasible in relation to what it is expected to accomplish?
- Does it cover the essential content required to meet the purpose of the training?
- Is the style of the media package appropriate to the tone sought for the training activity?
- Does the package format being considered include the capabilities and advantages needed for the purposes intended?
- Will the limits and disadvantages of the format affect the training design or results significantly?
- What expertise is required to make the media effective?
- Is that expertise available?
- How will the media package be integrated with other components?
- Will learner preparation and/or follow-up reinforcement be required to achieve the minimum level of performance sought? Is this feasible?
- Does the media package offer any benefits that are not otherwise obtainable?
- Is the package feasible for learners working individually as well as those working in a group training situation?

The answers to some of these questions require previewing the media training packages being considered. No matter how relevant a promotional brochure or a review may seem, it cannot ensure that the package will not be distractive or even counterproductive. Only pre-viewing can test this. For this reason, previews are essential.

The questions about the learning results sought and the media itself are not universally applicable, but they help in evaluating the possibilities of using media packages in general or the use of a specific media package. Answers cannot be reduced to a simple prescription of what will work unfailingly in any given situation. Too many uncontrollable elements are present: the motivation of the learners, the skills of the trainer, the resourcefulness of the group, the tenor of the organization. Using these questions, however, encourages a systematic exploration of some key factors that are within the trainer's control.

Equipment and Facilities

Media packages require equipment and/or facilities for their use. Planning must take these into account. Investment in these elements in addition to package rental or purchase fees can be costly. Appropriate equipment must be owned, leased, rented, or borrowed. Organizations without needed projectors for film, filmstrip or slides, or video players and monitors can rent or borrow equipment. Later, when the extent of media use warrants it, longer term arrangements such as lease or purchase can be explored for equipment most often required. Cooperative arrangements with related or nearby organizations or with various organizational divisions are often possible and cost effective.

The major consideration with equipment is its compatibility with the formats of the packages used, and the techniques the trainer wants to use. If the package and the equipment are compatible but do not allow the trainer to use a desired technique, equipment use will be frustrating and difficult because of its limitations. Thus, equipment capability, media formats, and training techniques need to be considered before equipment is acquired.

Selecting equipment is challenging. Justification must include both the type of anticipated use and the feasibility in terms of budget, workloads, and facilities. When the equipment will be used for organizational purposes in addition to training, budgeting is made easier but scheduling then may become difficult. However, not only must decision makers anticipate what formats will predominate for training purposes, but they must also anticipate future uses for the equipment (in addition to training). Then, once such specifications are clear, based on the anticipated uses, selection of specific brands and models should rest with a knowledgeable and experienced media specialist.

Related investments must also be considered. Once equipment such as projectors, players, and monitors are selected and purchased, skilled personnel must operate them. Provisions must also be made for servicing, maintenance, and storage. These responsibilities may, in turn, require training of in-house personnel. Or maintenance and servicing contracts outside the organization may be possible. Storage will require space allocation. All of these expenses are ongoing and proportional to the degree of equipment use.

In addition to audio and audiovisual equipment storage, the space in which training is done warrants review. Using media packages requires adequate space in which to accommodate training groups so they can see, hear well, and work comfortably. The usual conference room may not be sufficient for good media use because it has too few electrical outlets, has too much light, or is of the wrong shape and size. Three choices are apparent: making do, upgrading present facilities, or changing the training site. Once again, collaborative arrangements may be possible with other organizations or among in-house units. As with equipment, facilities can be rented in most areas. This, however, removes learners from the worksite, a move that may not be desirable due to travel arrangements or schedule adjustments.

Even a skilled trainer working with a high quality media package may find an inhospitable environment counterproductive for effective learning. Consequently, upgrading present training facilities may be a sound option. Particular aspects to address would be (1) room shape and size, (2) acoustics and visibility, and (3) lighting and temperature control. Each of these factors can limit the number of learners and media components that can be used effectively. Hanging screens and monitors from the ceiling saves floor space for group work and improves visibility. Audiovisual controls should be simple to operate and located where the presenter has easy access to them.

Since the use of media packages often opens up new possibilities for self-study by individual learners, facilities planning can include learning carrels, study areas, and access to the media packages. Media packages can be used to broaden training potential by videotaping role plays for feedback or even for in-house production of at least modest training segments. Trainers finding these potentials useful will want to incorporate them in their planning for facilities and equipment.

To make the most of media investments, planning for training equipment and facilities must accommodate today's needs and predict with some accuracy those of tomorrow. Once a commitment to mediated training goes beyond occasional use, the alert trainer must be knowledgeable about new trends and emerging frontiers of training. Developing technology and equipment advances, innovative training techniques, and trends in package development are all areas that affect the selection and planning of equipment and facilities needed for regular use of mediated training.

From the beginning, planning for the use of media packages requires the trainer to experiment with existing packages, test media approach to determine how to incorporate packages into specific learning activities, and explore their possibilities within an overall training program addressing a variety of learning needs. An experimental stage offers the trainer the opportunity to apply evaluative criteria to media packages, to build personal facilitative skills using media, and to explore equipment and facility capabilities. This stage tests hypotheses and yields experience vital to planning subsequent stages. Thus, using media packages on a limited scale builds decision-making capabilities for sound planning if more extended use seems warranted. The experimental stage brings to be surface the potentials in learners, in packages, in equipment, in facilities, and, most of all, in the trainer.

USING MEDIA PACKAGES

Planning provides a base for the overall training and development program and for the many specific training activities it includes. When well-planned resources such as relevant and effective media training packages are introduced into training activities, they enable learners to acquire needed knowledge, skills, and attitudes. A media package cannot do this alone, but it is one component—sometimes a major component—in an overall training design. Training design brings together content and appropriate methods, such as media, in a supportive learning environment ready for motivated and involved learners. The design comes alive when the trainer assembles the planned decisions and components and the concept is translated into action.

Media Package Formats

Presently, commercially available media training packages feature basic audio and audiovisual formats already familiar to us from school, mass media, consumer and adult education, and organizational communication channels. Although specialized variations in format are sometimes attempted for instructional purposes with both consumers and employees, these have been few and shortlived. In effect, a fair amount of standardization exists. This allows trainers to make use of such packages with reliable and relatively modest equipment investments.

A typical package is intended for instructional purposes, usually for a specified audience, such as first-time supervisors, clerical staff, retail clerks, office managers, or forklift operators. Or the topic may focus on building specific skills, such as machine transcription or delegation. It may stress safe equipment operation or serve to introduce employees with expanded responsibilities to a greater knowledge of the scope and implication of those responsibilities. It may demonstrate preferred behavior and attitudes for those involved with customer service. A few packages will have broad application to many audiences and may convey knowledge and skills and attitude development simultaneously, such as those on time management, career development, communication, and interpersonal relations.

Film or video often use a dramatized situation to illustrate a problem, such as one typically encountered by supervisors needing to delegate. Often, a character in the portrayal or a narrator offers the solution to the dilemma and resolves the dramatized problem situation, pointing out the principles at work. In the case of a typical skills development portrayal, the sequence of steps is demonstrated and narrated, highlighting the crucial points and pinpointing potential problem areas.

Audiocassettes are more likely to present narrated information, sometimes in a lecture style. Audio portrayals can often be used to demonstrate communication techniques, sales presentations, or memory devices. Presentations will often convene experts to discuss trends in a particular industry, in management styles, or in organizational problem-solving approaches. Discussion formats also use practitioners with guidance from a moderator. The presentation format usually uses professional narrators.

Both audiovisual and audio packages often include print materials to supplement the nonprint form. Print materials make the package a true package, as distinct from a film or an audiocassette alone. Print materials, although not standardized, do fall into patterns. Those intended for the trainer or instructor typically consist of a "leader's guide" that describes the content and offers suggestions for how to use the media effectively. Materials intended for the learner may include background readings, abstracts of the key points, or thought-provoking questions for individual or collective response. Print materials are not intended as the primary instructional tool. Rather, they are intended to aid the trainer in making full use of the media format.

The predominant media formats in training packages include films, videotapes/cassettes, audiocassettes, slides, filmstrips, and filmstrip cartridges. The following quick "snapshots" of each format provide basic descriptions and terminology, outline their primary training uses, and sketch their chief advantages and disadvantages. The end of the section describes typical print materials that often come with packages. Given the perspective of the trainer considering use of media training packages, only those aspects important to "off-the-shelf" packages are detailed.

Film. Film combines audio and visual capabilities bringing continuity, motion, sound, and color together in a single medium. Film widths most commonly used in training are 16mm and super 8mm, with 8mm a trailing third. The 8mm is one-half the size of the 16mm and is usually used for small groups only. Super 8mm increases the size of the projected image to three-eighths the size of 16mm, although the width of the film is still 8mm. Both 16mm and super 8mm give high quality image, color, and sound. Sound is recorded on film by either optical or magnetic methods. Special effects, such as slow motion or high speed and split or multiple images, are possible.

Film's best attributes are its permanence, quality, and usefulness for large audiences.

Equipment required for film use includes the appropriately sized projector with speakers and a screen or wall on which to project the image. Film may be threaded into the projector with a manual, semiautomatic, or automatic mechanism. Projection may be either front or rear. Super 8mm projectors are very compact; some include a built-in screen that makes the unit self-contained, particularly useful for individual or small group study, as well as possibilities for slow motion, stop action, and single-frame sequencing.

The primary use of films is to illustrate realistic events and processes. Training films often use dramatizations with commentary to present concepts, portray situations, and model behavior or attitudes. Technical training films show action sequences to demonstrate techniques and equipment use. Dramatization with motion, animation, graphics, and still pictures can all be incorporated into a single film.

The advantages of film include its ability to communicate directly and effectively and to show situations that individuals may not yet have experienced themselves. Consequently, through film, a group of learners share a common experience that can serve as a base for instructional exercises or discussion. Good equipment produces quality image and sound. Film can easily be edited and reproduced either on film or video, and it is not easily erased by accident. Because of standardization, projection equipment is easily obtainable.

The disadvantages of film include expense as a result of its high production costs. Films require maintenance and care in handling. They cannot be erased and reused. If they are not well-produced, the lack of "slickness" is apparent to audiences, possibly creating a distraction from learning. Super 8mm has diminished quality when projected on a large screen, limiting its use with large groups.

Video. Video, like film, combines audio and visual impressions and can integrate motion, still pictures, animation, and graphics. Images on tape are transmitted with a video player that connects with a cathode ray tube, such as a television monitor. The tape is either on reels or in cassettes, with the predominant trend toward cassettes. Image and sound quality (with good equipment) are equal to film. Video formats and equipment are in a great state of flux. Tape width was originally 2 inches, then one, then three-quarter inch. Now it is a half-inch. A quarter-inch width tape is also now being developed. Most media packages are now available in either three-quarter or half-inch tape widths; three-quarter inch U-matic and half-inch Beta or VHS have become virtually universal standards for commercial packages in cassettes. Each width can only be used with a compatible video player.

The primary training uses are similar to film, and most film packages are becoming available in video formats. Since random access to specific content areas within a videotape is relatively easy and quick, video is ideal for technical training sequences, individual learners, or other situations calling for such referral. Media viewing by larger groups requires either multiple monitors or projection equipment.

The advantages of video include its high quality sound and image and its moderate cost. It is easily handled and maintained and can be reproduced onto film or other video sizes relatively easily, although this process is sometimes expensive. Videotape can be erased and reused. In addition to advantages parallel to those of film, video equipment can be easily managed with minimal instruction. This, then, increases its ability to be used by individuals and small groups working alone as well as by larger groups working with an instructor.

Video's disadvantages include its variable formats and the need for a player for each different tape format used. Packages may not be available in the desired formats. Technological changes make new formats, equipment, and capabilities possible, making today's equipment obsolete. Thus, making choices for long-term investment may be risky.

Filmstrips. For 50 years, filmstrips have been used for instructional purposes. Filmstrips are a series of still images on a continuous strip of 35mm motion picture type film. They may be silent and scripted, or they may have a soundtrack available on audiocassette, on audiotape, or on a record synchronized with silent or audible (i.e., manual) advance signals that move the images forward. Filmstrips also come in cartridges for use with special projection equipment such as Audiscan and LaBelle. Filmstrip projectors may be either front or rear screen; some are self-contained and designed for individual or small group use.

Primary instructional uses are where coordination of words, concepts, and images are important for learning and reinforcement. Usually a filmstrip demonstrates step-by-step action, although motion itself cannot be shown. Complicated visual concepts are not easily achieved, but filmstrips offer visual focus that exhibits critical information and progressively builds knowledge. Thus, they are particularly useful for technical training of basic and routine tasks. Use of filmstrips often can incorporate self-instructional devices such as reading pacers and teaching machines.

The advantages of the filmstrip include its low cost and its use of equipment that requires little servicing and is easy to use. It is portable, compact to store, and easy to handle. The pace and rate of presentation can be controlled automatically with the possibility of stopping at discussion points. Alternative soundtracks can be made for audiences that require different languages, technical terms, or additional points of reference.

Disadvantages include the wide variety of projection equipment and the necessary match with various filmstrip formats. Image and sound are sometimes difficult to synchronize. Filmstrips require care in handling and maintenance.

Slides. Slides are mounted 35mm film images electronically coordinated with a soundtrack, usually audiocassette. As with filmstrips, the soundtrack may have silent or audible advance signals to move to the next slide. Carousels provide automatic feeding of slides. Projection can be onto a wall or screen; sound is amplified by speakers. The primary instructional uses are similar to filmstrips, with the major difference being the format of the images.

The advantages of slides include their low cost and high quality image. Again, alternative soundtracks can be made for different audiences and the rate of presentation can be controlled or stopped manually. Slides are easily reproducible. Substitute slides can be inserted.

Disadvantages include possible mix-up of slide sequence unless the slides are stored securely. Locating suitable projection equipment that is compatible with the slides and sound formats is sometimes a problem. The most common difficulty encountered is the synchronization of sound and image.

Audiocassettes. Audio has gone from wire to tape to reel-to-reel to audiocassette. Media packages are almost exclusively on cassettes that consist of one-eighth-inch tape wound on 2 small reels within a sealed plastic cartridge. Players can be for table top, automobile, or pocket use.

Primary audiocassette uses include group and self-instructional programs to explore ideas, such as new trends, to demonstrate communication techniques, or to help make crucial audio distinctions. Often used with repetition for learning reinforcement, audiocassettes help learners make good use of limited time, commuter habits, and portable players. Some organizations maintain libraries of useful cassettes for employees to "check-out" for use at home or while traveling. Audiocassettes more frequently supplement printed materials rather than provide the primary training medium.

Advantages include the low cost, the readily available players, and convenient portability. When used for large groups, sound can be projected through public address systems. The material is easily self-pacing because of the format, and the method is familiar to most learners.

Disadvantages include problematic use with a group without skilled leadership or substantive supporting materials. Effectiveness depends on the learner's ability to listen and to sustain interest without visual stimulus.

Print Materials. Media training packages focus their major instructional content on what the audio or audiovisual media convey. Print materials then supplement and reinforce the nonprint components, helping trainers and learners make effective use of the media. Content and format of print materials vary as widely as do the nonprint components. Similarly, their quality and style also vary. Media without accompanying print materials can be made into in-house packages by trainers who take advantage of the opportunity to tailor and adapt the media formats to specific learner groups and to link the media more closely to on-the-job specifics or organizational characteristics.

Print materials for the trainer usually consist of a "leader's guide," "instructor's handbook," "discussion leader's guide," or "program guide." These usually describe the media's content and may outline its learning objectives. Many print materials offer suggestions for preparing the learner to see and/or hear the presentation and suggest how the trainer can involve learners in focused discussion. Some materials will assist a trainer to adapt or modify media components to suit various purposes. Some packages include training exercises such as role play or case studies related to the nonprint presentation. With slides or filmstrips, scripts are often included even though narration is provided on tape or cassette.

Print materials for learners may include a "workbook," "notebook," or "handbook." These often include the highlights of the presentation, questions or written exercises, and suggestions of further references for continued study. Learner's materials used for preparation may include an introductory booklet of background readings or an abstract of key points. Less frequently, printed materials will include a closely related resource package or even a textbook. Reinforcement tools for learner follow-up may include "reminder" cards or posters. A few packages include pre- and posttests that measure the learning accomplished.

Learner's print materials should be attractive, easy to use, give clear instructions, and serve to reinforce the practical application of the media presentation. Often they come in kits. These kits can often be ordered in bulk; or, to supply each learner with a single copy, only one may be ordered, thus relying on the organization to reproduce the number of copies needed. Additional learner's print materials can be produced in-house. These might include a statement of organizational policy or regulations, directions for working with a particular process or equipment, or a procedure manual for a given employee level of responsibility. Print materials often provide the link to making the media package relevant to the specific organization.

Operating Guidelines

Broad operating guidelines for using media packages skillfully in training and development work are not altogether different from trainers' usual patterns. Nonetheless, although the principles are standard, use of media packages presents some unique perspectives that warrant such guidelines.

1. The use of any media package must be consistent with the objectives for the training activity. Training objectives must be carefully defined in terms of real needs and the possible outcomes the activity addresses. The media package must fit into the learning design rather than the design being fit to the media package. Within that design, the trainer must know the purpose for which the media is to be used: to deliver an expert's concept, to portray a common work dilemma, to provide a change of pace, to show the implications of particular attitudes and behavior, or to open a topic for discussion. The message and media must be congruent to convey clear direction to learners whether they work independently or as part of a group. While mutual accommodation naturally develops while planning and using media packages, if the package is allowed to distort the design, training validity is sacrificed. Despite package attractiveness, the design's purpose must be foremost in planning for its use as well as for selecting it. The trainer is the active agent to test and adapt the package to its design and its purpose.

2. The trainer using a media package must know the print and nonprint materials thoroughly—what they say, what they do, and how they do it. Each package requires preview. This is vital for design, sequence, and timing. Familiarity pinpoints inadequacies of the package, indicates what techniques can be used and where they fit, and helps the trainer make the most of what the package has to offer. In addition, in-depth knowledge enables the trainer to prepare learners working alone or together for what to anticipate, to set realistic expectations, and to achieve the package's potential as fully as possible. This includes appropriate preparation of physical facilities and equipment, supplementary print materials, and carefully designed exercises.

3. Media packages can be "custom tailored" to better meet the intent of a training activity, the needs of its learners, or the trainer's skills. Free adaptation can be considered, guided by sound learning principles and by the package's possibilities. Many packages themselves offer ideas for modifications and options for their use. The trainer inexperienced with different kinds of media usually becomes bolder after initial attempts at adaptation. Characteristically, learner preparation and follow-up reinforcement are least likely to be built into packages. A training session, and certainly a media package, is only part of the learning process. For in-depth learning, these must be supplemented by opportunities for continued systematic study by learners.

4. The use of media packages in general as well as of particular packages should be evaluated to test their usefulness. An evaluation process can guide future package selection, can reveal additional ways to adapt packages, and can indicate appropriate follow-up plans to assist learners when the package was inadequate. Evaluation will reveal how learners respond to various media, given their preferred learning style. Their perception of what is helpful and how it is helpful will surface. In addition, evaluation can give information about the package's quality in terms of content and presentation, give better understanding of the variables at work with package use, and provide feedback on trainer skills and awareness.

5. The trainer must manage the design, the package, and the learning environment in such a way as to make the most of each by focusing interest and learning. The trainer is the one responsible for "reading" the situation to see how the design is working, to identify its constraints, and to change direction if necessary. Balance, flexibility, and knowledge of the principles of adult learning are essential. Media packages require that the user has equipment ready for use (i.e., focus, sound, and threading), knows how to troubleshoot equipment difficulties, and recognizes what facilities are suitable for each part of the activity's design. The trainer is an active agent, serving as a "manager" to ensure the effective use of a package's capabilities.

Techniques to Increase Media Package Effectiveness

The success of a media training package often depends on the trainer's abilities more than it does on the media presentation itself. Techniques to increase and focus learning from media must be carefully planned and then skillfully used. Both planning and use require a trainer's skills. Without such skills, media presentations may be considered by learners as entertainment rather than as learning—and about as long remembered.

The trainer's skills enable techniques that enrich media package effectiveness by (1) increasing learner involvement—making media active rather than passive learning stimuli; (2) increasing learner interaction and practice of new knowledge and skills; (3) increasing the relevance of the package for learners by relating it to their on-the-job situation and personal learning goals; and (4) increasing the overall effectiveness of the total training activity with change of pace, reinforcement, and variety of learning opportunities. Ideally, the trainer works with media so that they act as catalysts in a controlled and measurable way.

Adaptive techniques may be used prior to, during, or following the media presentation. Most techniques used prior to the presentation prepare the context, focus attention, or intensify interest. Those used during a presentation highlight essential points, stimulate thought, offer practice opportunities, or strengthen its relevance to learners and their jobs. Techniques that follow a media presentation, either immediately or some time later, reinforce learning or facilitate its on-the-job application. To be valid, each technique must heighten the learning impact of the media presentation, making it more effective than it would be without the technique.

Planning which techniques to use with a media package requires a preview to determine whether the package is suitable and which techniques might be useful. Often a preview is needed to decide *if* and *which* to select. If not done initially, a second viewing may be needed to decide *how* to use it and which techiques would be appropriate. To technique decisions, the trainer must view the presentation from the perspective of a typical learner in the anticipated audience.

From a preview, the trainer can decide when during the training event to use the package: to open with it

because of its dramatic impact, to use it in the middle to deliver the information at the relevant moment, or to clinch the salient points at the end. Previewing will indicate the pacing and timing for the media presentation, when interaction techniques can best be introduced, what segments might be dropped, and what subtleties may need to be pointed out.

A preview will reveal the strong and weak points of the package. For example, only a preview would reveal if a package's use of terminology is inconsistent or contradictory with that of the organization. Only a preview will show how realistic a dramatization is in relation to the organization's actual work setting. Only a preview would indicate significant gaps in the content or if extraneous and misleading information is given. And, only a preview would reveal a portrayed caricature that matches a real life manager! From such a preview the trainer determines how best to prepare learners to accept what the package has to offer, what modifications and disclaimers are needed, and what techniques to use to bring out the strength of the package in relation to the learning objectives. (Evaluative preview criteria are more specifically examined in Chapter 3.)

PREPARING LEARNERS

Before the training event, the trainer might distribute an outline of the day's design and objectives together with related readings that are brief, specific, and interesting to the anticipated audience. In the day's design, a cogent description of the media presentation can point out its relevance to the work situation to heighten interest. Other preparatory materials might include a needs assessment form or a request that each learner identify typical or unusual problem situations encountered in relation to the topic or skill area. This helps learners determine their greatest interest (i.e., need) areas within the topic, perhaps set implicit personal learning goals, build their readiness to participate and learn, and enrich possibilities for salient discussion in relation to the package.

During the training event, but just prior to the media presentation, a briefing can prepare learners with guidance as to what to watch for, which prime concepts to identify, and what new or different terminology is used. This briefing is also an opportunity to indicate the significance of the presentation to the training event and why it is being used. The briefing is the logical time to indicate if learners will be expected to do anything such as create discussion questions, report observations, complete a questionnaire, or discuss a main point.

STIMULATING LEARNER INVOLVEMENT AND INTERACTION

Most media packages, both audio and audiovisual, include several logical points at which a "stop action" technique can be successful. Sometimes, the leader's guide will indicate these or the presentation itself may build in such points, but the trainer can also determine relevant points that warrant stop action using the interruption to review, to pose discussion questions, to highlight important content, or to prepare learners for the next concept to be portrayed. Stop action points can be used also for learners to fill in worksheets individually or collectively. Often, interruptions serve as a reminder that the presentation is for learning rather than for entertainment.

At stop action points used for discussion periods, the trainer can pose structured questions to individuals, to small groups, or to the total group. Effective questions are typically open ended questions rather than ones requiring a yes/no answer. For example: "What would you do here? Why?" "What is likely to result from the decision just made?" "What are the characters likely to be thinking? To be feeling?" Particularly in dramatized presentations, discussion can usefully center on problem solving and may use role play to act out different possible endings. For work in small groups, each group might be asked to plan the next step. Then, when the groups report, many different approaches can be seen. A different technique asks individuals of the group to identify similar situations in their work context and to speculate on how the approaches indicated might be useful.

The stop action technique includes several applications. Each use of it, however, increases the learner's involvement by changing a passive experience into an active one. Stop action creates a "freeze" on the visual or aural medium somewhere in the midst of the presentation or dramatization. Then, a discussion, led by the trainer with the use of key questions, shares the information and ideas sparked by the medium, or a role play is done with the solution being worked out by the learners. Once that is completed, the end of the media presentation may be given. As a whole, the presentation can be used to form the basis for action planning by the group. In any case, these techniques enable the learners to internalize concepts while relating them to their own colleagues, jobs, and organizations—and to themselves.

Technically, the use of stop action must take into account the capabilities of the equipment. Stopping a 16mm film projector midway with the lamp on will burn the film. Videocassette players are built to stop, start, reverse, and fast forward easily. Some super 8mm projectors are built for stop action; slide and filmstrip projectors also vary in their capabilities to stop action.

Brainstorming, another group technique, uses groups of 6 to 8 people with one person serving as a recorder. Their task is to come up with as many ideas, solutions, or alternatives as possible in a short amount of time. In the idea-generating phase, all ideas are recorded. No judgment is passed on any idea, no matter how wild it may seem. In the next phase, the group goes through each idea and asks: Is it feasible? This technique quickly involves everyone and provides an energizing change of pace. It can be used for planning subsequent action steps, identifying behavioral problems, or listing communication barriers.

INCREASING RELEVANCE AND APPLICATION

To prepare for discussion either at stop action points or at the presentation's conclusion, small groups can be given specific tasks. Each group might be assigned the same responsibility, or a number of tasks could be allocated so each group has a different assignment. For example, one group might observe specific topical areas of the media presentation, such as nonverbal communication behavior, indicators of a given management style, or ways in which relationships advance or impede tasks. Or, observer teams could be assigned responsibilities such as identifying questions raised by the presentation, areas that need clarification, where team members agree or disagree, or points that particularly apply to their jobs. Then, discussion within each group surfaces highlights that can then be shared with those of other groups in a general reporting and discussion session.

Another group technique is the "fishbowl." While seated in a circle, 5 to 10 learners address an issue raised by the presentation. Usually, their discussion is guided by a stated charge, such as "Identify the major implications in our organization for an effort similar to the one shown in the film" or "What would be necessary if we were to adopt this procedure?" Other learners from outside the circle observe and listen. After a specified time, perhaps 15–20 minutes, the observers exchange places with the discussants, and the latter become the observers. The learners in the new fishbowl address the same issue or a different one, or they may react to the previous discussion. With larger groups, several fishbowls can occur simultaneously.

If total group involvement is sought, but more focus on individuals is wanted, individual learners can be asked to identify questions raised by the presentation, to form discussion topics for the whole group to consider, or to write or speak about the ways one's job responsibilities relate to the material in the presentation. Any of these could lead to important contributions to discussion involving the total group, or the participants could work in small groups of 2 or 3 to assure everyone fair amounts of discussion.

Thus, group discussion is often used to help learners explore and understand the material introduced by the media presentation. However, where feasible, learners—either individually or in small or large groups—should practice the skills introduced by the media presentation. Models, demonstration units, and training exercises can simulate skills in the use of equipment, with procedures, or with processes. When individuals or groups use what they have learned to plan on-the-job application or the next steps they will take, the exercise not only gives a base of action planning but results in an implicit commitment to do something with what was learned, and individuals can apply new ideas and techniques on the job.

Discussion and practice opportunities provide the essential link between the realm of learning and that of work. Such opportunities deepen the understanding needed to apply that which is learned to job responsibilities. In some instances, practice opportunities offer a chance to do something with relatively low risk before trying it on the job where more may be at stake. Each practice example used benefits from the full use of a trainer's skills. These are vital to enable learning to occur and be shared through discussion and controversy. These are also vital to maintain a consistent focus on the training event's objectives and the topic(s) at hand.

INCREASING THE ACTIVITY'S OVERALL EFFECTIVENESS

Techniques involved in designing an effective training program include good pacing and movement. Media packages offer opportunities to accomplish these design factors and thus should be well placed within the training session. A complex media presentation with little drama or movement should not be on the agenda right after lunch or late in the day. In turn, such a presentation should be preceded and followed by activities that make its meaning personally relevant to learners. On the other hand, a brief animated media presentation on creative problem solving or motivation can connect with the day's theme yet provide an upbeat note for the close of a section, a coffee break, or general wrap-up.

Techniques that ensure an effective learning environment improve the smoothness of the activity, eliminate distractions, and keep the sequence on track. Such efforts as well-planned seating arrangements for both the media presentation and the discussion or practice sessions following it improve the trainer's and the learners' abilities to devote full attention to learning. Factors such as ventilation, adequate light to take notes, good visibility and acoustics, and having the equipment in good working order and ready to use increase the amount of training time and keep the learner's interest high.

Follow-through techniques prompt learning reinforcement. Print materials are often helpful after, as well as prior to, the media presentation. If the group has evolved important points or planned action in relation to the presentation or the day's activities, highlights could be written up and distributed some time after the training event. Tips for on-the-job application are often more meaningful following the presentation because they can relate more closely to the characters in the media presentation or make use of new terminology mastered during the training event.

No matter how learner evaluation is accomplished (organizations vary greatly on this), evaluation of the training activity as a whole is important. Both immediate impressions and later feedback are valid to help improve the trainer's skills in the use of media packages, to endorse or add to the criteria for the selection of such packages, or to raise design considerations that can make subsequent package use more effective. In addition, if carefully designed, evaluation often reinforces the learning process by helping learners internalize and analyze new information. Evaluation can pinpoint the most important points to be gained by the training session.

Trainers who know the guidelines, formats, and techniques for using media packages effectively increase their value to an organization. Media presentations portray processes and events that are often not able to be directly experienced. They introduce experts, concepts, and innovative ideas to the workplace; they can stimulate new interest by showing a real-life context, illustrating it more clearly than words alone; and they provide depth and reality to abstract topics and principles. Media can show procedural steps in sequence, doing it consistently and simultaneously for many learners. Effective use of media allows their potential to be more fully realized, and the trainer has the central role in realizing that potential.

RESOURCES FOR PLANNING AND USE OF MEDIA PACKAGES

The resources that follow include representative books, periodicals, periodical articles, and nonprint materials. They are intended to guide trainers to more effective use of media training packages. Nonprint materials are included in the directory section of this volume under the headings Audiovisual Techniques, Instruction and Instructional Methods, and Training and Development.

Resources with Comprehensive Coverage of Training and Development

The titles below are especially useful for sound overall program planning for training as well as for specific details relating to functional areas such as needs assessment, evaluation, and program management.

Craig, Robert L., ed. *Training and Development Handbook*. Sponsored by American Society for Training and Development. New York: McGraw-Hill Book Co., 1976.

Donaldson, Les, and Scannell, Edward E. *Human Resource Development; The New Trainer's Guide*. Reading, MA: Addison-Wesley Publishing Co., 1978.

Nadler, Leonard. *Developing Human Resources*. 2nd ed. Austin, TX: Learning Concepts, 1979.

Saint, Avice. *Learning at Work: Human Resources and Organizational Development*. Chicago: Nelson-Hall Co., 1974.

Warren, Malcolm W. *Training for Results: A Systems Approach to the Development of Human Resources in Industry*. 2nd ed. Reading, MA: Addison-Wesley Publishing Co., 1979.

Relevant articles consistently appear in the following journals.

Training and Development Journal, One DuPont Circle, Washington, DC 20036.

Training, The Magazine of Human Resources Development, 731 Hennepin Avenue, Minneapolis, MN 55403.

Resources in the Area of Adult Learning and Instructional Skills

Trainers will find the titles below useful in designing training activities and techniques.

Brinbrauer, Herman. *Training for Trainers: Increasing the Effectiveness of On-the-Job Training Instructors*. Bensalem, PA: Institute for Business and Industry, Inc., 1981.

Cross, Patricia. *Adults as Learners*. San Francisco, CA: Jossey-Bass, Inc., 1981.

Entwistle, Noel. *Styles of Learning and Teaching*. New York: John Wiley and Sons, 1981.

Knowles, Malcolm S. *The Modern Practice of Adult Education*. Revised. New York: Association Press, 1975.

McLagan, Patricia A. *Helping Others Learn*. Reading, MA: Addison-Wesley Publishing Co., 1978.

Schneier, Craig Eric. "Training and Development Programs: What Learning Theory and Research Have to Offer." *Personnel Journal* 53 (April 1974): 288–93.

Zemke, Ron, and Zemke, Susan. "30 Things We Know for Sure about Adult Learning." *Training: The Magazine of Human Resources Development* 18 (6) (June 1981): 45–52.

Relevant nonprint resources include the following:

Catching On (Roundtable Film and Video), 16mm film.

Cognitive Learning Styles (Nebraska Educational Television Council for Higher Education), 16mm film.

I'd Like a Word with You* (Video Arts), 16mm film/video.

Strategies in College Teaching (Indiana University), 16mm film

Train the Trainer* (Butler Learning Systems), slides/audiocassettes.

Current articles appear in *Training and Development Journal* and *Training: The Magazine of Human*

_____

* These titles are included in Part II of this volume.

Resources Development. See listing for address information.)

Resources for Using Media in Instruction

Allen, Sylvia. *A Manager's Guide to Audiovisuals*. New York: McGraw-Hill Book Co., 1979.

Anderson, Ronald H. *Selecting and Developing Media for Instruction*. New York: Van Nostrand Reinhold, 1976.

Bell, Norman T., and Abedor, Allan J. *Developing Audio-Visual Instructional Modules for Vocational and Technical Training*. Englewood Cliffs, NJ: Educational Technology Publications, 1977.

Brown, James W.; Lewis, Richard B.; and Harcleroad, Fred F. *AV Instruction Technology, Media and Methods*. 5th ed. New York: McGraw-Hill Book Co., 1977.

Cabeceiras, James, *The Multimedia Library: Materials Selection and Use*. New York: Academic Press, 1978.

Cavert, C. Edward. *An Approach to the Design of Mediated Instruction*. Washington, DC: Association for Educational Communications and Technology, 1974.

Cavert, C. Edward. *Procedural Guidelines for the Design of Mediated Instruction*. Washington, DC: Association for Educational Communications and Technology, 1974.

Davies, Ivor K. *Instructional Technique*. New York: McGraw-Hill Book Co., 1980.

Floyd, Steve, and Floyd, Betty, eds. *Handbook of Interactive Video*. White Plains, NY: Knowledge Industry Publications, Inc., 1982.

Gerlach, Vernon S., and Ely, Donald P. *Teaching and Media: A Systematic Approach*. 2nd ed. Englewood Cliffs, NJ: Prentice-Hall, 1980.

Heidt, Erhard U. *Instructional Media and the Individual Learner: A Classification and Systems Appraisal*. New York: Nichols Publishing Co., 1978.

Heinich, Robert; Molenda, Michael; and Russell, James D. *Instructional Media and the New Technologies of Instruction*. New York: John Wiley and Sons, 1982.

Kemp, Jerrold E. *Planning and Producing Audiovisual Materials*. 4th ed. New York: Harper and Row, 1980.

Kinder, James S. *Using Instructional Media*. New York: Van Nostrand Reinhold Co., 1973.

Laird, Dugan. *A-V Buyer's Guide: A User's Look at the Audio-Visual World*. 3rd ed. Fairfax, VA: National Audio-Visual Association, Inc., 1980.

Langdon, Danny G. *The Audio-Workbook*. (Instructional Design Library, vol. 5.) Englewood Cliffs, NJ: Educational Technology Publications, 1978.

McInnis, James. *Video in Education and Training*. Woburn, MA: Focal Press, 1981.

Romiszowski, A. J. *The Selection and Use of Instructional Media*. New York: John Wiley and Sons, 1974.

Several periodicals are concerned with planning for and using media in instruction, either from the viewpoint of the audiovisual materials or from the perspective of education and/or training. Articles and resources found in the following periodicals will be relevant. They are not focused on school instruction.

Audio-Visual Communications, United Business Publications, 475 Park Avenue South, New York, NY 10016.

Bulletin on Training, BNA Communications Inc., 9401 Decoverly Hall Road, Rockville, MD 20850.

DB—The Sound Engineering Magazine, Sagamore Publishing Co., Inc., 1120 Old Country Road, Plainview, NY 11803.

Educational Communication and Technology: A Journal of Theory, Research and Development, Association for Educational Communications and Technology, 1126 16th Street, NW, Washington, DC 20036.

Educational Technology, Educational Technology Publications, Inc., 140 Sylvan Avenue, Englewood Cliffs, NJ 07632.

Film Library Quarterly, Film Library Information Council, Box 348, Radio City Station, New York, NY 10019.

Instructional Innovator, Association for Educational Communications and Technology, 1126 16th Street, NW, Washington, DC 20036.

International Journal of Instructional Media, Baywood Publishing Co., 120 Marine Street, Farmingdale, NY 11735.

Media Adult Learning, College of Education, Kansas State University, Manhattan, KS 66506.

Media Memo: An Exchange of Audio Visual Techniques for Educational Purposes, Wisconsin Audiovisual Association, Shattuck Campus, 611 Division Street, Neenah, WI 54956.

Super-8 Filmmaker, PMS Publishing Co., Inc., 609 Mission Street, San Francisco, CA 94105.

Training and Development Journal, One DuPont Circle, Washington, DC 20036.

Training: The Magazine of Human Resources Development, 731 Hennepin Avenue, Minneapolis, MN 55403.

Relevant nonprint resources concerning media in instruction follow.

Don't Just Tell Them...Show Them * (BNA Communications Inc.).

Utilizing Instructional Television (Media Systems Corp.).

Utilizing the Tape Recorder in Education (Media Systems Corp.).

Resources for Using Media Equipment and Facililties

The titles below provide useful guides for purchasing and using media equipment or simply for learning more about the hardware needed to support media use in instruction.

Audio-Visual Equipment Directory. Fairfax, VA: National Audio-Visual Association, 1982–83.

AV Clearinghouse. Albany, NY: Parameters Unlimited, 1982–83.

Bensinger, Charles. *The Video Guide*. 2nd ed. Santa Fe, NM: Video-Info Publications, Inc., 1979.

Billboard Tape/Audio/Video Market Sourcebook. Los Angeles, CA: Billboard Publications, Inc., 1979.

Bullard, John, and Mether, Calvin. *Audiovisual Fundamentals: Basic Equipment Operation and Simple Materials Production*. 2nd ed. Dubuque, IA: William C. Brown Co., 1979.

Laird, Dugan. *A-V Buyer's Guide: A User's Look at the Audio-Visual World*. 3rd ed. Fairfax, VA: National Audio-Visual Association, Inc., 1980.

National Center for Audio Tapes. *Guidelines for Utilizing Audio Tapes*. Boulder, CO: National Center for Audio Tapes, 1967.

Oates, Stanton C. *Audiovisual Equipment: Self-Instruction Manual*. 4th ed. Dubuque, IA: William C. Brown Co., 1979.

Quinly, William J. *The Selection, Acquisition and Utilization of Audiovisual Materials*. 2nd ed. Pullman, WA: Information Futures, 1978.

Rosenberg, Kenyon C. *Media Equipment: A Guide and Dictionary*. Littleton, CO: Libraries Unlimited, Inc., 1976.

Schroeder, Don, and Lare, Gary. *Audiovisual Equipment and Materials: A Basic Repair and Maintenance Manual*. Metuchen, NJ: Scarecrow, 1979.

Video Register. White Plains, NY: Knowledge Industry Publications, Inc., 1981–82.

* This title is included in Part II of this volume.

Wyman, Raymond. *Mediaware: Selection, Operation and Maintenance* . Dubuque, IA: William C. Brown Co., 1976.

Resources for Using Equipment for Mediated Instruction

Helpful periodical articles can be found in *Audio Visual Communications, Educational Technology, Instructional Innovator, Training and Development Journal* and *Training: The Magazine of Human Resources.* (See above sections for address information.) In addition, the following are helpful.

Audio Visual Directions: The What's New and How To Magazine for the AV Communicator, Montage Publishing, 5173 Overland Avenue, Culver City, CA 90230.

A-V Guide: The Learning Media Magazine, 380 Northwest Highway, Des Plaines, IL 60016.

Educational Digest, Maclean Hunter Ltd., 481 University Avenue, Toronto, Ontario Canada M5W 1A7.

Journal of Educational Technology Systems, Baywood Publishing Co., 120 Marine Street, Farmingdale, NY 11735.

Video Trade News, C. S. Tepfer Publishing Co., 51 Sugar Hollow Road, Danbury CT 06810.

Some periodicals have annual special issues around the theme of media equipment. Examples of these are in *Audio-Visual Communications, Audio Visual Directions: The What's New and How To Magazine for the AV Communicator* and *Training: The Magazine of Human Resources Development.*

One useful nonprint source is Indiana University's *Media for Presentations* which reviews basic audiovisual equipment.

Resources to explore in surveying an organization's present training facilities or in planning for new arrangements include the following.

Ackerman, Norman A. "How to Choose the Right Sound System for Your Training Room." *Training* 17 (5) (May 1980): 45–47.

Davis, James L., and Hagaman, John W. "What's Right—and Wrong—With Your Training Room Environment." *Training* 13 (7) (July 1976): 28–31.

Finkel, Coleman L. "The Supportive Environment." *Training and Development Journal* 29 (1) (January 1975): 26–36.

Smith, Judson. "Designing and Installing a Training Room Sound System." *Training* 18 (1) (January 1981): 88–90.

Smith, Judson. "Locating, Designing and Equipping the Ideal Training Room." *Training* Part I 15 (8) (August 1978): 21–26; Part 2 15 (9) (September 1978): 91–98.

"Study Carrels." *Training* 14 (9) (September 1977): 97–98.

Sullivan, Janet. "Nine Design Factors for Better Learning." *Instructional Innovator* 26 (3) (March 1981): 14–19.

Wiegand, Richard. "Do Your Training Facilities Leave People in the Dark?" *Training* 18 (5) (May 1981): 69–74.

Chapter 3
Discovering, Selecting, and Acquiring Media Packages for Training

The trainer faces several challenges when deciding to use media training packages experimentally, occasionally, or regularly. What packages exist? How can one select wisely from what is available? How can such packages be obtained? This chapter is primarily a descriptive guide to the information sources and resources required to discover, select, and acquire media packages. Brief descriptions of these processes provide the context to lead trainers to key information sources they need to use media packages effectively.

The discovery section includes where to start finding out what packages are available and the information resources that provide such information. The next section describes the process of selecting packages, outlining evaluative criteria that guide selection, describing resources that review training media, and detailing how to preview packages. The third section describes acquisition—how packages can be obtained, under what terms they are available, and the sources from which they may be acquired.

An overview of where packages can be obtained and how to find out information about them is important for trainers inexperienced with media packages. Sources for packages are producers and/or distributors who often handle packages from several producers and libraries which maintain media collections. Dealers and suppliers are the sources of purchased or rented audiovisual equipment.

To make knowledgeable use of each of these sources, trainers require information resources. These resources include guides and directories listing available packages and how and where to obtain them, evaluative information to aid selection, manuals covering how to use media and equipment, and guides and catalogs for appropriate equipment. For trainers using packages regularly, such basic information resources must be on hand. For occasional use, libraries, current professional training periodicals, and even promotional materials from producers and distributors may be sufficient. Finding and using good information resources is a challenge to most

trainers. Inexperienced or impatient trainers may find such challenges sufficient reason to prevent their using media training packages.

The information resources cited here direct the user to useful, current, and generally available media materials that relate to adults learning work-related information and skills on the job. Thus, the lists largely bypass resources that lead to school-focused educational media, although such material is occasionally helpful for trainers.

DISCOVERY

A common question that many trainers who want to try media training ask is: Where do I start? As with most new topics, the answer is "anywhere" and "everywhere." An efficient approach is to gather segments of important information by using resources that are most readily available. From there, the move is to the less easily accessible information. For an organization close to a large public or university library, book sources would be the logical beginning. For a trainer who subscribes to professional periodicals, looking at them with a new focus would be helpful. For persons active in personnel or training associations, those organizations provide a good base for exploring and learning.

The resource tools described in this section are meant to assist trainers become familiar with the literature to use when beginning to systematically search for media training possibilities. Those seeking more specialized or obscure materials may wish to initiate their searches through colleagues or through some of the specialized associations or periodicals. Once a variety of packages have been used, trainers may find that catalogs from certain producers or distributors suffice. Which resources to acquire for regular in-house reference depends on the nature and degree of searches and the adequacy of the training budget. Many of these tools may be found in large libraries or might be collaboratively purchased with other organizations that have similar needs for them.

Discovering what is available in training media *should* lead one to a comprehensive directory giving full information and evaluation of such packages, but most directories to training media have limitations of one kind or another: the time span covered, the formats included, the currency, the amount or type of information given, or the basic arrangement. Both discovery and selection are impeded by these limitations; thus, it becomes necessary to search more than one resource to obtain adequate or essential information.

The limitation that affects all resources to some extent is keeping current with a fast-changing field. Some printed information is out-of-date virtually the moment it is available. For instance, price, format availability, and new releases are most often outdated. This common limitation requires that the information found in any print resource be checked directly with the learning package's producer.

The resource tools suggested in this section are a representative selection of valid basic guides, each with some strengths and limitations that trainers will want to weigh against their unique situations.

Basic Guides

Primary resources for finding what media training packages exist must, to be valuable, include current information in a useful format. They must reveal media primarily intended for training and must be generally available to trainers either for purchase or through libraries. The following resources meet these criteria and provide the trainer seeking media packages with basic information about ones that are available. Each has strengths and weaknesses.

Audio-Cassette Directory (Cassette Information Services, PO Box 9559, Glendale, CA 91206) lists spoken word programs for adult or college level listeners by producer. 1979. $12.00.

Business and Technology Videolog (Video-Forum, 145 East 49th Street, New York, NY 10017) provides a guide to 4,500 videotape programs from 135 producers/distributors. Basic entries are under title with indexes by subject. Gives formats available, prices, and brief content description. Includes a directory of producers and distributors. Earlier editions were titled *Videolog Programs for Business and Industry* (1979) and *Video Bluebook* (1976). 1981. $40.00.

Film Finder (Olympic Media Information, 70 Hudson Street, Hoboken, NJ 07030) lists 1,510 audiovisual training programs by title under 676 subject headings and includes a directory of sources. 1980. $24.00.

Management Media Directory: An Annotated Guide to Commercially Available Audiovisual Programs (Gale Research Co., Book Tower, Detroit, MI 48226) details 3,500 media programs for use in management training. Includes date, format, producer or distributor, and brief annotation for each title. Contains all media formats and a distributor directory. 1982. $85.00.

Media Profiles: The Career Development Edition (Olympic Media Information, 70 Hudson Street, Hoboken, NJ 07030) was entitled *Training Film Profiles* from 1968 to late 1982. Includes more than 2,000 descriptions and evaluations of films, slide sets, filmstrips, and videotapes for employee development. Each title has a separate report that describes the primary audience, content, and synopsis as well as the complete citation. Each annual cumulated volume includes about 250 profiles. Annual. First 14 volumes $596.00. $175.00 per year.

The Trainer's Resource: A Comprehensive Guide to Packaged Training Programs (Human Resource Development Press, 22A Amherst Road, Amherst, MA 01002) gives brief information about audience, description, media components, instructional strategies, costs, references, and source. The basic binder contains 322 one-page descriptions of off-the-shelf programs from 136 producers and distributors. Supplementary sheets update the basic volume. Consulting editor is Leonard Nadler. Basic volume $50.00. With supplements $75.00.

Video Source Book (Gale Research Co., Book Tower, Detroit, MI 48226) lists 35,000 videotape and disc programs in 8 major subject categories. Arranged by title, giving format, date, distributor, audience level, availability, language, and brief annotation. Includes entertainment, education, sports, health, as well as business and industry and instructional programs. Does not include prices, though an update "hotline" service is available for price information and consultation. Contains a producer directory. 3rd ed. 1982. $125.00.

The following resources are more specifically focused as to their source, date, or arrangement. This may enhance or limit their usefulness in particular situations.

Feature Films on 8mm and 16mm and Videotape (R.R. Bowker, 1180 Avenue of the Americas, New York, NY 10036) is a directory to commercial productions, documentaries, animations, and videocassettes. Regular updates appear in *Sightlines* (Educational Film Library Association). Index gives distributors by geographic area. Edited by James L. Limbacher. 1982. $65.00.

Guide to Free-Loan Training Films (Serina Press, 70 Kennedy Street, Alexandria, VA 22305) arranges entries by topic with an alphabetic title index. Includes a list of sources. Compiled by Daniel Sprecher. 1975. $7.95.

Guide to Government Loan Films (Serina Press, 70 Kennedy Street, Alexandria, VA 22305) consists of 2 parts: civilian agencies and defense agencies. Indicates borrowing sources. Compiled by Daniel Sprecher. 1976. $9.95.

List of Audiovisual Materials Produced by the United States Government for Business and Government Management (National Audiovisual Center, General Services Administration, National Archives and Records Service, Washington, DC 20409) is arranged by subject categories and gives, for each entry, full citations of producing agency, price, date, time, and brief annotation. 1980. Free.

Media for Corporate Film Programs (National Audiovisual Center, General Services Administration, National Archives and Records Service, Washington, DC 20409) is same format as above and focuses on subjects such as management training, labor/employee relations, business market development, and personnel. 1980. Free.

Media Profiles: Educational Media Catalogs on Microfiche (Olympic Media Information, 70 Hudson Street, Hoboken, NJ 07030) reproduces catalogs of audiovisual producers and distributors in all subjects at all levels. More than 400 catalogs for audio, video, slides, films, and filmstrips. Strong curricular emphasis. $87.50 each semi-annual update.

Motion Pictures and Filmstrips (Library of Congress Catalogs, National Union Catalog. Library of Congress, Washington, DC 20541) is a periodic and comprehensive listing giving title, date, producer, format, and subject headings.

National Center for Audio Tapes Catalog (National Center for Audio Tapes, 348 Stadium Building, Boulder, CO 80309) lists materials for sale in four sections: subject, entry with annotation, alphabetic title, producer. Covers 1974 to 1976. Later catalogs will be by subject categories rather than a complete catalog. The center's collection includes 15,000 tapes. 1977. $4.50.

National Information Center for Educational Media Index to... (National Information Center for Educational Media, University of Southern California, University Park, Los Angeles, CA 90004) NICEM indexes list commercially produced materials with format, producer/distributor, audience level, contents summary, release date. New editions come out periodically and include listings from earlier editions. Many are curricular but training and instructional materials are also covered. Volumes include: *Educational Audiotapes*, 5th ed., 1980, $54.00; *Educational Slides*, 4th ed., 1980, $49.00; *Educational Videotapes*, 5th ed., 1980, $34.00; *Eight-mm Motion Cartridges*, 6th ed., 1980, $54.00; *Health and Safety Education Multimedia*, 4th ed., 1980, $55.00; *Sixteen-mm Educational*

Films, 7th ed., 1980, $126.00; *Vocational and Technical Education Multimedia* 4th ed., 1980. $55.00.

Sightlines (Educational Film Library Association, 43 West 61st Street, New York, NY 10023) is a quarterly periodical with articles covering audiovisual aspects of topics and an extensive listing in each issue of "Recent Film/Video Releases." Gives full citation including price and brief annotation. Each issue has subject index to the entries. Quarterly. $15.00 per year.

Sources: A Guide to Print and Nonprint Materials Available from Organizations, Industry, Government Agencies and Specialized Publishers (Neal Schuman, 23 Cornelia, New York, NY 10014) describes organizational sources of materials and has a title index to all print and nonprint products. Issued 3 times a year since 1977. Has cumulative indexes. $70.00 per year.

Specialized Guides

Some directories come with a special focus on function, such as supervision, management, basic skills, or salesmanship; some focus on industry, such as utilities or data processing, banking, hotels, food service, or manufacturing; others specialize in motivational films, success audiotapes, or safety media. These are especially helpful in some specialized training situations. Three examples follow.

Media Profiles: The Health Science Edition (Olympic Media Information, 70 Hudson Street, Hoboken, NJ 07030) reviews all audiovisual formats for hospital, nursing, and health care education. Bimonthly installments are sheets of entries giving descriptions and evaluations. Includes over 2,000 entries. Volumes 1–9 $496.00. $87.50 per year.

Nonprint Materials on Communication: An Annotated Directory of Select Films, Videotapes, Videocassettes, Simulations and Games (Scarecrow Press, 52 Liberty Street, Metuchen, NJ 08840) arranges over 2,000 entries from 1,400 sources by form of media, then by subtopic. 1976. $21.00.

Sales Trainer's Media Handbook (Olympic Media Information, 70 Hudson Street, Hoboken, NJ 07030) contains full-length media profiles that pertain to sales training and marketing. Each entry has full descriptions and evaluative comments. 1983. $26.00.

These more specialized resources are usually discovered through information channels directed to the industry or function or special focus. Thus, industry and trade journals will feature articles, special bibliographies, and reviews of such resources as well as advertisements. Third class mailings often include flyers and brochures directed toward companies in a particular field or to organizational positions such as production unit head, accounting department, or marketing director. Industry associations are also often good sources of resources in their journals and newsletters. The same is true for the professional associations of data processors, personnel administrators, financial managers, or executives. Trainers alert to these information channels can watch for mention of specialized resources.

Associations

Media-related associations and others with significant audiovisual interests issue periodicals of general or specialized interest or single publications of useful or popular media information sources. Some associations serve as clearinghouses referring requests for information to their staffs or members with expert knowledge. Three general sources which include lists of such associations are listed below.

Audiovisual Market Place: A Multimedia Guide (R. R. Bowker, 1180 Avenue of the Americas, New York, NY 10036). 11th ed., 1981. $32.50.

Educational Media Yearbook (Libraries Unlimited, Inc., PO Box 263, Littleton, CO 80160). 7th ed., 1981. $36.00.

In-House Training and Development Programs Directory (Gale Research Co., Book Tower, Detroit, MI 48226). 1st ed., 1981. $98.00.

Some periodicals have an annual directory issue that lists associations. One is the annual August "Marketplace Directory" of *Training: The Magazine of Human Resources Development.*

The following list provides a representative sampling of media-related associations, in particular those with an interest in instructional media.

Agency for Instructional Television, Box A, Bloomington, IN 47402.

American Society for Training and Development, One DuPont Circle, Washington, DC 20036.

Association for Educational Communications & Technology, 1126 16th Street, NW, Washington, DC 20036.

Association of Media Producers, 1707 L Street, NW, Washington, DC 20036.

Audio-Visual Management Association, Box 821, Royal Oak, MI 48068.

Educational Film Library Association, Inc., 43 West 61st Street, New York, NY 10023.

Health Eduction Media Association, Inc., Box 771, Riverdale, GA 30274.

Industrial Audio-Visual Association, Box 656, Downtown Station, Chicago, IL 60690.

National Association for Industry-Education Cooperation, 235 Hendricks Boulevard, Buffalo, NY 14226.

National Audio-Visual Association, 3150 Spring Street, Fairfax, VA 22031.

National Committee on Films for Safety, 444 North Michigan Avenue, Chicago, IL 60611.

National Society for Performance and Instruction, 1126 16th Street, NW, Washington, DC 20036.

Training Media Distributors Association, 1258 North Highland Avenue, Los Angeles, CA 90038.

Videotape Production Association, 63 West 83rd Street, New York, NY 10024.

Producers and Distributors

Producers and distributors of media training packages are also useful resources. Most produce and readily supply catalogs or lists of their packages, although these vary in lavishness, specificity, and the amount of promotional information. In addition to catalogs, some issue, on either a regular or infrequent basis, newsletters or newspapers that are used to announce and promote new media products. Since these are specifically aimed at trainers, they give helpful information on how and where to use the producer's packages. Examples include *American Media Eagle* (American Media, Inc., 5907 Meredith Drive, Des Moines, IA 50324); *BNA Communicator* (BNA Communications, Inc., Rockville, MD 20850); *Professional Trainer* (CRM/McGraw-Hill, PO Box 641, Del Mar, CA 92014).

The directories listed below are useful for trainers seeking a list of media package producers and distributors. Such a list is useful for ordering catalogs or materials.

Educational Marketer Yellow Pages (Knowledge Industry Publications, Inc., Two Corporate Park Drive, White Plains, NY 10604) lists over 2,000 companies producing educational materials and services. Edited by Dantia Quirk. 4th ed., 1978–79. $17.95.

Index to Producers and Distributors (National Information Center for Educational Media, University of Southern California, University Park, Los Angeles, CA 90004) is a comprehensive listing of producers and distributors of all formats including school as well as training materials. 1980. $24.00.

Video Register (Knowledge Industry Publications/ Gale Research Company, Book Tower, Detroit, MI 48226) lists nearly 4,000 users, manufacturers, publishers, dealers, production services, and consultants. Edited by Eileen Gardiner. 1981–82. $47.50.

Periodicals often issue "who's who" lists on an annual or biennial basis. These are most often producers and distributors who advertise in the periodical, but sometimes they are not that restrictive. The May issue of *Audio Visual Communications* and the August "Marketplace Directory" issue of *Training: The Magazine of Human Resources Development* include such lists.

Periodicals

Consistent review and reading of periodicals can give a trainer depth and perspective. Reviewing periodicals in the fields of training and instruction, those in audiovisual and media, and those in special industry or professional fields are invaluable in the search to discover useful, current learning package titles. Since most educational periodicals are for curricular purposes in school level education rather than adult and professional use, it becomes a challenge to find those titles most useful for the latter purpose. *Audiovisual Market Place* includes a list of periodicals and trade journals in the audiovisual field. It is a useful place to start looking for periodicals that include information about media packages. The prime periodicals for the trainer, however, are *Training and Development Journal* (American Society for Training and Development, One DuPont Circle, Washington, DC 20036) and *Training: The Magazine of Human Resources Development* (731 Hennepin Avenue, Minneapolis, MN 55403). Both titles contain articles, advertisements, and reviews of training media.

Periodicals offer the advantage of currency. In addition, they offer special columns, resource information sections, and theme issues or special surveys which focus on topics or techniques of particular interest to trainers. Furthermore, some periodicals review media packages, aiding the trainer's selection. (See the following section for more specific information about reviews.)

SELECTION

Selection is closely linked with planning. Both planning for the use of media and then planning for specific media training packages require knowing the purpose media are intended to serve. When inadequate planning is combined with either good or poor media packages, the results will be disappointing. The impact that can be achieved through the use of media is sufficiently great to warrant its careful selection. This section will explore the key factors to be considered in selection, the evaluative criteria that should guide selection, and the resources for effectively using reviews and previews.

Key Factors

Once the purpose of the training activity and use of a media package have been determined, other factors must also be considered. The first is the anticipated audience. Its characteristics, such as the number of learners, the group's makeup with respect to their function and level, their degree of awareness or knowl-

edge or experience, and their receptivity to mediated training, are all significant. The second factor is the trainer's capabilities. How much of the content responsibility can rest on the trainer? Is the trainer skilled in the techniques required to make the media approach work effectively? Is the trainer capable enough to work with the equipment required by the package? The third factor involved is the media package itself. A decision must be made about which media package will best do the job, yield the needed results, and be available within budget. The fourth factor is closely connected with the package format—the equipment needed. This factor is included in the selection of a media package because equipment requires investment (purchase or rental), skilled handling and use, suitable space, and accessibility. The equipment and the space in which it is used affect the environment of the learners and the trainer throughout the training activity.

Selection Criteria

Some specific criteria to observe when previewing or reviewing the media components of a package follow. Since no established or standardized criteria exist, and since other factors also will guide a trainer's decision making, these should not be applied uniformly but with flexibility, depending on the situation at hand.

1. Message

- What is the message?
- Is the message clear or ambiguous?
- Is this the message sought?
- Is its tone and style appropriate for the purpose for which it will be used?
- Is it relevant to the situation and the learners?
- Are there any hidden messages?
- Will it seem important and interesting to the learners?
- Is the message cogent?
- Does it offer insight?
- Is it creative?

2. Content

- Is the scope and coverage of the content adequate?
- Is it at the appropriate level (concepts, vocabulary) for the anticipated learners?
- Is the content objective?
- Is the sequence clear?
- Is the content accurate?
- Is it presented in such a way that it will hold a learner's interest?
- Is the content current? Up to date?
- Is the pace of presentation right?
- Does it have unity and cohesiveness?
- Is it believable?
- Is its modeling appropriate to the purpose?

3. Technical Aspects

- Are images clear and effective?
- Is sound clear and effective?
- Are sound and image synchronized?
- Has it been cleanly edited?
- What is the overall effect of the technical approach?

4. Design

- Does the structure reveal the content satisfactorily?
- Is it well organized and edited?
- Is the script natural or forced?
- Is the tempo and pace appropriate?
- Is it creative?

5. General Characteristics

- Will it fit the design of the training as anticipated?
- Will it stimulate learners to involvement and interaction?
- Will it provoke but not outrage?
- Is it in good taste?
- Does it present outdated social attitudes such as racism or sexism?
- Will the media component and its activities fit the time allocated?
- Is it a good representative of the genre?
- Does the audio or visual information outweigh any technical deficiencies?

Although the above criteria are important, media components should not be measured by their "slickness" alone. For learners (and trainers) familiar with quality movies, television, and cable, "slickness" is often overrated. The message and content and overall impression may be more effective from a less polished performance than from one that dazzles with its show-off style. Remember, the purpose of a media training package is to effect learning, not to offer a gimmick.

In addition to the media component itself, the accompanying printed materials are important and should be examined with care. Whether for learner or instructor, they should give instructions clearly, be easy to use, well organized, and attractive. As with media, the message and content are significant and should be top-rated.

Often, printed materials are developed somewhat independently of the media and may not integrate in a truly supportive way. If the printed materials do not meet the need, adaptations can be made. In almost every instance, a trainer will want to consider the available materials, but s/he should not feel confined to using them. Often, the most useful materials are those that offer a number of selected alternatives and leave the choice open.

Reviews

Reviews provide descriptive and sometimes evaluative information about the package or, more often, its media components. A number of problems reduce the effectiveness of relying on reviews to make final purchase decisions, yet relying on reviews to make a decision concerning previewing a package is useful.

Indexes, directories, guides, and publishers' catalogs are valid sources for discovering what training media exist. Only a small portion of those that exist are reviewed. In the field of instructional media, the greatest number of media products are aimed at the school child or adult. As such, they are geared toward a predictable curriculum and audience level. Thus, producers can, with some security, produce media for a given market; media evaluators can, with some confidence, develop criteria and procedures to review the available materials; and publishers can, with some boldness, compile these reviews and market reference tools that lead to them.

The availability of such tools for the much less predictable training media market is very limited. Sources of reviews of that media are scattered and few, and the directories that exist are not evaluative, although they are, for the most part, descriptive. Reviews sometimes appear in business and professional periodicals, but these sources mostly review only what they wish to recommend. At times, the reviews do not reflect training uses so much as educational uses in the classroom sense.

Another significant problem is that a reviewer is likely not be be able to project (or predict) usefulness as closely as a trainer. Accuracy is not the question so much as relevance. Although a greater measure of bibliographic control and reviewing is evident now than has been in the past, the challenge is still great for the trainer wishing to select either prior to or instead of previewing.

To some extent, the review seeking process is an expense. Trainer time to seek reviews, given the "relevance return," is substantial. Although some tools may be provided in-house, saving such time, most tools that review media products are expensive and may require using a local library.

However, such resources do exist. Some are one-time-only publications; some are issued serially; and some are brought up-to-date with regular or occasional supplements. Their scope and specialty varies, as some include the reviews and others only index where the media were reviewed. Film is reviewed more often than other formats, but since many training films are also available in video formats, those perforce are also reviewed.

BASIC RESOURCES

The chief evaluative resources in the training field follow.

Choice (100 Riverview Center, Middletown, CT 06457) is a monthly book and nonprint selection journal that reviews college level nonprint materials, including computer software. Evaluations are prepared by undergraduate faculty members. Nonprint reviews, which began to be included in *Choice* during the late 1980s, are indexed separately, although the reviews are included in subject categories with print reviews. $55.00 per year.

EFLA Evaluations (Educational Film Library Association, 43 West 61st Street, New York, NY 10023) covers about 400 reviews per year, giving full information on films plus synopsis and critical comments. Issued for several years on cards, it is now a quarterly publication. The evaluations were previously issued as *Film Evaluation Guide*, with supplements 1 and 2. 1946–65 $30.00. Supplement 1, 1965–67 $12.00. Supplement 2, 1967–71 $12.00. $50.00 per year.

Filmfacts (University of Southern California, Los Angeles, CA 90007) issued from 1958 to 1977 reviewed films, a few of which were applicable for training.

The HRD Review: A Journal of Professional Opinion (105 Berkley Place, Glen Rock, NJ 07452) is a new venture begun in January 1983. It is an 8-page monthly publication including 6 to 8 reviews by experienced training practitioners. Reviewed books, audiocassettes, films, and video packages include those from large and small producers. The major emphasis throughout is on training and development. Annual subscription is $72.00.

Media Profiles: The Career Development Edition (Olympic Media Information, 70 Hudson Street, Hoboken, NJ 07030) issues bimonthly profile sheets, each giving full information on a training film, filmstrip, slide/tape program, video, or audiocassette program for management development or employee training. Some 2,000 titles from more than 200 producers or distributors have been issued, each with a content analysis, synopsis, and evaluation. From 1973 to late 1982, this publication was entitled *Training Film Profiles* ; from 1968 to 1972, it was entitled *Olympic Training Film Profiles*. The bimonthly profile sheets total about 250 per year. Annual. First 14 volumes $596.00. $175.00 per year.

Media Profiles: The Health Science Edition (Olympic Media Information, 570 Hudson Street, Hoboken, NJ 07030) contains more specialized evaluations of audiovisual programs of interest to health care professionals. Its format is similar to the above title, as is its frequency. It was formerly entitled *Hospital/Health Care Training Media Profiles*. Annual. First 9 volumes $496.00. $87.50 per year. (A collection of programs suitable for the education of patients and the lay public in general has been selected from *Media Profiles: The Health Science Edition*. It is entitled *Patient Education Media Handbook* and costs $26.00.)

Previews: News and Reviews of Non-Print Media (R. R. Bowker Co., 1180 Avenue of the Americas, New York, NY 10036) covers audio, films, slides, and graphics, with 9 issues per year from 1972 through December 1980.

Sightlines (Educational Film Library Association, 43 West 61st Street, New York, NY 10023) provides explicit evaluations of films and video that are entered into competitions such as the annual American Film Festival. Winners are noted in some competitions for substance as well as technical quality. $18.00 per year or $5.00 per issue.

The reviewing resources above concentrate on evaluating media materials. Periodicals in the training field, in the media field, in the education field, and in special professional fields also feature occasional reviews. The blend of evaluative information and promotional efforts is sometimes subtle, but some include critical reviews in a special section that appears regularly or in an occasional article reviewing several titles simultaneously. Both *Training and Development Journal* and *Training: The Magazine for Human Resources Development* are giving more attention to media for training though neither has a regular monthly column of reviews. Other periodicals with reviews follow.

Audio Visual Directions: The What's New and How To Magazine for the AV Communicator, Montage Publishing, 5173 Overland Avenue, Culver City, CA 90230.

A-V Guide: The Learning Media Magazine, 380 Northwest Highway, Des Plaines, IL 60016.

Booklist, American Library Association, 50 East Huron Street, Chicago, IL 60611.

Business Screen Magazine, Back Stage Publications Inc., 165 West 46th Street, New York, NY 10036.

Community College Social Science Journal, Community College Social Science Association, Grossmont College Drive, El Cajon, CA 92020.

Educational Technology, Educational Technology Publications, Inc., 140 Sylvan Avenue, Englewood Cliffs, NJ 07632.

Film News, Open Court Publishing Co., Box 619, La Salle, IL 61301.

Industrial Education, Macmillan Professional Magazines, Inc., 77 Bradford Street, Stamford, CT 06901.

Instructor, 757 Third Avenue, New York, NY 10017.

International Journal of Instructional Media, Baywood Publishing Co., 120 Marine Street, Farmingdale, NY 11735.

Journal of Educational Technology Systems, Baywood Publishing Co., 120 Marine Street, Farmingdale, NY 11735.

Media Digest, National Film and Video Center, Inc., 4321 Sykesville Road, Finkburg, MD 21048.

Media Mix Newsletter: Idea and Resource for Media Communication, Claretion Publications, 221 West Madison Street, Chicago, IL 60606.

Super-8 Filmmaker, PMS Publishing Co., Inc., 609 Mission Street, San Francisco, CA 94105.

Video News, Phillips Publishing, 8401 Connecticut Avenue, Washington, DC 20015.

Videoscope, Gordon and Breach Science Publishers Inc., One Park Avenue, New York, NY 10016.

Wilson Library Bulletin, H. W. Wilson, 950 University Avenue, Bronx, NY 10452.

Finding an isolated review in a periodical seems a discouraging task, but for some periodicals the *Media Review Digest* (Pierian Press, 5000 Washtenaw Avenue, Ann Arbor, MI 48104) indexes reviews from 147 periodicals and services, giving full information about the title, brief excerpts of the reviews, and citations of where the reviews can be found. All entries are arranged by format and are indexed by and subject. Volumes are issued annually. Until 1974, the title was *Multi-Media Reviews Index*. Volumes 5 to 12 cover 1975 to 1982. $189.00 per volume.

The *International Index to Multi-Media Information* was issued from 1973–1975 by Audio-Visual Associates of Pasadena, CA. It incorporated the earlier *Film Review Index* and provided a source for locating media and media reviews by subject and title with a producer/distributor index. The same editors, Wesley A. Doak and William J. Speed, and publisher issued the *Film and Video Review Index*. It included motion picture and video reviews, as well as television programing.

Finally, *Media Review* (346 Ethen Allen Highway, Ridgefield, CT 06877) gives in-depth evaluations of audiovisual programs for classroom use through the college level. Each month's issue focuses on a special area. Full citations are given with suggested discussion topics, content summaries, and evaluative comments from several reviewers. Includes cumulative indexes by title, producer, and subject. $59.00 per year.

Even when they are available, reviews are not the final solution to selecting the most suitable media package for a given training situation. There are several reasons for this. First, so few titles are actually reviewed that selection on that basis alone is very limited. Presently, training and development journals review very few titles; however, there is a trend to include more frequent and better reviews. Second, reviewers reflect their personal perspectives in their reviews. Even though a review may yield a description of the media package, the reviewer may comment on its usefulness from a view-

point different from that of a trainer; thus, it may be misleading. Third, a review of a title for a classroom context may not consider the same factors that a trainer would consider when reviewing the same title. Training and development journals clearly use the worksite training situation and, for that reason, they are prime sources for reviews.

Even when a review is available, the selection preview is not precluded. Reviews can help a trainer decide what to preview and perhaps suggest ideas on how to use the media. But only the preview can determine how suitable the media package will be in view of the training objectives and how it can be fit and adapted to achieve the results sought. The selection process is an essential part of planning and requires the trainer's judgement using the criteria for selection described above.

Previews

The steps of selection covered so far are (1) to make a relatively broad selection of package "candidates" that, given initial available information, seem to be suitable, then select more specific titles with information gathered from directories, sales representatives, promotional brochures, producers' catalogs, or convention exhibits; (2) to apply the selection criteria; and (3) to check review sources. Rather than making a decision on the basis of this information-gathering process only, previewing the top choices ensures substantially better decisions. Too often what sounds good from the available information (especially the producer's catalog) turns out to have important weaknesses in the situation in which the trainer wishes to use it.

Previewing incurs costs, but it should be considered more investment than expense. In addition to the preview fee, there are the costs of shipping, previewing time, record keeping, and the risk of damaging the product. Remember though that previews are invaluable for providing the trainer with an opportunity to plan the techniques to be used as well as to apply the selection criteria—before the rental or purchase price is paid. Previews allow the trainer to weigh the message and content, to consider the possible ways to use the package, and to compare various packages.

Previewing may be done by the trainer, a group of instructors, or a group of previewers. A group will serve to balance the preferences, prejudices, and perspectives of its members. The American Film Festival uses 3 types of jurors for each film: one for the technical qualities, one for the subject area, and one for the usefulness of the film. For the trainer working with a review group, it will be important to be very clear on who makes the final decision concerning purchase or use of the package, whether it is the trainer or the group.

Group evaluation may call for an increase in awareness or skill of the evaluators. A comprehensive and definitive source is Emily S. Jones's *Manual on Film*

Evaluation (Educational Film Library Association, New York, NY, revised ed., 1974). This source includes a number of evaluation forms that can be used to collect the information on which decisions can be made.

ACQUISITION

After discovering and selecting specific media training opportunities, trainers must obtain what they have decided to preview, rent, or purchase. Of the 3 processes—discovery, selection, and acquisition—the latter is the least complex. It is important, however, for if it is not successful, the training package cannot be used. This section covers obtaining packages through primary sources, such as producers or distributors, as well as secondary sources such as libraries. It also explores briefly 2 issues raised by acquisition: compatibility and duplication.

A trainer using several media packages might wish to order some directly from producers yet borrow others through local resources. The most direct and popular route is ordering from the producer or distributor since, with few exceptions, this route offers standardized prices, predictable access and availability, and ensured technical quality of the product. Alternative routes involve borrowing from local public or university libraries, library consortiums (i.e., networks), or commercial clearinghouses. These have the advantage of substantially lesser cost, since usually only rental arrangements are possible. Disadvantages involve additional checking and handling, possible scheduling conflicts, and, at times, problems with technical quality and availability of print materials. The significance of these factors varies with the trainer's requirements and the scope of local resources.

Producers/Distributors

As explained in the section on selection, previews are always advisable. The procedure for requesting a preview through a commercial producer or distributor resembles renting or purchasing procedures. Media directories or producers' catalogs usually include the information needed to order the wanted materials. The producer or distributor is able to respond more quickly and accurately when full information is given, including title, required format, and whether a preview, rental, or purchase is being requested. Format specificity is vital, e.g., "¾″ U-Matic" or "½″ VHS" or "slides in a Kodak Carousel." When unsure about what format to order, supply the brand, type, and model of the available equipment and leave it to the producer to supply what is most suitable. Orders are placed through correspondence or by telephone; several major producers and distributors now have toll-free (800) numbers.

The preview entitles trainers or decision makers to examine the package to judge if it is suitable for the purpose they intend; preview prices are often substantially lower than rental or purchase fees. In fact, previews were once almost universally free, but their misuse for "free" showings or violation of copyright has led all but a few producers and distributors to now charge. Most film and video producers, however, indicate that the preview cost will apply to subsequent rental or purchase. It is important to note that previews are usually not available for audiocassettes, and sometimes previews are available on only one of the many formats that may be available for purchase or rental, i.e., often film is supplied, although video may be available for rental or purchase. Previewing time is often limited, and prompt return of materials is important.

Like previews, rentals are usually for a specified period of time such as 24 hours, 3 days, or one week. Sometimes producers limit the number of times a media component may be used during a specified period, but usually any number of uses is permitted. The borrower incurs liability for damages sustained during use. No modifications are allowed and prompt return of materials is important.

In many cases, outright purchase of a media package is not possible. Rather, the producer, and often the distributor, chooses to "lease" the package to ensure limitations on the use of the work. (Lease terms are spelled out in producers' catalogs and, usually, on order forms.) Producers such as BNA Communications, Inc., National Educational Media, Inc., and Dartnell emphasize that their films and video must be used within the purchaser's organization only. Given the high cost of producing audiovisual training materials, particularly films, producers do not wish their work to be duplicated, loaned to colleagues in other organizations, modified, or given pubic showings for profit. The copyright law supports producers' rights. Many are reluctant to sell to libraries or clearinghouses.

Producer/distributor catalogs give the specific terms and cost of preview, rental, purchase, and lease arrangements, as well as the desired form of payment and other procedural options. Because of price and format changes, however, it is advisable to confirm this information.

Other Sources

In addition to the possibility of ordering directly from producers and distributors, media packages can often be obtained for loan through public, college, or university libraries with audiovisual collections. The media component, though not always the print supportive materials, is loaned either for preview or use with a group. Limitations on library use and loan policies vary locally, but publicly supported institutions are generally accessible. Major limitations may exist, however, such as whether they have the title wanted, how heavily its use is scheduled, what formats are available, and producer-assigned conditions, such as minimum rental fees or restricted circulation (e.g., "for classroom use only").

Most institutions have catalogs of their holdings either in book or card form. Some with statewide obligations issue book catalogs for distribution. Some examples follow:

Colorado Video Resources (Video Clearinghouse, Public Library Media Center, Boulder, CO) lists statewide holdings available to individuals and groups within the state.

Film Catalog, 1979–81 (University of Colorado Educational Media Center) also loans films nationally at a reasonable cost.

Iowa Films, 1981–1983 (University of Iowa/Iowa State University) makes films available for modest cost on a national basis.

Media Resources, 1980–1982 (University of California Extension Media Center) includes 4,000 films and 200 videotapes available throughout the United States.

In addition to such general catalogs, some institutions distribute select lists in specialized areas, e.g., Pennsylvania State University Audio Visual Services' *Films for Business and Industrial Organization and Management* (5th ed., 1980) or The University of Illinois Film Center's *Business and Economics Films* (1980).

Discovering what institutions and organizations build and maintain media collections in a given locale is a challenge. Although it is dated (published in 1976), the *North American Film and Video Directory: A Guide to Media Collections and Services* (R. R. Bowker, 1180 Avenue of the Americas, New York, NY 10036) identifies over 2,000 college, public, special, museum, or archival libraries and media centers with collections of more than 25 16mm films or videotapes. Each listing gives the subject emphasis, loan and rental policies, budgets, publications, income, and facilities; arrangement is geographical, and an appendix lists film cooperatives.

National, regional, and local collaborative efforts have developed as groups seek to share their resources. Such efforts formed the Consortium of University Film Centers. Its 50-member institutions hold 40,000 16mm films that are listed in the *Educational Film Locator* (R. R. Bowker, 1180 Avenue of the Americas, New York, NY 10036, 1980). Although its major focus is curricular, many training titles are available.

Both academic institutions and corporations can be members of the Intercollegiate Video Clearinghouse (PO Drawer 33000R, Miami, FL 33133) which seeks to increase the availability and exchange of instructional programs. To do so, it issues catalogs of "educationally sound" video programs, many in the business area that are suitable for training. Videotape programs are available for the cost of reproduction.

An example of a local business initiative is Videocenters (1401 Madison, Seattle, WA 98104) which includes over 1,000 video programs from 30 major companies available for rental or purchase. In addition to making these programs available, Videocenters works with organizations to help them develop employee train-

ing using the cross-section of media in their collection and beyond it.

Compatability and Duplication

Acquisition raises 2 significant issues, one technical and one legal. The first is the need to ensure compatibility between media package format and the equipment available to play or project it. For the organization with access to all types of such equipment, no special consideration is necessary. More typically, where available equipment is limited, compatibility becomes an important selection criteria. If acquiring new equipment is not feasible, 3 approaches are possible: limit selection possiblities to formats that can be used, obtain the required equipment temporarily, or special order the desired format from the producer if it cannot be regularly supplied.

The second issue, the legal one, is that of duplication. The federal Copyright Law, effective 1978, prohibits copying of the media or the print materials in training packages without explicit permission. Many producers include specific stipulations in their lease or purchase agreements. Although some systems are designed to prevent the making of copies, none are totally effective. That fact, plus the high cost of media and the ease of duplication, can be tempting to trainers.

Two resources are helpful for trainers wishing to explore this issue.

Association for Educational Communications and Technology. *Copyright and Educational Media: A Guide to Fair Use and Permissions Procedures.* Washington, DC: Association for Educational Communications and Technology and Association of Media Producers, 1977.

Johnston, Donald F. *Copyright Handbook.* 2nd ed. New York: R. R. Bowker, 1982.

Concern about illegal duplication has caused the National Audio Visual Association to take an active step by establishing an information exchange to identify and circulate the names of violators to its member producers, enabling them to refuse to service orders from violators. Similarly, the Training Media Distributors' Association shares information on film piracy incidents and legal proceedings, seeks stronger criminal penalties for copyright infringement, and has established a $1,000 reward program for information leading to film piracy convictions. Duplication is an ethical issue, as well as a legal one, for trainers using media.

The trainer experimenting with the use of media to test its feasibility need only use a few basic guides to discover, select, and acquire useful media packages. The trainer planning regular use of media would need more comprehensive and specialized resources. Luckily, new resources appear each year to assist discovery and selection. Thus, the resources listed above are just a beginning.

Chapter 4
Developing Media Training Packages In-House

After using "off-the-shelf" media training packages and finding them of significant value, trainers may also wish to explore in-house production of audiovisual or audio units. Certainly, this approach may result in media that meets an organization's specific needs better than any prepackaged program, for scenes from the organization's worksite can demonstrate functions and equipment as no outside effort can. Of course, cost and the other elements necessary to develop and produce in-house media as well as the print exercises, cases, workbooks, and manuals to enhance their effectiveness, must be explored.

Generally speaking, in-house media development is warranted when there are large numbers of learners with common needs for training. If these learners are spread over a wide geographic area, in-house media could become vital. A major factor favoring in-house development is substantial long range use of the hardware and facilities that will be needed. Often, such equipment will be used for other organizational functions, such as management and communication. This possibility will probably increase as new technologies arrive to change how organizations communicate, manage, and train.

Developing in-house media offers new potentials that are worth noting. One potential is that of using portions of training media for external public relations, lay education, customer education, or stockholder information reports. Multiplying the uses of training media often diminishes the cost factor. Another potential is the possibility of marketing the developed media program to other organizations in the same or parallel fields. This can serve to reduce the expense, or even make a profit, if it is successful.

Several important aspects face the trainer contemplating the possibility of developing, producing, distributing, and even marketing training media. In addition to the need for a budget, specialized skills are required. Technical skills of instructional design, educational technology, and audiovisual techniques are needed in the preproduction or planning stages. In this same stage, script writing and editing, organization, and detail work are required, as is talent selection. Production demands coordinating and directing talent, lighting, sound, staging, and graphics development and editing. Throughout, there is the constant need to remain aware of the needs of the learners and the organization.

For trainers and organizations wanting to consider the alternative avenues for developing in-house media, there are at least 4 such avenues. One is to contract for media consultants to come into the organization to plan and produce training media. This alternative assumes that preliminary investigation has been done by the trainer and that s/he understands the needs to be met and that nonprint media are most capable of fulfilling them. [Two resources mentioned in Chapter 3 would provide good starting places to find media firms and consultants: *Audiovisual Market Place* and *Training Marketplace Directory*. Additional resources include the *Annual Directory of Commercial Producers/Production Companies* issued each August by *Audio-Visual Directions* (25550 Hawthorne Boulevard, Suite 314, Torrance, CA 90505), *Who's Who in AV Presentation* issued in June by *Audio-Visual Communications* (475 Park Avenue South, New York, NY 10016), and *Annual Directory of Production Houses* issued in the spring by *Educational and Industrial Television Magazine*, C.S. Tepfer Publishing Co. (51 Sugar Hollow Road, Danbury, CT 06810).]

A second alternative is to develop an idea for the training needed, frame a proposal, and use it to approach outside producers. It is equally important when using this alternative to know the media to be used—slides, filmstrip, video, film, or audio—since selection helps when choosing a producer. In this and the first alternative, knowing and making expectations clear will be extremely important. Those expectations must be specified in a contractual relationship with the producer and/or consultant to protect both parties.

The third alternative is to open new professional staff positions. This, of course, will be a longer term budget commitment and will call for regular office facilities as well as production equipment and facilities. This level of commitment would indicate extensive involvement of the in-house training program to mediated training and would require major organizational decisions to back the move.

The final alternative is for the trainer to explore how in-house media development might be possible with present staff, equipment, and facility expenditures. Producing audiotapes is feasible for most organizations of modest size, and videotaping is becoming more feasible. This alternative implies that the trainer will be learning and building skills in new areas, a process which includes academic work, short courses, self-directed reading and study, apprenticeship—all demanding of time and funds.

With each of these alternatives, the change from using prepackaged training materials to developing and maybe producing one's own is a tremendous leap. Such an important personal and organizational change warrants preparation through careful study, discussion with colleagues who have made the change, and visiting other organizations with in-house production facilities. Exploratory talks with outside producers will be helpful.

The following list gives titles of books that focus on the techniques, the skills, and the equipment and facilities required for audiovisual development and production in-house.

Association for Educational Communications and Technology. *Producing Slide and Tape Presentations*. Washington, DC: Association for Audiovisual Communications and Technology, 1980.

Basic Filmmakers Packet. Rochester, NY: Eastman Kodak Company, n.d.

Combes, Peter. *Television Production for Education*. Woburn, MA: Focal Press, 1978.

Ertel, Robert E. *The Multi-Image Production*. Laguna Niguel, CA: WTI Corporation, 1977.

Film Animation: A Simplified Aprproach. New York: Unipub, 1976.

Gordon, Roger. *The Art of Multi-Image*. Abington, PA: Association for Multi-Image, 1978.

Harwood, Don. *Everything You Always Wanted to Know about Portable Videotape Recording*. 3rd ed. Syosset, NY: VTR Publishing Company, 1978.

Harwood, Don. *Video as a Second Language: How to Make a Video Documentary*. Rev. ed. Syosset, NY: VTR Publishing Company, 1979.

Kemp, Jerrold E. *Planning and Producing Audio Visual Materials*. 4th ed. New York: Harper & Row, 1980.

Klein, Walter J. *The Sponsored Film*. New York: Hastings House Publishers, 1976.

Laybourne, Kit. *The Animation Book*. New York: Crown Publishers, 1979.

Levitan, Eli L. *Handbook of Animation Techniques*. New York: Van Nostrand Reinhold Co., 1979.

Manvell, Roger, and Huntley, John. *The Technique of Film Music*. 2nd ed. New York: Hastings House Publishers, 1976.

Mayer, Michael F. *The Film Industries: Practical Business-Legal Problems in Production, Distribution and Exhibition*. 2nd ed. New York: Hastings House Publishers, 1978.

Media Profiles: The Audiovisual Marketing Newsletter. New York: Olympic Media Information, annual.

Millerson, Gerald. *Basic Television Staging*. New York: Hastings House Publishers, 1974.

Millerson, Gerald. *The Technique of Television Production*. 10th ed. Woburn, MA: Focal Press, 1979.

Minor, Edward O. *Handbook for Preparing Visual Media*. New York: McGraw-Hill, 1978.

Nisbett, Alec. *The Technique of Sound Studio*. Woburn, MA: Focal Press, 1979.

Planning and Producing Slide Programs. Rochester, NY: Eastman Kodak, n.d.

Q, Pat, and Q, Mike. *Manual of Slide Duplicating*. Garden City, NY: Amphoto, 1978.

Robinson, J. F., and Lowe, Stephen. *Videotape Recording: Theory and Practice*. 3rd ed. Woburn, MA: Focal Press, 1981.

Russell, James D. *The Audio-Tutorial System*. (Instructional Design Library, Vol. 3.) Englewood Cliffs, NJ: Educational Technology Publications, 1978.

Samuelson, David. *Motion Picture Camera Techniques*. (Media Manuals) Woburn, MA: Focal Press, 1978.

Schmidt, William D. *Designing the Film*. Pullman, WA: Information Futures, 1978.

Stecker, Elinor. *The Master Handbook of Still and Movie Titling for Amateur and Professional*. Blue Ridge Summit, PA: Tab Books, 1980.

Stolovitch, Harold D. *Audiovisual Training Modules*. (Instructional Design Library, Vol. 4.) Englewood Cliffs, NJ: Educational Technology Publications, 1978.

Sunier, John. *Slide, Sound & Film Strip Production*. Woburn, MA: Focal Press, 1981.

Swain, Dwight V. *Film Scriptwriting: A Practical Manual*. New York: Hastings House Publishers, 1976.

Swain, Dwight V. *Scripting for Video and Audiovisual Media*. Woburn, MA: Focal Press, 1981.

Utz, Peter. *Video User's Handbook*. 2nd ed. Englewood Cliffs, NJ: Prentice-Hall, 1982.

Wilkie, Bernard. *Creating Special Effects for TV and Films*. Woburn, MA: Focal Press, 1977.

Yulsman, Jerry. *The 8MM Movie Book*. New York: Coward, McCann & Geoghegan Inc., 1979.

Zettl, Herbert. *Television Production Handbook and Workbook*. Belmont, CA: Wadsworth Publishing Co., 1977.

The following periodicals include articles which focus on the production of audiovisual products.

Bulletin for Film and Video Information, Anthology Film Archives, 80 Wooster Street, New York, NY 10012.

Business Screen: Back Stage Magazine Supplement, Back Stage Productions, Inc., 165 West 46th Street, New York, NY 10036.

Business Screen Magazine, Back Stage Publications, Inc., 165 West 46th Street, New York, NY 10036.

Educational and Industrial Television Magazine, C. S. Tepfer Publishing Co., 51 Sugar Hollow Road, Danbury, CT 06810.

Video Trade News, C.S. Tepfer Publishing Co., 51 Sugar Hollow Road, Danbury, CT 06810.

Videography, United Business Publications, Inc., 475 Park Avenue South, New York, NY 10016.

Chapter 5
Conclusion

Trainers skeptical of and resistant to the use of media packages in employee training may hamper their own effectiveness, both long term and short term. On a short term basis, using media can enhance an employee's learning experiences and a trainer's capabilities. By refusing to consider media package use, both may be impeded. Further long term implications exist. Integrating media in training design now sets a pattern for the learner and the trainer, preparing both for the new training technologies that are becoming increasingly available. With the advent of early audiovisual methods in schools, some instructors and learners were blockers— suspicious of technology's promises, awed by the expense or complexity, and anxious about their own status and ability. Conversely, enthusiasts found audiovisual methods brought the promise of individualized learning, introduced a new aspect of "reality" into the learning situation, and offered useful instructional support. Now, similar blockers and enthusiasts emerge in relation to computer-assisted instruction, interactive videodisc, and satellite possibilities.

"During the next decade, virtually all audiovisual equipment will be affected by computer technology. Already, computers permit highly individualized training and learning programs, generate graphics and animation, edit videotape, and program multi-image systems, to mention a few applications. The integration of video and computers will eventually provide the ultimate communications and information network."[1] This statement by Harry McGee, an officer of the National Audio Visual Association, points to the new dimension facing—and challenging—today's trainers. Each month, the training literature becomes more and more prolific with descriptions of the wonders and dangers of this new dimension. Changes, as well as challenges, are certain in the way training is developed and done, in who does it, and how it is done.

A major area for change and challenge from the trainer's perspective involves a shift in roles. Tomorrow's trainer will relate to the learner, the training and development effort, and the organization different from the way s/he relates today. Some roles may simply be extensions of present roles; others will be new. New training technologies, particularly those that are interac-

tive, enable learners to work with suitably designed programs to improve their performance. Logically, the trainer is likely to continue to connect learners with resources from which to learn through guidance and counseling. Though this is not a new role, it will certainly exist at a new level, since many learners will not be familiar with learning via media programs and special equipment.

Tomorrow's trainer will find that the planning and production of training events requires new skills, knowledge of new resources, and knowledge of how to use them. Those skilled in instructional design and presentation will need to work in close collaboration with specialists in computers and video and with content specialists. This type of team approach will be necessary to address the changing needs of learners and organizations and to take advantage of the possibilities of the new technologies.

Within the organizational structure, tomorrow's trainer will find new roles. The means by which an organization communicates and manages will shift to accommodate new technologies, opening up new possibilities for assessing training needs, evaluating learners' performance, and, perhaps most exciting, closely linking learning with on-the-job application. The trainer will find ways to integrate the training and development function more significantly with the organization's communications and management functions.

These areas of role change in store for trainers point up the importance of media training packages and their skillful use. "Through design, education will be making an ironic turnabout of major proportions: live instruction, which has to this point in history seemed the most interactive learning, will become the least interactive, and packaged media, which has to this point seemed the least interactive, will become the most interactive."[2] The experience and expertise gained by using media training packages will prepare a trainer for using new technologies.

Whereas predominant use of audiovisual techniques began with the school, application of audiovisual interactive learning is more likely to take place in industry and government because of their more rapid adoption of interactive communication. The degree of media use in business, industry, and government is estimated at 20 percent. Of that, 70 percent is estimated as applied to continuing education and training.[3] The trainer who uses media packages now can experiment and explore the opportunities for these new roles, new methods, and new approaches to training.

This exploration allows trainers themselves to become transition tools, preparing themselves, their functions, their learners, and their organizations for the future. All of these will be affected by the changes ahead and, as such, aware trainers can become vital instruments of change as educators for the future.

References

1. Harry McGee, "The AV Communications Revolution," *Photomethods* 24 (1) (January 1981): 39.

2. Willard Thomas, " Use of Media in Business, Government, and Medicine," in *Providing Continuing Education by Media and Technology* , New Directions for Continuing Education, No. 5, 1980 (San Francisco, CA: Jossey-Bass, 1980), pp. 56–57.

3. David Hon, "The Videodisc, Microcomputer and the Satellite," *Training and Development Journal* 34 (12) (December 1980): 28.

Part II
Directory of Media Packages

How to Use This Directory

This directory provides a tool for managers and trainers who are seeking learning opportunities that are relevant for personnel in the workplace. Entries that are included address typical training needs in today's organizations: current business, management, and personnel trends and practices. These audio and audiovisual media packages offer methods for general information and instruction, skills development, and attitude formation. Those responsible for training and development can use this guide to aid their efforts in locating commercially available audiovisual training packages for preview, rental, or purchase.

Each entry features an audio or audiovisual product as the primary training vehicle rather than offering them as supplementary tools. Formats include films, videocassettes, slides, filmstrips, and audiocassettes, most of which have been released since 1970. Computer software is not included, nor are overhead transparencies, posters, models, and realia, unless they supplement other audio or audiovisual formats.

Certain categories of material have also been excluded. Materials produced by universities and colleges are usually curricular and of limited value and acceptance by adults at work. Those produced primarily for network broadcast or entertainment purposes, career and vocational guidance, and language training focus on specialized purposes and are not directly work oriented. Audiocassettes from association, conference, or convention meetings are not included. Technical and safety practice training or materials relating to specific equipment models are omitted since industry-specific training materials are widely publicized through trade journals and vendors. Promotional materials from industries or organizations are excluded for the same reason.

Materials about motivation are included but not those for "inspiration" or personal growth unless their focus is primarily on the workplace. Sales training materials are included only if they emphasize general customer service principles. Packages where vendors require specific training or licensure of trainers, either in-house or with the vendor, are excluded as are those noted as restricted for certain audiences and not generally available.

DIRECTORY ARRANGEMENT

Entries are arranged by topic, then alphabetically by title. A single title may be listed in more than one subject category, although only one listing will be that title's "main listing." Each main listing includes a unique entry number. Users can browse within a given topic, or they can use the indexes to seek specific titles through their citation numbers.

Entry information is as complete, accurate, and current as possible, with information gleaned from producers' and distributors' catalogs, promotional material, published reviews, and direct personal contact. Priority has been given to listing producers of the material; when that was not feasible, distributors were listed. Although useful as a guide, information about price, availability, and format becomes out of date quickly. Consequently, direct contact with the producer or distributor is the best source for the latest, most accurate information. Annotations are descriptive, not evaluative, since few materials were previewed. Entries are for informational purposes only and not intended to advertise or promote specific materials, producers, or distributors.

To ensure that materials are suitable for an intended and specific purpose, users of this directory are strongly urged to preview selected materials. Guidelines for evaluating materials when previewed are given in Part I.

THE CITATION

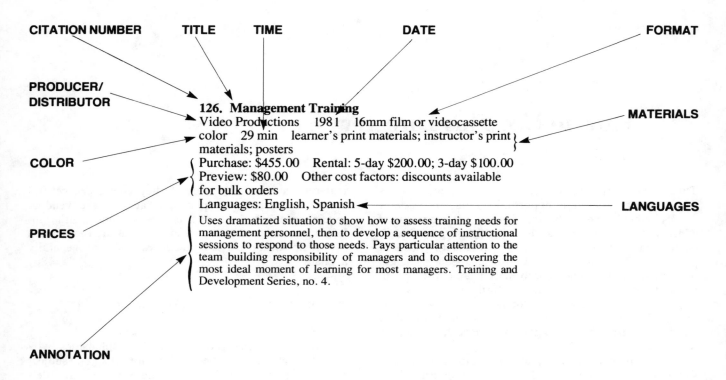

CITATION NUMBER   TITLE   TIME   DATE   FORMAT

PRODUCER/
DISTRIBUTOR

COLOR

PRICES

ANNOTATION

MATERIALS

LANGUAGES

126. Management Training
Video Productions   1981   16mm film or videocassette
color   29 min   learner's print materials; instructor's print
materials; posters
Purchase: $455.00   Rental: 5-day $200.00; 3-day $100.00
Preview: $80.00   Other cost factors: discounts available
for bulk orders
Languages: English, Spanish

Uses dramatized situation to show how to assess training needs for
management personnel, then to develop a sequence of instructional
sessions to respond to those needs. Pays particular attention to the
team building responsibility of managers and to discovering the
most ideal moment of learning for most managers. Training and
Development Series, no. 4.

Date: When known, the date of release is indicated. No date designation does not necessarily indicate an older film.

Producer or Distributor: Although a title may be available from many suppliers, only one is listed here. Addresses are in the Appendix for ordering or inquiry.

Format: Formats are indicated in general terms. The availability of formats changes frequently and producers or distributors will often transfer from one format to another on special order. Consequently the term "videocassette" may refer to 1-inch, 2-inch, ½-inch Beta or ½-inch VHS or ¾-inch U-Matic cassettes. Videocassette is used here as a generic term, even though videotape would be the larger term and would encompass videocassette. Filmstrip cartridge refers to materials that combine filmstrip and sound for use with Audiscan or La Belle equipment (projectors). Slides and audiocassettes are usually packaged as a set and will also require specific equipment to use. Audiocassettes are almost always cartridges, rather than tapes, for use in cassette players. When inquiring about or ordering materials, the producer can be more helpful if told the equipment they will be used with.

Prices: The indicated purchase price may be a lease purchase arrangement or an outright purchase. Similarly with rental. The producer or distributor will indicate current policies in response to an inquiry or order. The prices shown are those that are current rather than those

at special discount rates. Some packages consist of modules that can be purchased and rented separately. In these cases both rates are given. Sometimes different formats can be purchased at different rates and those also are indicated. Rental periods vary; sometimes more than one rental period is available from a given producer or distributor. In most cases rental and preview prices will apply to purchase if done promptly. Most producers have restrictions, such as purchase from resale or rerental, or use of products on television or radio. Previews are not used for training purposes but for consideration for purchase. Other information about cost, such as membership only prices or discounts, is also included.

Language: English is assumed on all materials. When versions are available in other languages, they are also indicated.

Materials: Instructor's print materials usually include such varieties as leader's guides, discussion guides, training exercises, scripts, briefing manuals, or facilitator's guides. Learner's print materials usually include worksheets or work books, quiz booklets, case studies, narratives or guides. Materials that are not able to be categorized in either of these groupings are listed by name.

Annotation: The annotation describes the content and coverage and the primary method used, such as dramatization, panel discussion, etc. It identifies, if possible, the intended audience, if that is not clear from the title or description. It indicates who is featured if s/he is well-known generally or in the field. Where the title is one of a series, the series note is indicated, or if it is to be used in conjunction with another title, that information is given. Series are not listed under series names.

List of Media Packages

ABSENTEEISM

1. Absenteeism
BNA Communications, Inc 1978 16mm film or videocassette color 18 min learner's print materials
Purchase: $630.00 Rental: 5-day $150.00; 3-day $105.00 Preview: $35.00

A dramatized open-ended case study, "The Unexcused Absence," on film is supplemented with a decision sheet to involve learners working on the case. The following additional written cases offer further practice: "The Conscientious Bible Student," "The Moonlighting Policeman," and "The Incarcerated Employee." Final arbitrators' decisions are given. Audiocassette gives a round table discussion on absenteeism. Preventive Discipline Training Program, no. 2.

2. Absenteeism
Xerox Education Publications 1979 16mm film or videocassette color 12 min
Purchase: film $255.00; video $155.00 Rental: $28.00 Preview: $28.00

Following Charlie through a typical office day reveals the physical and psychological stresses that he faces, and the causes for his chronic absenteeism become clear. Insights about the causes and cures of this expensive malady open the possibility for discussion between employees and management. Particularly useful for supervisors.

3. Controlling Absenteeism
BNA Communications, Inc 1974 16mm film or videocassettes color 32 min instructor's print materials
Purchase: $550.00 Rental: 5-day $150.00; 3-day $105.00 Preview: $35.00
Languages: English, Spanish

Identifies 5 types of absentees, and Saul Gellerman shows, through dramatized portrayals, their motivations and how to deal with them. Offers 3 general rules for supervisors to reduce absenteeism. Advanced Supervision Series, no. 3.

4. Controlling Absenteeism
Bureau of Business Practice 1977 audiocassette 30 min
Purchase: $9.95

Demonstrates ways to detect phony excuses and confront repeat offenders. Offers a follow-up technique to get absentees back on the job and "make up for lost time."

5. How to Eliminate and Control Absenteeism
Bureau of Business Practice 1976 16mm film or videocassette color 20 min
Purchase: $450.00 Rental: $95.00 Preview: $49.00

Shows the fine line between valid and questionable absence and offers a check-off and follow-up system to reduce the problem. Intended for supervisors faced with excessive employee absenteeism.

How to Reduce Absenteeism and Turnover. For complete citation, see EMPLOYEE PERFORMANCE.

6. Rx for Absenteeitis
Dartnell 1978 16mm film or videocassette color 15 min instructor's print materials; learner's print materials
Purchase: $475.00 Rental: $95.00
Languages: English, Portuguese

Dramatized "on the job" incidents illustrate 5 techniques supervisors can use to avoid unwarranted absences. Identifies the symptoms of "absenteeitis" and its consequences. Shows how to use preventive medicine and enforce company rules for best results.

7. Weber's Choice
Motivision, Ltd 1975 16mm film or videocassette color 23½ min instructor's print materials
Purchase: $475.00 Rental: $25.00
Languages: English, French

Shows plant foreman and an employee in conflict over absenteeism. The foreman tries to handle it "his way," is unsuccessful, and then discovers the effectiveness of the employee counseling program.

ACCOUNTING

8. Accounting Principles
HBJ Media Systems Corporation 1981 100 slide/audiocassette presentations instructor's print materials; learner's print materials
Purchase: $15,000.00

Gives a comprehensive survey of accounting principles and practice covering accounting procedures for service, merchandising, and manufacturing businesses. Includes in-depth analysis of accounting for proprietorships, partnerships, and corporations and gives the concepts of financial and managerial accounting. Introduces cost accounting, budgeting, departmental accounting, and analysis and interpretation of financial statements. Intended for employees who are training for management or administrative positions. Includes 24 modules; suggested for 180–200 hours.

9. Basic Accounting Cycle
HBJ Media Systems Corporation 1981 19 slide/audiocassette presentations instructor's print materials; learner's print materials
Purchase: $2,850.00

Introduces accounting and financial statements and how to prepare them. Includes 7 modules. Intended for entry-level employees in accounting and financial services departments. Suggested for 25–35 hours.

10. Basic Accounting: Introduction
Prentice Hall Media 6 filmstrips and 6 audiocassettes instructor's print materials; learner's print materials
Purchase: $199.00

Intended to give beginners a firm foundation in theory and basic skills. For use as individual self-study or small group instruction. Explains double entry bookkeeping, defines key terms, and demonstrates common procedures. Offers valuable practice in preparing a balance sheet, making the opening entry in a general journal, and recording transactions in a service business.

11. Basic Accounting: The Accounting Cycle
Prentice Hall Media 12 filmstrips and 12 audiocassettes instructor's print materials; learner's print materials
Purchase: $199.00

After a brief review of basic terms and principles, modules lead beginners step-by-step through the procedures required to record the financial data of a service business in general journal, ledger, and worksheets.

12. Depreciation and Inflation
Xicom-Video Arts 1980 16mm film or videocassette color 18 min
Purchase: $475.00 Rental: $100.00 Preview: $35.00

Shows how overstatements of company profitability can be corrected to account for inflation. Diagrams, models, and John Cleese's humor reveals how to accommodate the distortion. Illustrates depreciation errors, such as depreciating at cost rather than replacement value, and their consequences. Describes current cost accounting—what it means and how it works.

Finance and Accounting for Nonfinancial Managers. For complete citation, *see* FINANCIAL MANAGEMENT.

Finance and Accounting Overview for Non-Financial Managers. For complete citation, *see* FINANCIAL MANAGEMENT.

Fundamentals of Finance and Accounting for Non-Financial Executives. For complete citation, *see* FINANCIAL MANAGEMENT.

13. Maintaining Payroll Records
HBJ Media Systems Corporation 1981 3 slide/audiocassette presentations instructor's print materials; learner's print materials
Purchase: $895.00

Shows how to compute salaries, wages, and deductions for standard payroll accounting records and how to make journal entries for payroll and for payroll taxes. Suggested for 5–6 hours.

14. Practical Accounting Skills
HBJ Media Systems Corporation 1981 50 slide/audiocassette presentations instructor's print materials; learner's print materials
Purchase: $7,500.00

Shows the basic accounting cycle and use of special journals and subsidiary ledgers, accounting for merchandise inventory, payroll accounting, internal control of cash, accounts receivable and payable, and depreciation methods. Intended for accounting and financial clerks. Includes 13 modules. Suggested for 80–100 hours.

15. What Every Profit-Oriented Manager Should Know about Accounting
Instructional Dynamics, Inc 1978 10 audiocassettes 6 hrs learner's print materials
Purchase: $125.00

Explains key business accounting processes in a clear, straightforward language. Includes balance sheets, inventory, income statements, financial analysis, budgeting, value concepts and capital budgeting, product costing, and specialized decisions. For those who must interpret financial data.

AFFIRMATIVE ACTION
See EQUAL EMPLOYMENT OPPORTUNITY

ALCOHOLISM

Addictions, Compulsions and Alternative Highs. For complete citation, *see* HEALTH.

16. Alcohol: Drug of Choice
BNA Communications, Inc 1972 16mm film or videocassette color 27 min instructor's print materials
Purchase: $475.00 Rental: 5-day $150.00; 3-day $105.00 Preview: $35.00

Alcoholism is costly to the individual and to the organization. This film alternates dramatization and narration to show how a potential alcoholic feels and reasons, the dangers of addiction, and how to estimate how much alcoholism costs organizations annually. Practical focus on how to spot and deal with an alcoholic. Supplementary booklet available separately. Project Health Series, no. 2.

17. Alcohol, Drugs or Alternatives
Barr Films 16mm film or videocassette color 26 min
Purchase: $490.00   Rental: $100.00   Preview: $50.00

Brings out the values in a life lived without alcohol or drugs. Offers ways to handle stress and develop confidence and self-worth. Encourages use of outside help in solving problems.

18. Alcoholism: Almost Everything You Need to Know to Recognize It
Salenger Educational Media 1975 16mm film or videocassette color 15 min   instructor's print materials
Purchase: $410.00   Rental: 10-day $90.00   Preview: 5-day $30.00

Three dramatized stories reveal the signs of alcoholism and courses of corrective action. Defining alcoholism as a disease, the film identifies signs of alcoholism, where professional help is available, and when and how to use it.

19. Alcoholism and the Supervisor
NPL, Inc 79 slides and audiocassette 12 min instructor's print materials
Purchase: $50.00

Helps supervisors detect alcohol-related problems and solve them in subtle, effective ways. Embodies input from the National Council On Alcoholism and several industrial companies.

20. Alcoholism Film
Barr Films 16mm film or videocassette color 23 min
Purchase: $460.00   Rental: $100.00   Preview: $50.00

Creates a checklist of alcoholism's symptoms. Through a supportive and nonjudgmental tone, emphasizes the importance of recognizing the symptoms and taking responsibility for overcoming it. Hosted by Rod Serling.

21. America on the Rocks
National Audiovisual Center 1973 16mm film or videocassette color 29 min
Purchase: film $250.00; video $65.00   Rental: $25.00

Presents the dimensions of alcoholism as a problem in the work environment. Terms it America's number one drug problem. Narrated by Robert Mitchum.

22. How to Handle the Problem Drinker
Bureau of Business Practice 1974 16mm film or videocassette color 20 min
Purchase: $425.00   Rental: $95.00   Preview: 15-day $45.00

Gives supervisors a realistic approach for achieving positive results. To help problem drinkers become productive employees, typical plant and office scenes recreate situations supervisors may have faced. Presents proven steps to motivate the alcoholic employee to bring performance back up to par.

23. Problems of Alchoholism in Industry
Development Digest audiocassette
Purchase: $13.75

Donald F. Godwin examines traditional attitudes and remedies for alcoholism and ways they encourage drinking. Describes a program to identify employees having problems with alcoholism.

24. Something of the Danger that Exists
National Audiovisual Center 1978 videocassette color 59 min
Purchase: $165.00

Conveys a broad understanding of the many problems of alcohol abuse. Stresses that alcoholism is a treatable disease, discusses pharmacological aspects of alcohol in combination with other drugs, and addresses questions in a small group setting.

25. Thanks for the One Time
LCA Video/Films 16mm film or videocassette 45 min   instructor's print materials
Purchase: $495.00   Rental: $100.00   Preview: $50.00

Low-keyed intense docudrama which supports employee assistance programs to help alcoholic or drug-dependent workers recover and return to productive work. Illuminates the special problems involved when a high-ranking employee or professional person is an alcoholic and points out the importance of the employer in motivating the alcoholic to seek treatment. Deals with the difficult problems faced by the co-workers of alcoholics.

APPRAISAL
See PERFORMANCE APPRAISAL

ARBITRATION AND LABOR RELATIONS
See also NEGOTIATION; GRIEVANCE

Anatomy of a Grievance. For complete citation, *see* GRIEVANCE.

26. Arbitration of a Grievance
National Audiovisual Center 1974 16mm film or videocassette color 36 min   instructor's print materials
Purchase: film $229.50; video $132.00   Rental: $30.00

Demonstrates a mediator's arbitration of the grievance shown in *Anatomy of a Grievance*. Emphasis is on techniques of preparation and presentation for arbitration. Important for persons handling arbitration cases.

27. Arbitration: The Truth of the Matter
BNA Communications, Inc   1975   16mm film or videocassette   color   50 min   instructor's print materials; learner's print materials
Purchase: license $610.00   Rental: 5-day $150.00; 3-day $105.00   Preview: $35.00   Other cost factors: discounts available for bulk orders of materials

Enacted case shows how an arbitration hearing is conducted, what really takes place, how principals and witnesses should prepare for and conduct themselves during the hearing, examination and cross-examination of witnesses, introduction of exhibits, and what to avoid. Labor mediator Adolph Koven acts as arbitrator. Useful tool to review management practices or prepare witnesses for arbitration hearings.

28. At the Table
National Audiovisual Center   1974   16mm film or videocassette   color   45 min
Purchase: film $261.00; video $148.50   Rental: $17.50

Depicts the negotiation of 2 federal bargaining issues: subcontracting and work schedules. Views tactics and techniques of negotiations as practiced at the bargaining table.

Button, Button. For complete citation, *see* GRIEVANCE.

Case of Barbara Parsons. For complete citation, *see* GRIEVANCE.

29. Collective Bargaining
Development Digest   audiocassette
Purchase: $13.75

General presentation by Leonard Woodcock from labor point of view covering labor bargaining and legislation affecting workers.

30. Dimensions of Bargaining
National Audiovisual Center   1978   16mm film or videocassette   color   29 min
Purchase: film $198.75; video $65.00   Rental: $25.00 (film only)

Outlines the various dimensions of collective bargaining. Demonstrates the different levels: horizontal (between teams), internal (with each team), vertical (between each team and its constituency), and external (between each team and the community). Purpose is to generate thought and discussion about the ways in which each dimension manifests itself and the impact each has on the structure, content, and tone of negotiations. Out of Conflict—Accord Series.

Equal Opportunity. For complete citation, *see* EQUAL EMPLOYMENT OPPORTUNITY.

Handling Health and Safety Grievances. For complete citation, *see* GRIEVANCE.

31. Inside Look at Collective Bargaining
NPL, Inc   16mm film   color   45 min   instructor's print materials
Purchase: $595.00   Rental: $95.00

Explores the dynamics of contract negotiations in detail. Portrays labor and management at the bargaining table on the eve of a strike deadline trying to hammer out an agreement on 7 issues: management rights, no-strike clause, discipline, sex discrimination, hospitalization insurance, maternity benefits, and skilled trades wage adjustment.

32. Labor Relations for Supervisors
Management Resources, Inc   2 audiocassettes   instructor's print materials; learner's print materials
Purchase: $75.00

Five-hour course provides disciplined and practical training in 4 areas of labor relations where many supervisors are weak: the labor contract, the arbitration process, proper grievance procedures, and effective discipline. Includes case studies. Useful for first-line supervisors.

33. People at Work...A Right to Refuse
CRM/McGraw-Hill Films   16mm film or videocassette   color   13 min
Purchase: $425.00   Rental: $95.00   Preview: free

Dramatizes the dilemma of the supervisor when workers and senior management have legitimate but conflicting views on a work solution. Raises the question of how to represent the needs of management and workers in crucial situations.

34. Supervisor and Arbitration
Bureau of Business Practice   16mm film or videocassette   color   20 min
Purchase: $425.00   Rental: $95.00   Preview: $45.00

Documented grievance cases reveal the 5 leading reasons why disciplinary penalties are often reversed at arbitration. Shows how to plug these lax areas and build penalties on a foundation that's so solid it virtually eliminated grievances from ever going to arbitration.

35. Waldenville I
National Audiovisual Center   1978   16mm film or videocassette   color   38 min
Purchase: film $260.25; video $75.00   Rental: $30.00

Dramatizes realistic picture of collective bargaining between a public employees union and city officials. Shows mechanics of bargaining—how proposals and counter proposals are made and responded to, how agreements on various issues are reached at the bargaining table, and what happens when a deadlock develops and negotiations break down. Companion film to *Waldenville II*. Out of Conflict—Accord Series.

36. Waldenville II
National Audiovisual Center   16mm film or videocassette   color   31 min
Purchase: film $212.25; video $75.00   Rental: $25.00

Continues from the deadlock reached in *Waldenville I* by showing the involvement of a mediator and how he referees the negotiations. The dynamics of mediation are illustrated—with the film ending short of total agreement between the parties. Shows the mediation process and how the mediator works to assist the parties in reaching agreement. Out of Conflict—Accord Series.

37. Waldenville III
National Audiovisual Center   1980   16mm film or videocassette   color   36 min
Purchase: film $246.50; video $75.00   Rental: $30.00

Portrayal shows how factfinding can be used when arbitration ends in deadlock. Shows the process in which a third and neutral party intercedes and recommends a settlement that considers the positions of each of the negotiating parties. Recommended for use with *Waldenville I* and *Waldenville II*.

Waldenville Jogger. For complete citation, *see* GRIEVANCE.

ASSERTIVENESS

38. Assertion Skills: Tintypes
Salenger Educational Media   16mm film or videocassette   color   20 min   instructor's print materials; learner's print materials
Purchase: $455.00   Rental: $125.00   Preview: $35.00

Useful for starting assertion training sessions; serves as a learning aid and to motivate people to think and act assertively. Designed to help viewers identify and recognize passive, aggressive, and assertive patterns of behavior in themselves and others. This awareness may then create the desire for personal change to become more effective.

39. Assertion Training
Lansford Publishing Company, Inc   2 audiocassettes   instructor's print materials; learner's print materials
Purchase: $69.95

Developing assertive behavior can be important for employees at all levels in an organization. Covers nonassertive and aggressive behavior, rights, irrational and rational beliefs, blocks to assertiveness, relaxation techniques, steps to assertive behavior, and application of assertion training in different situations.

40. Assertive Management
Professional Resources   6 audiocassettes   learner's print materials
Purchase: $90.00

Focuses on managing relationships at work, managing conflict, giving and receiving performance feedback, and becoming a pro-active manager. Taped seminar features Jim Lewis. Intended for both men and women in management or those aspiring to managerial positions.

41. Assertiveness for Career and Personal Success
American Management Associations   6 audiocassettes   learner's print materials
Purchase: $145.00   Other cost factors: AMA members $135.00; discounts available for bulk orders of materials

Emphasizes how to use proven assertiveness skills to improve job performance and increase satisfaction with personal life through a wide choice of responses to difficult situations.

Exercises, self-evaluations, personal inventories, and self-awareness sessions help build assertive behavior habits.

42. Assertiveness Training for Managers
Applied Management Institute, Inc   audiocassettes
Purchase: $65.00

Audiocassettes of one-day seminar on replacing ineffective nonassertiveness or aggressiveness with assertive behavior. Covers range of responsible assertive options for different situations, the importance of better listening, and the challenge of constructive confrontation. Primarily lecture format.

43. Birds of a Feather
CRM/McGraw-Hill Films   16mm film or videocassette   color   5 min
Purchase: $195.00   Rental: $75.00   Preview: free

Presents a nonnarrated fable about a bird who becomes dissatisfied with looking like the rest of the flock. Shows how it is learned that it is foolish to be something that one is not. Animated.

44. Learning to Walk
International Film Bureau, Inc   16mm film   color   8 min
Purchase: $130.00   Rental: $10.00   Preview: free

Brief animated vignette of protagonist with an unorthodox walk. As others try to correct the walk, he first accommodates and then assumes his natural gait, resisting others' attempts to change him. Useful for assertiveness training.

45. Mallet
International Film Bureau, Inc   16mm film   color   10½ min
Purchase: $145.00   Rental: $12.50   Preview: free

Animated portrayal of sorting chickens into healthy and culls. Mallet destroys the culls. Black chick emerges, is sorted as a cull, and rebels. Useful for assertiveness training.

46. Resistance
International Film Bureau, Inc   16mm film   color   6½ min
Purchase: $120.00   Rental: $10.00   Preview: free

Shows tools coping with a nail resistant to being driven. Not narrated.

47. Responsible Assertion
Research Press   16mm film or videocassette   color   28 min
Purchase: $495.00   Rental: $50.00

Examines different styles of behavior through 3 dramatic scenes. Demonstrates the different consequences of nonassertive, aggressive, and assertive behaviors. Uses such assertion training techniques as cognitive restructuring and behavioral rehearsal. Includes documentary footage of an assertion training workshop conducted by Arthur Lange.

48. Spinnolio
National Film Board of Canada   16mm film or videocassette   color   10 min
Purchase: film $210.00; video $250.00   Rental: $80.00   Preview: $40.00

Spinnolio, a puppet, goes through life without planning his own avenue of growth. He allows other people to pull all the strings in his life and to see in him whatever they want to see. Presents an allegory giving provocative metaphors about planning, passivity, and personal projection. Shows how people use others without regard for their feelings, needs, and fears. Animated.

49. Strong but Gentle
Didactic Systems, Inc   6 audiocassettes
Purchase: $89.50

Presents assertiveness to the point of negotiating, whereby one is able to express what is on one's mind without guilt while also respecting the rights of others. Strength with gentleness thus becomes a realistic pattern of positive behavior.

50. What Could I Say?
Research Press   16mm film or videocassette   color   18 min   instructor's print materials
Purchase: $295.00   Rental: $50.00

Useful to develop assertion perceptions and skills. Presents 20 vignettes that illustrate common situations in social, work, marital, family, sexual, and consumer problems. Stops after each provide time to discuss appropriate responses.

51. When I Say No, I Feel Guilty
Cally Curtis Company   1976   16mm film or videocassette   color   30 min
Purchase: film $550.00; video $525.00   Rental: $130.00   Preview: $40.00

Shows how to cope with every day problems and conflicts at work or in life by using the special verbal skills of Systematic Assertive Training. Features Dr. Manual J. Smith and June Lockhart.

ASSESSMENT CENTER
See CAREER PLANNING AND DEVELOPMENT

ATTITUDINAL CHANGE

52. BE-ATTITUDES
Carlocke/Langden, Inc   1969   9 videocassettes or filmstrips or slides and audiocassettes   10 min ea
Purchase: video $145.00 ea; filmstrip $75.00 ea; slides $115.00 ea   Rental: $5.00 ea (filmstrip only)

Short, animated presentations intended to help employees recognize and build desired personality traits and attitudes such as self-esteem, integrity, safety, courtesy, productivity, dependability, responsibility, awareness, and enthusiasm. Messages presented with humor.

53. Grab Hold of Today
Ramic Productions   1980   16mm film or videocassette   color   28 min   instructor's print materials; learner's print materials

Purchase: $650.00   Rental: $150.00   Preview: $65.00

Eden Ryl demonstrates the Pike Syndrome, the problem of negative attitudes and behaviors. Breaking free of the syndrome enables managers and employees to stay open to new ideas, to reexamine, and to adjust and revise their attitudes and behaviors. Presents "how to" guidelines to break away from negative attitudes.

54. Joy of Development
Ramic Productions   1981   16mm film or videocassette   color   30 min   poster
Purchase: $650.99   Rental: $150.00   Preview: $65.00

Addresses indifference with the Double Helix behavioral model. Model shows difference between active and passive behavior and the implications of each. Features Dr. Eden Ryl. For employees of all levels.

55. Light Your Own Fire
Continental Film Productions   slides or filmstrip and audiocassette   15 min
Purchase: filmstrip $75.00; slides $95.00

Points out the importance of attitudes and how to adopt a new attitude. Uses humorous animation to present insights and suggestions that help every employee deal more effectively with others and with him/herself.

56. Making It in the Organization
Salenger Educational Media   1980   16mm film or videocassette   color   18 min   instructor's print materials; poster
Purchase: $455.00   Rental: $125.00   Preview: $35.00

Designed to help people see how their attitudes toward their work influence their performance. Humorous lecture encourages a close look at behavior in the organization. Shows how attitudes toward work help determine the rewards and satisfactions received from it. Helps employees explore and develop alternative strategies to deal with their work environment.

57. Man in the Mirror
BNA Communications, Inc   1969   16mm film or videocassette   color   25 min
Purchase: $525.00   Rental: 5-day $150.00; 3-day $105.00   Preview: $35.00

Illustrates a middle manager's negativism at home and on the job. Joe Batten argues for a more positive approach to our whole lives if we are to succeed. Raises issues such as managerial obsolescence, conformity vs. individuality, creativity, selling a new idea, turnover, and the generation gap.

58. Strategy for Winning
National Educational Media, Inc   1977   16mm film or super 8mm or videocassette   color   20 min   study guide
Purchase: $540.00   Rental: 5-day $125.00; 3-day $115.00   Preview: free
Languages: English, Japanese, Spanish

Stresses the importance of positive attitude, persistence, and sensitivity to the opinions of others in gaining acceptance of new ideas. Offers a valuable lesson in leadership—pinpointing the need for effective, positive, interpersonal communications. Describes the rejection of a proposal prepared by a new manager and how he turns that disappointment into success. Outlines his approach.

That's Not My Job. For complete citation, *see* TEAM BUILDING.

What You Are Is... For complete citation, *see* COMMUNICATION.

What You Are Is Where You Were When. For complete citation, *see* COMMUNICATION.

What You Are Isn't Necessarily What You Will Be... For complete citation, *see* INTERPERSONAL RELATIONS.

When You're Smilin'. For complete citation, *see* INTERPERSONAL RELATIONS.

59. Winning Attitudes for the 80's
Nightingale-Conant Corporation audiocassette learner's print materials
Purchase: $50.00

Suggests the importance of positive self-image, self-direction, and self-discipline as well as the ability to earn respect from others and project one's self. Features principles from *Denis Waitley's Psychology of Winning*.

60. Winning Combination
BNA Communications, Inc 1963 16mm film or videocassette color 12 min booklets
Purchase: $250.00 Rental: 5-day $150.00; 3-day $105.00 Preview: $35.00
Languages: English, Spanish

Deals with the importance of employee attitudes and how they can be influenced by a sales approach to motivate employees. The winning combination is good supervision and good salesmanship. Modern Management Series, no. 7.

61. You Can Build a Better You
Singer Management Institute 4 audiocassettes learner's print materials
Purchase: $60.00 Preview: $15.00

Prompts individuals to discover and tap their potential, turn problems into opportunities, and reach for larger goals. Promotes a positive expectant attitude, replacing unproductive habits and self-imposed limitations.

62. You Pack Your Own Chute
Ramic Productions 1979 16mm film or videocassette color 30 min
Purchase: $595.00 Rental: $130.00 Preview: $45.00

Those who "pack their own chute" create their own successes and failures. Deals with fear of change and challenges as well as the excitement of achievement. Dramatizes the fact that most people are their own biggest obstacles to accomplishment and brings home the truth that all of us are responsible for our own behavior and have the power to change. Features Eden Ryl.

63. Your Attitude Is Showing
CRM/McGraw-Hill Films 16mm film or videocassette color 19 min
Purchase: $395.00 Rental: $100.00 Preview: free

Deals with the practical principles of good human relations utilizing a problem-solving approach. Developed with Elwood Chapman, author of *Your Attitude Is Showing*.

64. Your Erroneous Zones
Twentieth Century-Fox Video, Inc 1977 16mm film or videocassette color 97 min instructor's print materials; book
Purchase: film $1,195.00; video $750.00 Rental: film $200.00; video $160.00 Preview: film $75.00; video $50.00

Emphasizes that personal attitudes are a function of individual choice. Unhealthy behavior patterns result from attitude and may block individuals from freedoms and experiences. Wayne Dyer, author of the book by the same title, outlines several plans which will eliminate such zones.

AUDIOVISUAL PRODUCTION

65. AV Script Writing Kit
Hass-Haus Productions 2 audiocassettes 50 min learner's print materials
Purchase: $42.00

Discusses how to write scripts for slide/tape programs. Describes how to develop a project proposal, do the needed research, develop a preliminary narrative, and finalize visualization and narrative.

66. Basic Art Techniques for Slide Production
Eastman Kodak Company 1979 78 slides and audiocassette 15 min
Purchase: $62.00 Rental: $20.00

Illustrates basic concepts, tools, and techniques of preparing slide artwork. Provides a foundation for those with little or no experience.

67. Basic Copying
Eastman Kodak Company 76 slides and audiocassette 18 min script
Purchase: $70.00 Rental: $20.00

Step-by-step guide to producing 2x2-inch slides from artwork. Principles outlined apply to large slide labs as well as to small producers.

68. Basic Lighting
Eastman Kodak Company 16mm film color 5 min
Purchase: $40.00 Rental: $10.00

Shows beginning filmmakers and photography students the fundamentals of lighting. Uses a miniature set, character, and lights to illustrate how to place and direct lights.

69. Basics of Cinematography
Eastman Kodak Company 16mm film color 21 min
Purchase: $150.00 Rental: $35.00

Important facts about continuity, sequence development, and the basic techniques of cinematography including how to handle a camera properly, how to use different shots to develop effective pictorial continuity, and how to create smooth transitions that prevent viewer confusion. Teaching and review aid for filmmaker directly involved in producing training films, documentaries, feature-length films, or news for television.

70. Camera Handling
Eastman Kodak Company   16mm film   color   5 min
Purchase: $40.00   Rental: $10.00

Offers the basics of motion picture production, a variety of ways to get started, and how to get the best results from a camera through skilled camera handling.

71. Creating Slide/Tape Programs
Association for Educational Communications and Technology   1980   filmstrip and audiocassette   color   15 min   learner's print materials
Purchase: $25.95

Illustrates how to develop slide/tape programs with ideas for scripting, photography, and audio production. Gives many options, hints, and resources.

72. Development of a Slide-Tape Instructional Presentation
National Audiovisual Center   1979   71 slides and audiocassette   16 min
Purchase: $49.00

Outlines basic steps involved in developing content material for slide-tape presentations. Stresses use of audiovisual tools to convey knowledge and principles in a clear, concise manner.

73. Optical Titling
Eastman Kodak Company   1979   64 slides and audiocassette   15 min   script
Purchase: $65.00   Rental: $20.00

Introduces the hardware and techniques needed to create simple but professional-looking title slides. Emphasizes the use of existing slides and materials.

74. Photography for Audiovisual Production
Eastman Kodak Company   120 slides and audiocassette   35 min   script
Purchase: $120.00   Rental: $30.00

Discusses factors that make visuals more effective including the proper selection of visuals, the equipment to use, and the photographers.

75. Presentation of Data
Lansford Publishing Company, Inc   40 slides and audiocassettes   instructor's guide
Purchase: $169.00

Covers use of graphic presentations, methods to improve graphic presentations, applications of basic charting methods, and how to avoid creating misleading impressions in graphic presentations.

76. Synchronizing a Slide-Tape Program
Eastman Kodak Company   72 slides and audiocassette   12 min   script
Purchase: $70.00   Rental: $20.00

Gives step-by-step instructions for synchronizing slide-tape presentations with a cassette tape recorder, a self-contained slide projector/viewer with tape, or a reel-to-reel tape recorder with a synchronizer. Synchronization makes a more professional presentation, coordinates all components consistently, and frees operators of timing responsibility.

77. Use of the Overhead Projector and How to Make Do-It-Yourself Transparencies
Schwan-STABILO   80 slides and audiocassette   15 min
Purchase: $79.50

Shows how to take full advantage of the unique benefits of the overhead projector and do-it-yourself transparencies. Can be used as an introduction or a refresher.

AUDIOVISUAL TECHNIQUES

78. Can We Please Have That the Right Way Round?
Xicom-Video Arts   1977   16mm film or videocassette   color   22 min   instructor's print materials; learner's print materials
Purchase: $530.00   Rental: $100.00   Preview: $35.00

Demonstrates the design and use of slides and overhead transparencies for presentations. Shows the principal errors and their consequences through John Cleese's humor.

Communicating Successfully. For complete citation, *see* PRESENTATIONS.

79. Don't Just Tell Them...Show Them
BNA Communications, Inc   16mm film   color   20 min
Purchase: $525.00   Rental: 5-day $150.00; 3-day $105.00   Preview: $35.00

Shows the advantages and disadvantages of different types of visual aids and points out which is best for a particular presentation. Audiovisual techniques are demonstrated with instruction. British production.

80. Effective Projection
Eastman Kodak Company   160 slides and audiocassette   45 min   script
Purchase: $120.00   Rental: $30.00

Describes the do's and don'ts of effective projection: room size and shape, screen selection and surface characteristics, ambient light, room light control, and their effect on image legibility. Covers the 3 principal classes of images, image keystoning, projection lamps, lenses, slide mounts, control of audio reproduction, and room acoustics.

81. Effective Visual Presentations
Eastman Kodak Company 1980 138 slides and
audiocassettes and 16mm filmstrip 18 min
instructor's print materials
Purchase: $120.00 Rental: $30.00

Illustrates the creation of effective visual presentations, noting
objectives, audience considerations, and appropriateness of
content. Useful for those new to production of audiovisual
presentations.

82. Flick Facts
Thompson-Mitchell and Associates filmstrip and
audiocassette 10 min
Purchase: $45.00

Instructs the novice how to set up room and projection
equipment to ensure smooth, effective use of 16mm films.

83. Impact of Visuals on the Speechmaking Process
Eastman Kodak Company 100 slides and
audiocassette 20 min script
Purchase: $120.00 Rental: $30.00

Overview of the ways visual messages will improve presentations. Discusses all forms of audiovisual presentations from
overhead transparencies to 35mm slides. Helps the presenter
decide which type of visual to use. Other issues discussed are
cost justification, residual use, slide libraries, and how to deal
with a producer.

So You're Going on Camera? For complete citation,
see PRESENTATIONS.

84. Visual Aids
BNA Communications, Inc 1966 16mm film or
videocassette color 27 min
Purchase: $550.00 Rental: 5-day $150.00; 3-day
$105.00 Preview: $35.00

A humorous presentation of the right and wrong ways to use
chalk boards, flannel boards, magnetic boards, charts, diagrams, models, and actual products as well as still, movie, and
overhead projectors. Useful in giving more effective talks,
briefings, and presentations.

AUTHORITY
See POWER AND AUTHORITY

AUTOMATION
See also TECHNOLOGY; COMPUTERS

85. Ballet Robotique
Pyramid Films 1982 16mm film or
videocassette color 8 min
Purchase: $225.00 Rental: $55.00

Offers a nonthreatening introduction to computers and robots
in the workplace. Classical music and special lighting personify
robots, showing their teamwork and productivity.

86. Industrial Robot, an Introduction
Society of Manufacturing Engineers 1982
videocassette color 20 min

Purchase: $150.00 Rental: $40.00 Other cost
factors: SME members $120.00 (rental $35.00)

Introductory program that covers the basics of industrial robot
memory capabilities and shows the physical make-up of what is
considered to be a reprogrammable industrial robot. Can be
used to introduce industrial robots to any level of manufacturing employee from board of directors to shop floor employees.
Footage used was supplied by leading manufacturers of industrial robots and shows each unit at work in a factory
environment.

87. Industrial Robot Applications
Society of Manufacturing Engineers 1982
videocassette color 20 min
Purchase: $150.00 Rental: $40.00 Other cost
factors: SME members $120.00 (rental $35.00)

Shows major industrial applications for using robots such as
material removal, spot welding, material palletizing, painting
and deburring, die casting, and machine loading. All are
demonstrated by a host of different robots. Applications in dirty
and unpleasant jobs will raise productivity, increase quality,
and improve the quality of working life.

88. Mr. Money
MTI Teleprograms, Inc 1980 16mm film or
videocassette color 4 min
Purchase: film $140.00; video $125.00 Rental:
$40.00 Preview: free

Introduces an automatic teller machine that has a personality.
Spoof on the machine age. Useful for meeting openers or
breaks.

89. Robots VI: Tomorrow's Technology on Display
Society of Manufacturing Engineers 1982
videocassette color 40 min
Purchase: $260.00 Rental: $125.00 Other cost
factors: SME members $230.00 (rental $110.00)

Designed to update manufacturing executives on the state-of-
the-art in industrial robot capabilities. Interviews with 2
pioneers, Joe Engleberger and George Devol, outline the
development of the robot market and its future. Shows laser and
video-sensing equipment demonstrated for the first time outside
the laboratory. New equipment overcomes the previous obstacles that have limited the use of industrial robots in bin picking
and parts sorting. Demonstrates small robots designed specifically for training and educational purposes.

BEHAVIOR MODIFICATION

**90. Approaches to Organizational Behavior Modifica-
tion (OBM)**
Document Associates 1978 16mm film or
videocassette color 26 min
Purchase: $400.00 Rental: $45.00

Reveals inefficiencies that affect a work unit's productivity.
Filmed training sessions in 3 organizations show use of
techniques to identify, analyze, and change problem behavior
patterns. Stresses use of operant conditioning and positive and
negative reinforcements.

91. Behavior Modification Skills
Research Media, Inc   5 slides and
audiocassettes   10–15 hrs   instructor's print
materials; learner's print materials
Purchase: $395.00 plus materials

Presents the basics of behavior modification: observing behavior, increasing behavior, decreasing behavior, creating new behavior, and implementing the system. A self-contained multimedia program to administer in-house. Each of 5 units can be purchased separately.

92. Business, Behaviorism and the Bottom Line
CRM/McGraw-Hill Films   1972   16mm film or
videocassette   color   23 min
Purchase: $425.00   Rental: $95.00   Preview: free

B.F. Skinner explains how actions and attitudes of all individuals are conditioned by their environments. The film shows how this highly systematic, scientific approach can be applied to typical organizational problems. Uses specific examples to show how feedback and positive reinforcement serve as strong inducements toward productivity.

93. Power of Positive Reinforcement
CRM/McGraw-Hill Films   1978   16mm film or
videocassette   color   26 min   instructor's print
materials; learner's print materials
Purchase: $560.00   Rental: $95.00   Preview: free

Describes the spontaneous and natural bases of positive reinforcement and behavior modification and examples. Show supervisors and managers how to use behavior modification techniques within the organization. Confronts the controversy and criticism surrounding the subject, but the numerous successes outlined in the film attest to an overriding positive acceptance of these behavioral systems.

94. Rewards of Rewarding
Roundtable Films, Inc   16mm film or
videocassette   color   24 min
Purchase: $495.00   Rental: $100.00   Preview:
$40.00   Other cost factors: supervisor's guidebook
Languages: English, French, Spanish

Western ranch setting demonstrates humorously how and when to properly reward employees. Provides a practical explanation of modern psychological concepts such as stimulus/response, feedback, and reinforcement. Thanks A'Plenty Boss Series, Part I.

95. You Can Lead a Horse to Water
American Media, Inc   1977   16mm film or super
8mm or videocassette   color   30 min   instructor's
print materials
Purchase: $495.00   Rental: $95.00   Preview:
$30.00

Designed for managers and supervisors instituting or implementing a system of performance feedback with positive reinforcement intended to improve employee performance. Uses vignettes to illustrate a 6-step approach in effective use of behavior modification to increase productivity.

BUDGETING
See FINANCIAL MANAGEMENT

BURNOUT
See STRESS AND STRESS MANAGEMENT

BUSINESS ENVIRONMENT

96. Acquiring, Merging and Selling Companies
AMR International, Inc   1977   12 audiocassettes
learner's print materials
Purchase: $350.00

Merger and acquisition offer opportunities for growth but may present problems for the uninformed. Cassettes present basic practices in acquiring, merging, and selling companies. Includes approaches used by the professionals: negotiating strategies, financial reporting, tax aspects, valuation, the contract, and closing. Emphasizes the importance of planning for external growth.

Age of Uncertainty. For complete citation, *see* ECONOMIC CONDITIONS.

Bricklin Story. For complete citation, *see* COMPETITION.

97. Business Civilization in Decline
Audio-Forum   audiocassette   56 min
Purchase: $10.95

Robert Heilbroner and Heywood Hale Broun discuss how capitalism's success has depended on its growth. Now that resources are running out, they anticipate more control of science and technology by the state.

98. Crisis of the American Board: How It Grew—And What We Can Do About It
AMACOM   3 audiocassettes   3 hrs   booklet
Purchase: $75.00   Other cost factors: AMA members
$63.25

Warren Bennis suggests how corporate boards can effectively arm themselves against the devastating crossfire of today's business, social, economic, and political demands.

Encounters with the Future. For complete citation, *see* SOCIETAL CHANGE.

99. Enterprise 1
LCA Video/Films   1981   13 16mm films or
videocassettes   color   30 min ea   instructor's print
materials
Purchase: $500.00   Rental: $100.00   Preview:
$50.00

Profiles companies, industries, and individuals as they confront critical decisions that can make business fail or succeed. Includes situations of dealing with unions, expansion into foreign markets, and operating more productively. Hosted by Eric Sevareid. Enterprise Series, Part I.

100. Enterprise II
LCA Video/Films   1982   12 films or
videocassettes   color   30 min ea

Purchase: $4995.00 ($500.00 ea) Rental: $100.00
ea Preview: $50.00 ea

Portrays entrepreneurs in oil, space, clothing, baseball, entertainment, diamonds, and restaurants. Also covers issues such as defaults, bankruptcy, outplacement, bidding, and corporate reorganization. Enterprise Series, Part II.

Focus on Ethics: The Role of Values in Decision-Making. For complete citation, *see* ETHICS AND VALUES.

Free Enterprise Economics. For complete citation, *see* FREE ENTERPRISE SYSTEM.

Fully Functioning Society. For complete citation, *see* FREE ENTERPRISE SYSTEM.

101. Jamestown Story: Improved Human Relations Can Change a Community
Document Associates 16mm film color 26 min
Purchase: $400.00 Rental: $45.00

Offers an eye-witness report of how Jamestown using a "quality of work" program, effected a unique economic turnaround in the face of local recession and unemployment. Shows how profit-sharing and worker training programs were instituted along with increased communication between employees and management.

102. Japan Inc. Lessons for North America
National Film Board of Canada 1983 16mm film or videocassette color 28 min
Purchase: film $500.00; video $300.00 Rental: $120.00 Preview: $40.00

Examines productivity in Japan, its level of organization, efficiency, and discipline. Then, it prompts discussion about which lessons from the Japanese experience can be successfully applied to North American business and industry.

103. Japan: The Collective Giant
Films, Inc 1973 16mm film or videocassette color 20 min
Purchase: film $365.00; video $185.00 Rental: $45.00

The productive labor force in Japan has made it a serious competitive threat, but industrial prosperity brings mixed blessings: traffic and smog as well as a sense of urgency and achievement.

104. Making Things Happen
Chamber of Commerce of the United States 73 slides and audiocassette 13 min script
Purchase: $25.00

Explains the leadership role of the voluntary business organization—how it is structured, the role of components within the organization, and how and why the local chambers of commerce work in the public interest.

105. Marvelous Mousetrap
BNA Communications, Inc 1963 16mm film or videocassette color 25 min learner's print materials

Purchase: $450.00 Rental: 5-day $150.00; 3-day $105.00 Preview: $35.00

Aims to better the understanding of our economic system, the importance of employee-employer cooperation, and many factors involved in the growth and success of a business. Highlights topics such as customer service, quality control, economic education, and employee attitudes toward work. Features Wally Cox.

106. Open System Re-Design
Development Digest audiocassette
Purchase: $13.75

Theoretical discussion of the application of open system concepts and terms to induce traditional organizations to think of themselves as socio-technical systems. Socio-technically organized work units consist of a few workers with the same capability, working in a common environment with a supervisor.

107. Problem
Films, Inc 16mm film or videocassette color 12 min
Purchase: film $280.00; video $140.00 Rental: $40.00 Preview: free

Examines with insight the dehumanizing effect of bureaucracies and the individual's reaction to it. An animated puppet film that centers on the question of what color the trash box in a large organization should be painted.

108. Sense of Saving
Chamber of Commerce of the United States 80 slides and audiocassette 15 min script
Purchase: $25.00

Illustrates the way savings of business and individuals interact to keep the economy moving, influence business growth, and create new jobs as well as what happens to this pool of capital when government borrowing occurs.

109. Social Needs as Business Opportunities
BNA Communications, Inc 1971 16mm film or videocassette color 33 min
Purchase: $385.00 Rental: 5-day $150.00; 3-day $105.00 Preview: $35.00

Shows businesspeople who are moving into socially responsible roles how problems involving minority employment, vocational school development, environment protection, and community development can be business opportunities. Peter Drucker, Elizabeth Hall, and Robert Hansberger discuss how ultimate control of a business must be people-oriented and not solely dominated by standard accounting principles. Managing Discontinuity Series, no. 5.

110. Understanding the Business World
Singer Management Institute filmstrip and audiocassette or slides
Purchase: filmstrip $29.50; slides $49.00 Preview: $15.00

Discusses the roles of consumers, business, and government in the free enterprise system as well as the goals of a business concern and the means it uses to achieve them. Useful to help new employees understand their role in the business world and learn how business fits into the whole economic picture.

111. Understanding the Social Responsibility of Business
Audio-Forum   audiocassette   27 min
Purchase: $10.95

An explanation of why modern society expects responsible decisions from the managers of its organizations.

You and Your Job. For complete citation, *see* ECONOMIC CONDITIONS.

BUSINESS MANAGEMENT
See MANAGEMENT

CAREER PLANNING AND DEVELOPMENT

112. ABC Man: The Manager in Mid-Career
BNA Communications, Inc   1969   16mm film or videocassette   color   22 min
Purchase: $535.00   Rental: 5-day $150.00; 3-day $105.00   Preview: $35.00
Languages: English, Spanish

Dramatization of a mid-career manager confronting possible obsolescence. Raises the importance of career development and personal growth in a technological age. Motivation to Work Series, no. 5.

113. ...and It Works
Creative Media   audiocassette   30 min
Purchase: $13.75

Joe Batten describes his formula for success. Useful as a motivational meeting opener.

114. Applying for a Public Service Job
National Audiovisual Center   1977   16mm film   28 min   learner's print materials
Purchase: $162.50   Rental: $12.50

Shows how to get started in an entry level public service position and gives information on how to apply. Promotion policies are discussed with practical advice on how to learn about job openings and what to do during an interview. You in Public Service Series.

Appraisal & Career Counseling Interviews. For complete citation, *see* INTERVIEWING.

115. Art Pell Weekly Workshops
Employment Training Corporation   audiocassette   instructor's print materials; learner's print materials
Purchase: $249.00

Intended for training placement counselors in groups of 3 to 8 persons once a week for an hour and a half at a time. Cassettes and materials include exercises, role play, and demonstrations to illustrate principles being learned. Emphasis is on group participation and on-the-job application for placement agencies.

116. Assessing Employee Potential
Resources for Education and Management, Inc   5 videocassettes or slides and audiocassettes or 5 filmstrips or 5 filmstrip cartridges   color   instructor's print materials
Purchase: video $305.00 ($75.00 ea); filmstrips $280.00 ($64.00 ea); filmstrip cartridges $425.00 ($85.00 ea); slides $&295.00 ($67.00 ea)   Preview: $20.00

Points out the importance of recognizing employee potential and effectively developing it. Offers a number of practical and effective assessment techniques. Modules present different facets including general problems, matching people and positions, assessment methods, on-the-job assessment, and the assessment center.

Assessing Management Potential. For complete citation, *see* MANAGEMENT DEVELOPMENT.

117. Assessment/Career Development Centers
Development Digest   3 audiocassettes
Purchase: $41.25

An extensive open discussion of the assessment center movement and its relationship to human resource development. Gives special depth and emphasis in relation to the Syntex Center in terms of its goals, organization, techniques, feedback, and use of data for personnel development as well as assignment.

118. Becoming a Successful Businesswoman
Audio-Forum   audiocassette   48 min
Purchase: $10.95

Betty L. Harragan discusses how and why business is a game and offers concrete pointers on how to approach the challenges of job hunting, promotions and raises, and moving up the corporate ladder.

119. Career Awareness for Women
Instructional Dynamics, Inc   1977   12 audiocassettes   instructor's print materials; learner's print materials
Purchase: $79.50

Group- or self-study program on affirmative action. Helps women identify barriers they face and employ techniques to overcome them. Focuses on leadership, communication, decision making, and conflict management. Role play and exercises offer practice opportunities.

120. Career Development
Management Decision Systems, Inc   1980   2 16mm films or videocassettes   color   15 min ea   instructor's print materials
Purchase: $5,700.00

Leads employees through goal setting and action step development that apply to any job level. Intended to build supervisor's skills in developmental counseling and career planning.

121. Career Development: A Part of OD?
Development Digest   audiocassette
Purchase: $13.75

John H. Zenger describes one approach that can discover and develop potential managers. Necessary steps include assessing developmental needs and then negotiating with supervisors.

122. Career Development: A Plan for All Seasons
CRM/McGraw-Hill Films   1978   16mm film or
videocassette   color   26 min   instructor's print
materials; learner's print materials
Purchase: $560.00   Rental: $95.00   Preview: free

Highlights the problems of continual worker turnover, mid-career changes, and financial instability, showing the adverse effects all of these factors have on productivity. Dr. Beverly Kaye traces career development programs as one of the best means to analyze an employee's desires and coordinate those with organizational goals.

123. Career Management: When Preparation Meets Opportunity
EFM Films   1982   16mm film or
videocassette   color   20 min   instructor's print
materials; learner's print materials
Purchase: $545.00   Rental: $120.00   Preview:
$40.00

Introduces pro-active, 3-step career management process of self-assessment, research, and planning that enables each employee to take control of and responsbility for his/her own career. Each step is detailed to show method. Emphasizes ability to develop individual goals within the framework of the organization's needs and directions.

124. Career Success: A Manager's Guide to Upward Mobility
AMACOM   2 audiocassettes
Purchase: $39.95   Other cost factors: AMA members
$33.95

Presents Gene Jennings's total career game plan of 9 simple rules. Concern is with upward mobility, following the rules, and making moves at the right time and place.

Confidence Game. For complete citation, *see*
PERSONNEL MANAGEMENT.

125. Developing Personal Effectiveness
BNA Communications, Inc   10 audiocassettes
Purchase: $100.00 ($12.00 ea)

Emphasizes personal growth for managers on the job. Cassettes on achieving, career and life-style goals, communication, and time management skills. For group or individual use. Effective Management Program Series, no. 3.

Executive Development and Training Issues—Government and Industry. For complete citation, *see*
MANAGEMENT DEVELOPMENT.

126. Fine Art of Keeping Your Cool
National Educational Media, Inc   1977   16mm film
or super 8mm or videocassette   color   20 min
instructor's print materials; learner's print materials
Purchase: $499.00   Rental: 5-day $120.00; 3-day
$110.00
Languages: English, French, Japanese, Spanish,
Portuguese

Gives guidelines for managing a temper in one's self and others. Demonstrates the likely adverse consequences of showing hostility toward others. Offers stop-gap and long-term procedures to build good relationships with others on the job.

Intended for those interested in creating and advancing a career.

127. Fully Functioning Individual
BNA Communications, Inc   1969   16mm film or
videocassette   color   22 min
Purchase: $525.00   Rental: 5-day $150.00; 3-day
$105.00   Preview: $35.00

Dramatization and comment by Joe Batten reveals responsibilities of an individual to one's self and to the organization. These include risk taking. The organization, in turn, is responsible for providing the individual opportunities for growth and development plus a fair appraisal based on results. Tough-minded Management Series, no. 3.

128. Get Them Moving
Goodmeasure, Inc   1980   slides and
audiocassette   13 min   instructor's print materials
Purchase: $425.00   Rental: $125.00

Graphically illustrates 7 ways employees get "stuck" despite their potential. Points out barriers to career progress and how they can be bypassed. Shows how to generate new opportunites in the organization. Companion to *The Moving and the Stuck*. P/QWL Series, no. 2.

129. Getting Ahead: The Road to Self Development
Roundtable Films, Inc   16mm film or
videocassette   color   28 min
Purchase: $400.00   Rental: $75.00   Preview:
$30.00

Includes interviews with people who describe the techniques, education, and preparation they needed for success in their present positions. Presents a step-by-step action plan for self-development, self-evaluation, goal setting, and continuing education.

130. Helping People Perform, What Managers Are Paid For
BNA Communications, Inc   1977   16mm film or
videocassette   color   23 min   instructor's print
materials
Purchase: $560.00   Rental: 5-day $150.00; 3-day
$105.00   Preview: $35.00
Languages: English, Spanish, French

Shows Peter Drucker advising managers about coaching employees and selecting personnel for advancement and performance appraisal. Gives Drucker's views on training and motivation plus the issue of performance vs. potential. Manager and the Organization Series, no. 3.

131. How to Make the Organization Work for You
BNA Communications, Inc   1977   16mm film or
videocassette   color   22 min   instructor's print
materials
Purchase: $560.00   Rental: 5-day $150.00; 3-day
$105.00   Preview: $35.00
Languages: English, Spanish, French

With dramatization and comment, Peter Drucker illustrates why employee goals should be accomplishment instead of promotion and how rules, procedures, and good manners allow an organization to function efficiently. Deals with career planning and organizational coping. Manager and the Organization Series, no. 6.

132. If You Don't, Nobody Else Will
EFM Films   16mm film   color   13 min
instructor's print materials
Purchase: $425.00   Rental: $120.00   Preview:
$40.00

Demonstrates that development is the personal responsibility of each employee. Urges that each create specific career objectives and concrete plans to reach goals. Issues challenge to trainers to provide guidance and resources. Clarifies relationship between employees and training department and lays basis for continued interaction.

133. Job Story
National Audiovisual Center   1971   16mm film or
videocassette   color   22 min
Purchase: $127.50

Shows operation of the job information service and the job bank that supports it. Discusses advantages to the employer and to applicants. Career Job Opportunity Series.

Lead the Field. For complete citation, *see*
DECISION MAKING/PROBLEM SOLVING.

134. Life/Work Goals Exploration Workbook Kit
Development Publications   1977   7 audiocassettes
learner's print materials
Purchase: $155.00   Preview: $15.00

Through a career planning process, an individual collects information about self and develops realistic life and work goals that most satisfy self-values, needs, and wants. Then, these goals become action plans to achievement—while pursuing organization goals. A process designed for 2 or more persons working together and experiencing giving and receiving feedback throughout the exploration. Uses interactive learning approach.

135. Lifelines: A Career Profile Study
Document Associates   1977   16mm film or
videocassette   color   26 min
Purchase: $400.00   Rental: $45.00

Uses illustrations from 3 case histories to explore Edgar Schein's concept of "career anchors," patterns by which individuals discover what they are good at and what they would like to do for the rest of their lives. Explores 5 categories of career anchors: technical or functional, managerial competence, security, creativity, and autonomy.

136. Managing Career Developoment of Professionals
Center for the Management of Professional and Scientific Work   1977   16mm film and
audiocassette   color   instructor's print materials;
learner's print materials; transparencies
Purchase: $2,500.00

Designed to assist managers in learning to deal effectively with the needs of professional employees. Includes strong emphasis on conducting career interviews, information on adult life cycles, creative problem solving, organizational change, and career stages. Suggested as a 3-day program.

137. Mature Executive
AMACOM   3 audiocassettes   60 min ea
Purchase: $80.00   Other cost factors: AMA members
$68.00

Gives advice on how to stay on top—of the heap, the competition, new opportunities, and the state of the art.

138. Now That's Upward Mobility
National Audiovisual Center   1974   67 slides and
audiocassettes   15 min   instructor's print materials;
learner's print materials
Purchase: $25.50

Introduces the concepts and program components of upward mobility for lower-level employees in private industry, state and local governments, and federal agencies. Intended for the orientation and training of supervisors, managers, EEO specialists, and employee representatives.

139. Twelve Like You
Cally Curtis Company   1973   16mm film or
videocassette   color   25 min
Purchase: film $395.00; video $380.00   Rental:
$120.00   Preview: $30.00

Discusses career opportunities for women by women. Asks each woman to analyze and appraise her own assets and liabilities and help her find answers to some crucial career questions. Outlines a systematic and pragmatic approach to assist women get the answers to some of the crucial questions that affect their careers. Useful for self-improvement, orientation, and affirmative action programs.

140. Violinist
LCA Video/Films   16mm film or
videocassette   color   8 min
Purchase: $175.00   Rental: $60.00   Preview:
$30.00

An instructive and amusing look at the way we shape our personal values and beliefs. Useful for career planning and development workshops. The characterization of Harry, a "normal guy who likes to play the violin," aptly illustrates the role others play in developing personal goals. Features Carl Reiner.

141. What Have You Done for Yourself Lately?
EFM Films   1982   16mm film or
videocassette   color   15 min   instructor's print
materials; script
Purchase: $465.00   Rental: $120.00   Preview:
$40.00

Proposes that employees seek to develop within their current jobs rather than only striving for upward mobility. Jack Falvey offers self-development techniques useful for job enrichment and personal growth. Useful where turnover and job hopping is prevalent. Especially for computer personnel, salespeople, and high-tech employees.

142. Where Do I Belong?
BNA Communications, Inc   1981   16mm film or
videocassette   color   20 min   instructor's print
materials; learner's print materials
Purchase: $650.00   Rental: $245.00

Suggests that managers develop themselves personally and professionally by finding out what they excel in, redefine their jobs, and take advantage of career development opportunities offered by their organizations and communities. Emphasizes the importance of increased knowledge of finance, marketing, planning, psychology, and budgeting. Uses case study of a company losing the business of one of its oldest customers and how the problem gets solved. Emphasizes importance of obtaining information essential to make effective decisions. Uses discussion stops to involve viewers. Features Peter Drucker. Managing for Tomorrow Series, no. 5.

143. Where Do I Go from Here?
EFM Films   1980   16mm film or videocassette   color   23 min   instructor's print materials; learner's print materials
Purchase: $525.00   Rental: $120.00   Preview: $40.00

Introduces the concept of employee review and realistic self-appraisal. Presents a 3-step program for achieving career success and personal satisfaction and will help employees use the training department as a resource for growth. Shows how management can provide guidance and resources necessary for goal attainment. Features Jack Falvey.

CHANGE
See also ORGANIZATIONAL CHANGE AND DEVELOPMENT; PERSONAL GROWTH

144. Better Train of Thought
CRM/McGraw-Hill Films   1976   16mm film or videocassette   color   9½ min
Purchase: $250.00   Rental: $75.00   Preview: free
Animated film without narration offers a parable on problem solving, reactions to new ideas, and the value of seeking new directions for innovative solutions. Intended to stimulate discussion about change and acceptance of new ideas.

Cave. For complete citation, *see* LEADERSHIP.

145. Challenge to Change
Roundtable Films, Inc   16mm film   color   23 min
Purchase: $475.00   Rental: $85.00   Preview: $30.00

Reveals impact change can have including a sense of desperation, diminished ability to think clearly, and impaired self-confidence. Dramatization is of a promoted woman executive who must develop new values and goals. Useful for management development and preparing people for change.

146. Changing Attitudes through Communication
BNA Communications, Inc   1965   16mm film or videocassette   color   25 min   learner's print materials
Purchase: $525.00   Rental: 5-day $150.00; 3-day $105.00   Preview: $35.00
Languages: English, Dutch, Portuguese, Spanish
Dramatizes employee behavior in the face of change and how to deal with various behavior patterns. David Berlo explains rejection, distortion, and avoidance as major resistance forces that can be overcome through communication. Useful for experienced supervisors and managers.

Competition: Planning for Changes in Business. For complete citation, *see* COMPETITION.

147. Coping with Change
BNA Communications, Inc   1969   16mm film or videocassette   color   24 min
Purchase: $495.00   Rental: 5-day $150.00; 3-day $105.00   Preview: $35.00

Identifies 2 types of change and 11 reasons why people resist change. Shows how to analyze organizational forces that resist change and then build strategies to diminish those forces. Organization Renewal Series, no. 4.

148. Coping with Technological Change
BNA Communications, Inc   1971   16mm film or videocassette   color   32 min   instructor's print materials
Purchase: $350.00   Rental: 5-day $150.00; 3-day $105.00   Preview: $35.00

Peter Drucker and Charles De Carlo question the nature and direction of technological society. Intended to stimulate discussion of concerns about "over-extended" technology, planned obsolescence, safety, the impact of foreign competition, and how to approach technological changes in the factory. Managing Discontinuity Series, no. 3.

Creative Thinking System. For complete citation, *see* CREATIVITY.

149. Energy Carol
National Film Board of Canada   16mm film or videocassette   color   11 min
Purchase: film $275.00; video $250.00   Rental: $80.00   Preview: $40.00

Useful for a focus on energy, change, problem solving, and interpersonal relations. Satires a Scrooge-like president of a power company who has a block on energy conservation.

150. Hundredth Monkey
Hartley Film Foundation   1983   16mm film or videocassette   color   28 min
Purchase: $400.00   Rental: $45.00

Introduced the concept that, when a critical mass of people believe and act alike, the awareness spreads exponentially and becomes universal. Based on research. Features Robert Theobald.

151. I Want to Change but I Don't Know How
Cally Curtis Company   1982   16mm film or videocassette   color   25 min   instructor's print materials
Purchase: film $550.00; video $525.00   Rental: $130.00   Preview: $40.00

Helps viewers understand why they have resisted change and then provides them with practical guidelines on how to change—whether they want to break a habit or change in any other way. Offers tested ideas that work and help people get unstuck and improve their lives.

152. If It Is to Be, It Is Up to Me
BNA Communications, Inc   1978   16mm film or videocassette   color   26 min   instructor's print materials
Purchase: $525.00   Rental: 5-day $150.00; 3-day $105.00   Preview: $35.00

Points out the effect change is having on our lives, our work, and our organizations. Joe Powell discusses why the law of change governs our lives, where most change takes place, why we must unlearn as we learn, and why we should never underrate ourselves. Joe Powell Films, no. 6.

153. Introduction of Change
Resources for Education and Management, Inc   3 filmstrips or slides and audiocassettes or videocassettes or filmstrip cartridges   9–10 min ea   instructor's print materials
Purchase: video $245.00 ($95.00 ea); filmstrips $220.00 ($75.00 ea); filmstrip cartridges $255.00 ($85.00 ea); slides $235.00 ($80.00 ea)   Preview: $20.00

Shows how people react to change and what determines their reaction. Offers 5 simple steps to avoid the major pitfalls of introducing change. Intended for supervisors who face conflict and resistance to organizational change.

154. Joshua and the Blob
CRM/McGraw-Hill Films   16mm film or videocassette   color   7 min
Purchase: $225.00   Rental: $75.00   Preview: free

Animated, nonnarrated story shows Joshua's initial reaction to the Blob as fearful aggression. Then, as he comes to know it, his response changes. Suggests the value of an open and positive attitude in response to new ideas, change, and the unknown. Useful as meeting opener or discussion starter. Joshua Trilogy Series.

155. Management of Change
Harris International, Ltd   1965   videocassette and audiocassettes   color   60 min   instructor's print materials; learner's print materials
Purchase: $5,000.00

Offers methods of planning for change with organizations and our cultures. Delves into the why of managing change, how to plan for change, and strategies for changing. Advocates designing the organization of the future now. Suggested for a one- to 3-day program, with 10–35 participants.

156. Managing Change
International Film Bureau, Inc   16mm film or videocassette   color   23 min   discussion guide
Purchase: $450.00   Rental: 3-day $50.00   Preview: free

Illustrates and suggests solutions to some of the special problems that confront managers when it is their responsibility to manage change. Shows how managers can share responsibility and coordinate efforts to effect change successfully. Dramatizes concepts as a new assembly line is installed and new products are introduced.

157. Overcoming Resistance to Change
Roundtable Films, Inc   1962   16mm film or videocassette   color   30 min
Purchase: $425.00   Rental: $85.00   Preview: $30.00

Shows supervisors how to recognize the emotional factors which breed resistance to change and how to prevent and overcome such resistance. Demonstrates how resistance should be handled by clearing up misperceptions, opening communica-tion channels, developing participation, and permitting the ventilation of feelings.

158. Overmanagement
Salenger Educational Media   1976   16mm film or videocassette   color   10 min   instructor's print materials
Purchase: $410.00   Rental: $125.00   Preview: $35.00

Amusing and instructive parable created by Warren Schmidt and narrated by Hans Conreid. Animated film about a simple man who had a simple idea—until he became entangled in the red tape and bureaucracy of his own organization. A film to help managers become more aware of how they treat new ideas or people with new ideas. Alternate title is *How an Exciting Idea Can Become a Dull Project*.

159. People Don't Resist Change
BNA Communications, Inc   1967   16mm film or videocassette   color   24 min   instructor's print materials
Purchase: $450.00   Rental: 5-day $150.00; 3-day $105.00   Preview: $35.00

Allan H. Mogensen outlines how involving people in planning, recognizing good ideas, and providing strong motivational factors enable maximum job satisfaction. Intended for supervisors who must persuade others that change is important.

160. Real Security
BNA Communications, Inc   1963   16mm film or videocassette   color   26 min   instructor's print materials; learner's print materials
Purchase: $450.00   Rental: 5-day $150.00; 3-day $105.00   Preview: $35.00
Languages: English, German, Portuguese, Spanish

Addresses the causes of employee lethargy. Intended to help overcome resistance to change by encouraging adaptability and acceptance. Joe Powell Films, no. 3.

161. Releasing Human Potential
General Cassette Corporation   4 audiocassettes
Purchase: $59.50

Focuses on how to change patterns of behavior that stand in the way of success, set goals, and respond positively to pressures. Features James Newman.

Research and the Change Process. For complete citation, *see* ORGANIZATIONAL CHANGE AND DEVELOPMENT.

162. Ten—The Magic Number
National Film Board of Canada   16mm film or videocassette   color   13 min
Purchase: film $350.00; video $250.00   Rental: $80.00   Preview: $40.00

Portrays how a clear and diplomatic demonstration of the advantages of a new method can be convincing. In this case, a man is strongly attached to his old way of measuring water and resists adopting the metric system.

163. This Thing Called Change
Cally Curtis Company 1973 16mm film or
videocassette color 9 min
Purchase: film $325.00; video $300.00 Rental:
$100.00 Preview: free

Helps viewers recognize, understand, and accept change. Shows
historical examples of individuals and societies that could not or
would not adapt to change. Useful for meeting opener or
discussion starter.

CLERICAL SKILLS

164. Basic Clerical Skills
Prentice Hall Media 10 filmstrips and 10
audiocassettes instructor's print materials
Purchase: $299.00

Covers filing systems and records management, written communication, and telephone techniques. Each segment progresses
from simple to complex allowing learners to find the level at
which they need to learn. Useful as refresher. Segments are also
available separately.

Desk Set. For complete citation, *see*
COMMUNICATION.

165. Electric Typewriter Series
Thompson-Mitchell and Associates slides and 6
audiocassettes
Purchase: $600.00

IBM Selectric used to demonstrate typical competencies needed
for any electric typewriter: corrections, centering, carbons, and
advanced techniques.

166. Printing Calculator
HBJ Media Systems Corporation 1981 8 slide/
audiocassette presentations instructor's print
materials; learner's print materials
Purchase: $2,380.00

Shows how to perform computations quickly and accurately.
Suggested for 14–18 hours.

167. Ten-Key Adding Machines
HBJ Media Systems Corporation 1981 8 slide/
audiocassette presentations instructor's print
materials; learner's print materials
Purchase: $2,380.00

Shows how to perform calculations quickly and accurately.
Includes the various functions as well as speed and accuracy
building. Suggested for 14–18 hours.

COACHING

**168. Face to Face; Coaching for Improved Work
Performance**
Cally Curtis Company 1981 16mm film or
videocassette color 27 min instructor's print
materials

Purchase: film $550.00; video $525.00 Rental:
$130.00 Preview: $40.00

Demonstrates in 3 instances how a supervisor can coach
employees for improved work performance. Based on Ferdi-
nand Fournies's *Coaching for Improved Performance*. Discusses why managers traditionally avoid "face to face" performance
discussions with employees. Uses specific techniques for a 2-
part process that deals with behavior.

169. To Try Again—And Succeed
CRM/McGraw-Hill Films 16mm film or
videocassette color 7½ min
Purchase: $295.00 Rental: $75.00 Preview: free

A little eagle fears to fly yet yearns to soar. Guided by another
who knows how to inspire self-confidence, the eaglet tries and
finally succeeds. Narrated by Orson Welles. For supervisors
who need to learn to coach for productivity. Animated.

COMMUNICATION
See also LISTENING; NONVERBAL
COMMUNICATION; LANGUAGE; TELEPHONE
USAGE; WRITING

170. AAAARK—Something about Communication
National Audiovisual Center 1969 16mm film 18
min
Purchase: $104.50

Defines communication and elaborates on the art of communicating. Shows how communication gives purpose and meaning to life. Highlights ways of getting ideas across to others.

171. Avoiding Communication Breakdown
BNA Communications, Inc 1965 16mm film or
videocassette color 26 min learner's print
materials
Purchase: $450.00 Rental: 5-day $150.00; 3-day
$105.00 Preview: $35.00
Languages: English, Dutch, Portuguese, Spanish,
Swedish

Dramatizes loss of a key account to show significance of
communications flow in an organization. Useful for managers
and those concerned with customer relations. Effective Communication Series, no. 1.

172. Berfunkle
Thompson-Mitchell and Associates 1968 16mm
film or videocassette color 10 min
Purchase: $195.00 Rental: $35.00 Preview: $7.50

Animated communication program dealing with interpreting
word meanings, the importance of clear and common understanding, and the consequences of misunderstanding.

173. Blowing Hot and Cold
BNA Communications, Inc 1973 16mm film or
videocassette 24 min instructor's print materials
Purchase: $495.00 Rental: 5-day $150.00; 3-day
$105.00 Preview: $35.00

Points out the importance of good communication between
work groups. Portrays struggle between sales and production

units to illustrate the problem and its solution. Part of the Communicating Series.

174. Bob Knowlton Story
Roundtable Films, Inc 16mm film or videocassette color 28 min
Purchase: $450.00 Rental: $85.00 Preview: $30.00

Real life dramatized case study about the psychological barriers that interrupt communication and job performance. Shows the disastrous effects of poor organizational development and planning on production, communication, and interpersonal relations. Points out the importance of managers and subordinates keeping the channels of communication mutually open.

175. Boss/Secretary
Educational Resources Foundation 1972 2 16mm films or videocassettes color 21 min and 23 min
Purchase: $400.00 ea Rental: $65.00 ea Preview: $15.00 ea

Two program series, *Opening the Door* and *Combination for Results,* which focus on office communications between office assistant or secretary and manager. Objective is to build a well-coordinated team. Specific situations are shown and alternative solutions given with viewers making decisions.

176. Bottom Line Communicating: Get to the Point
Barr Films 16mm film or videocassette color 18½ min
Purchase: $450.00 Rental: $100.00 Preview: $50.00

Demonstrates a strategic system of communication that meets the different needs for communicating. Stresses value of direct message (i.e., bottom line) placed initially, delayed, or last.

177. Building a Working Team: "Let's Get Engaged"
BNA Communications, Inc 1975 16mm film or videocassette color 31 min
Purchase: $550.00 Rental: 5-day $150.00; 3-day $105.00 Preview: $35.00

Focuses on communication relationships on the job. Such relationships are vital to the exchange of information. Offers ways to maintain and budget for these relationships. Useful for supervisors in particular but all employees in general. Two Person Communication Series, no. 3.

178. Business Communication Series
Thompson-Mitchell and Associates filmstrip or slides and audiocassette
Purchase: filmstrips and audiocassettes $180.00; slides and audiocassettes $300.00

Three units intended for managerial levels or for office and secretarial training: (1) Business Communications Overview; (2) Art of Dictation; (3) Introduction to Telecommunications. Each unit can be purchased separately.

Case of Insubordination. For complete citation, *see* GRIEVANCE.

179. Case Studies in Communication
Salenger Educational Media 1976 16mm film or videocassette color 18 min instructor's print materials; learner's print materials; poster
Purchase: $455.00 Rental: $125.00 Preview: $35.00

Two dramatized case histories illustrate the major barriers to effective communication: the way we see ourselves and the way we see others. Heightens awareness of the need for feedback and active listening in order to avoid potential blocks to communication.

Changing Attitudes through Communication. For complete citation, *see* CHANGE.

Chris Argyris on Organization Predictions/Prescriptions. For complete citation, *see* ORGANIZATIONAL CHANGE AND DEVELOPMENT.

180. Citizen Chang
BNA Communications, Inc 16mm film b/w 26 min
Purchase: $250.00 Rental: 5-day $150.00; 3-day $105.00 Preview: $35.00

Instance of a small boy alerting town mayor to problem. Shows importance of listening, interpersonal communication, and gathering facts in making decisions.

181. Clear as Mud
CRM/McGraw-Hill Films 16mm film or videocassette color 10 min
Purchase: $250.00 Rental: $75.00 Preview: free

Life-sized puppets reveal pitfalls that prevent clear verbal communication. Focuses on use of appropriate language and eliciting feedback. Useful as meeting opener or discussion starter.

182. Communicate What You Think
Nightingale-Conant Corporation 6 audiocassettes
Purchase: $60.00

Discusses how to transmit messages from one person to another without sacrificing meaning or intent. Offers techniques for effective presentations, including the use of visuals.

183. Communicating Effectively
Barr Films 1978 16mm film or videocassette color 21 min
Purchase: $430.00 lease Rental: $100.00 Preview: $25.00

Focuses on verbal and nonverbal forms of communication and analyzes how on-the-job behavior influences the way others see us. Useful for orientations, entry-level personnel, and customer relations.

184. Communicating for Profit
Edupac, Inc 2 audiocassettes instructor's print materials; learner's print materials
Purchase: $75.00

Includes verbal and nonverbal communication with subordinates, superiors, and peers. Emphasizes the supervisor's role in communication. Suggest how to map guidelines for communicating with subordinates and gives techniques for conducting interviews and negotiations.

185. Communicating for Profit
Management Resources, Inc 2 audiocassettes instructor's print materials; learner's print materials
Purchase: $75.00 Other cost factors: discounts for additional learner's printed materials

Emphasizes that good oral and written communication skills downward, upward, and laterally are essential in a successful business. Special focus is given to the supervisor's role.

186. Communicating Management's Point of View
BNA Communications, Inc 1965 16mm film or videocassette color 24 min learner's print materials
Purchase: $525.00 Rental: 5-day $150.00; 3-day $105.00 Preview: $35.00
Languages: English, Dutch, Portuguese, Spanish

Dramatized examples show how effective managers can and must be as persuaders. Dr. David K. Berlo outlines the basic principles of effective persuasion, affecting and changing people's beliefs, attitudes, and behavior. Effective Communication Series, no. 5.

187. Communicating Non-Defensively: Don't Take It Personally
CRM/McGraw-Hill Films 1982 16mm film or videocassette 22 min instructor's print materials
Purchase: $595.00 Rental: $95.00 Preview: free

Looks at defensiveness as a roadblock to effective communication. Details why defensiveness occurs, showing examples of behaviors. Suggests ways to preserve employee self-esteem during criticism.

188. Communicating Skills
Resources for Education and Management, Inc 1981 6 audiocassettes instructor's print materials
Purchase: $75.00 Preview: $10.00

Indicates that people can learn to fill organizational needs for oral and written communication providing they receive proper direction and apply themselves. Points out many of the "do's and don'ts" in communicating and offers suggestions for avoiding or correcting a number of communication problems.

189. Communicating through Objectives
Practical Management Associates, Inc 6 audiocassettes 4½ hrs
Purchase: $125.00

Taped seminar stresses value of the communicating process to affect performance. Weaves setting and achieving performance objectives with on-the-job communication at managerial, supervisory, and worker levels.

190. Communication and Motivation
Lansford Publishing Company, Inc 1981 60 slides and audiocassettes learner's print materials
Purchase: $245.00

Analyzes nature of the human element in the organization, role and importance of communication, and interrelationships between communication and motivation. Includes wide range of communication topics plus foundations for successful motivation and positive reinforcement theory.

191. Communication: Barriers and Pathways
PCI 16mm film color 16 min
Purchase: $350.00 Rental: $50.00

Dramatization of a work conflict due to common communication breakdowns. Reveals the complexity of interpersonal communication, how feedback can be helpful, and the importance of nonverbal messages. Primarily for managerial and supervisory employees.

192. Communication Generation Gap
Monad Trainer's Aide 1977 16mm film or videocassette color 20 min
Purchase: $485.00 Rental: $100.00 Preview: $25.00

General overview of communication through lifelike situations that show inadequacies and ways to improve communications within the organization.

193. Communication: Getting in Touch
CRM/McGraw-Hill Films 1979 16mm film or videocassette color 13½ min
Purchase: $295.00 Rental: $75.00 Preview: free

Illustrates 3 major barriers to communication. Shows an alien colony settling on earth, presenting language differences as a real problem. This challenges residents' ability to build bridges to meaningful and effective communications. Useful as meeting opener or discussion starter.

194. Communication in Management
Classroom World Productions 4 audiocassettes
Purchase: $27.50

Offers basic pointers for conducting small meetings, giving instructions, eliciting feedback, and guarding against misinterpretation.

195. Communication Lectures
Lansford Publishing Company, Inc 4 audiocassettes instructor's print materials; learner's print materials
Purchase: $79.95

Lecture format covers this overview of communication. Emphasis is on persuasion and attitude change, listening, and audience analysis.

196. Communication Skills for Managers
Time-Life Video 1980 6 videocassettes color 30 min ea instructor's print materials; learner's print materials
Purchase: $3,950.00 Rental: $500.00 Preview: free

Dramatized typical office situations are presented to stimulate managers to analyze the communication process and strategize how to achieve results through communication. Includes preparation, speaking effectively, listening, presentation skills, and managing meetings.

197. Communication: The Name of the Game
Roundtable Films, Inc 1981 16mm film or videocassette color 28 min instructor's print materials
Purchase: $550.00 Rental: $125.00 Preview: $30.00 Other cost factors: learner's printed materials

Uses vignettes of communication problems and a game show format that involves learners along with 3 "contestants" on film. Five rounds focus on the importance of organizing thoughts before communicating, selecting the appropriate media, using feedback, reading body language, and listening with an open mind.

198. Communications or Confrontations
Barr Films 1978 16mm film or videocassette color 18 min
Purchase: $300.00 Rental: $31.62 Preview: free

Three vignettes demonstrate how one's point of view can get in the way of meaningful communication. Uses school, home, and business examples. Film is open-ended to stimulate audience discussion.

199. Critic
LCA Video/Films 16mm film or videocassette color 4 min
Purchase: $175.00 Rental: $60.00 Preview: $30.00

Group discussion starter for training activities involving communications and performance appraisal. Mel Brooks offers a parody of how critics can sometimes be their own worst enemies. Animated.

200. Dealing with the Unexpected
Centron Films 1975 16mm film color 10 min
Purchase: $205.00

Dramatization of an unexpected series of events and how 2 men handle the change in direction. Intended to give insight into how to deal effectively with the unexpected. Especially useful for communication skill development. Handling Information at the Personal Level Series.

201. Desk Set
Educational Resources Foundation 1981 3 videocassettes color 25–29 min ea instructor's print materials
Purchase: $1,100 ($400.00 ea) Rental: $65.00 ea Preview: $15.00 ea Other cost factors: printed materials not included with media
Languages: English, Spanish

Intended for professional secretaries, clerks, and supervisors. Effective communication techniques shown in situations with superiors, peers, and subordinates. Printed exercises help learners apply those techniques to daily work experience. For individual or group study.

202. Doubletalk
LCA Video/Films 16mm film or videocassette color 9 min
Purchase: $220.00 Rental: $60.00 Preview: $30.00

Brief humorous film reveals what might happen if management and labor were on a "blind date" and spoke exactly what they thought. Useful to encourage open communication among employees and employers.

203. Effective Communicating Skills
Resources for Education and Management, Inc 5 filmstrips or slides and audiocassettes or videocassettes or filmstrip cartridges 8–12 min ea instructor's print materials
Purchase: video $305.00 ($75.00 ea); filmstrip $280.00 ($64.00 ea); filmstrip cartridges $425.00 ($85.00 ea); slides $295.00 ($67.00 ea)

Combines case studies and exercises to point out some common failures in communicating and how they can be overcome. Modules cover general principles, barriers, improving personal and group communications, and the supervisor as communicator.

204. Elephant
Salenger Educational Media 1981 16mm film or videocassette color 5 min instructor's print materials
Purchase: $155.00 Rental: $60.00 Preview: $35.00

Modern-day fable to show the importance of communication between specialists and teamwork in problem solving. Rhymed animation also points up the dangers in a narrow point of view.

205. Executive Writing, Speaking and Listening Skills
American Management Associations 1974 6 audiocassettes 1 hr ea learner's print materials
Purchase: $145.00 Other cost factors: AMA members $135.00; additional materials available at bulk rates

Gives a unified approach to integrate speaking, writing, listening, and reading. Begins with a refresher course in word usage, grammar, tone, memos, proposals, letters, and oral presentations. Intended for experienced managers.

206. Getting Change through Communications
Classroom World Productions 4 audiocassettes
Purchase: $27.50

Concerns the importance of a good climate for communication and why arguments do not work. Relates communication to problem solving especially when done with employees.

207. Grapevine
Xicom-Video Arts 1982 16mm film or videocassette color 25 min instructor's print materials
Purchase: $625.00 Rental: 5-day $140.00; 3-day $100.00 Preview: $35.00

Dramatization shows the birth and growth of a damaging rumor about management's intentions. The manager portrayed feeds the rumor but finally shows the grapevine can be an ally and reveals how effective a communication channel it can be.

I Told 'Em Exactly How to Do It. For complete citation, *see* SUPERVISION.

I'd Rather Not Say. For complete citation, *see* INTERVIEWING.

208. If—For Anyone Who Makes Excuses
Cally Curtis Company   16mm film or videocassette   color   10 min
Purchase: film $325.00; video $300.00   Rental: $100.00   Preview: $40.00

Points out that excuses waste energy and block solutions. Suggested for programs on communication skills, assertiveness training, interpersonal relationships, and management training.

209. Improving Communication Skills
Training by Design   5 audiocassettes   instructor's print materials; learner's print materials
Purchase: $95.00

Basic communication skills including overcoming barriers and using nondirective questioning techniques, active listening skills, and descriptive feedback. Approaches communication as an interpersonal process and shows how to analyze effective and ineffective self-expression. Suggested for 5 hours in 4 units.

210. Improving Communication Skills: The Skills of Effective Communication
Management Resources, Inc   5 audiocassettes   instructor's print materials; learner's print materials
Purchase: $150.00

Practical techniques for overcoming barriers to effective communication, using communication as an interpersonal process, nondirective questioning, active listening, generating descriptive feedback, and analyzing self-expression. Intended for supervisors and managers. Recommended for 5 hours.

211. Improving Management Communication Skills
Edupac, Inc   3 audiocassettes   study manual
Purchase: $70.00

Shows steps involved in the vital process of communication, gives the concepts of behavioral communication, and examines the impact of images of self, role, and organization. Illustrates how perception influences human interaction. Creates an awareness of what is involved in human transactions to help managers become more professional and sensitive communicators.

212. In the Company of Men
Didactic Systems, Inc   16mm film   b/w   52 min
Purchase: $350.00   Rental: 5-day $130.00; per-day $45.00

Examines conflicting attitudes between minority-group employees and supervisors. Uses sensitivity training and role playing to explore the breakdown and reconstruction of communication between new employees and their direct supervisors.

213. Information Interview
AMACOM   audiocassette   60 min
Purchase: 30.00   Other cost factors: AMA members $25.50

Shows how to troubleshoot, mediate, negotiate, maintain control, and safeguard vital communication channels. Simple yet invaluable techniques to assure wide-open 2-way communication between manager and employees. Features John R. Hinrichs. Productive Interviewing Series.

214. Instructions or Obstructions
BNA Communications, Inc   1961   16mm film or videocassette   color   15 min   booklet
Purchase: $250.00   Rental: 5-day $150.00; 3-day $105.00   Preview: $35.00
Languages: English, French, Spanish, Swedish

Illustrates that most errors are the fault of the giver of instructions, not the receiver. Dr. Paul Pigors shows 7 steps to give orders that will get people to work with, instead of for, supervisors. Useful for training in how to give instructions, execute a performance appraisal, and eliminate barriers to interpersonal communications. Modern Management Series, no. 4.

215. Interpersonal Communication
Lansford Publishing Company, Inc   6 audiocassettes   instructor's print materials
Purchase: $129.95

Lectures examine the factors that influence our contacts with others and show ways to deepen and enrich that contact. Includes the self and its expression; orientations to others; effects of dominance, power, and authority; the encounter group; group functions and phases; and I-Thou relationship through dialog.

216. Interpersonal Communications
Learning Consultants, Inc   audiocassette   learner's print materials
Purchase: $17.50

Shows how to develop listening and communicating skills. Discusses the 10 common blocks to effective communication. Features Clay Hardesty. Recording of a seminar. Woman in Management Series.

217. Intrapersonal Communication
Lansford Publishing Company, Inc   25 slides and 6 audiocassettes   instructor's print materials
Purchase: $139.95

Proposes that the heart of the communication process is what happens inside the listener as s/he responds to information according to a personal understanding of that information. Lectures deal with the inner workings of the communicator and the intrapersonal aspects of communication.

218. Leadership Problems in Communication
Audio-Forum   audiocassette   25 min
Purchase: $10.95

Franklin S. Haiman discusses the nature and importance of communications in industrial and business organizations.

219. Maintaining the Organization: "How Far Should I Trust You?"
BNA Communications, Inc   1975   16mm film or videocassette   color   33 min   instructor's print materials
Purchase: $550.00   Rental: 5-day $150.00; 3-day $105.00   Preview: $35.00

Challenges conventional wisdom about personal trust and its cost benefit and points out why personal relationships and trust are not enough to manage a complex organization. Includes topics such as the appraisal interview, trust and intimacy in interpersonal relationships, and risks in sharing and receiving information. Two Person Communication Series, no. 4.

220. Managerial Communication—How to Master It
AMACOM   6 audiocassettes   45 min ea   learner's print materials
Purchase: $120.00   Other cost factors: AMA members $102.00

Offers 22 communication secrets of successful business executives. Includes time-saving techniques. Features Glenn A. Bassett.

Managing through Leadership & Communications.
For complete citation, *see* LEADERSHIP.

221. Meanings are in People
BNA Communications, Inc   1965   16mm film or videocassette   color   24 min
Purchase: $525.00   Rental: 5-day $150.00; 3-day $105.00   Preview: $35.00
Languages: Dutch, English, Portuguese, Spanish, Swedish

Shows how misunderstandings occur by presenting dramatic reenactments of what was said and what was thought by several managers and employees at cross-purposes in typical work situations. Vignettes portray a series of events that result in costly foul-ups. Aids study of topics such as nature of communication, assignment of work, feedback, interpersonal relations, and perception. Effective Communication Series, no. 2.

222. Measure of Understanding
Roundtable Films, Inc   16mm film or videocassette   color   29 min   learner's print materials
Purchase: $450.00   Rental: $85.00   Preview: $30.00

Focuses on the problems involved in communicating meaning, attitudes, and intentions. Emphasizes how meaning is communicated on an informational and behavioral level and that communication is clear only when both information and behavior "say" the same thing. Dramatization shows the necessity of preventing assumptions and summarizing communication and information logically. Provides reliable techniques for clearing up conflicting meanings.

223. Meeting of Minds
Xicom-Video Arts   1979   16mm film or videocassette   color   15 min
Purchase: $390.00   Rental: $100.00   Preview: $35.00

Shows 2 kinds of barriers that obstruct communication and result in disappointment, frustration, or anger for the customer and lost business for the company. Portrays how an employee can identify and remove barriers to achieve a meeting of minds.

224. More than Words
Monad Trainer's Aide   1968   16mm film or videocassette   color   15 min   learner's print materials
Purchase: $195.00   Rental: $45.00

Uses a combination of animated and live sequences. Outlines basic methods of good communication that are applicable to activities where dealing with people plays a key role in management, supervision, sales, and public and community relations.

225. One-Sided Triangle
BNA Communications, Inc   1973   16mm film or videocassette   color   24 min   instructor's print materials
Purchase: $550.00   Rental: 5-day $150.00; 3-day $105.00   Preview: $35.00

Focuses on group communication patterns and building of trust and teamwork through open and shared communication. Communicating Series, no. 2.

226. Open the Door
Cally Curtis Company   1972   16mm film or videocassette   color   28 min   instructor's print materials
Purchase: film $550.00; video $525.00   Rental: $130.00   Preview: $40.00

Through dramatization, Bill Welp illustrates an OPEN communication system (objectives, planning, expectancy, needs). Its focus is to eliminate barriers, reduce mistakes, and promote understanding. Provides an introduction to roles managers play in filling their responsibilities.

227. Oral Communication
National Audiovisual Center   1977   16mm film or videocassette   color   28 min   learner's print materials
Purchase: $162.50   Rental: $12.50

Emphasizes the important aspects of oral communication and applies them to the 3 types of oral communication: person-to-person, informal interviews, and group discussion. You in Public Service Series.

228. Oral Communication Skills
Lansford Publishing Company, Inc   6 audiocassettes
Purchase: $25.95 ea

Covers 6 basic skills: speechmaking, voice improvement, reading aloud, parliamentary procedure, group discussion, and debating.

229. Pass It On
Cally Curtis Company   16mm film or videocassette   color   12 min
Purchase: film $325.00; video $300.00   Rental: $100.00   Preview: $40.00

Demonstrates that unclear and misunderstood messages or instructions result in losses of time, money, and productivity. Suggests a clarify-and-verify technique to ensure that understanding occurs. Offers tips to help with the verification process. Features Ed Carrol as a well-intentioned, well-educated manager whose instructions often sound like double-talk.

230. Person to Person
Barr Films   16mm film   color   11 min
Purchase: $190.00

Explores facial expression, body language, eye contact, and vocal enthusiasm. Gives examples of both positive and negative communication in the 4 areas.

231. Person to Person Communication

Roundtable Films, Inc 1956 16mm film or videocassette color 14 min
Purchase: $295.00 Rental: $75.00 Preview: $30.00
Languages: Danish, Dutch, English, German, Norwegian, Swedish

Shows how to analyze communications for assumptions, viewpoints, and feelings. Helps improve listening habits for better understanding. Dramatization shows unspoken thinking behind a work incident.

232. Powers of Persuasion

Human Productivity Institute, Inc 1982 audiocassettes learner's print materials
Purchase: $69.95

Presents state-of-the-art communication techniques and strategies. Shows how to take control of any situation immediately, establish trust and credibility, get other people to understand, and avoid being manipulated.

233. Psychology of Communication

Learning Consultants, Inc 2 audiocassettes 50 min ea
Purchase: $29.95

Points out the importance of good and effective communication in business and personal lives. Covers styles of communicating, nonverbal messages, and communicating feelings. One tape is a presentation and the other a discussion with businessmen giving practical applications and suggestions.

234. Question of May

BNA Communications, Inc 1973 16mm film or videocassette 22 min instructor's print materials
Purchase: $550.00 Rental: 5-day $150.00; 3-day $105.00 Preview: $35.00

Dramatization of work crisis that develops during communication breakdown. Provides guidelines for clear communication between individuals. Communicating Series, no. 1.

235. Read Your Way Up

Manpower Education Institute 1970 30 videocassettes color 28 min ea learner's print materials
Purchase: $3,000.00 Rental: $500.00

Successively builds work skills, meanings, and study skills. Intended to strengthen communication skills and is suitable for working adults.

236. Replay

CRM/McGraw-Hill Films 16mm film or videocassette color 8 min
Purchase: film $145.00; video $110.00 Rental: 10-day $50.00; 5-day $30.00 Preview: free

Brief musical film designed to encourage open communication between unlike groups. Shows uninhibited young adults and the comments of their elders to demonstrate the misunderstandings of the generation gap.

237. Seeking Understanding and Acceptance: "Try to Tell It Like It Is"

BNA Communications, Inc 1975 16mm film or videocassette color 33 min
Purchase: $550.00 Rental: 5-day $150.00; 3-day $105.00 Preview: $35.00

Stresses the importance of presenting information in ways that are concise and clear. Reveals how cogency in interpersonal communication is essential to the effectiveness of the organization. Uses dramatization. Two Person Communication Series, no. 2.

238. Speak Up and Communicate: A System of Oral Communication

Butler Learning Systems 1980 624 slides and audiocassettes instructor's print materials; learner's print materials
Purchase: $2,595.00 plus $70.00 per learner Preview: free

Provides a systematic and practical method to follow when a person has to give a presentation. Emphasizes organizing and delivering a speech, the importance of word power, voice and gestures, and how to break communication barriers.

239. Speaking Effectively...To One or One Thousand

CRM/McGraw-Hill Films 1980 16mm film or videocassette color 21 min
Purchase: $495.00 Rental: $95.00 Preview: free

Shows that speaking need not be painful and gives clear, concise keys for improving communication skills. Christopher Hegarty explains and demonstrates that the intention of each spoken communication must be clear from the start. Key areas emphasized are body language, vocal quality, intonation, and, finally, the words spoken.

240. Straight Talk

Andragogy Press 1981 audiocassette instructor's print materials; learner's print materials
Purchase: $385.00

Emphasizes the communication exchange and the fundamental purpose of that exchange. Strategies suggested are practical but require an honest assessment of one's current communication practices as well as a commitment to improve. Focuses on what is involved in good communication, how to identify communication problems they are having in the workplace and their causes, and how to develop and use strategies for improved communication. Suggested for 4 hours.

241. Strictly Speaking

Cally Curtis Company 1979 16mm film or videocassette color 30 min instructor's print materials
Purchase: film $550.00; video $525.00 Rental: $130.00 Preview: $40.00

Argues for direct, lucid, and imaginative language and against jargon, verbiage, and trick phrases. Loss of productivity is staggering when communication is confusing. Suggests that too much language of business, government, and education in America is unclear and wasteful. Based on Edwin Newman's book.

242. Supervisory Communication Skills
Phoenix-BFA Films and Video, Inc   1982   16mm
film or videocassette   color   24 min
Purchase: film $495.00; video $375.00   Rental:
$50.00

Addresses the problems of communication between supervisors and employees and presents basic tenets of successful communication that should be followed: consider the message and its impact; look for a reaction; criticize constructively and in private; build employee self-esteem by praising in public; remain tactful; present ideas effectively; anticipate and interpret change; provide support and appropriate retraining when required by a changing job situation. Supervising for Results Series, no. 3.

243. Tell-Sell-Resolve
General Motors Corporation   2
videocassettes   color   1 hr and 26 min   instructor's
print materials; learner's print materials
Purchase: $1,100.00   Preview: $60.00
Languages: English, Spanish

Designed to improve a supervisor's ability to communicate more effectively with employees. The skill of telling imparts information effectively, the skill of selling considers the employee's reaction, and the skill of resolving accomplishes the objective. Suggests that these improve relationships and the quality of work life.

244. Ten Commandments of Meaningful Communication
Audio-Forum   audiocassette   23 min
Purchase: $10.95

Examines the communication process in terms of receiving, sending, understanding, and accepting.

245. This is Marshall McLuhan: The Medium is the Message
CRM/McGraw-Hill Films   16mm film or
videocassette   color   53 min
Purchase: film $695.00; video $525.00   Rental:
$53.00

Visual interpretations and examples of McLuhan's explosive ideas about the manner in which all media of communication shape and alter society. Concentrates particularly upon the new electronic media and instruments that are speeding up our lives, processing information, and most fundamentally, shaping our sensibilities. Opposing viewpoints are also aired.

246. To Be a Winner, Back Your Winners
EFM Films   16mm film or videocassette   color   17
min   instructor's print materials
Purchase: $465.00   Rental: $125.00   Preview:
$40.00

Emphasizes the importance of people and communication. Promotes idea that the 3 most important jobs managers do is to communicate expectations, inspect results, and provide feedback. Features Jack Falvey. Intended for new and prospective managers.

Transactional Analysis: Better Communication for Organizations. For complete citation, *see* TRANSACTIONAL ANALYSIS.

Transactional Analysis in Social and Communications Training (TASC). For complete citation, *see* TRANSACTIONAL ANALYSIS.

247. Verbal Communication
CRM/McGraw-Hill Films   16mm film or
videocassette   color   30 min
Purchase: $560.00   Rental: $95.00   Preview: free

Uses animation, vignettes, and dramatized slices of organizational life to illustrate the 4 critical parts of every verbal exchange: the speaker, the language used, the atmosphere, and the listener.

248. What Do You Mean, What Do I Mean? Case Studies in Communication
Salenger Educational Media   1976   16mm film or
videocassette   color   18 min   instructor's print
materials; learner's print materials; poster
Purchase: $455.00   Rental: $125.00   Preview:
$35.00

Presents 2 dramatized cases dealing with communication, both illustrating major barriers to effective communication. Looks at and evaluates communication as an interpersonal process. Demonstrates the major factors which impede or block effective communication and suggests ways to improve and facilitate effective communication.

249. What You Are Is...
Twentieth Century-Fox Video, Inc   3 16mm film or
videocassettes   color   30–60 min   instructor's print
materials; learner's print materials
Purchase: film $2,150.00; video $1,500.00   Rental:
film $250.00; video $200.00   Preview: film $120.00;
video $90.00

Focuses on values and human behavior. Morris E. Massey examines each generation and the rules they lived by and formulated. Shows what the differences are and how to overcome those differences through better communication. Positive framework for building relationships to bridge differences.

250. What You Are Is Where You Were When
Twentieth Century-Fox Video, Inc   1976   16mm
film or videocassette   color   89 min   instructor's
print materials; book
Purchase: film $1,195.00; video $750.00   Rental: film
$200.00; video $160.00   Preview: film $75.00; video
$50.00

Compares groups of people with similar values to show how attitudes, prejudices, and ways of reacting to change are "programed" into each generation. Uses examples to prompt individuals to examine their values and attitudes. Designed to help people improve communication, understand motivation and perception, and better cope with change. Features Morris Massey. Companion film to *What You Are Isn't Necessarily What You Will Be....*

251. Who's on First
Salenger Educational Media   16mm film   b/w   7½
min   booklet
Purchase: $155.00   Rental: $60.00   Preview:
$35.00

Classic case of reciprocal misunderstanding demonstrating some of the inherent problems in effective communication. Reinforces the need for training in the area of communication. Features Bud Abbott and Lou Costello.

252. You're Not Communicating
Barr Films   1980   16mm film or videocassette   color   19½ min
Purchase: $415.00   Rental: $100.00   Preview: $50.00

Delineates the responsibilities of both message sender and speaker and those roles in the communication process. Narrator intervenes in 4 situations where people are having problems communicating and points out just why the breakdowns occur. Focuses on tailoring messages to the listener's level of knowledge, understanding and using feedback, choosing the right time and place for communication, and honestly sharing feelings.

COMPETITION

253. Bricklin Story
Vantage Communications, Inc   1974   16mm film or videocassette   color   24 min
Purchase: $375.00

Shows impact of innovative style, optimism, and energetic style in business. Real-life story of automobile entrepreneur who made safety sports cars in competition with the Big Three.

254. Business of Competition
Chamber of Commerce of the United States   67 slides and audiocassette   11 min   instructor's print materials
Purchase: $25.00

Emphasizes importance and benefits of freedom of competition in pricing, products, and new business opportunities. Written materials include script.

255. Competition: Planning for Changes in Business
CRM/McGraw-Hill Films   1979   16mm film or videocassette   color   12 min
Purchase: $295.00   Rental: $75.00   Preview: free

Animated narrated film shows impact on the Bell Factory when a competitor moves into the territory. After initial frenzy, planning and response show how dealing with change prompts an organization to shape its own destiny. Good for meeting opener or to deal with resistance to change.

Competitive Spirit. For complete citation, *see* MANAGEMENT.

COMPUTERS
See also AUTOMATION

Achieving Computer Security. For complete citation, *see* SECURITY.

Ballet Robotique. For complete citation, *see* AUTOMATION.

256. Basic
Prismatron Productions, Inc   4 videocassettes or 240 slides and 4 audiocassettes   20–25 min ea   instructor's print materials
Purchase: video $360.00; filmstrip $235.00; slides $270.00   Preview: free

Concentrates on the most important instructions for the newcomer to computer programing. Includes realistic examples and encourages writing one's own programs from the start. Emphasizes the importance of clarity in coding. Analyzes common mistakes. Includes numerous review questions to assess students' progress. Audiovisual Library of Computer Education, no. 12–15.

257. Basic Computer Terms
Pyramid Films   1976   16mm film or videocassette   color   16 min
Purchase: film $250.00; video $235.00   Rental: $30.00
Languages: English, Spanish

Introduces beginners to the parts, processes, and terminology of today's computers. Large and small computers are being used in many professions for routine tasks. Humor is used to remove the mystique surrounding computers.

258. Central Processor
Prismatron Productions, Inc   videocassette or 60 slides and audiocassette or 2 filmstrips   20 min   instructor's print materials
Purchase: video $99.50; slides $75.00; filmstrips $65.00   Preview: free

Describes the structure of digital computers and the role of the central processor. Discusses computer binary devices. Considers program execution and the function of registers. Explains read/write operations and reviews semiconductor memories. Audio Visual Library of Computer Education Series, no. 10.

259. Computer
Prismatron Productions, Inc   1981   videocassette or 60 slides and audiocassette or 2 filmstrips   20 min   instructor's print materials
Purchase: video $99.50; filmstrips $65.00; slides $75.00   Preview: free

Provides a highly visual introduction to the world of computers. Diagrams demonstrate the fundamental structure of digital computer systems. Describes how computers can be used to process information. Shows computers at work in laboratories, factories, and offices. Audio Visual Library of Computer Education Series, no. 1.

260. Computer and You
BNA Communications, Inc   1972   16mm film or videocassette   color   34 min
Purchase: $260.00   Rental: 5-day $150.00; 3-day $105.00   Preview: $35.00

Provides background relative to adapting to a new system, maximizing use of the computer, improving internal flow of information, and solving problems of the staff. Sets to rest many of the myths about computers, discusses fundamental problems, and illustrates how to make data processing systems more productive and effective. Uses dramatization. Features John Humble and Isaac Auerbach. Companion film to *Drowning in*

Data but Starved for Information. Management Practice Series A, Part II.

261. Computer Basics for Management
American Management Associations   1982   6 videocassettes   color   instructor's print materials; learner's print materials
Purchase: $1,585.00 (for 5 people)   Preview: $50.00   Other cost factors: AMA members $1,385.00 (preview $40.00)

Emphasizes use of computer as a management tool. Video supplements expand material in AMA course of the same title which is included in printed materials that accompany the video. Shows hardware, charts, slides, and other visuals to make concepts clear. Features William J. O'Neill.

262. Computer Fundamentals for the Manager
AMACOM   6 audiocassettes   learner's print materials
Purchase: $145.00   Other cost factors: AMA members $135.00; discounts available for bulk orders of materials

Designed for the manager who is not and does not intend to be a computer expert but finds it useful to be able to evaluate information and know when to double check. Basic course to enable the manager to communicate effectively with EDP personnel and to use computers for information and problem solving.

263. Computer in Business and Managerial Data Processing
Audio-Forum   audiocassette   47 min
Purchase: $10.95

Review of the role of the computer in business management. Discussion of EDP as the focal point of the management information system by Richard Schmidt and William Meyers.

264. Computer Numbers
Prismatron Productions, Inc   videocassette or 60 slides and audiocassette or 2 filmstrips   20 min   instructor's print materials
Purchase: video $99.50; filmstrips $65.00; slides $75.00   Preview: free

Explains the relationship between the binary, decimal, and hexadecimal systems. Describes different number systems and the storage and transmission of binary information inside a digital computer. Describes binary arithmetic and the use of the twos complement method. Includes photographs, cartoons, and a representation of the twos complement method. Audio Visual Library of Computer Education Series, no. 11.

265. Computer Programme
Films, Inc   1982   10 16mm films or videocassette   color   25 min ea
Purchase: film $4,995.00 ($500.00 ea); video $2,990.00 ($400.00 ea)

Presents the basic concepts of microcomputers and their applications in clear, concise terms and shows the effects they are having, and will continue to have, on our lives. Presents why computers have become so important to all of us and what we, as noncomputer experts, should know about them and how to use them. Covers how to communicate with a computer, its

value in storing information, the electronic media, graphics, modeling, and many areas of application.

266. Computer Terminals
Prismatron Productions, Inc   videocassette or 60 slides and audiocassette or 2 filmstrips   20 min   instructor's print materials
Purchase: video $99.50; filmstrips $65.00; slides $75.00   Preview: free

Utilizes both diagrams and photographs to explore characteristics of online computing. Describes the use of terminals and the nature of communication channels. Illustrates terminal applications by examples that include real time, information retrieval, program development, and CAD. Audio Visual Library of Computer Education Series, no. 8.

267. Computers at Work
Creative Venture Films   16mm film   color   12 min
Purchase: $175.00   Preview: free

Capsule glimpse of some of the many ways computers are being used in a variety of fields. Companion film to *You and the Computer.*

268. Computers in Your Life
Association for Computer Machinery   1982   16mm film   color   13 min
Rental: free

Intended for those with little or no technical knowledge about computers. Illustrates how computers are productive tools within the society. Offers an introductory examination for general audiences. Includes humorous touches.

269. Data Processing Series
HBJ Media Systems Corporation   1978   42 slide/audiocassette presentations   1½ hrs per module   instructor's print materials; learner's print materials
Purchase: $7,500.00

Offers an overview of computer components and functions and the development of modern-day computers and the future impact of data processing. Introduces computer languages, flowcharting, and writing simple code. Shows uses of computers in business. Includes 4 self-contained modules. Intended for employees who handle data processing input or output or their administrators.

270. Distribution and Retention
Prentice Hall Media   1981   2 filmstrips and 2 audiocassettes   color   program guide
Purchase: $90.00

Explains the methods used to distribute documents and surveys different types of magnetic storage media with emphasis on disks. Two modules cover document distribution and document retention. Word Processing Series.

271. Drowning in Data, but Starved for Information
BNA Communications, Inc   1972   16mm film or videocassette   color   19 min
Purchase: $540.00   Rental: 5-day $150.00; 3-day $105.00   Preview: $35.00

Portrayal of an organization that installs its first computer when its managers do not understand either the computer or what they want from it. Illustrates how to get managers involved and how much involvement is necessary. Addresses problems associated with instituting data processing systems including systems trade-offs. Companion film to *The Computer and You*. Management Practice Series A, Part I.

272. GIGO
Dartnell   16mm film or videocassette   color   30 min
Purchase: $525.00   Rental: $120.00

Takes the viewer into the world of the computer to see what it is, how it works, and, most importantly, how it will affect our lives and our jobs. Designed to allay fears and doubts about what's going on. Intended for all employees and community groups.

273. How Does a Computer Work?
Xicom-Video Arts   1981   16mm film or videocassette   color   15 min
Purchase: $390.00   Rental: $100.00   Preview: $35.00

Seeks to solve a major computer problem—underuse—by helping managers understand computer basics and see how computers fit into business. Uses animation and humor to present the computer as a positive influence to help managers improve their own effectiveness. Intended for nonspecialists.

274. Human Side of Computer Graphic Design
Society of Manufacturing Engineers   1981 videocassette   color   16 min
Purchase: $150.00   Rental: $40.00   Other cost factors: SME members $120.00 (rental $35.00)

Developed to assist managers and users of computer graphics in how to deal with the new pressures this system creates. A help to identify problem areas before they boil over and reduce skepticism about the system allowing it to operate as it was designed.

275. Industrial Microcomputer Systems
Society of Manufacturing Engineers   1980   36 videocassettes   color   40–50 min ea   learner's print materials
Purchase: $1,500.00   Rental: $50.00   Other cost factors: SME members $1,400.00; manual $49.95; microcomputer trainer unit $590.00

Examines the programing techniques for using microcomputers to control machine tools and monitor processing and inspection devices. Describes memory technology, programmable controllers, and writing programs. Emphasizes basics and application in manufacturing situations. Microcomputer training unit can be used to program, debug, and run actual automation exercises.

276. Information Processing and the Computer: A Survey
Charles E. Merrill Publishing Company   1979   15 videocassettes   color   15–30 min ea   learner's print materials
Purchase: $2,495.00   Preview: free

Provides a basic introduction to computers—their history and applications today including science, the arts, and business. Addresses information processing, computer concepts, and societal implications.

277. Input and Output Units
Prismatron Productions, Inc   videocassette or 60 slides and audiocassette or 2 filmstrips   20 min instructor's print materials
Purchase: video $99.50; filmstrips $65.00; slides $75.00   Preview: free

Discusses the structure of digital computers and the role of peripheral devices. Describes the appearance and use of typical input and output units. Enables a computer user to make a knowledgeable, rational choice of an input/output unit. Audio Visual Library of Computer Education Series, no. 7.

278. Introduction to BASIC: A Four Part Course
Prismatron Productions, Inc   240 slides or 8 filmstrips and audiocassettes   learner's print materials
Purchase: filmstrip $200.00; slides $235.00   Preview: free

Concentrates on the most important instructions for the newcomer to computing. Completely independent of any particular make of computer and compatible with most available versions of BASIC. For group or self-study.

279. Introduction to Industrial Microcomputers
Society of Manufacturing Engineers   20 videocassettes   color   60 min ea
Purchase: $1,250.00   Other cost factors: SME members $1,150.00; student manual $14.95

Discusses the basics of microcomputers and their use in manufacturing. Offers an understanding of the abilities and limitations of microcomputers as well as information to correctly identify successful applications. Includes the technology review of microcomputers, fundamentals of microprocessor operation, simple programing structures, estimating software costs, input and output elements, and future trends in industry. Goes step-by-step through the development of a simple program for a PET microcomputer. Designed for the practicing engineer.

280. Introduction to Programming
Prismatron Productions, Inc   videocassette or 60 slides and audiocassette or 2 filmstrips   20 min instructor's print materials
Purchase: video $99.50; filmstrips $65.00; slides $75.00   Preview: free

Provides beginners with clear, language-free independent guidelines for good programing practice. Explains the function of programs in a computer's operation. Discusses the principles of flowcharting, coding, testing, and documentation. Audio Visual Library of Computer Education Series, no. 6.

281. Making It Count
Boeing Computer Services Company   1975–1983   23 videocassettes   color   30 min ea   instructor's print materials; learner's print materials
Purchase: $8,600.00 ($495.00 ea)   Rental: $1,500.00 ($80.00 ea)   Preview: $200.00 ($30.00 ea)

Presents broad overview of data processing concepts and problems. Covers fundamentals of hardware and software, programing languages, and logic. Introduces and defines data processing terms in context. Shows role of computers in management decision making and how to acquire computing capability. Intended to help employees assume a more active role in defining their own computing requirements and evaluating systems.

282. Matter of Survival
National Film Board of Canada   16mm
film   color   26 min
Purchase: $350.00   Rental: $30.00   Preview: free

Portrays a situation in a company where the computer methods that are about to be introduced to take over much of the paperwork will result in a surplus number of responsible, long-time employees. Poses the problem from the points of view of management and of the employees concerned.

283. Micro Revolution
Prismatron Productions, Inc   videocassette or 60 slides and audiocassette or 2 filmstrips   20 min instructor's print materials
Purchase: video $99.50; filmstrips $65.00; slides $75.00   Preview: free

Discusses how microelectronic technology has revolutionized our lives. Describes the appearance and function of different types of integrated circuits. Explains why silicon chips have become so important and how they are used. Audio Visual Library of Computer Education Series, no. 4.

284. Microcomputer Literacy Program
CRM/McGraw-Hill Films   1983   9 audiocassettes   60 min ea   learner's print materials
Purchase: $195.00

Gives overview of microcomputing history, functions, and components. Explains how to select the personal computer and software to suit specific needs. Includes a short course in computer programing using BASIC. Intended for self-study.

285. Microcomputers
Prismatron Productions, Inc   videocassette or 60 slides and audiocassette or 2 filmstrips   20 min instructor's print materials
Purchase: video $99.50; filmstrips $65.00; slides $75.00   Preview: free

Explains the structure of microcomputers in clear, simple terms and includes pictures of the very latest equipment. Diagrams demonstrate how the different components of a microcomputer contribute to its operation. Shows examples of microcomputers employed in a range of situations. Audio Visual Library of Computer Education Series, no. 3.

286. Microcomputers: An Introduction
CRM/McGraw-Hill Films   1983   16mm film or videocassette   color   26 min   instructor's print materials
Purchase: $495.00   Rental: $75.00   Preview: free

Introduces basic terminology and initial questions asked about microcomputers on the job. Shows the possibilities computers offer for word processing, accounting, and financial applications. Combines animation and live footage. Intended to create acceptance for computers in the workplace.

287. Now The Chips are Down
Films, Inc   1981   16mm film or videocassette   color 50 min

Purchase: film $860.00; video $430.00   Rental: $100.00   Preview: free

Shows how microprocessors are made and the different kinds of applications already in use or being researched. Surfaces issues and problems that arise from sophisticated machines such as the choice whether to advance applications of the computer or to stop the advance.

288. Painting by Numbers
Films, Inc   16mm film or videocassette   color   60 min
Purchase: film $900.00; video $450.00   Rental: $100.00   Preview: free

Introduces the fascinating world of computer graphics that makes it possible for computers to translate swathes of numbers to the kind of pictures that human eyes and brains can readily understand. Shows how computers are programed to produce video games, NASA space-simulation films, dimensional scientific examination of DNA (dioxyribonucleic acid), and more.

289. Powersharing: The Microcomputer
Martha Stuart Communications, Inc   1983 videocassette   color   50 min
Purchase: $225.00   Rental: $55.00

Provides a starting point for understanding the microcomputer—what it is and what it does. Demonstrates its power and versatility in action using an Apple II as a representative system. Shows word processing, graphics, database management, spread sheet, and news wire services. Nontechnical.

290. Secondary Storage
Prismatron Productions, Inc   videocassette or 60 slides and audiocassette or 2 filmstrips   20 min instructor's print materials
Purchase: video $99.50; filmstrips $65.00; slides $75.00   Preview: free

Provides a complete guide to the magnetic storage devices: tape, disk, and drum. Explains how computers store information. Discusses the role of secondary storage. Describes the appearance and applications of mainframe and micro-compatible units and compares various storage media. Audio Visual Library of Computer Education Series, no. 9.

291. Silicon Chip
Prismatron Productions, Inc   videocassette or 60 slides and audiocassette or 2 filmstrips   20 min instructor's print materials
Purchase: video $99.50; slides $75.00; filmstrips $65.00   Preview: free

Describes the use and appearance of silicon chips. Explains at an introductory level the structure of integrated circuits. Illustrates the steps involved in designing, producing, packaging and testing integrated circuits. Audio Visual Library of Computer Education Series, no. 5.

292. Silicon Factor: And What of the Future?
Films, Inc   1981   16mm film or videocassette   color   40 min
Purchase: film $690.00; video $345.00   Rental: $75.00   Preview: free

Raises issues about the effects of microelectronics on employment, life styles, or the economy over the next few years. Gives examples such as the Washington Metro, a Dallas supermarket, and a Scottish hospital.

293. Silicon Factor: So What's It All About?
Films, Inc 1981 16mm film or videocassette color 40 min
Purchase: film $690.00; video $345.00 Rental: $75.00 Preview: free

Looks at how evolution has become revolution as the silicon chip continues to become less expensive and more sophisticated every year. Provides a detailed look at the silicon chip—its development, design, production, and mushrooming applications. Examines the potential gains in levels of productivity and competitiveness with microelectronics as well as what long-term effects this revolution could have on employment, life styles, and the economy. Asks how far computer-controlled machines can go on imitating human functions.

294. Techniques for Systems Design and Implementation
Q.E.D. Information Sciences, Inc 10 audiocassettes 60 min ea instructor's print materials; learner's print materials
Purchase: $275.00

Intended for those responsible for computer systems design. Includes how to formulate an overall design, select devices, establish controls, define data requirements and match them with hardware and software capabilities, develop a systems test plan, and work effectively with users.

295. Understanding Computers
Prismatron Productions, Inc 1981 videocassette or 60 slides and audiocassette or 2 filmstrips 20 min instructor's print materials
Purchase: video $99.50; filmstrip $65.00; slides $75.00 Preview: free

Uses a mix of cartoons and photographs. Describes in clear nontechnical terms exactly what computers can and can't do. Examples show why computers are more suitable for some applications than others. Emphasizes the programer's responsibility for efficient utilization of the computer. Audio Visual Library of Computer Education Series, no. 2.

296. Understanding the Computer
Ibis Media 157 slides and 2 audiocassettes instructor's print materials
Purchase: $165.00

Introduces the computer and demonstrates its wide range of applications. Includes programing basics and computer languages. Surveys computer's present and future impact on society.

297. What Is a Computer?
Xicom-Video Arts 1979 16mm film or videocassette color 18 min instructor's print materials
Purchase: $390.00 Rental: 3-day $100.00 Preview: $35.00

Designed for training staff who are coming into contact with the computer for the first time or who work alongside it without really understanding just what it does or is capable of doing. Humorous cartoon explains the relationship between the central processing unit and the computer's peripherals—the video

console, the printer, card reader, magnetic tape unit, and disk unit. Deals with software, hardware, and data preparation.

298. What Is a Word Processor?
Xicom-Video Arts 1982 16mm film or videocassette color 28 min learner's print materials
Purchase: $625.00 Rental: $120.00 Preview: $40.00

Dramatizes the difference in performance that a word processor can make from the office worker's point of view. Uses humorous, realistic office situations relating to keeping files, updating correspondence, and making corrections. Features John Cleese.

CONFERENCE LEADERSHIP
See MEETING MANAGEMENT

CONFLICT AND CONFLICT MANAGEMENT
See also NEGOTIATION

Affirmative Action and the Supervisor: It's Not Simply Black and White. For complete citation, *see* EQUAL EMPLOYMENT OPPORTUNITY.

Case of Insubordination. For complete citation, *see* GRIEVANCE.

299. Chairy Tale
National Film Board of Canada 16mm film or videocassette b/w 10 min
Purchase: film $110.00; video $130.00 Rental: $10.00 Preview: free

Mimed portrayal of a youth and a chair that eludes him as he tries to sit. The initial struggle for mastery grows into understanding.

Chris Argyris on Organization Predictions/Prescriptions. For complete citation, *see* ORGANIZATIONAL CHANGE AND DEVELOPMENT.

300. Conflict: Causes and Resolutions
Roundtable Films, Inc 1974 16mm film or videocassette color 34 min
Purchase: $525.00 Rental: $100.00 Preview: $30.00
Languages: English, Dutch, Spanish, Swedish

Identifies major causes of conflict and 3 major approaches to conflict resolution: win-lose, negotiation, and problem solving. Brings out how conflict can become an opportunity for creative solutions. Dramatizations illustrate points made and open-ended format encourages viewer involvement.

301. Conflict on the Line, a Case Study
CRM/McGraw-Hill Films 1982 16mm film or videocassette color 15 min instructor's print materials
Purchase: $425.00 Rental: $95.00 Preview: free

Two employees explode their conflict on the line. One is a key person on a project and the other is an upwardly mobile supervisor. Suggests this is typical in an industrial system pressured by changing technologies and economies. Explores fundamentals influencing the workplace at supervisor/staff interface levels.

302. Conflict Resolution
Lansford Publishing Company, Inc   2 audiocassettes   instructor's print materials
Purchase: $55.95

Explores how and why conflict develops, identifies conflict patterns, and describes methods for reducing conflict. Useful for management and supervisory personnel.

303. Confrontation, Search and Coping
BNA Communications, Inc   1969   16mm film or videocassettes   color   26 min   learner's print materials
Purchase: $525.00   Rental: 5-day $150.00; 3-day $105.00   Preview: $35.00

Dramatized portrayal shows how to bring internal conflicts into the open and find solutions. Illustrates openness, trust, and privacy as being important to daily interactions. Emphasizes how seeking alternatives increases an organization's viability and flexibility. Organization Renewal Series, no. 2.

304. Confronting Conflict
BNA Communications, Inc   1971   16mm film or videocassettes   color   32 min
Purchase: $550.00   Rental: 5-day $150.00; 3-day $105.00   Preview: $35.00
Languages: English, Spanish, Swedish

Dramatization that shows consultant Sheldon Davis's techniques of dealing with conflict and building a productive team. Illustrates the role of the team leader in facilitating communication and helping team identify issues. This film continues the situation shown in *Team Building*. Effective Organization Series, no. 5.

305. Coping with Conflict
International Film Bureau, Inc   1980   16mm film or videocassette   color   22 min   instructor's print materials
Purchase: $450.00   Rental: 5-day $60.00; 3-day $45.00   Preview: free

Illustrates several areas of conflict in an industrial setting (a textile plant). Dramatization presents the chain of events leading to various stages and degrees of conflict between employees and management. Gives guidelines for resolving conflicts using intervention and problem-solving skills.

306. Effective Supervisor: Dealing with Conflicting Value Systems
Edupac, Inc   2 audiocassettes   study manual
Purchase: $60.00

Presents a 4-step approach to "people problems" that deal with interpersonal conflicts, focus on unacceptable behavior and the values that underlie it, show respect for employees' attitudes and values, and request behavioral change. Intended for first-level supervisors.

307. Five Ways to Manage Conflict
Xicom-Video Arts   16mm film or videocassette   color   30 min   instructor's print materials
Purchase: $390.00   Rental: $100.00   Preview: $35.00   Other cost factors: additional copies of conflict mode instrument

Three behavioral scientists elaborate on 5 approaches to handling conflict and demonstrate their possible applications in turning conflict situations into creative opportunities. Suggested for a 2–4 hour exercise involving group discussion. Includes Thomas-Kilmann Conflict Mode Instrument, a self-administered, self-scoring instrument revealing styles of dealing with conflict.

308. Grid Approach to Conflict Solving
BNA Communications, Inc   1974   16mm film or videocassette   color   33 min
Purchase: $550.00   Rental: 5-day $150.00; 3-day $105.00   Preview: $35.00

Demonstrates the application of the managerial grid to management team building. Dramatized situation shows a group working through several conflicts enroute to effective problem solving. Features Jane S. Mouton and Robert R. Blake. Managerial Grid Series, no. 2.

Guinea Pigs Is Pigs! For complete citation, *see* CUSTOMER RELATIONS.

309. Harmonics of Conflict
National Audiovisual Center   1978   16mm film or videocassette   color   25 min
Purchase: film $171.25; video $65.00   Rental: $25.00

Overview of the nature of conflict and the valuable role of negotiation. Combines commentary with a series of vignettes to explain and illustrate. Probes negotiation as the productive way of managing conflict, suggests the universality of negotiations, and considers the similarities and differences between private- and public-sector collective bargaining. Not for the experienced negotiator.

310. Interpersonal Relations
Resources for Education and Management, Inc   6 audiocassettes   9–16 min ea   instructor's print materials
Purchase: $75.00   Preview: $10.00

Addresses common causes of workplace conflict. Whether between supervisor and employee or between peers, conflict causes and is caused by poor interpersonal relations. Deals with major areas of conflict caused by lack of information, delegating of responsibilities, lack of empathy, and job enrichment opportunities.

311. Is It Always Right to Be Right?
CRM/McGraw-Hill Films   1970   16mm film or videocassette   color   8 min
Purchase: $295.00   Rental: $75.00   Preview: free

Brief animated portrayal of the powerful role emotions play in perpetuating conflict situations and blocking communication and shared efforts. Stresses importance of openness and receptivity. Meeting opener or discussion starter.

312. Likerts on Managing Conflict
AMACOM   5 audiocassettes   45–60 min ea
learner's print materials
Purchase: $135.00   Other cost factors: AMA
members $114.75

Rensis and Jane Likert discuss their System 4—a practical method to deal with organizational conflict. System 4 focuses on motivation, decision making, communication, and group problem solving.

313. Managing Conflict
American Management Associations   6
audiocassettes   learner's print materials
Purchase: $145.00   Other cost factors: AMA
members $135.00

Identifies those management practices and styles that encourage conflict. Shows how to define conflicts before they create absenteeism, work slow-downs, low morale, high turnover, and poor work quality. Suggests 7 basic steps of rational problem solving in conflict resolution.

314. Managing Conflict between Groups
Development Digest   audiocassette
Purchase: $13.75

Describes in detail an approach used for managing conflict in such diverse systems as an aluminum company, an electrical manufacturing company, and a medical center. Features Warner Burke.

315. Managing Conflict: How to Make Conflict Work for You
Salenger Educational Media   1978   16mm film or videocassette   color   15 min   instructor's print materials; learner's print materials
Purchase: $455.00   Rental: $125.00   Preview: $35.00

Introduces the concept that, when it is managed properly, conflict can be productive. Shows how to explore and develop alternative strategies to deal with conflict effectively. Identifies and illustrates several strategies and analyzes these strategies in terms of their advantages.

316. Managing Conflict Productively
Human Productivity Institute, Inc   audiocassettes
learner's print materials
Purchase: $59.99

Shows how the potential of conflict is possible in any situation. Offers negotiation techniques that produce win/win resolution and interorganizational communication skills. Suggests how to analyze power control and maximize positive outcomes of conflict.

317. Neighbors
International Film Bureau, Inc   16mm film or videocassette   color   9 min
Purchase: film $155.00; video $140.00   Rental: $10.00   Preview: free

Shows 2 neighbors in conflict over a flower. Their conflict destroys them and they find equality only after death. Illustrates consequences of unresolved conflict.

318. Plant Shutdown
BNA Communications, Inc   1972   16mm film or videocassette   color   34 min   instructor's print materials
Purchase: $525.00   Rental: 5-day $150.00; 3-day $105.00   Preview: $35.00

Dramatization of a needless plant shutdown due to personal conflict. Manager demonstrates coaching and interviewing skills to resolve the conflict. Shows techniques such as probing and reflecting back to get to the root of a problem and how to move people of different age, education, experience, and outlook to work together and develop further as managers. Interviewing Series, no. 2.

319. Positive No: A Manager's Guide to Dealing with Superiors, Peers, and Subordinates
AMACOM   1981   3 audiocassettes   60 min ea
booklet
Purchase: $57.95   Other cost factors: AMA members $49.25

Shows how to turn confrontations into cooperation, dissent into team spirit, conflicts into opportunities for growth, and refusals into new and better understandings. Demonstrates situations when NO is unavoidable. Illustrates what went wrong and points out simple, easy-to-implement techniques to make it go right the next time. Features Auren Uris.

320. Power and Conflict in the Organization: We Can Work It Out
Document Associates   1977   16mm film or videocassette   color   26 min
Purchase: $400.00   Rental: 2-day $45.00

Documents an actual training lab session with participants developing an understanding of the dynamics of conflict and its resolution. As they attempt to work out their interpersonal and intergroup differences, they develop an understanding of the nature of all power struggles and gain insight into the difficulties of communicating across power lines.

321. Solving Employee Conflict
Creative Media   16mm film or videocassette   color   10 min   instructor's print materials
Purchase: $250.00   Rental: $60.00   Preview: $20.00

Shows 2 employees in conflict—one having been promoted over the other. The supervisor, using an expective rather than a directive approach, resolves the conflict and improves cooperation in the department. Advocates resolving conflict promptly, building on employee strengths, and recognizing human wants, needs, and problems.

Supervising and People Problems. For complete citation, *see* SUPERVISION.

Supervisor and Interpersonal Relations. For complete citation, *see* SUPERVISION.

322. Talking Out Conflict
EFM Films   16mm film or videocassette   color   15 min   instructor's print materials; learner's print materials

Purchase: $445.00   Rental: $120.00   Preview:
$40.00

Shows how to analyze problems that give rise to conflict,
confront conflict, and evaluate and understand attitudes in
order to handle them objectively. Emphasizes that conflict is
better dealt with than delayed.

323. Through Conflict to Negotiation
National Film Board of Canada   1970   16mm
film   b/w   47 min
Purchase: $665.00   Rental: $65.00   Preview: free

Examines Saul Alinsky's method of organizing communities
into effective action units based on participatory democracy. A
community action group in Rochester, New York confronts the
community's largest employer, Eastman Kodak, on the issue of
corporate responsibility and the employment of minority
groups.

324. When Will They Realise We're Living in the Twentieth Century
Xicom-Video Arts   1980   16mm film or
videocassette   color   24 min
Purchase: $625.00   Rental: $100.00   Preview:
$35.00

Dramatization of an unnecessary industrial dispute. Shows the
assumptions, attitudes, and actions of a shop steward and
production director, both portrayed by John Cleese. Avoidable
but classic errors cause disputes and stoppages, resentment, and
discontent. British production but applicable elsewhere.

CORPORATIONS

325. Corporation
National Film Board of Canada   1973   7 16mm
films or videocassettes   b/w   29 min ea (78 min for
last one)
Purchase: $1,450.00 (1st 6 $280.00 ea; 7th
$430.00)   Rental: $160.00 (1st 6 $20.00 ea; 7th
$40.00)   Preview: free

Intimate observation of management, operations, and social
role of a major Canadian corporation that includes supermar-
kets, retailing, manufacturing, and real estate. Includes films on
bilingualism, growth, international operations, real estate, marketing, motivation, and the step down of the president. Each
film/videocassette can be purchased or rented separately.

**Crisis of the American Board: How It Grew—And
What We Can Do About It.** For complete citation,
see BUSINESS ENVIRONMENT.

326. Freedom River
CRM/McGraw-Hill Films   1972   16mm film or
videocassette   color   8 min
Purchase: $250.00   Rental: $75.00   Preview: free

Intended to stimulate discussion of the role of the corporation
and the individual in the community and the environment.
Allegory is the river of our freedoms, responsibilities, and
environment. Narrated by Orson Welles.

327. Henry Ford's America
National Film Board of Canada   16mm film or
videocassette   color   57 min
Purchase: film $775.00; video $450.00   Rental:
$160.00   Preview: $40.00

Provides a penetrating close-up of the day-to-day activities of
Ford Motor Company through interviews with executives,
marketing strategists, government and consumer representatives. Shows how a single product has affected an entire culture.

328. How to Stop the Corporation from Stifling People and Strangling Profits
AMR International, Inc   12 audiocassettes
Purchase: $350.00

Robert Townsend explores various dimensions of the relationships between corporations and the people who are involved.
He discusses people, leadership, getting things done, motivation
and incentive compensation, fairness and justice, investors,
boards of directors, and financial statements.

329. Social Responsibility—Myth or Reality?
BNA Communications, Inc   1975   16mm film or
videocassette   color   10 min   learner's print
materials
Purchase: $140.00   Rental: 5-day $150.00; 3-day
$105.00   Preview: $35.00

Gives an overview of the social responsibility of business and
the role of the corporation in a free enterprise society. Features
John Humble.

COST CONTROL
See also FINANCIAL MANAGEMENT

Controlling Costs for Profit. For complete citation,
see PERSONNEL MANAGEMENT.

Cost, Profit and Break-Even. For complete citation,
see FINANCIAL MANAGEMENT.

330. Fundamentals of Cost Control
Penton/IPC Education Division   3 audiocassettes
learner's print materials
Purchase: $60.00

Intended for managers who must know what cost control is,
how to use it, and how to make the best decisions based on the
facts that a cost control system gives. Emphasizes standards,
feedback, control, and planning.

Guide to Operational Auditing. For complete
citation, *see* FINANCIAL MANAGEMENT.

331. Peter Hill Puzzle
National Educational Media, Inc   1976   16mm film
or super 8mm or videocassette   color   32 min
instructor's print materials; learner's print materials
Purchase: $595.00   Rental: 5-day $130.00; 3-day
$120.00   Other cost factors: complete course
planner
Languages: English, French, Japanese, Portuguese,
Spanish

Shows the impact serious management problems can have on all employees. Dramatization reveals the close interlacing of cost management with all other aspects of the organization. A professional manager is sent in to save a troubled organization in a modern high-technology setting. Film is open-ended.

COUNSELING
See also INTERVIEWING

332. Counsel Interview
Roundtable Films, Inc   16mm film or videocassette   color   15 min
Purchase: $400.00   Rental: $75.00   Preview: $30.00

Distinguishes between a counsel interview and a discipline interview. Portrays the skills and 6 steps needed to conduct a counsel interview that gets at the root of the problem.

Discipline Interview. For complete citation, *see* DISCIPLINE.

333. Helping: A Growing Dimension of Management
CRM/McGraw-Hill Films   1979   16mm film or videocassette   color   30 min
Purchase: $560.00   Rental: $95.00   Preview: free

Overview of the problems, benefits, and overall impact of formalized helping relationships. Discussions and interviews filmed in major organizations feature Dr. Malcolm Knowles. Topics include mentoring relationships, organizational environments that help or hinder helping relationships, and the benefits and pitfalls of helping relationships.

334. Helping People Develop: "Don't Tell Me What's Good For Me"
BNA Communications, Inc   1975   16mm film or videocassette   color   33 min   instructor's print materials
Purchase: $550.00   Rental: 5-day $150.00; 3-day $105.00   Preview: $35.00

Gives rationale for effective counseling plus practical steps in counseling and development. Identifies what can and can't be accomplished, the limitations of reward and reinforcement, and the effect of rule changes on the role of manager, coach, and referee. Two Person Communication Series, no. 5.

335. Helping Skills for Human Resource Development
University Associates   1981   audiocassette   30 min   instructor's print materials
Purchase: $49.95

Intended for professional and nonprofessional helpers. Provides assistance for giving helping skills training and feedback. As a facilitator's package, it presents the theory and process for helping as well as training activities and procedures for presentation.

336. Intervene if You Care
Motivision, Ltd   16mm film or videocassette   color   10 min
Purchase: $237.00   Preview: $25.00

Demonstrates impact of a problem employee in co-workers. Shows example of peer referral to an employee counseling program. Useful for management training. Edited from *Call Walsh.*

CREATIVITY
See also DECISION MAKING/PROBLEM SOLVING

337. Beginning
CRM/McGraw-Hill Films   1972   16mm film or videocassette   color   5 min   learner's print materials
Purchase: $195.00   Rental: $75.00   Preview: free

Intended to prompt creative problem solving in an organization. Discusses, through animation, the signs that indicate a need for change and how one idea will generate others.

Brain Power. For complete citation, *see* PERCEPTION.

Creative Problem Solving. For complete citation, *see* DECISION MAKING/PROBLEM SOLVING.

338. Creative Problem Solving: How to Get Better Ideas
CRM/McGraw-Hill Films   1979   16mm film or videocassette   color   28 min
Purchase: $560.00   Rental: $95.00   Preview: free

Uses various film techniques, animation, dramatization, and lecture to describe the sources of creativity and how to enhance them. Covers major psychological stages of creative thought, blocks and how to break through them, and brainstorming as a technique. Synectics, a group problem-solving method, is described by George Prince.

339. Creative Thinking
Nightingale-Conant Corporation   6 audiocassettes
Purchase: $65.00

Offers practical, time-tested creative principles and procedures to enhance problem-solving skills and creative abilities. Features Mike Vance.

340. Creative Thinking System
Creative Media   6 audiocassettes
Purchase: $72.00

A common sense approach to observation and planned change. Mike Vance explores creativity from both a philosophical and "nitty gritty" point of view.

341. Creativity
Salenger Educational Media   16mm film or videocassette   color   7 min   instructor's print materials
Purchase: $ 275.00   Rental: $125.00   Preview: $35.00

Focuses on need for organizations to recognize and nurture the creative person as a valuable resource. Creative people help increase productivity and solve major problems.

Discover Your Hidden Talents. For complete citation, *see* GOALS AND GOAL SETTING.

Doubling Idea Power. For complete citation, *see* DECISION MAKING/PROBLEM SOLVING.

Ego Trap. For complete citation, *see* DECISION MAKING/PROBLEM SOLVING.

342. Everyday Creativity
AMACOM   7 audiocassettes   30 min ea   learner's print materials
Purchase: $115.00   Other cost factors: AMA members $99.00

Ernest Dichter offers 12 steps to innovative thinking. Gives tips and exercises to activate creativity and provides new solutions to everyday business problems.

343. How to Change Ideas
Audio-Forum   audiocassette   55 min
Purchase: $10.95

Edward DeBono discusses the yes-no system usually used for basic thinking. He then introduces lateral thinking and explores how this can be used as a creative alternative.

344. Imagination at Work
Roundtable Films, Inc   16mm film or videocassette   color   21 min
Purchase: $295.00   Rental: $85.00   Preview: $30.00

Illustrates how anyone can do more creative thinking and improve imagination, ingenuity, and initiative. Teaches practical methods for developing new ideas. Explains how to recognize and reduce major perceptual, cultural, and emotional barriers to creative thinking. Stimulates suggestion programs, methods improvement, and problem solving.

345. Joshua in a Box
CRM/McGraw-Hill Films   16mm film or videocassette   color   5 min
Purchase: $225.00   Rental: $75.00   Preview: free

Animated, nonnarrated story shows Joshua escaping from one box only to find himself in another. Illustrates the importance of recognizing personal limitations. Designed to promote creative and critical thinking rather than bog down in the face of changing business or life conditions. Joshua Trilogy Series.

346. Lemon Sequence
Eastman Kodak Company   16mm film   2 min
Purchase: $22.00   Rental: $10.00

Brief imagination stimulator using the response generated from closeups of a lemon being cut and squeezed.

347. Managing for Creativity in Organizations: Problems and Issues in Training and OD
Development Digest   audiocassette
Purchase: $13.75

Discusses ways of managing for creativity and presents designs for training people more effectively in this managerial process. Features William G. Dyer.

Possibility Thinking. For complete citation, *see* DECISION MAKING/PROBLEM SOLVING.

Problem Solving Strategies: The Synectics Approach. For complete citation, *see* DECISION MAKING/PROBLEM SOLVING.

348. Why Man Creates
Pyramid Films   16mm film or videocassette   color   25 min   instructor's print materials
Purchase: 16mm $395.00; video $275.00   Rental: $35.00   Preview: $35.00

Poetic, imaginative exploration of creativity. Subject to a wide variety of interpretations. Includes a management study guide that offers new approaches to creative thinking.

CREDIT AND COLLECTIONS

349. Credit and Collection: Taking Charge
National Audiovisual Center   1981   16mm film or videocassette   color   15 min
Purchase: film $130.00; video $55.00   Rental: $25.00

Offers advice from business owners and staff members of wholesale, retail, and service-oriented organizations in relation to the use of credit. Gives advantages and disadvantages of extending credit. Includes commentary from bank officials and credit experts.

350. Seventh Chair
National Audiovisual Center   1971   16mm film   color   13 min
Purchase: $75.50   Rental: $12.50

Dramatizes the credit and collection problems of 5 small business owners and flashbacks to their places of business. Ultimate answers to the questions raised are left up to the viewing audience.

CRIME PREVENTION
See also SECURITY

351. Arson Investigation
National Fire Protection Association   1979   16mm film   color   22 min
Purchase: $375.00   Rental: $50.00

Documents suggested procedures in investigating arson cases. Stresses the need to develop a systematic approach to arson investigation and the importance of gathering evidence for successful arson prosecutions.

352. Holdups: What to Do
BNA Communications, Inc   1972   16mm film or videocassette   color   16 min
Purchase: $275.00   Rental: 5-day $150.00; 3-day $105.00   Preview: $35.00

With dramatizations, shows how to act during a holdup to reduce risks to self and others. Shows how to observe keenly in ways that will help to identify and apprehend the robber.

Includes simulated holdups to give viewers practice in identification.

CUSTOMER RELATIONS
See also INTERPERSONAL RELATIONS

353. Awkward Customers
Xicom-Video Arts   16mm film or videocassette   color   24 min   instructor's print materials
Purchase: $475.00   Rental: $100.00   Preview: $35.00

Portrayals by John Cleese and Angharad Rees demonstrate the most common errors in dealing with difficult customers. These vignettes show special ways of dealing with the rude, the angered, and the talkative. Through these examples, they illustrate general principles that apply in serving all customers. Intended for retail sales and service staff. Companion film to *More Awkward Customers.*

354. Boss
Nightingale-Conant Corporation   1974   16mm film or videocassette   color   11 min
Purchase: $375.00   Rental: $95.00

"The Boss" is the customer in this presentation by Earl Nightingale. He presents 4 simple rules for the care and feeding of the boss and stresses the importance of good customer relations. For those who have contact with customers.

355. Can You Help Me?
American Media, Inc   16mm or super 8mm or videocassette   color   22 min
Purchase: $495.00   Rental: $95.00   Preview: $30.00

Offers techniques to assist retail sales personnel help customers more effectively. Dramatizations illustrate skills related to merchandise knowledge, customer greeting, discovering wants and needs, overcoming objections, and closing.

356. Count to Ten
Roundtable Films, Inc   16mm film or videocassette   color   26 min   learner's print materials
Purchase: $450.00   Rental: $85.00   Preview: $30.00

Demonstrates to those who contact the public the techniques that make their work easier and more pleasant and maintain customer good will. Focuses on the problems of maintaining customer good will while upholding company policy. Examples are from hotels, airlines, government agencies, and utilities.

357. Courtesy Is the Answer
National Educational Media, Inc   1977   16mm film or super 8mm or videocassette   color   17 min   instructor's print materials; learner's print materials
Purchase: $399.00   Rental: 5-day $100.00; 3-day $90.00
Languages: English, French, Spanish

Shows how courtesy keeps a service industry operating successfully and demonstrates its importance through dramatic situations with hotel employees. Includes suggestions for developing personal qualities of courtesy and for improving teamwork.

358. Customer Relations
S&L Communications, Inc   3 videocassettes   color   15 min ea   instructor's print materials; learner's print materials
Purchase: $375.00   Rental: $75.00

Presents an overview of customer relations. Focuses on guiding the customer interview with active listening, questioning, using the telephone, and interpreting nonverbal cues. Illustrates problem interviews. Intended for those with customer contact.

359. Customer Service Is Everybody's Business
BNA Communications, Inc   1977   16mm film or videocassettes   color   20 min
Purchase: $475.00   Rental: 5-day $150.00; 3-day $105.00   Preview: $35.00

Dramatized situations in a restaurant, office, department store, and hospital show how customer service is a team effort. Illustrates how to gain leverage through making creative contacts, how to save time, and how to keep complaints from becoming battles.

360. Dealing with Angry Customers
Salenger Educational Media   1982   16mm film or videocassette   color   16 min   instructor's print materials; learner's print materials
Purchase: $495.00   Rental: $125.00   Preview: $35.00

Demonstrates a simple method for dealing with angry customers: deal with the person's feelings then deal with the person's problem. Features William Windom.

361. Dealing with People
Salenger Educational Media   16mm film or videocassette   color   12 min   learner's print materials; booklet
Purchase: $455.00   Rental: $125.00   Preview: $35.00

Introduces and illustrates basic interpersonal skills important for effective customer service. Suggests that the customer is the judge of whether the service is effective and that job satisfaction is an important by-product of good service.

362. Effective Customer Service Skills
American Learning Systems, Inc   5 filmstrips or slides and audiocassettes or videocassettes or filmstrip cartridges   color   7–11 min ea
Purchase: video $150.00; slides $125.00; other formats $95.00   Preview: free

Dramatizations show how to handle negative situations positively and tactfully, build solid teamwork with each other, and attract new customers as well as satisfy the present ones. Stresses the importance of attitude in serving customers. Intended for retail employees.

363. Everybody's a Salesbody
Roundtable Films, Inc   16mm film or videocassette   color   16 min   learner's print materials

Purchase: $400.00 Rental: $75.00 Preview: $30.00

Stresses that all employees have an impact on good customer relations and the image of the organization. Presents 5 crucial factors to help employees improve their attitudes toward customers. Ross Tew discusses employee attitudes that make the difference between satisfied and dissatisfied customers. Dramatized examples highlight common mistakes as well as model behavior.

364. Feelings
Singer Management Institute 3 audiocassettes instructor's print materials; learner's print materials; poster
Purchase: $110.00 Preview: $15.00

Dramatizations to help employees understand their role in customer relations. Shows techniques of good customer service. Illustrates how attitudes are telegraphed to customers, types of stroking, and how to deal with angry customers. Suggested for 3 60–90 minute sessions spaced 3–7 days apart.

365. Gift from Mrs. Timm
Dartnell 1983 16mm film color 16 min
Purchase: $474.00 Rental: $135.00 Preview: $45.00

Reveals the importance of being helpful and courteous to the public. Demonstrates how thoughtful, considerate treatment of others pays off. Shows several typical job situations.

366. Guinea Pigs Is Pigs!
Barr Films 16mm film or videocassette color 15½ min
Purchase: $345.00 Rental: $100.00 Preview: $25.00

Humorous dramatization about the problems caused by inflexible rules and bureaucratic mismanagement. Useful for customer relations, problem solving, and conflict management. Companion film to *Listening—The Problem Solver*.

Handling Checks. For complete citation, *see* LOSS PREVENTION.

367. Handling Complaints
National Educational Media, Inc 1974 16mm film or super 8mm or videocassette color instructor's print materials; learner's print materials
Purchase: $330.00 Rental: 5-day $80.00; 3-day $70.00
Languages: English, French, Spanish, German, Japanese

Gives specific directions for handling complaints for every person on "the front lines" dealing with customers, clients, or associates. Complaints shown contain emotions from shyness and incoherence to outrage and anger. Dramatic presentations illustrate procedures in typical situations.

Handling Credit Cards. For complete citation, *see* LOSS PREVENTION.

368. Have a Nice Stay
Xicom-Video Arts 1979 16mm film or videocassette color 25 min instructor's print materials; learner's print materials; booklet
Purchase: $625.00 Rental: $100.00 Preview: $35.00

Dramatization features John Cleese and Dinsdale Landen in a situation where the staff of a hotel must be not only ambassadors but also salespeople for the facilities of the hotel. Intended to train staff to understand the importance of giving good service to customers. Companion film to *See You Again Soon*. Welcome Customer Series.

369. How to Improve Customer Service
American Management Associations 6 audiocassettes learner's print materials
Purchase: $145.00 Other cost factors: AMA members $135.00; discounts available for bulk orders of materials

Provides guidelines for managers and employees involved with customer relations. Includes effective staffing, procedures, standards, and evaluation techniques useful to the manager. Shows employees how to solve customer problems and manage conflict skillfully as well as use contacts to generate added business. Suggested for 10 hours of self-study.

370. Human Factor
MTI Teleprograms, Inc 1979 16mm film 15 min guide
Purchase: $275.00 Rental: $50.00

Designed to motivate financial institution employees to better customer relations. Uses typical "slice-of-life" situations to illustrate why courtesy and common sense are essential to every banking transaction and what can happen if customers are not treated properly.

371. I Just Work Here
Roundtable Films, Inc 1963 16mm film or videocassette color 17 min learner's print materials
Purchase: $375.00 Rental: $75.00 Preview: $30.00
Languages: Dutch, English, German, Japanese, and Swedish

Shows the damaging effects of negative, self-centered attitudes in dealing with the public and demonstrates how helpfulness, readiness to listen to others, and sincere concern open the way to achieving solutions comfortable to everyone. Shows scenes from banks, public utilities, and government agencies.

372. Improving Customer Relations
Singer Management Institute 1980 140 slides or filmstrip and audiocassette instructor's print materials; learner's print materials
Purchase: $180.00

Shows how good service generates repeat customers, new customers, and increased sales and profits. Focuses on how to exhibit knowledge and skill and how to inspire confidence. Emphasizes that customers do care.

373. Improving Customer Relations II
Creative Universal, Inc   140 slides and audiocassette or filmstrip   instructor's print materials; learner's print materials
Purchase: $180.00

Focuses on effective customer interaction techniques. Suggests upgrading customer relations to a professional standard within an organization to yield reduced complaints and increased sales, referrals and profits. Recommended for 3–4 hour program.

374. In Two Minds
Xicom-Video Arts   1973   16mm film or videocassette   color   18 min
Purchase: $390.00   Rental: $100.00   Preview: $35.00

Shows the possibility of misunderstanding when dealing face-to-face with customers. Humorous portrayals show how the employee's job must accommodate and resolve misunderstandings.

375. It's All Right, It's Only a Customer
Xicom-Video Arts   1973   16mm film or videocassette   color   29 min
Purchase: $530.00   Rental: $100.00   Preview: $35.00

Demonstrates the proper way to handle customer inquiries on the telephone. Ronnie Baker portrays a long-suffering customer passed from one employee to another in an attempt to get an answer to a simple question. Features John Cleese.

Listening Makes a Difference. For complete citation, *see* LISTENING.

376. Making the Customer Your Friend
S&L Communications, Inc   videocassette   color   37 min   instructor's print materials
Purchase: $250.00   Rental: $35.00   Other cost factors: SLCI members $125.00 (rental $25.00)

Dramatizes some of the most common and important customer-teller situations to illustrate how to handle them properly. Portrays incidents handled correctly and then incorrectly. Stresses sound customer relations as key to effective marketing.

377. More Awkward Customers
Xicom-Video Arts   1974   16mm film or videocassette   color   31 min
Purchase: $475.00   Rental: $100.00   Preview: $35.00

Shows the importance of knowing your stocks or services—professional knowledge. Shows snooty, silent, and finicky customers. Companion film to *Awkward Customers*.

New Employees and the New Customers. For complete citation, *see* PERSONNEL MANAGEMENT.

378. Prescription for Complaints
Xicom-Video Arts   1974   16mm film or videocassette   color   21 min
Purchase: $175.00   Rental: 3-day $100.00   Preview: $35.00

Shows how complaints can be handled without creating a crisis even in difficult and emotional situations. Useful for employees who deal with customers with complaints and offers a simple 6-stage formula. Features John Cleese.

379. Remember Me
CRM/McGraw-Hill Films   1982   16mm film or videocassette   color   10 min
Purchase: $295.00   Rental: $75.00   Preview: free

Vignettes cover many types of retail service situations so that the fundamental principles of customer service come through. Useful for retail stores.

380. See You Again Soon
Xicom-Video Arts   1979   16mm film or videocassette   color   23 min   instructor's print materials; learner's print materials; booklet
Purchase: $625.00   Rental: $100.00   Preview: $35.00

Dramatization with John Cleese and Dinsdale Landen shows how important service is in a hotel situation. Lessons are fundamental but useful for experienced staff and for management as well as new employees. Uses humor to put the essential points across. Companion film to *Have a Nice Stay*. Welcome Customer Series.

381. Take Care
American Media, Inc   1982   16mm film   30 min
Purchase: $550.00   Rental: $110.00   Preview: $35.00

Emphasizes the importance of good customer relations and how to build them. Dramatization of a fantasy demonstrates both sales and service situations. Includes face-to-face and over the telephone interpersonal contact as well as how to deal with irate customers.

382. What Do They Really Want?
BNA Communications, Inc   1977   16mm film or videocassette   color   20 min   instructor's print materials
Purchase: $525.00   Rental: 5-day $150.00; 3-day $105.00   Preview: $35.00

Illustrates through dramatized situations how focusing on the customer's needs and paying attention to feelings gives an advantage. Shows situations at a museum, hotel, and bank. Helpful to reduce tensions and frustrations of customer service personnel. Winning with Customers Series, no. 1.

383. "When I'm Calling You..."
Xicom-Video Arts   1975   16mm film or videocassette   color   16 min   instructor's print materials
Purchase: $390.00   Rental: $100.00   Preview: $35.00

Alerts personnel who take outside calls to the 11 principal ways in which they are liable to offend or enrage the caller before they ever get through to the person they want to contact. Deals with the situation when the customer initiates the call. Companion film to *"...Will You Answer True?"*

384. When the Customer Complains
National Educational Media, Inc   108 slides or filmstrip and audiocassette   13 min
Purchase: filmstrip 35mm $90.00; 16mm $95.00; slides $115.00

Looks at the positive side of a customer's complaint. Shows typical situations encountered by clerks, sales personnel, managers, and others. Describes guidelines for clarifying complaints and taking immediate action, steps that reassure the customer that something is being done.

385. Who Sold You This, Then?
Xicom-Video Arts   1972   16mm film or videocassette   color   23 min   instructor's print materials
Purchase: $625.00   Rental: $100.00   Preview: $35.00

Shows how a service engineer can destroy the reputation of his company and its products every time he talks to a customer. Also shows how he could be his company's best ambassador. Emphasizes importance of customer relations with technical support people and installation staffs.

386. You and Your Customers
National Audiovisual Center   1970   16mm film   color   14 min
Purchase: $81.25   Rental: $12.50

Dramatizes situations which small retailers may encounter involving customer relations. Stimulates audience involvement by providing opportunity to stop film for discussion, then presents possible solutions to the problems presented on the screen.

DECISION MAKING/PROBLEM SOLVING
See also CREATIVITY; GROUP PROCESS

387. ABC's of Decision Making
Creative Media   1974   16mm film or videocassette   color   30 min   instructor's print materials
Purchase: $475.00   Rental: $90.00   Preview: $30.00
Languages: English, Spanish

Decisions are important to any organization in terms of 5 resources: people, money, materials, time, and space. Formula and steps for practical decision making in these areas are presented by Joe Batten. Steps include gathering facts, analyzing alternative solutions, balancing benefits with costs, and devising a contingency plan.

388. Action-Oriented Problem Solving
Butler Learning Systems   291 slides and audiocassettes   instructor's print materials; learner's print materials
Purchase: $2,595.00 plus $50.00 per learner   Preview: free

Shows a team approach with interaction between supervisors and workers in order to attain measurable objectives and to solve problems. Covers major areas of decision making, troubleshooting preventive practices, and improvement projects.

Adapts Quality Circles concept to American workers. Chuck Noll.

389. Advice without Consent
CRM/McGraw-Hill Films   videocassette   color   5 min   instructor's print materials
Purchase: $195.00   Rental: $75.00   Preview: free

Animated, nonnarrated film addresses problem solving through the dilemma of a motorist with car problems. Advice and solutions of others do not solve the problem. Points out the need to identify the problem and develop a solution specifically related to the situation. Good for meeting opener or discussion starter.

390. Avoiding Decisions!
LCA Video/Films   1982   16mm film or videocassette   color   15 min   instructor's print materials; learner's print materials
Purchase: $350.00   Rental: $70.00   Preview: $35.00

Demonstrates common decision-avoiding ploys used in business. Dramatizes how to become a decision-maker in a humorous but practical fashion. Australian production. Funny Business Series.

Beginning. For complete citation, *see* CREATIVITY.

Better Train of Thought. For complete citation, *see* CHANGE.

391. Buck Stops Here
Cally Curtis Company   16mm film or videocassette   color   6 min
Purchase: film $225.00; video $200.00   Rental: $75.00   Preview: $40.00

Chuck Connors stresses the importance of making a decision. Useful for meeting starter or companion piece for a straightforward presentation of how to make a decision.

392. Case of the Snarled Parking Lot
CRM/McGraw-Hill Films   1982   16mm film or videocassette   color   22 min   instructor's print materials
Purchase: $425.00   Rental: $95.00   Preview: free

The snarled parking lot is a symptom of snared supervision and tangled management, and the chief traps that have led to this situation are exposed in this case study. Intended to exercise problem-solving abilities of supervisors and managers. Case Study Series.

393. Challenger: An Industrial Romance
National Film Board of Canada   1983   16mm film or videocassette   color   28 min
Purchase: film $500.00; video $300.00   Rental: $100.00   Preview: $50.00

Follows a high-risk project showing the development of the technical components of manufacturing and marketing and sales strategy. The project, a new executive jet, is an example of all business endeavors in terms of its decision making, problem solving, and team building.

Citizen Chang. For complete citation, *see* COMMUNICATION.

394. Creative Problem Solving
American Management Associations   6
audiocassettes   learner's print materials
Purchase: $145.00   Other cost factors: AMA
members $135.00; discounts available for bulk orders
of materials

Self-study to improve creative problem-solving skills. Includes
exercises, experiences, and cognitive learning to generate and
select ideas and strategize to win support for them.

Creative Problem Solving: How to Get Better Ideas.
For complete citation, *see* CREATIVITY.

Decision Making: Alternatives and Information. For
complete citation, *see* INFORMATION SYSTEMS.

395. Decision Making: Outcomes and Action
Barr Films   16mm film or videocassette   color   18
min
Purchase: $440.00   Rental: $100.00   Preview:
$50.00

Explores the final steps in the decision-making process: predicting outcomes and taking action. Demonstrates how to predict
outcomes from each alternative, determine its desirability and
probability, and make plans for action after making a decision.
Companion film to *Decision Making: Values and Goals* and
Decision Making: Alternatives and Information.

396. Decision-Making Process
Lansford Publishing Company, Inc   1981   60 slides
and audiocassette   learner's print materials
Purchase: $255.95

Looks at decision making from a behavioral viewpoint and
analyzes individual and group decision making in terms of
sociological, psychological, and quantitative aspects. Covers the
steps in the decision-making process, and the role of individual
perception, expectations, power, persuasion, communication,
and influence in group decision making.

Decision Making: Values and Goals. For complete
citation, *see* GOALS AND GOAL SETTING.

397. Decision Theory
Audio-Forum   audiocassette   1 hr   learner's print
materials
Purchase: $15.50

Presents an introduction to analyzing decisions under certainty.
Colin C. Blaydon offers analytical tools of statistical decision
theory that enable decision makers to select strategies considering the uncertainties of the problem.

398. Decisions
CRM/McGraw-Hill Films   16mm film or
videocassette   color   28 min
Purchase: $560.00   Rental: $95.00   Preview: free

Examines the decision-making process from both practical and
psychological points of view and analyzes why decisions are so
difficult. Suggests how we can counteract the anxiety that
accompanies them.

399. Decisions, Decisions
Xicom-Video Arts   1978   16mm film or
videocassette   color   28 min   instructor's print
materials; booklet
Purchase: $625.00   Rental: $100.00   Preview:
$35.00

John Cleese's portrayal illustrates that making decisions is only
one-half of the problem. Getting people to go along with
decisions and making them work is the other half. Shows how
decision making has 5 stages, none of which can safely be
omitted: fact gathering, consulting people, making the decision,
communicating it, and following up.

Discover Your Hidden Talents. For complete
citation, *see* GOALS AND GOAL SETTING.

400. Divided Man
CRM/McGraw-Hill Films   1971   16mm film or
videocassette   color   5 min   instructor's print
materials
Purchase: $195.00   Rental: $75.00   Preview: free

Animated, nonnarrated presentation showing the difficulty
decision making presents when choice and indecisiveness is
involved.

401. Doubling Idea Power
Idea Development Associates   1975   3 filmstrips or
slides and 4 audiocassettes   instructor's print
materials; learner's print materials
Purchase: filmstrip $350.00; slides and audiocassettes
$386.00 or $410.00   Preview: $15.00

Designed to improve creative behavior in problem solving and
decision making. Fundamental principles and procedures are
given in separate modules intended for workshop format. Deals
with overcoming mental blocks, encouraging the creative
process, solving problems creatively, free associating, and
applying creative problem solving.

Drawing Conclusions Is a Tricky Art. For complete
citation, *see* PERCEPTION.

402. Effective Decisions
BNA Communications, Inc   1968   16mm film or
videocassette   color   25 min
Purchase: $525.00   Rental: 5-day $150.00; 3-day
$105.00   Preview: $35.00

Dramatization shows how decisions start out as opinions
instead of facts. Illustrates how problems can be turned into
opportunities by encouraging dissent, choosing among alternatives, handling personality factors, and using participative
management.

403. Ego Trap
CRM/McGraw-Hill Films   1977   16mm film or
videocassette   color   5 min
Purchase: $195.00   Rental: $75.00   Preview: free

Animated film without narration reveals how creativity of an
airplane designer is curtailed. Intended to raise awareness of
how ego can affect decisions and the introduction of new ideas.

Elephant. For complete citation, *see*
COMMUNICATION.

Everyday Creativity. For complete citation, *see* CREATIVITY.

404. Focus on Decisions
BNA Communications, Inc   1973   16mm film or videocassette   color   25 min   instructor's print materials; learner's print materials
Purchase: $535.00   Rental: 5-day $150.00; 3-day $105.00   Preview: $35.00

Dramatization of aircraft company considering expansion. Provides opportunity for brainstorming, decision tree analysis, and heuristic analysis. Points out new ways to set objectives, collect data and information, forecast outcomes, develop alternatives, and estimate sales, cash outlay, and profit probabilities.

405. Focus on Organization
BNA Communications, Inc   1974   16mm film or videocassette   color   31 min   instructor's print materials
Purchase: $535.00   Rental: 5-day $150.00; 3-day $105.00   Preview: $35.00

Dramatization of woman manager confronting organizational and operational problems. Presents issues for decision making, developing alternatives, and deciding profitability. British case study. Focus on Management Series, no. 3.

Getting Change through Communications. For complete citation, *see* COMMUNICATION.

Grid Approach to Conflict Solving. For complete citation, *see* CONFLICT AND CONFLICT MANAGEMENT.

Guinea Pigs Is Pigs! For complete citation, *see* CUSTOMER RELATIONS.

406. How to Apply the Tough-Minded Decision-Making Process
Creative Media   audiocassette   30 min
Purchase: $7.95

Demonstrates how good decisions can lead to higher productivity.

407. How to Take the Right Risks, the Manager as Decision Maker
BNA Communications, Inc   1977   16mm film or videocassette   color   23 min   instructor's print materials
Purchase: $560.00   Rental: 5-day $150.00; 3-day $105.00   Preview: $35.00
Languages: English, French, Spanish

Dramatization illustrates bad decision making by a manufacturing company manager. Peter Drucker outlines the steps to take before making a decision, discusses how to determine if a decision is needed at all, describes the importance of feedback, and defines the goals every decision should achieve. Manager and the Organization Series, no. 5.

Joshua in a Box. For complete citation, *see* CREATIVITY.

408. Krasner, Norman
MTI Teleprograms, Inc   1974   16mm film or videocassette   color   6 min
Purchase: film $150.00; video $130.00   Rental: $35.00

A businessman "copes" with stress in a monumental battle with a men's room. Shows problem solving without dialog. Useful for meeting opener or discussion starter.

409. Lead the Field
Nightingale-Conant Corporation   6 audiocassettes   learner's print materials
Purchase: $50.00

Discusses creative thinking, problem solving, and furthering both career and personal development. Offers guidelines to direct achievement. Tells how to recognize and capitalize on opportunities.

410. Making of a Decision
Roundtable Films, Inc   1968   16mm film or videocassette   color   32 min
Purchase: $450.00   Rental: $85.00   Preview: $30.00
Languages: Dutch, English, Arabic, French, German, Japanese, Spanish, Swedish

Explores rational, informed decision making by middle and top management. Analyzes the decision-making processes of 3 individuals for strengths and weaknesses. Highlights the essential steps of a rational decision-making process and factors which affect the success of the decision-making process.

411. Managing in a Crisis
BNA Communications, Inc   1974   16mm film or videocassette   color   28 min
Purchase: $550.00   Rental: 5-day $150.00; 3-day $105.00   Preview: $35.00

Covers the basics for conducting a planning fact-finding or problem-solving sessions with small and large groups. Richard Beckhard shows how to dig out the facts, tone down emotions, and convert antagonism into positive, constructive action. Advance Supervision Series, no. 1.

412. Modern Life: Choices and Conflicts
CRM/McGraw-Hill Films   16mm film or videocassette   color   10 min
Purchase: $250.00   Rental: $75.00   Preview: free

Includes symbolic illustrations of the everyday kinds of conflicts and decisions that a person in Western society faces and emphasizes their roles in self-development. Animated and not narrated. Useful for meeting opener.

413. Participative Problem Solving Skills
General Motors Corporation   1974   2 16mm films or videocassettes   color   40 min   instructor's print materials; learner's print materials
Purchase: $800.00   Rental: $60.00   Preview: $25.00
Languages: English, Flemish

Shows the use of routine conversation to identify causes and solve problems and the use of employees as a problem-solving resource to retain supervisory control during conflict. Suggested for 11 hours. Intended for first and second-line managers and for troubleshooters.

414. Possibility Thinking
Singer Management Institute 6 audiocassettes guide
Purchase: $62.50

Offers techniques for achieving immediate and long-range goals. Shows techniques to recognize and capitalize on opportunities. Features Robert H. Schuller.

415. Practical Decision Making
Learning Consultants, Inc audiocassette learner's print materials
Purchase: $17.50

Gives principles for determining what level of management should make a given decision. Points out 10 traps in the decision-making process. Develops a simple but effective system of factor analysis for determining priorities, weighing alternatives, and discovering and solving problems. Recording of a seminar. Features Clay Hardesty. Women in Management Series.

Problem. For complete citation, *see* BUSINESS ENVIRONMENT.

416. Problem Solving
CRM/McGraw-Hill Films slides and audiocassettes 15 min instructor's print materials; learner's print materials; transparencies
Purchase: $200.00 Preview: free Other cost factors: bulk rates for extra learner's materials

Presents proven methods for identifying, analyzing, and ultimately solving different types of problems. Applicable to a wide range of business, governmental, and institutional users. Includes skills and techniques to determine the real cause of a problem and to distinguish between problems and symptoms of problems. Also presents the kinds of questions to ask in analyzing and prioritizing problems. Management Productivity Series.

417. Problem Solving—A Case Study
Roundtable Films, Inc 16mm film or videocassette color 22 min
Purchase: $400.00 Rental: $75.00 Preview: $30.00

Applies basic problem-solving principles to locate and correct a quality control problem. Illustrates how to obtain information essential to making clear, effective decisions. Companion film to *Problem Solving—Some Basic Principles.*

418. Problem Solving: A Case Study
Roundtable Films, Inc 1973 16mm film or videocassette color 22 min instructor's print materials
Purchase: $400.00 Rental: $90.00 Preview: $30.00

Portrays a situation when a company loses the business of one of its oldest customers. Shows how to obtain essential information for making clear decisions and how to apply the principles of problem solving under realistic situations. Video has several suggested breaks for discussion and analysis.

419. Problem Solving—A Process for Managers
National Educational Media, Inc 1982 16mm film or super 8mm or videocassette color 22 min
Purchase: $525.00 Rental: 5-day $125.00; 3-day $115.00

Seeks to restate traditional problem-solving methods into people-oriented terms. Uses group discussion portrayal to bring out how personal politics can cloud a management situation and how to reason out solutions systematically.

420. Problem Solving
National Educational Media, Inc 1981 16mm film or super 8mm or videocassette color 20 min instructor's print materials; learner's print materials
Purchase: $520.00 Rental: 5-day $110.00; 2-day $85.00
Languages: English, Spanish

Shows how to evaluate information to solve a problem the most direct way. Points out the high cost of creating "original solutions" when acceptable solutions exist. Stresses the importance of testing possible solutions. Identifies emotional barriers to efficient problem solving.

Problem Solving Skills for Supervisors. For complete citation, *see* SUPERVISION.

421. Problem Solving: Some Basic Principles
Roundtable Films, Inc 16mm film or videocassette color 18 min
Purchase: $400.00 Rental: $85.00 Preview: $35.00

Uses humorous vignettes to focus on the points necessary in developing reliable methods of data collection and problem solving. Provides a set of principles to help solve problems. Shows how to define a problem in terms of the present situation. Presents factors that can obscure the real problem. Gives specific methods for reaching a solution: collecting alternatives and considering analytical, judicial, and creative thought approaches.

422. Problem Solving Strategies: The Synectics Approach
CRM/McGraw-Hill Films 1979 16mm film or videocassette color 28 min
Purchase: $405.00 Rental: $95.00 Preview: free

Documentary of a problem-solving laboratory demonstrating the synectics method of problem solving through a structured brainstorming format. Shows innovative strategies that can be used to stimulate organizational creativity and streamline problem solving. Useful for individual and group idea-generating sessions in all settings. Features George Prince.

423. Productive Person: A Choice Awareness Workshop
Guidelines Press 1978 audiocassettes instructor's print materials; learner's print materials
Purchase: $175.00 (for 12 learners) Other cost factors: additional learner's materials; specialized activities packet available

Highlights creative use of choices in problem solving to improve personal productivity. Includes listening, feedback and involvement, and how to influence consequences. Useful for all levels of personnel as a 16-hour program with audio presentations and structured exercises.

424. Reviewing Past Efforts
BNA Communications, Inc   16mm film   color   22 min   instructor's print materials; learner's print materials; book
Purchase: $630.00   Rental: 5-day $230.00; 3-day $185.00   Preview: $35.00

Company managers conduct a postmortem to find the failures of a program to increase productivity and efficiency. Presents a technique for finding the true cause of any program failure and what to avoid and offers 10 concrete points for better productivity. Shows how to use risk analysis and reality analysis and contains postmortem guides for a management work team. Increasing Productivity and Efficiency Program, no. 1.

425. Solving Problems Creatively
CRM/McGraw-Hill Films   1981   16mm film or videocassette or 3 audiocassettes   color   44 min   instructor's print materials; learner's print materials
Purchase: $1,495.00   Preview: free

Stresses the importance of developing answers to problems through clearly defining the problem and asking the right questions. Includes sections on generating ideas, evaluating them, and choosing and implementing a solution. Multimedia package integrates print, audio, and audiovisual components. Suggested for full- or half-day scheduling.

426. Thinking It Through
Roundtable Films, Inc   16mm film   color   23 min
Purchase: $475.00   Rental: $85.00   Preview: $30.00
Languages: Dutch, English

Provides a 7-step process for making decisions and solving problems. Shows a model approach to handling each step of the problem solving/decision making process. Open-ended dramatization shows a manager as he employs the step-by-step method to properly identify the problem as well as evaluate and choose the correct course of action. Helps managers at all levels in any type of organization systematically tackle complex problems and decisions.

427. To See or Not to See (Facing Problems)
LCA Video/Films   16mm film   15 min
Purchase: $245.00   Rental: $35.00   Preview: $20.00

Dramatizes typical situation of workers and managers choosing to ignore problems in the hopes they will go away or solve themselves.

428. Uncalculated Risk
Roundtable Films, Inc   16mm film or videocassette   color   26 min   learner's print materials
Purchase: $400.00   Rental: $85.00   Preview: 2-day $30.00
Languages: English, French

Dr. William Haney coaches, interviews, and counsels a young manager faced with a problem employee. The example shows how to reduce risk in decision making by separating fact and observation from inference. Outlines key concepts in manage-

ment communication such as consultive and participative management, handling and clarifying changes, and receptivity to feedback. Printed materials include "The Uncritical Inference Test."

429. Undoing
LCA Video/Films   16mm film   color   7 min
Purchase: $150.00   Rental: $30.00   Preview: $20.00

Illustrates the importance of thinking through a problem to anticipate end results as well as short-term objectives. Animation shows a man paving over the world then shows implications of this and his efforts to remedy the first solution with a second, equally disastrous one.

Where Do I Belong? For complete citation, *see* CAREER PLANNING AND DEVELOPMENT.

DELEGATION

430. Breaking the Delegation Barrier
Roundtable Films, Inc   1962   16mm film or videocassette   color   30 min   learner's print materials
Purchase: $425.00   Rental: $85.00   Preview: $30.00

Highlights most supervisors' problems in giving up responsibility and authority to subordinates. Three dramatized situations show main barriers to delegation: fear of mistakes by subordinates, fear of loss of authority, and the reluctance to delegate favored tasks. Participant's workbook must be purchased separately.

431. Case of Working Smarter, Not Harder
CRM/McGraw-Hill Films   1982   16mm film or videocassette   color   16 min   instructor's print materials
Purchase: $425.00   Rental: $95.00   Preview: free

Provides a practical role model how-to lesson for supervisors and managers who are uncertain about how to delegate. Makes clear the difference between delegating and dumping. Case Study Series.

432. Delegate—Don't Abdicate
National Educational Media, Inc   1974   16mm film or super 8mm or videocassette   color   12 min   instructor's print materials; learner's print materials
Purchase: $380.00   Rental: 5-day $90.00; 3-day $80.00
Languages: English, French, Spanish, Greek, Italian, Japanese, Norwegian, Portuguese

Demonstrates that delegation is a vital management function and responsibility. Presents a case study of a manager who abdicates responsibility, then examines the results when he delegates properly, i.e., assigns duties clearly, grants authority to execute them, and creates a sense of obligation to carry them out. Encourages managers to reevaluate the vital supervisor-subordinate relationship.

433. Delegating
CRM/McGraw-Hill Films   1981   16mm
film   color   28 min
Purchase: $560.00   Rental: $95.00   Preview: free

Examines delegation through various scenarios to reveal hidden traps in delegation. Provides basic steps for managers to ease their workloads, improve their finished products, and build stronger, more efficient work units.

434. Effective Delegation
CRM/McGraw-Hill Films   slides and
audiocassettes   15 min   instructor's print materials;
learner's print materials; transparencies
Purchase: $200.00   Other cost factors: discounts available for bulk orders of materials

Emphasizes that delegation is important to the growth and effectiveness of the manager, the employees, and the organization as a whole. Covers delegation and productivity, responsibility and authority, and the contribution delegation makes to employee development and motivation. Gives techniques for deciding which subordinates are best able to assume additional responsibilities. Management Productivity Series.

435. Handoff: A Study in Delegation
Salenger Educational Media   16mm film or
videocassette   color   11 min   instructor's print
materials; learner's print materials
Purchase: $410.00   Rental: $125.00   Preview:
$35.00

Dr. Warren H. Schmidt uses a football analogy, illustrated by vignettes, to propose important guidelines for delegating authority. Shows when it is most effective and how to do it. Corporate setting. Useful for new and experienced supervisors.

How to Fail in Managing without Really Trying.
For complete citation, *see* MANAGEMENT.

436. No-Nonsense Delegation
Creative Media   16mm film or
videocassette   color   30 min   instructor's print
materials
Purchase: $475.00   Rental: $90.00   Preview:
$30.00

Shows how to overcome obstacles in order to decide how and when to delegate. Dramatic sequences provide 4 keys to effective delegation. Intended to help managers to delegate effectively. Features Dale McConkey and is based on his book *No-Nonsense Delegation.*

437. Process of Delegation
Addison-Wesley Publishing Company, Inc   1980   6
audiocassettes
Purchase: $75.00

Integrates theory and practice. Explains the steps involved in learning to delegate more effectively and presents a comprehensive program designed to aid managers to organize their work, understand power and its use, and identify the authority levels of their bosses and the authority they have and can assign. Includes how to set up a plan to delegate and then make the process work. Features John Wells.

438. Successful Delegation
EFM Films   16mm film or videocassette   color   15
min   instructor's print materials; learner's print
materials
Purchase: $425.00   Rental: $120.00   Preview:
$40.00

Demonstrates how to save time on jobs that could be done better or less expensively by subordinates through a combination of animation, dramatization, and graphics. Uses humor to overcome the threatened feeling managers have about relinquishing authority and shows that they can actually enhance their own positions by giving subordinates the authority to act independently.

439. Successful Delegation
American Management Associations   6
audiocassettes   learner's print materials
Purchase: $145.00   Other cost factors: AMA
members $135.00

Covers effective delegation, how not to delegate, the manager's role, and rules and tools of effective delegation. Includes importance of atmosphere, games managers play, and the new philosophy of management. Emphasizes importance of delegation to a manager.

DICTATION

440. Art of Dictation
Addison-Wesley Publishing Company, Inc
audiocassette   learner's print materials
Purchase: $15.95

Identifies techniques for clear, concise, and logical dictation. Emphasizes the retention of ideas through dictation. Dictation exercises on cassette together with workbook offer practice. A self-evaluation checklist provides self-assessment and refresher possibilities.

Business Communication Series. For complete citation, *see* COMMUNICATION.

441. Effective Dictation
BNA Communications, Inc   1978   3
audiocassettes   1 hr ea   learner's print materials
Purchase: $125.00

Extensive workbook (232 pages) and cassettes are basis for this self-paced instructional course. Intended to sharpen dictating skills for letters, reports, and speeches. Strong emphasis on how to get organized.

442. Reinforcement of Gregg Symbols and Theory
Reinforcement Learning, Inc   12 audiocassettes
learner's print materials
Purchase: $158.50

Designed to supplement the Gregg text and provide rapid and automatic response to dictation. Useful for building effective speed, identifying where additional reinforcement and practice are needed, and reviewing brief forms, phrases, and word beginnings and endings.

443. Shorthand Refresher
HBJ Media Systems Corporation   1981   10 videocassettes or 18 audiocassettes   instructor's print materials; learner's print materials
Purchase: $7,145.00

Offers a review of Gregg shorthand skills. Suggested for 20–25 hours.

444. Shorthand Speed Development
Reinforcement Learning, Inc   10 audiocassettes
Purchase: $128.00

Sets speed objectives for dictated material that includes a wide variety of business correspondence, reports, and memos. Aim is to build to commercial speeds. Given in 5-word increments (40–135 WAM).

DISCIPLINE

445. Challenge of Discipline
CRM/McGraw-Hill Films   slides and audiocassette   15 min   instructor's print materials; learner's print materials; transparencies
Purchase: $200.00   Preview: free

Classifies workers into 3 categories: the self-disciplined, the undisciplined, and the average performers. Gives different techniques for dealing with each group. Offers 7 steps to improved discipline and tips on motivation. Stresses importance of timing and establishing clearly defined performance standards. Management Productivity Series.

446. Constructive Discipline for Supervisors
American Management Associations   6 audiocassettes   learner's print materials
Purchase: $145.00   Other cost factors: AMA members $135.00; discounts available for bulk orders of materials

Designed to help supervisors make discipline a positive force for improving morale and productivity as well as correcting such problem behavior as absenteeism, loafing, and insubordination. Includes how to establish a disciplinary policy, rules and fair penalties, preventive and disciplinary interviews, and preparing for arbitration.

447. Correct Way of Correcting
Roundtable Films, Inc   1973   16mm film or videocassettes   color   24 min   instructor's print materials
Purchase: $495.00   Rental: $100.00   Preview: $40.00
Languages: English, French, Spanish

Dramatizes work situation on a ranch to show how to appropriately deal with employee mistakes and errors in judgement. Positive approach to discipline and the impact a supervisor can have on employee attitudes and performance. Thanks A Plenty Boss Series, Part II.

448. Corrective Job Coaching Skills
Drake Beam Morin   1980   videocassette   55 min   instructor's print materials; learner's print materials
Purchase: $595.00 (for 12 learners)   Preview: $75.00

Deals with effective criticism of subordinates and corrective interviews. Special emphasis on identifying problems, getting agreement on them, and arriving at effective solutions. Intended for experienced supervisors and managers.

449. Discipline—A Matter of Judgment
National Educational Media, Inc   1973   16mm film or super 8mm or videocassette   color   11 min   instructor's print materials; learner's print materials
Purchase: $365.00   Rental: 5-day $90.00; 3-day $80.00
Languages: English, French, Spanish, Japanese

Dramatizes the basic principles of employee discipline from first reprimand to termination using a courtroom and judge to show managers and supervisors how to discipline effectively and fairly. Emphasizes an over-all systematic approach: putting rules in writing, disciplining in private, and keeping a file of employee infractions.

450. Discipline and Discharge
BNA Communications, Inc   16mm film or videocassette   color   19 min   instructor's print materials; learner's print materials
Purchase: $630.00   Rental: 5-day $150.00; 3-day $105.00   Preview: $35.00

Reveals how discipline must be backed by practice of management principles to avoid equal opportunity quicksand. Printed materials furnish exercises on discipline and discrimination plus a situation to "solve."

451. Discipline Interview
Roundtable Films, Inc   16mm film or videocassette   color   16 min
Purchase: $400.00   Rental: $75.00   Preview: $30.00

Intended to assist supervisors and managers in developing positive approach to interviewing, performance appraisal, and counseling. Emphasizes how to plan and adapt correct procedures through a dramatized situation.

452. Fair Warning
Dartnell   16mm film or videocassette   color   15 min   instructor's print materials; learner's print materials
Purchase: $425.00   Rental: $95.00

Offers 4 basic steps supervisors can use to deal with employee complaints correctly and effectively: give full attention, look employee in the eyes, listen, and state what is to be done. Stresses the importance of significant warnings about problems on the job.

453. Firm...But Fair
Dartnell   16mm film or 8mm or super 8mm or videocassette   color   15 min   instructor's print materials; learner's print materials
Purchase: $425.00   Rental: $95.00   Preview: $20.00

Guidelines for supervisors who discipline employees. Dramatizations and narration describe how and when discipline is warranted, the impact of temper, the importance of knowing the facts, and acting promptly. The question of fairness is emphasized, and equal discipline is shown as fairer than uniform discipline.

454. Handling "Problem Employees": How to Take Corrective Action
Singer Management Institute   2 audiocassettes   instructor's print materials
Purchase: $125.00   Preview: $15.00

Useful for supervisors in correcting employees whose off-the-job problems interfere with on-the-job productivity. Helps supervisors identify employees with problem behavior, take appropriate corrective action, establish a record of equal treatment, and protect against charges of discrimination.

How Good Is a Good Guy? For complete citation, *see* SUPERVISION.

455. I'd Like a Word with You
Xicom-Video Arts   1979   16mm film or videocassette   color   28 min   instructor's print materials
Purchase: $625.00   Rental: $100.00   Preview: $35.00

Humorous dramatizations illustrate the use of the discipline interview. Points out typical problems such as failing to check facts before the interview, jumping too quickly to conclusions and reprimands, and becoming emotionally involved. Useful for supervisors whose employees are not performing up to standard. Features John Cleese.

456. Insubordination
BNA Communications, Inc   1978   16mm film and audiocassette or videocassette   color   18 min   learner's print materials
Purchase: $630.00   Rental: 5-day $150.00; 3-day $105.00   Preview: $35.00

Defines insubordination and describes how to handle it, including those instances where behavior falls just short of being pure insubordination. Points out the situations where an employee can legitimately refuse to obey direct orders. Useful to address employee discipline, supervisor-employee relations, coaching, counseling, and grievances. Audiocassette includes roundtable discussion of the problem. Preventive Discipline Training Program, no. 1.

Motivation & Discipline. For complete citation, *see* MOTIVATION.

457. Positive Discipline
CRM/McGraw-Hill Films   1978   audiocassette   instructor's print materials; learner's print materials; transparencies
Purchase: $445.00   Preview: free

Describes how to recognize, prevent, and deal with discipline problems. Emphasizes how to use discipline to improve rather than punish performance. Includes preventing discipline problems, positive discipline process, discharge, and administering discipline. Includes self-study exercises and group discussion. Intended for supervisors. Suggested for 2-day program.

458. Problem—Employee Interview
AMACOM   audiocassette   60 min   learner's print materials

For supervisors who must cope with absenteeism, insubordination, discouragement, and all other personal "hangups" that can prevent valuable workers from doing their best. Helps supervisors spot the early warning signs of personnel problems and deal with them fairly and constructively. Features Glenn A. Bassett. Productive Interviewing Series.

459. Productive Discipline
Resources for Education and Management, Inc   3 videocassettes or slides and audiocassettes or filmstrips or filmstrip cartridges   color   10–11 min ea   instructor's print materials
Purchase: video $245.00 ($95.00 ea); filmstrip $220.00 ($75.00 ea); filmstrip cartridge $255.00 ($85.00 ea); slides $235.00 ($80.00 ea)

Offers a practical and realistic approach to the art of discipline. Module on the reasons for discipline, its relation to performance, and ways to discipline productively.

460. Supervisor's Responsibility for Maintaining Discipline
Continental Film Productions   slides or filmstrip and audiocassette   12 min
Purchase: filmstrip $105.00; slides $125.00

A group is made aware of how to recognize and handle the 2 distinct types of discipline. Supervisor Training Series.

461. Supervisory Interview
Advance Learning Systems   1978   4 videocassettes   color   10 min ea   instructor's print materials
Purchase: $1,980.00   Rental: $95.00

Presents dramatizations that show supervisors in corrective interviews with employees. Groups interviews around topics such as selling performance, communications, productivity, and assessing performance. Includes group discussion and suggests a 4–8 hour program.

462. Trouble with Archie
BNA Communications, Inc   1963   16mm film or videocassette   color   11 min   booklet
Purchase: $250.00   Rental: 5-day $150.00; 3-day $105.00   Preview: $35.00
Languages: English, French, Spanish

Dramatizes how a supervisor's use of discipline motivates a potential troublemaker to become a first-class worker. Shows how to change employee attitudes with disciplinary approaches. Modern Management Series, no. 6.

Unsatisfactory Work. For complete citation, *see* EMPLOYEE PERFORMANCE.

DISCRIMINATION
See also EQUAL EMPLOYMENT OPPORTUNITY

463. Bill Cosby on Prejudice
Pyramid Films   16mm film or videocassette   color   24 min
Purchase: film $375.00; video $275.00   Rental: $35.00
Languages: English, German

Bill Cosby, portraying America's composite bigot, disparages each minority and majority group in turn. Monolog serves as catalyst for thought and discussion about attitudes. Humor is biting and satirical.

464. Black Policeman: The Writing on the Wall...Black Exemplars

American Educational Films   1973   16mm film or videocassette   color   16 min   learner's print materials
Purchase: $350.00   Rental: $40.00

Portrays a diligent policeman who finds prejudice within his work situation. He deals with it in an honest and intelligent way useful for white and minority employees. Narrated by Dennis Weaver.

465. Management Workshop for Minority Workers

Instructional Dynamics, Inc   1973   audiocassette   instructor's print materials; learner's print materials; exercise materials
Purchase: $57.50

Presents clear step-by-step instructions to help employees see things as a new employee would. Includes exercises that apply problem-solving skills to specific situations that surface, such as attitudes of prejudice and how to cope constructively with them. Intended for those responsible for supervising minority group employees.

466. Prejudice/A Lesson to Forget

American Educational Films   16mm film or videocassette   color   17 min
Purchase: $360.00   Rental: $40.00

Includes interviews and documentary approach to the present nature of discrimination as well as how it came to this country. Shows how we learn prejudice. Narrated by Joe Campanella.

467. Tale of "O": On Being Different

Goodmeasure, Inc   1979   videocassette or slides   color   27 min or 19 min   instructor's print materials; learner's print materials
Purchase: 27 min $560.00; 19 min $550.00   Rental: $150.00   Preview: $50.00

Deals with managing the element of difference in the workplace. Important for supervisors of women and minorities to understand the group dynamics and performance problems that arise in such work situations. Suggested as a 3-hour program. The 19-minute version is termed "training version."

468. Understanding Institutional Racism

Racism/Sexism Resource Center for Educators   1980   filmstrip   color   17 min   instructor's print materials; learner's print materials
Purchase: $32.50

Justice, jobs, and housing are 3 areas examined in terms of how institutionalized racist patterns distribute unequal rewards to minorities and to Whites. Shows how an organization's racist practices are perpetuated deliberately and inadvertently. Printed materials include discussion guide and group activities useful to examine the practices and policies of organizations and to plan for organizational change.

469. Who Do You Think Should Belong to the Club?

CRM/McGraw-Hill Films   16mm film or videocassette   color   17 min   instructor's print materials
Purchase: $345.00   Rental: $75.00   Preview: free

Addresses issues of cultural stereotyping which raise awareness of negative attitudes toward minorities in hiring, working, and living relationships. Shows the straightforward way that children deal with the sensitive issue of negative interpersonal behavior. Earlier title was *Prejudice and Stereotyping*.

DISMISSAL

470. Alternatives to Discharge: A Case Study

Salenger Educational Media   1976   16mm film or videocassette   color   13 min   instructor's print materials; learner's print materials
Purchase: $395.00   Rental: 5-day $100.00; 3-day $35.00

Dramatization shows conflict between employee and supervisor, in which the company must decide to retain or discharge the employee. Film focuses on the costs of discharge and the concept of establishing proper cause when discharging an employee. The employee as a company human resource is emphasized. Useful for supervisors.

Discipline—A Matter of Judgment. For complete citation, *see* DISCIPLINE.

Discipline and Discharge. For complete citation, *see* DISCIPLINE.

471. Is It All Over—The Termination Interview

Creative Media   16mm film or super 8mm or videocassette   color   6 min   instructor's print materials
Purchase: $100.00   Rental: $35.00   Preview: $15.00

Illustrates how to conduct the termination interview. A case study shows how to terminate the employment of a person in a way that provides hope and guidance for the future. Intended for managers and supervisors. Companion film to *Face-to-Face Payoff: Dynamics of the Interview*.

472. Termination Interview

Dialogue Systems, Inc   videocassette   color   45 min   instructor's print materials
Purchase: $270.00   Rental: $225.00

Deals with the critical problems that managers face when terminating employees. Three dramatizations show the investigation and documentation required, the interpersonal skills needed, an awareness of possible employee reactions, and effective procedures to deal with them. Also addresses outplacement counseling.

DRUG ABUSE

Addictions, Compulsions and Alternative Highs. For complete citation, *see* HEALTH.

Alcohol, Drugs or Alternatives. For complete citation, *see* ALCOHOLISM.

473. Controlling Drub Abuse on the Job
Washington Film Company   16mm film or videocassette   color   27 min   instructor's print materials
Purchase: film $585.00; video $495.00

Dramatized episodes of the types of drug abuse most commonly found in work-related situations. Shows supervisors what actions to look for on the job to identify sustained low-dosage users. Asks a commitment from management to deal with drug control.

474. Drug Information Film Series
Southerby Productions, Inc   3 16mm films or videocassettes   color   16–27 min ea   instructor's print materials
Purchase: $850.00 ($350.00 ea)

Describes drug abuse as a major work problem affecting losses in time and money. Identifies signs and symptoms of abuse for most-used drugs. Discusses and demonstrates proper disciplinary procedures when dealing with drug affected employees.

475. First Step
Motivision, Ltd   16mm film or videocassette   color   28½ min   instructor's print materials
Purchase: $475.00   Preview: $25.00
Languages: English, French

Portrays teenagers and parents in troubled family raising questions about which came first, the trouble or the substance abuse. Points employee and/or family members toward help and motivates action.

476. Just One More Time
BNA Communications, Inc   1972   16mm film or videocassette   color   24 min   instructor's print materials
Purchase: $525.00   Rental: 5-day $150.00; 3-day $105.00   Preview: $35.00

Shows how use of "ordinary" substances like aspirin and tranquilizers can be dangerous and addictive if overused. Details one organization's drug abuse program. Identifies key signals to know who may be abusing drugs. Project Health Series, no. 8.

ECONOMIC CONDITIONS

477. Age of Uncertainty
Films, Inc   1976   12 16mm films or videocassettes   60 min ea
Purchase: film $7,776.00; video $3,888.00   Other cost factors: films with "Weekend in Vermont" $9,261.00; video with "Weekend in Vermont" $4,630.50

Offers a perspective and insight into modern economic problems through film, animation, and special effects as well as dramatizations. Includes basic economic theories, the nature of capitalism and competition, the role of corporations, and current issues. An additional 2½ hour film/cassette, "Weekend in Vermont," is a discussion by world leaders on these topics. Features John Kenneth Galbraith.

478. Conversation with Milton Friedman
Audio-Forum   audiocassette   89 min
Purchase: $11.95

Criticizes the immorality and ineffectiveness of wage price controls and discusses the gold standard, deflation, devaluation, and the draft.

479. Economics and the Public
Audio-Forum   audiocassette   56 min
Purchase: $10.50

John K. Galbraith discusses the problems with our modern consumer economy and the need to redirect the system toward the public interest and a more equitable and humane way of life.

Free Enterprise Economics. For complete citation, *see* FREE ENTERPRISE SYSTEM.

480. Hayek's Theory of the Business Cycle
Audio-Forum   audiocassette   52 min
Purchase: $10.95

Provides lucid explanantion of Hayek's theory of the business cycle as it relates to the money supply.

481. Introduction to Economics
Audio-Forum   10 audiocassettes   9½ hrs
Purchase: $88.00

Surveys economic policies in the past decade with particular view of the nature of unemployment and inflation, tax reform and money supply, balance of payments, and international value of the dollar. Features George J. Viksnins.

482. Milton Friedman Speaks on Economics
Instructional Dynamics, Inc   2 audiocassettes   instructor's print materials
Purchase: $28.40

Discusses the basics of economics and the marketplace, kinds of markets, macroeconomics, and the function of prices.

483. More
Films, Inc   16mm film or videocassette   color   3 min
Purchase: film $125.00; video $65.00   Rental: $35.00   Preview: free

Sums up the ills of a consumer-oriented society. Portrays the national syndrome of conspicuous consumption.

484. Reckoning
American Federation of Labor and Congress of Industrial Organizations   1980   16mm film   26 min
Rental: $5.00

Documents studies that show correlation between joblessness and the increase of deaths from heart attacks, suicide, liver disease, and other stress-related ailments.

485. We Didn't Want It to Happen This Way
International Association of Machinists and
Aerospace Workers   1978   16mm film or
videocassette   28 min
Rental: free

Shows the impact on American jobs lost due to multinational
corporations expansion to foreign countries. Illustrates its point
through the Zenith Radio Corporation's laying off thousands of
workers to seek cheaper labor abroad.

486. You and Your Job
Educational Resources Foundation   slides and
audiocassette
Purchase: $110.00   Rental: $50.00   Preview:
$15.00

Explains the American economic system and what it means to
those in business and industry. Relates the importance of each
and every job to the economic system. Helps employees see
where they fit in the company and in the overall economic
picture. Useful for orientation or motivation.

EFFICIENCY
See PRODUCTIVITY

EMPLOYEE PERFORMANCE
**See also PERFORMANCE APPRAISAL;
PRODUCTIVITY**

Case of the Missing Person. For complete citation,
see SUPERVISION.

487. Employee Inaccuracy Elimination
American Learning Systems, Inc   1981   filmstrip or
slides and audiocassette or videocassette or filmstrip
cartridge   12 min   instructor's print materials
Purchase: video $150.00; other formats
$125.00   Preview: free

Shows how to reduce losses to an organization by motivating
personnel to perform their work tasks with proper discipline
and diligence so that errors and omissions do not occur.
Emphasizes importance of encouraging employees to do their
jobs properly.

488. How to Reduce Absenteeism and Turnover
Professional Resources   6 audiocassettes   learner's
print materials
Purchase: $90.00

Presents facts about offenders and the causes and costs.
Suggests a control program after determining the patterns and
building commitment. Discusses when to use job redesign and
job reassignment and how to train supervisors.

489. Industry's Perennial Problem
Tampa Manufacturing Institute   16mm
film color   56 min   instructor's print materials;
learner's print materials
Purchase: $675.00   Rental: 5-day $105.00; each
additional day $20.00

Defines the fair day's work level (100% performance) and
demonstrates examples of 100%, 120%, and 70% performances

on a drillpress job. Develops a logical case for reasonable
acceptance of the industrial engineering profession's concept of
"normal" pace and answers typical questions about rate-setting
and standards administration. Useful to lay a foundation for the
use of performance rating films.

490. Learning the Principles of MTM
Maynard Management Institute   16mm film   color
17 min
Purchase: $490.00   Rental: $49.00

Introduces Methods-Time Management as a tool for improving
methods and setting consistent time standards. Shows examples
of typical shop and office jobs where it can be applied to
improve methods, set fair time standards, and plan assembly
methods before production.

491. MTM for Better Methods and Fair Standards
Maynard Management Institute   16mm film   color
16 min
Purchase: $460.00   Rental: $46.00

Demonstrates Methods-Time Measurement in observing and
analyzing an operation to improve methods and set a fair time
standard. Uses slow motion and close-ups to show analysis.

492. Make Fewer Motions—Motion Economy
National Audiovisual Center   1973   16mm film   color
18 min
Purchase: $104.50

Shows the principles of motion economy which enables workers
to perform tasks with less fatigue and increased output. Shows
how to select a job for analysis and how to use a motion
economy chart.

Pay for Performance. For complete citation, *see*
MOTIVATION.

Personal Productivity, The Key to Success. For
complete citation, *see* PRODUCTIVITY.

493. Planning Tomorrow's Methods Today
Maynard Management Institute   16mm film   color
17 min
Purchase: $490.00   Rental: $49.00

Shows how operational methods and standards can be developed in a laboratory before going to shop or assembly line,
thereby saving time and money. Uses Methods-Time Measurement to analyze motions and set time standards.

494. Pursuit of Efficiency
Roundtable Films, Inc   1980   16mm film or super
8mm or videocassette   color   25 min   instructor's
print materials
Purchase: $450.00   Rental: $85.00   Preview:
$30.00

Helps employees to think more consciously about the efficiency
of their own work methods, systems, and procedures. Encourages managers and supervisors to seek the opinions of their
employees on how they would change or improve upon the way
things are done. Demonstrates the importance of feedback and
rewards to stimulate employee suggestions. Visible results
include improved morale, reduced costs, and greater productivity. Uses office and manufacturing setting for dramatized
illustrations.

Road Ahead. For complete citation, *see* GOVERNMENT EMPLOYMENT.

Setting the Right Climate. For complete citation, *see* TEAM BUILDING.

Skill and Effort Rating. For complete citation, *see* PERFORMANCE APPRAISAL.

Troubled Employee. For complete citation, *see* PERSONNEL MANAGEMENT.

495. Unsatisfactory Work
BNA Communications, Inc 1978 16mm film or videocassette color 18 min   learner's print materials; audiocassette
Purchase: $630.00   Rental: 5-day $150.00; 3-day $105.00   Preview: $35.00

Major focus is on incompetence and how supervisors can detect and correct it. Delves into the reasons for which the employee is responsible and those for which the supervisor is responsible. Accompanied by a workbook with 3 cases and decision sheets. Audiocassette contains a round table discussion on the cases. Preventive Discipline Training Program, no. 3.

496. Work Sampling Technique
Maynard Management Institute 16mm film color 16 min
Purchase: $610.00   Rental: $61.00

Explains work sampling principles and procedures, including form used. Shows where it can be applied to rate efficiency, allocate time, and identify problems. Intended for supervisors, forepersons, and operators.

EMPLOYEE RELATIONS
See INTERPERSONAL RELATIONS

EMPLOYEE SELECTION AND PLACEMENT

497. Applicant Evaluation
American Learning Systems, Inc 1981 filmstrip or slides and audiocassette or videocassette or filmstrip cartridge 12 min ea   instructor's print materials
Purchase: video $150.00; other formats $125.00   Preview: free

Goes into the techniques of reviewing the personal, educational, military, and employment background of applicants to determine their suitability as nonsecurity risk employees. Includes the evaluation of application information, interview data, and facts learned in conducting a background investigation to make a judgment of the prospective employee's character and integrity. Intended for managers and supervisors.

498. Are You a Position Manager?
National Audiovisual Center 1976 slides and audiocassettes 26 min
Purchase: $28.75

Managers and supervisors must assign duties and responsibilities to various positions in their units. This program covers the assignment of title, series, and grades to government positions.

499. Executive Selection
Audio-Forum audiocassette 31 min
Purchase: $10.95

Robert N. McMurry discusses how to recruit, screen, select, and place qualified incumbents in positions.

500. Hiring High Performers
AMR International, Inc 1981 8 audiocassettes program manual
Purchase: $295.00

Discovery and development of outstanding candidates for well-defined jobs adds substantially to the organization's effectiveness. This requires skills such as interviewing, selection, presenting job offers, communicating job needs, and problem-solving methods.

501. How to Get a Job
Films, Inc 1970 16mm film or videocassette color 58 min
Purchase: film $750.00; video $375.00   Rental: $75.00

Job hunting as a skill requires the assessment of personal skills, strengths, and accomplishments. Critical analysis of practical techniques: how to generate interviews by telephone and how to take a positive approach by stressing accomplishments and the reasons one should be hired.

502. Man or Woman for the Job
National Audiovisual Center 1969 16mm film or videocassette color 15 min
Purchase: $87.00   Rental: $12.50

Points out the importance of effective employee recruitment and selection procedures through the experiences of a small print shop owner. Brief vignettes of other types of business reflect various sources of employees.

Management Guide to Successful Recruiting and Interviewing. For complete citation, *see* INTERVIEWING.

Peter Principle: Why Things Always Go Wrong. For complete citation, *see* MANAGEMENT.

503. Professional Placement for Profit
Employment Training Corporation 14 audiocassettes   learner's print materials
Purchase: $309.00; without clerical level materials $249.00

Presents all elements of successful placement for both clerical and professional level applicants. Includes real interviews and demonstrates present techniques and procedures. Basic employment counselor training program.

504. Recruitment, Selection and Placement
BNA Communications, Inc 16mm film 19 min instructor's print materials; learner's print materials
Purchase: $630.00   Rental: 5-day $246.00; 3-day $201.00   Preview: $35.00

Reveals the consequences of word-of-mouth recruiting through dramatization of a supervisor's action causing a discrimination complaint against the company. Several cases present the criteria for job tests, do's and don'ts of interviewing, and how to avoid charges of discrimination based on race, ethnic origin, or sex. Fair Employment Practice Training Program, no. 1.

505. Remember My Name
National Audiovisual Center 1972 16mm
film color 18 min
Purchase: $104.50 Rental: $12.50

Illustrates frustrations of employees in lower level, dead-ended job situations. Stresses the need for management and supervisory actions to bring about equality of opportunity in employment and upward mobility within the federal government. Short version.

506. Secrets of Executive Search
Employment Training Corporation audiocassettes
Purchase: $149.00

Shows how executive search consultants, good placement agencies, and management consulting firms throughout the country are able to locate the exact candidates they want without advertising. Includes book of case histories which provides illustrations of how actual searches are conducted from beginning to end.

507. Select the Best
WMI Corporation 1978 9 videocassettes and 3 audiocassettes color
Purchase: $1,000.00 Other cost factors: administrator's kit $500.00; learner's printed materials

Provides an interviewing model demonstrating the employment interview as developing criteria, gathering information, and evaluating information and applicant. Illustrates practical skills for opening and closing interviews, in-depth questions, documentation, handling special problems, and complying with equal employment opportunity laws. Audiocassettes offer practice opportunities. Suggested for 1½–2-day program.

508. Selecting Personnel for a "System 4" Organization
Development Digest audiocassette
Purchase: $13.75

Describes one organization's experience in creating a Likert System 4 organization by selecting people who would be compatible to such a style.

Selecting the Right Supervisor. For complete citation, *see* SUPERVISION.

509. Selection Interview: Hiring without Regrets
Dialogue Systems, Inc videocassette color 45 min instructor's print materials
Purchase: $750.00 Rental: $225.00

Presents the essential skills that lead to wise hiring decisions. Using 3 dramatized vignettes, reviews necessary preinterview arrangements and preparation. Offers ways to verify resumes, build unique questioning strategies, and keep the interview "on track."

510. Selection Interviewing
Management Resources, Inc 6 audiocassettes instructor's print materials; learner's print materials; book
Purchase: $295.00

For those with responsibility for selection interviewing. Designed for any level of applicant or job. Includes 4 learner's audiocassettes and 2 instructor's audiocassettes as well as printed materials and a hardbound text, *Interviewing for Managers* by Dr. John Drake. Emphasizes skills to get beyond resume facts. Intended for individual or group study.

Selection Interviewing Program. For complete citation, *see* INTERVIEWING.

511. Selection of Men
Classroom World Productions 24 audiocassettes 12–15 min ea
Purchase: $160.00

Identifies the 5 inner qualities important to look for in selecting personnel for any job. Discusses pitfalls of first impressions. Emphasizes the importance of job descriptions, employment forms, and aptitude tests.

512. Transitions: Letting Go and Taking Hold
CRM/McGraw-Hill Films 16mm film or videocassette color 29 min
Purchase: $560.00 Rental: $95.00 Preview: free

Examines the psychological and structural interrelationships affected by job transition. Particularly helpful for those affected by transitions within an organization. Uses dramatization of an hourly employee just promoted to a supervisory position.

513. Uniform Guidelines on Employee Selection Procedures
National Audiovisual
Center 1979 videocassette color 48 min guide
Purchase: $148.50

An overview of both the purpose and the scope of the new guidelines. Experts discuss the guidelines developed by the Office of Personnel Management.

514. "Who's Gonna Collect the Garbage?"
BNA Communications, Inc 16mm film or videocassette color 44 min instructor's print materials
Purchase: $385.00 Rental: 5-day $150.00; 3-day $105.00 Preview: $35.00

Discusses problems of humanpower selection, use, and development as well as the unique problems of women, Blacks, skilled and unskilled workers, and the knowledge worker. Panel participants representing labor, management, education, and minority groups discuss the heterogeneous new work force with Peter Drucker. Managing Discontinuity Series, no. 4.

EMPLOYEE TRAINING
See TRAINING AND DEVELOPMENT

ENERGY

Energy Carol. For complete citation, *see* CHANGE.

515. Save America's Valuable Energy
NPL, Inc   100 slides and audiocassette   25 min
script
Purchase: $19.50

Addresses how energy can be saved in processing operations and how to anticipate, prevent, and remedy energy losses. Covers furnaces, steam, electric motors vs. steam turbines, water and compressed air conservation, and heat exchangers of all types. Illustrated in refinery and petrochemical plant setting. Designed to impress employees with the importance of saving energy.

516. This is an Emergency
National Film Board of Canada   1983   16mm film
or videocassette   color   29 min
Purchase: film $550.00; video $350.00   Rental:
$120.00   Preview: $40.00

Combines live action and animation to raise energy consciousness of business, industry, and consumers. Offers practical solutions to the energy crisis and provides information on controlling energy costs that affect the price of goods.

ENVIRONMENTAL POLLUTION

517. An Act of Congress
LCA Video/Films   16mm film or
videocassette   color   52 min   instructor's print
materials
Purchase: $650.00   Rental: $150.00   Preview:
$75.00

Traces the progress of a bill—Clear Air Act of 1977—to record the nation's lawmakers at work. Shows how the system protects a multitude of interests, in this case, both business and the environmenalists. Two Congressmen battle over which is more important, a healthy environment or a secure automobile industry. Features E.G. Marshall. Follow-up film is *Regulators*.

518. No Fuelin'—We're Poolin'
National Audiovisual Center   1976   16mm film or
videocassette   color   8 min
Purchase: $46.50

Describes the role of the employer in vanpool programs, including carpool matching, driver selection, and determining fares. Encourages employees to participate in the program.

519. Pollution Control—The Hard Decisions
BNA Communications, Inc   1971   16mm film or
videocassette   color   30 min
Purchase: $385.00   Rental: 5-day $150.00; 3-day
$105.00   Preview: $35.00

Considers the challenges executives face in dealing responsibly with problems of the environment. They are required to make difficult and in most cases unpopular decisions to effect courses of action on related issues of environmental concern. Covers broad societal aspects and how each manager may contribute professionally and as a citizen. Features Peter Drucker. Managing Discontinuity Series, no. 6.

520. Regulators
LCA Video/Films   1982   16mm film or
videocassette   color   50 min   instructor's print
materials
Purchase: $750.00   Rental: $150.00   Preview:
$75.00

Focuses on one provision of the Clean Air Act to show how lobbied bureaucrats put regulations into effect. This specific provision generated 27 pages of regulations, 33 pages of explanations, and 2000 pages of background papers—from 5 pages of law. Sequel to *An Act of Congress*. Features E.G. Marshall as narrator.

521. Serpent Fruits
American Federation of Labor and Congress of
Industrial Organizations   1979   16mm
film   color   30 min
Rental: $5.00

Documents 3 case histories of the disastrous effect of toxic chemicals to which people are unknowingly exposed on the job and in the community.

EQUAL EMPLOYMENT OPPORTUNITY
See also DISCRIMINATION; WOMEN

522. Affirmative Action and the Supervisor: It's Not Simply Black and White
Thompson-Mitchell and Associates   1975
videocassette   color   20 min
Purchase: $240.00   Rental: $55.00

A frank and candid discussion of reasons for dissatisfaction and conflict between White supervisors and non-White employees. Suggestions offered for reducing such conflicts. Basic premise is that cultural and social differences are more influential than lack of skills and abilities in such conflicts. Designed for use by supervisors and management personnel.

523. Awareness Training for Managers—Minority Relations
Development Digest   audiocassette
Purchase: $13.75

Awareness of supervisors together with action programs help meet organizational commitment to affirmative action. Describes the Affirmative Action Awareness Training Program of TRW's Systems Division including the methods used to prepare for training and follow-up as well as the development of action programs.

524. Beyond Black and White
Motivational Media   16mm film or
videocassette   color   32 min   instructor's print
materials
Dramatized vignettes portray the psychological, sociological, and historical origins of prejudice against minorities and women. Clarifies employee rights under EEO and Affirmative Action provisions of the law. Intended for frontline supervisors and management.

525. Bill of Rights in Action: Equal Opportunity Series
Thompson-Mitchell and Associates   1970
videocassette   color   22 min
Purchase: $375.00   Rental: $50.00   Preview:
$30.00

An arbitrated case of a personal grievance involving seniority and equal employment practices. Raises basic question of special minority recruitment and employment programs when a minority employee is selected for the job despite the White man's seniority.

526. Can You Make that Decision?
S&L Communications, Inc   1980   videocassette
color   10 min   instructor's print materials; learner's print materials
Purchase: $300.00   Rental: $75.00

Deals with affirmative action and equal employment opportunity in financial institutions. Addresses 5 major areas: hiring and promoting the disabled, age discrimination, sex discrimination, proper documentation, and commitment of management. Each is dramatized.

Career Awareness for Women. For complete citation, *see* CAREER PLANNING AND DEVELOPMENT.

527. Conducting Lawful Interviews: Guidelines for Non-Discriminatory Hiring Practices
Singer Management Institute   2 audiocassettes
instructor's print materials; learner's print materials
Purchase: $125.00   Preview: $15.00

Addresses how to conduct lawful and effective selection interviews and then prevent or defend against charges of discrimination that may be brought under equal employment laws. Units include EEO laws and regulations, planning the interview, conducting the interview, evaluating results, and follow-up. Case studies are given with exercises. For group or self-study. Suggested time is 3 hours.

Discipline and Discharge. For complete citation, *see* DISCIPLINE.

528. EEOC Story
Didactic Systems, Inc   16mm film   38 min
Purchase: $325.00   Rental: 5-day $110.00; per-day $40.00

An informal yet systematic look at the machinery of the Equal Employment Opportunity Commission. Interviews with key officials concern corporate and union discrimination against minorities and women seeking employment. Dramatizes typical violations of Title VII of the Civil Rights Act.

529. Equal Employment and the Law
Instructional Dynamics, Inc   6 audiocassettes
learner's print materials
Purchase: $69.95

Guide to employment practices and laws that apply to equal employment. Prepared and presented by Elmer Ellentuck.

530. Equal Employment Opportunity and Affirmative Action
National Audiovisual Center   1973   16mm film or videocassette   b/w   28 min   learner's print materials
Purchase: film $92.50; video $110.00   Rental: $12.50

Provides statutory authority for affirmative action and enforcement to assure that personnel actions are free from discrimination. Highlights agency and commission responsibilities for meaningful affirmative action programs under the law.

531. Equal Opportunity
Barr Films   16mm film or videocassette   color   22 min
Purchase: $450.00   Rental: $100.00   Preview: $50.00

Dramatization illustrates the dilemmas presented by equal opportunity in the context of affirmative action, discrimination, union contracts, seniority, and fairness. Situation presented goes to arbitration, and the decision is left to viewers. Discussion Film.

532. Equal Opportunity and Control of the Work Place
Development Digest   2 audiocassettes
Purchase: $27.50

Describes equal opportunity as an employment standard. Illustrates need for legislation on equal opportunity and describes effect of the Philadelphia Plan. Insists management must get on with the program or lose control of the workplace to the courts. Presented by Arthur A. Fletcher.

533. Equal Opportunity
Salenger Educational Media   1970   16mm film or videocassette   color   22 min   instructor's print materials; learner's print materials
Purchase: $380.00   Rental: $90.00   Preview: $35.00

Open-ended dramatization to encourage group discussion. Presents a case of reverse discrimination and the problems connected with it. Designed to help managers and supervisors understand the reasons behind the Civil Rights Acts of 1964 and 1966 and to understand that discrimination can cut both ways. Major focus is on reverse discrimination.

534. Equal Rights for Women
Bureau of Business Practice   1973   16mm
film   color   19 min
Purchase: $425.00   Rental: $95.00   Preview: $45.00

On-the-job scenes show how practices accepted for years are discriminatory today. Supervisors see where mistakes are being made, which actions violate the law, and what to do to avoid charges of discrimination.

535. Games
National Audiovisual Center   1973   16mm
film   color   32 min
Purchase: $185.50   Rental: $12.50

Discusses obstacles to equal employment opportunity. Exposes the games people play that keep minority members from advancing as their abilities would allow.

536. Goals, Quotas, and Merit Principles
National Audiovisual Center   1974   42 slides and audiocassette   script
Purchase: $15.00

Deals with the provisions of the memorandum "Federal Policy on Remedies concerning EEO in State and Local Government Personnel System." Identifies 4 agencies and the authorities under which they operate.

537. Hispanic Employment Program
National Audiovisual Center   1979   59 slides and audiocassettes   11 min   program guide
Purchase: $24.75

Designed to aid agencies fulfill their obligation for training Hispanic minorities for supervisory and management positions in the goverment. Useful for international training or briefing sessions for management personnel.

In the Company of Men. For complete citation, *see* COMMUNICATION.

Increasing Job Options for Women. For complete citation, *see* WOMEN.

538. Interview
Xicom-Video Arts   1975   2 16mm films or videocassettes   color   35 min ea   instructor's print materials
Purchase: $475.00 ea   Rental: $100.00   Preview: $35.00

Each contains a live interview which demonstrates potentially unfair employment practices, followed by a discussion of the implications of these practices with regard to EEO legislation. Intended for personnel managers or those responsible for interviews. Each suggested for a 2-hour program.

539. Legal Responsibilities—Affirmative Action and Equal Employment
National Audiovisual Center   1976   72 slides and audiocassette   12 min   script
Purchase: $29.00

Presents drawings illustrating the legal responsibility of employees to eliminate unfair and illegal employment practices that often affect women. Explains affirmative action plans and equal employment opportunity enforcement of sex discrimination laws.

540. Legal Rights of Women Workers
National Audiovisual Center   1976   64 slides and audiocassette   6 min   script
Purchase: $25.50

Cartoon drawings illustrate women in nontraditional jobs to explain the legal rights of women workers to equal employment opportunity, equal training and promotion opportunity, and equal pay. Important information about placement interviews and testing. For women preparing to enter the job market and those who are presently employed.

541. Motivating Employees: Understanding Legal Requirements
Singer Management Institute   1980   2 audiocassettes   instructor's print materials; learner's print materials
Purchase: $125.00   Preview: $15.00

Focuses on motivating and upgrading protected employee groups. Addresses how equal employment laws and regulations affect employers and supervisors and necessary record keeping. Suggested for a 4–6 hour program.

542. Moving Women into the Organization Mainstream for Profit
Development Digest   audiocassette
Purchase: $13.75

Suggests the critical issue is no longer equal pay for equal work but equal access to jobs. Describes a way to blow the whistle on the games businesses play with women. Points out an important role for the corporation in bringing about social reforms. Features Liz Carpenter.

543. One by One
Tylie Jones   16mm film or videocassette   color   28 min   instructor's print materials
Purchase: $300.00   Rental: $100.00   Preview: $25.00

Defines and exposes unconscious prejudice and examines why it still exists. Dramatic documentary about a middle manager and a minority employee on his staff. The film explores emotional prejudice. Helps managers recognize and deal with negative feelings.

544. Opportunity for All: Making a Go of EEO
Roundtable Films, Inc   1981   slides and audiocassette or videocassette   instructor's print materials; learner's print materials
Purchase: $595.00   Rental: $125.00   Preview: $30.00

Presents a fundamental understanding of EEO law and practice. Gives specific guidelines for performance, documentation, career development planning, defining minimum job qualifications, recognizing and correcting equal pay problems, and identifying nonprofessional behavior which results in discriminatory practices. Intended to help managers and supervisors avoid discrimination complaints. Suggested for 4-hour or 1-day session.

Recruitment, Selection and Placement. For complete citation, *see* EMPLOYEE SELECTION AND PLACEMENT.

Remember My Name. For complete citation, *see* EMPLOYEE SELECTION AND PLACEMENT.

545. Role of the Female in the World of Work
Development Digest   audiocassette
Purchase: $13.75

Three women point out opportunities and problems of "working women" and interpret discriminatory practices and new legislation involving women in the work force.

546. Supervisor and Equal Employment Opportunity
Thompson-Mitchell and Associates 16mm film or
super 8mm or videocassette color 35 min
Purchase: $265.00 Rental: $35.00

Discusses equal employment opportunity and some of the
problems involved. Brings out the honest objections and
concerns in many supervisors' minds. Portrays unsuspected
feelings and inner attitudes that color supervisors' attitudes.
Clearly details situation of the Black, the Spanish American,
and the women. Emphasizes the importance of 2-way communication.

**547. Women in the Corporation: On a Par, Not a
Pedestal**
Document Associates 1977 16mm film or
videocassette color 26 min
Purchase: $375.00 Rental: $45.00

Case history of a successfull affirmative action program involving women in clerical positions at Connecticut General Insurance Company. Presents the problems, the methods instituted,
and the solutions in developing this effective ongoing program.

ETHICS AND VALUES

**Adapting Training and Development to Changing
Values.** For complete citation, *see* TRAINING AND
DEVELOPMENT.

548. Business Ethics
Lansford Publishing Company, Inc 1981 slides and
audiocassettes instructor's print materials; learner's
print materials
Purchase: $265.95

Examines most critical business ethics problems such as bribes,
payoffs, graft, and employee theft. Can be used, with discussion
guide and games furnished, for half-day or full-day session.

**Effective Supervisor: Dealing with Conflicting Value
Systems.** For complete citation, *see* CONFLICT
AND CONFLICT MANAGEMENT.

**549. Focus on Ethics: The Role of Values in Deci-
sion-Making**
Salenger Educational Media 1977 3 16mm films or
videocassettes color 45 min instructor's print
materials; learner's print materials
Purchase: $695.00 Rental: $175.00 Preview:
$60.00

Intended to increase sensitivity to potential business/society
problems and improve understanding of the importance of
public image and public/society relations. Assists managers to
clarify their own values, increase their awareness of the value
system of others, improve their interpersonal and organizational relations, and improve their ability to make realistic decisions
for the greatest personal, social, and corporate benefit.

550. Fully Functioning Organization
BNA Communications, Inc 1969 16mm film and
videocassette color 23 min
Purchase: $525.00 Rental: 5-day $150.00; 3-day
$105.00 Preview: $35.00

Joe Batten describes his 7-phase "servo-climate for results" and
applies them to the dramatized case on film. Stresses the
importance of a "grand design," a set of beliefs or values that
set the style of organization. Intended for managers. Tough-
minded Management Series, no. 4.

551. Values and Decisions: The Roger Berg Story
Salenger Educational Media 1977 16mm film or
videocassette color 16 min instructor's print
materials; learner's print materials
Purchase: $455.00 Rental: $125.00 Preview:
$35.00

Explores a possible conflict of interest situation of a young
executive. Illustrates the role values play in the decision-making
process and how they influence the way we deal with the
consequences of our decisions. Shows factors in decision
making.

EXPORTS
See INTERNATIONAL BUSINESS

FEEDBACK

552. Communication Feedback
BNA Communications, Inc 1965 16mm film or
videocassette color 23 min
Purchase: $525.00 Rental: 5-day $130.00; 3-day
$105.00 Preview: $35.00
Languages: English, Dutch, Portuguese, Spanish,
Swedish

Feedback is essential to attain good management communication and to gain attention, understanding, acceptance, and
action. Dramatizations alternate with David Berlo's discussion
of principles of feedback and how to elicit it. Intended for
managers. Effective Communication Series, no. 3.

553. Dealing with Criticism
Centron Films 1975 16mm film color 11 min
Purchase: $210.00

A supervisor's criticism of a project is well-intended but is
taken differently by each of the production team members.
Shows how 3 people perceive feedback and the consequences.
Handling Information at the Personal Level Series.

Farewell to Birdie McKeever. For complete citation,
see INTERPERSONAL RELATIONS.

554. Feedback: Making Your Comments Count
Andragogy Press 1981 audiocassette 15 min
instructor's print materials; learner's print materials;
transparencies
Purchase: $385.00

Deliberate and careful use of feedback can become a powerful
management tool. Focuses on the essence of feedback and how
to plan the kind of feedback to give. Aims to help understanding of the usefulness and limitations of giving feedback based on
opinions and to build skills for giving feedback. Audiocassette is
"Tips for Trainers." Suggested for 3½-hour program.

555. Feedback Systems: Big, Fast Performance Improvements, Large Payoffs, Low Cost
Development Digest   audiocassette
Purchase: $13.75

Edward J. Feeney proposes how to apply feedback systems to improve worker performance in less than 5 days, create a benefit-cost ratio of 100 to one, and sustain performance at high levels over long periods.

FINANCIAL MANAGEMENT
See also COST CONTROL

556. Balance Sheet Barrier
Xicom-Video Arts   1977   16mm film or videocassette   color   29 min   instructor's print materials; learner's print materials
Purchase: $625.00   Rental: $100.00   Preview: $35.00

Intended to show nonfinanacial managers what business finance is all about. Visually links balance sheet lines with company events and objects. Actors John Cleese and Ronnie Corbett portray the naive and the sophisticate. Plain language and animation help expose the simplicity of business finance.

557. Basic Budgeting
Management Resources, Inc   2 audiocassettes   instructor's print materials; learner's print materials
Purchase: $75.00

Identifies the objectives and techniques of budgeting. Illustrates 3 ways of achieving flexibility in budgets. Focuses on kinds of investments in capital budgets and how to evaluate proposed investments.

558. Basics of Finance and Accounting
AMACOM   4 audiocassettes   1 hr ea   learner's print materials
Purchase: $79.95   Other cost factors: AMA members $67.95

Gives overview of key aspects of finance and accounting and insights into financial management including specific analysis techniques, cash flow management principles, cost control procedures, and knowledge about sources of funds.

559. Basics of Finance and Accounting
AMACOM   3 audiocassettes   3 hrs   learner's print materials
Purchase: $69.95   Other cost factors: AMA members $59.45

Overall coverage of financial management and the ins-and-outs of financial statements. Includes specific analysis techniques, sources of funds, and cost controls. Useful for self-study. Features Theodore Cohn. AMA Management Basics Series.

560. Blueprint for Financial Independence
Twentieth Century-Fox Video, Inc   1979   videocassette   color   51 min   instructor's print materials; learner's print materials
Purchase: $475.00   Rental: $160.00   Preview: $50.00

Outlines the basic mistakes people make with their money and presents a formula for financial independence. Venita Van Caspel urges planning with financial objectives and wise investments. Purchase includes copy of Van Caspel book, *New Money Dynamics* as well as financial planning worksheet, outline, glossary, and leader's guide.

561. Break-Even Point Analysis
Salenger Educational Media   1977   16mm film or videocassette   color   14 min   instructor's print materials; learner's print materials
Purchase: $420.00   Rental: $100.00   Preview: $35.00

Introduces nonfinancial managers and supervisors to the concept of break-even point (BEP) analysis, a simple and valuable tool for management decision making. Shows how important quantification is for supplying information used in decision making.

562. Collecting Money by Telephone
Schrello Associates   1977   audiocassette   learner's print materials
Purchase: $69.95

Techniques for using the telephone to collect delinquent accounts. Uses role play and self-instructional methods. Emphasizes strategy, motivation, efficiency, and handling difficult situations firmly but tactfully.

563. Control of Working Capital
Xicom-Video Arts   1978   16mm film or videocassettes   color   26 min   instructor's print materials; learner's print materials
Purchase: $625.00   Rental: $100.00   Preview: $35.00

Humorous portrayal by John Cleese and Ronnie Corbett shows how understanding the basic simplicities of business finance can increase the profitability of a business. Essentials of business finance for people without any financial background. Film follows *Balance Sheet Barrier*.

Corporate Planning I. For complete citation, *see* PLANNING.

Corporate Planning II. For complete citation, *see* PLANNING.

564. Cost, Profit and Break-Even
Xicom-Video Arts   1980   16mm film or videocassette   color   22 min
Purchase: $625.00   Rental: $100.00   Preview: $35.00

Demonstrates key factors that determine profit on a product or in a business. Cost, price, and volume all affect each other. The technique of costing is not a magic formula but is one that helps strike the right balance. Intended for line managers as a conceptual tool, for senior executives who are responsible to implement it, and for all staff as a basic explanation.

565. Depreciation
HBJ Media Systems Corporation   1981   4 slide/audiocassette presentations   instructor's print materials; learner's print materials
Purchase: $1,190.00

A practical introduction to a basic understanding of what depreciation means and the most common methods of calculating depreciation: straight-line, units-of-production, sum-of-the-years digits, and declining-balance. Intended for general accounting clerks, cost accounting clerks, and others whose duties involve them with issues of depreciation. Suggested for 6–9 hours.

566. Eagle on the Street
National Audiovisual Center 1975 69 slides and audiocassette 12 min script
Purchase: $25.00

Traces the development of the securities industry in the US from its origins on Wall Street in the late 18th century through the precipitous 1929 crash of the stock market. Relates the reasons for the creation of the Securities and Exchange Commission (SEC) in 1934 and how the SEC, an independent, bipartisan, quasi-judicial regulatory agency of the federal government administers the various laws that relate to field securities and finance.

567. Economic Purposes of Commodity Futures Trading
National Audiovisual Center 1978 55 slides script
Purchase: $16.50

Discusses cash trades and forward contracts, futures trading, and speculation. Describes the functions of the Commodities Future Trading Commission.

568. Finance and Accounting for Nonfinancial Managers
American Management Associations 1974 6 audiocassettes 1 hr ea learner's print materials
Purchase: $145.00 Other cost factors: AMA members $135.00

Presents basic concepts and language of accounting, financing business, inventory valuation and profit management, and budgeting. Includes pre- and posttest. Suggested as a 10-hour self-study program or 14 hours for groups.

569. Finance and Accounting Overview for Non-Financial Managers
Schrello Associates 6 audiocassettes learner's print materials
Purchase: $295.00

Presents the principles, practices, and vocabulary of business finance in a logical manner that requires no prior knowledge of accounting, finance, or higher mathematics. Includes practical exercises that translate finance and accounting concepts into concrete terms.

Five 'M's. For complete citation, *see* MANAGEMENT.

Focus on Organization. For complete citation, *see* DECISION MAKING/PROBLEM SOLVING.

570. Fundamentals of Budgeting
American Management Associations 6 audiocassettes 10 hrs learner's print materials

Purchase: $145.00 Other cost factors: AMA members $135.00; discounts available for bulk orders of materials

Explains what budgets are, how they work, how to prepare and present them, and most important, how to use them as powerful management tools to increase executive effectiveness.

571. Fundamentals of Finance and Accounting for Non-Financial Executives
AMR International, Inc 1981 10 audiocassettes learner's print materials
Purchase: $350.00

The ability to understand, interpret, and communicate vital financial facts is essential for successful businesspeople. Offers the basics in understanding cost behavior, budgeting, and control in managerial decisions. Useful for planning, distinguishing between financial alternatives, and justifying funding requests.

572. Futures in the Balance
National Audiovisual Center 1978 16mm film color 20 min
Purchase: $116.00

Discusses commodity futures and the functions of the Commodity Futures Trading Commission.

573. Guide to Operational Auditing
American Management Associations 6 audiocassettes learner's print materials
Purchase: $145.00 Other cost factors: AMA members $135.00; discounts available for bulk orders of materials

Intended to help managers discover, evaluate, and report on those areas where cost reductions, operating improvements, or increased profit opportunities are possible. Gives tips to spot uncorrelated policies and practices, poorly utilized resources, unclear objectives and priorities, and fraudulent activities.

574. Heartbeat of Business
National Audiovisual Center 1971 16mm film 15 min
Purchase: $87.00 Rental: $12.50

The importance of good financial management is dramatized through conversations between 2 businessmen.

575. How to Interpret Financial Statements
American Management Associations 6 audiocassettes learner's print materials
Purchase: $145.00 Other cost factors: AMA members $135.00; discounts available for bulk orders of materials

Builds an understanding of financial statements and the use of analysis tools. Covers comparison of statements, horizontal and vertical percentage analysis, and various ratio tools to analyze financial data accurately. Points out the potential impact of various decisions on a company's total financial situation.

576. How to Plan an Investment Program
Audio-Forum audiocassette 60 min learner's print materials
Purchase: $15.50

Explains mutual funds, stock and bonds, second mortgages, and tax shelters in a humorous, nontechnical manner.

577. Inventories
HBJ Media Systems Corporation 1981 5 slide/audiocassette presentations instructor's print materials; learner's print materials
Purchase: $1,490.00

A practical introduction to concepts of perpetual and periodic inventory systems; methods for valuing inventory, such as FIFO, LIFO, and Weighted Average; the retail and gross profit methods for estimating inventory; and computing inventory turnover. Intended for general accounting clerks, cost accounting clerks, and others who work with inventory. Suggested for 9–12 hours.

578. Managing Cash Flow
American Management Associations 6 audiocassettes learner's print materials
Purchase: $145.00 Other cost factors: AMA members $135.00

Provides an up-to-date understanding of cash flow techniques, new insights into the management of working capital, and the ability to prepare an analysis showing how improved management of working capital can result in an opportunity for savings. Shows how to predict the timing of cash flows, turn inventory into cash, and utilize assets and liabilities effectively as possible. Increases awareness of the relationships among accounting, control, financial management, and economics.

579. Managing to Survive
International Film Bureau, Inc 16mm film or videocassette 27½ min
Purchase: $495.00 Rental: 5-day $67.00; 3-day $50.00 Preview: free

Dramatizes the events which lead to the bankruptcy of an English furniture manufacturing firm. Points out the importance of an adequate information system for financial management. Financing for Managers Series.

580. Micawber Equation
International Film Bureau, Inc 16mm film or videocassette color 25 min
Purchase: $495.00 Rental: 5-day $67.00; 3-day $50.00 Preview: free

Shows how a hi-fi manufacturing company in England is able to use its budget to uncover losses and then discover causes, alter plans, and rectify the situation. Various managers become involved in deciding and implementing changes, thereby achieving control and coordination of efforts. Useful to prompt discussion on budgetary planning, coordination, and control. Finance for Managers Series.

581. Money Management Workshop
Creative Universal, Inc 1977 audiocassettes instructor's print materials; learner's print materials; transparencies
Purchase: $1,995.00 (for 10 learners) Preview: $20.00

Focuses on the responsibilities of money management, improving cash and capital, debt management, increasing profit, tax reductions, and long-term financial stability. Includes exercises and case studies.

582. Origin and History of Program Budgeting
National Audiovisual Center 1970 16mm film b/w 25 min
Purchase: $82.50

Traces the history of planning, programing, and budgeting. Describes the fundamentals of the system.

What Every Profit-Oriented Manager Should Know about Accounting. For complete citation, *see* ACCOUNTING.

583. Why the Price?
Chamber of Commerce of the United States 80 slides and audiocassette 16 min script
Purchase: $25.00

Shows that business costs, availability, competition, and consumer demand play important roles in product pricing. Looks at other influential factors: inflation, taxes, government regulation, and the impact of consumer choices.

584. Zero Base Budgeting
AMR International, Inc 10 audiocassettes learner's print materials
Purchase: $350.00

Presents zero base budgeting as a general management tool that provides a systematic way to evaluate all operations and programs. Explains the concept, implementation, and organizational impact. Audio portion of a workshop presented by Peter A. Pyhrr.

FRAUD

585. Billion Dollar Bubble
Films, Inc 1981 16mm film or videocassette color 60 min
Purchase: film $900.00; video $450.00 Rental: $100.00 Preview: free

Details the story of the Equity Funding Corporation's 1959–1973 computer fraud. Illustrates how the picture of the ideology of success was carried too far.

586. The Bunco Boys—And How to Beat Them
BNA Communications, Inc 16mm film color 22 min instructor's print materials
Purchase: $450.00 Rental: 5-day $150.00; 3-day $105.00 Preview: $35.00

Dramatizes 3 common confidence games that frequently victimize individuals and organizations, and the leader's guide exposes more. Describes how to recognize them and counter them.

587. Games People Play: Currency and Check Schemes
MTI Teleprograms, Inc 1978 16mm film and 20 slides color 26 min instructor's print materials; script
Purchase: film $435.00; video $395.00 Rental: $80.00

Dramatizations show how to identify fraudulent instruments, how to evaluate customer behavior, and how to take effective action when suspicions are aroused. Addresses counterfeit and altered currency, checks which have been forged, stolen, or written against nonexistent accounts, counterfeit securities and traveler's checks, and stolen passbooks.

$9+ $1=$20: Shortchanged. For complete citation, *see* LOSS PREVENTION.

588. Stop the Short Change Artist
Classroom World Productions   2 filmstrips and/or audiocassette
Purchase: filmstrips and audiocassette $45.00; audiocassette $12.95

Describes short change artists and the step-by-step methods they employ. Shows how to stop these crooks cold, without personal or business risk.

589. That Final Touch
Continental Film Productions   slides or filmstrip and audiocassette   14 min
Purchase: filmstrip $95.00; slides $75.00

Shows how to make change correctly, how to spot doctored bills and counterfeits, and how to recognize and deal with short-change artists. Stresses courtesy and accuracy.

590. You Catch a Thief
S&L Communications, Inc   4
videocassettes   color   10–32 min ea
Purchase: $175.00 ea   Rental: $25.00   Other cost factors: SLCI members $60.00 ea (rental $25.00 ea)

Shows and discusses 4 frauds: forged checks, counterfeit money and traveler's checks, identification papers, and shortchanging. Each shows how to detect the frauds and how to take steps to safeguard against them. Uses a retired con man to explain the frauds common in white-collar crime.

FREE ENTERPRISE SYSTEM

591. Decision Making by Workers
Development Digest   audiocassette
Purchase: $13.75

Presentation by Irving Bluestone suggests that the drive that moves people and nations toward political freedom exists at the workplace and that maximizing profit obstructs democracy there.

592. Free Enterprise Economics
Educational Resources Foundation   1975   9   16mm films or videocassettes   color   23–30 min ea
Purchase: $3,575.00 ($450.00 ea)   Rental: $65.00   Preview: $15.00 ea   Other cost factors: printed materials for instructors and learners priced separately

Presents the basics of the US economic system, its fundamental structure, and the economic problems we face as a nation. Specific aspects include productivity, competition, inflation, and profits.

593. Fully Functioning Society
BNA Communications, Inc   1969   16mm film or videocassette   color   23 min
Purchase: $525.00   Rental: 5-day $150.00; 3-day $105.00   Preview: $35.00

Joe Batten discusses business's responsibility to government, the social responsibility of business, and the nature of the free enterprise system.

Social Responsibility—Myth or Reality? For complete citation, *see* CORPORATIONS.

594. Some Call It Greed
LCA Video/Films   16mm film or videocassette   color   52 min   instructor's print materials
Purchase: $750.00   Rental: $120.00   Preview: $60.00

Looks at the history of 4 American enterprises (Morgan, Carnegie, Rockefeller, and Ford) and shows how they succeeded by responding to need—overcoming obstacles with imagination and creativity. Tells the story of how America moved from a rural, agricultural society to the world's most industrialized nation through depression, postwar boom, aviation, superhighways, and electronic brains. Produced by *Forbes* magazine for its 60th anniversary.

Understanding the Business World. For complete citation, *see* BUSINESS ENVIRONMENT.

FRINGE BENEFITS

595. American Valley
American Federation of Labor and Congress of Industrial Organizations   1979   16mm film   color   12 min
Rental: $5.00

Talks about the Trade Adjustment Assistance program that provides financial benefits for workers whose jobs have been destroyed or hours of work reduced and how they qualify for benefits under the Trade Act of 1974.

596. Benefits You Earn
National Audiovisual Center   16mm film or videocassette   color   16 min   instructor's print materials
Purchase: film $102.00; video $64.00   Rental: $12.50

Discusses health insurance, life insurance, injury insurance, leave, and retirement for government employment. Working for the US Series.

597. Cash on the Barrel Head
BNA Communications, Inc   1962   16mm film or videocassette   color
Purchase: $395.00   Rental: 5-day $150.00; 3-day $105.00   Preview: $35.00

Humorous dramatization of employee who insists on trading company fringe benefits for "cash on the barrel head." Illustrates the importance of company benefits package. Employee Orientation Series.

598. Check Your Paycheck
Chamber of Commerce of the United States   71 slides and audiocassette   13 min   instructor's print materials
Purchase: $25.00

For new employees, people preparing to enter the job market, or long-time employees. Gives idea of what's built into paychecks and the importance of employee productivity to maintain and expand benefits.

599. Flexible Compensation
Development Digest   audiocassette
Purchase: $13.75

Thomas Wood describes various approaches to flexible compensation. Outlines several supplements including health benefits, profit sharing, educational assistance, and survivor benefits. Points out the necessity of tailoring benefits for the individual. Discusses the theories of Maslow and Herzberg as they apply to management of compensation and benefits.

600. Social Security: Change and Exchange
National Audiovisual Center   1981   16mm film or videocassette   color   15 min
Purchase: film $130.00; video $55.00   Rental: $25.00

Uses format of call-in radio show to answer questions about social security. Provides insight about the system that is undergoing continuous evaluation and change.

601. You're Covered! Social Security Protection at Any Age
BNA Communications, Inc   1973   16mm film or videocassette   color   25 min   instructor's print materials
Purchase: $510.00   Rental: 5-day $150.00; 3-day $105.00   Preview: $35.00

Intended to orient employees to vital fringe benefits provided by the organization and the government.

GOALS AND GOAL SETTING

602. Decision Making: Values and Goals
Barr Films   16mm film or videocassette   color   17 min
Purchase: $415.00   Rental: $100.00   Preview: $50.00

Focuses on the first steps to good decision making showing the relationship of values to goals and decisions. Emphasizes the importance of goals congruent with values. Companion film to *Decision Making: Alternatives and Information* and *Decision Making: Outcomes and Action*.

603. Defining the Manager's Job
BNA Communications, Inc   1970   16mm film or videocassette   color   21 min
Purchase: $495.00   Rental: 5-day $150.00; 3-day $105.00   Preview: $35.00

Languages: English, Portuguese, Spanish
Dramatized "how to" portrayals of goal setting for managers. Emphasizes winning managers over to management by objectives, setting performance goals and controls, and eliciting suggestions for improvement and cooperation. British production. Companion film to *Performance and Potential Review*. Management by Objectives Series, no. 3.

604. Discover Your Hidden Talents
Classroom World Productions   4 audiocassettes
Purchase: $27.50

Emphasizes the importance of self-image, goal setting, and enthusiasm. Links creativity and problem solving.

605. Establishing Goals and Game Plans
BNA Communications, Inc   16mm film or videocassette   color   22 min   learner's print materials
Purchase: $630.00   Rental: 5-day $150.00; 3-day $105.00   Preview: $35.00

Dramatization illustrates a management team setting goals and developing a game plan. Uses an action research model. Shows how to monitor progress and make changes and adjustments. Increasing Productivity and Efficiency Program Series, no. 3.

606. Flower
International Film Bureau, Inc   16mm film   color   1½ min
Purchase: $65.00   Rental: $10.00   Preview: free

Animated film of a man's struggle to obtain a flower, i.e., goal. Meeting opener.

Getting Ahead: The Road to Self Development. For complete citation, *see* CAREER PLANNING AND DEVELOPMENT.

607. Getting Your Act Together: Goal Setting for Fun, Health and Profit
MOR Associates   16mm film or videocassette and audiocassettes   color   17 min   instructor's print materials; learner's print materials
Purchase: $495.00; audiocassettes $75.00   Rental: $125.00   Preview: $35.00

Focuses on the importance of the ability to set and achieve goals. Uses dramatizations to demonstrate a step-by-step process. Emphasizes the application of the goal setting approach to both professional and personal life. Features George Morrisey.

608. Goal Setting for Fun, Health, and Profit
Salenger Educational Media   1979   16mm film   17 min
Purchase: $495.00   Rental: $125.00   Preview: $35.00

Explains and illustrates a simple step-by-step process for setting and achieving goals: get agreement and commitments, reduce goals to "bite size," state the goals in terms of measurable results, and initiate an "action plan." Features George Morrisey who developed the model. He stresses that the ability to set and achieve goals is an essential personal and professional skill.

609. Heritage of the Uncommon Man
BNA Communications, Inc   1967   16mm film or videocassette   color   29 min
Purchase: $450.00   Rental: 5-day $150.00; 3-day $105.00   Preview: $35.00
Languages: English, Portuguese, Spanish

Joe Powell shows how uncommon people committed to uncommon goals have given us a legacy of achievement that can be tapped to unleash individual potential and achieve organization goals. Points out the value of a desire for excellence and pride of accomplishment that increases productivity. Joe Powell Films, no. 2.

610. How to Be a No-Limit Person
Nightingale-Conant Corporation   1981   6 audiocassettes   learner's print materials
Purchase: $62.50

Dr. Wayne Dyer presents a game plan for developing a purpose and pursuing it, turning aside setbacks and delays. Material is based on his book "The Sky's the Limit" and is taped from a public presentation. Addresses both personal and professional areas.

Life/Work Goals Exploration Workbook Kit. For complete citation, *see* CAREER PLANNING AND DEVELOPMENT.

611. Managing Priorities
Professional Resources   6 audiocassettes
Purchase: $90.00

Points out the power of goals and priorities for those with leadership responsibilities. Outlines how individual goals and organizational goals can be integrated. Includes how setting priorities assists a leader's management of time and pressure.

612. Psychling
CRM/McGraw-Hill Films   1981   16mm film or videocassette   color   25 min
Purchase: $495.00   Rental: $95.00   Preview: free

Shows how to set manageable goals, how to be realistic about personal expectations, and how to cope with that "crisis" point that can come at any time during a career. Chronicle of a cross-country bicycle trip made in record time.

613. Putting It All Together—Integrating Your Objectives
National Audiovisual Center   1973   16mm film or videocassette   color   22 min
Purchase: film $127.50; video $100.00

Demonstrates a top-down, deductive means of developing a hierarchy of objectives. Shows that a hierarchy is useful to relate objectives to the fundamental purpose of the school system. Putting It All Together Series.

Putting It All Together—It All Depends. For complete citation, *see* PLANNING.

614. Putting It All Together—Nature of Objectives
National Audiovisual Center   1973   16mm film or videocassette   color   14 min
Purchase: film $81.25; video $79.25

Presents the criteria for evaluating an objective. Emphasizes the problem of evaluating the validity of an objective and the problem of tying an objective to a specific position in the organization. Putting It All Together Series.

615. Setting Operational Goals and Objectives
CRM/McGraw-Hill Films   slides and audiocassettes   15 min   instructor's print materials; learner's print materials; transparencies
Purchase: $200.00   Preview: free

Shows managers how to clearly define realistic goals for employees and themselves. Emphasizes setting goals, gaining support and acceptance, planning techniques for monitoring performance, and giving feedback on performance in light of objectives. Management Productivity Series.

616. Take Aim—Goals for Success
Lee Boyan and Associates   1976   100 slides and audiocassette   instructor's print materials; learner's print materials
Purchase: $285.00   Rental: $25.00

Presents how teams set goals and make them work. Highlights techniques useful to teams and those that can improve individual goal-setting capability. Suggested for a 2–3 hour program for those who need practice in goal setting.

617. Women and MORe—Winning Techniques for Goal Setting
MOR Associates   2 audiocassettes   learner's print materials
Purchase: $35.00

Deals with special psychological factors women face in contributing to results using the MOR approach. Features Dru Scott and George Morrisey.

GOVERNMENT EMPLOYMENT

618. Factor Evaluation System for Position Classification
National Audiovisual Center   1976   75 slides and audiocassettes   12 min   instructor's print materials; learner's print materials; transparencies
Purchase: $50.00

Explains the Factor Evaluation System (FES) for all federal general schedule positions. Provides needed materials for supervisors, managers, professionals, and other employee groups.

619. Launching Civil Service Reform
National Audiovisual Center   1978   7 videocassettes   color   18–31 min ea   instructor's print materials
Purchase: $660.00 ($100.00 ea)

Offers an overview of the major changes affecting civil service regulations. Each covers a specific area of civil service reform such as merit pay, performance appraisal, and labor-management relations in the federal government. Designed primarily for federal managers, supervisors, and personnel specialists, this series is useful for any audience interested in the evolution of the civil service.

620. Orientation to Civil Service Reform—A Discussion of the Highlights
National Audiovisual
Center 1978 videocassette 31 min program guide
Purchase: $100.00

Follows the development and highlights of the reform bill from its signing by the president. Launching Civil Service Reform Series.

Remember My Name. For complete citation, *see* EMPLOYEE SELECTION AND PLACEMENT.

621. Road Ahead
National Audiovisual Center 1976 16mm film or videocassette color 17 min instructor's print materials
Purchase: film $108.25; video $64.00 Rental: $12.50

Describes federal government programs that respond to employees' performance and potential: merit promotion, upward mobility, incentive awards, within-grade increases, training and development opportunities, and performance requirements.

622. Working for the US
National Audiovisual Center 1976 16mm film or videocassette color 25 min instructor's print materials
Purchase: film $159.50; video $82.50 Rental: $12.50

Explains the executive branch and its relationship with other branches, the role of the federal employee in the political system, and the make-up, location, and nature of the activities of the federal workforce. Working for the US Series.

623. You and the Merit System
National Audiovisual Center 1978 16mm film or videocassette color 15 min instructor's print materials
Purchase: film $95.75; video $64.00 Rental: $12.50

Discusses federal merit principles, probationary period, career status, pay systems, classification systems, and equal opportunity. Working for the US Series.

624. Your Rights and Responsibilities
National Audiovisual Center 1976 16mm film or videocassette color instructor's print materials
Purchase: film $102.00; video $64.00 Rental: $12.50

Discusses federal employee conduct, grievance procedures, equal employment opportunity complaints, adverse actions, reduction in force, privacy, political activity, unions, and safety. Working for the US Series.

GRIEVANCE
See also ARBITRATION AND LABOR RELATIONS; NEGOTIATION

625. Anatomy of a Grievance
National Audiovisual Center 1974 16mm film or videocassette color 22 min instructor's print materials
Purchase: film $140.00; video $110.00 Rental: $25.00

Dramatized case of a union steward in the hospital who is disciplined for spending 40% of available time on union business. Based on an actual case, it focuses on the interpretation and application of a contract clause. Designed for use in public-sector labor/management relations training. Companion film to *Arbitration of a Grievance*.

Arbitration of a Grievance. For complete citation, *see* ARBITRATION AND LABOR RELATIONS.

Bill of Rights in Action: Equal Opportunity Series. For complete citation, *see* EQUAL EMPLOYMENT OPPORTUNITY.

626. Button, Button
National Audiovisual Center 1975 16mm film or videocassette color 29 min
Purchase: film $185.00; video $110.25 Rental: $25.00

One of the confrontations from *Scenes from the Workplace* is that of an employee given a disciplinary layoff for wearing a button supporting a tax increase bill. Dramatizes the treatment of a grievance up to second level procedures. Issue is unresolved at the end.

627. Case of Barbara Parsons
National Film Board of Canada 1979 16mm film or videocassette color 52 min
Purchase: film $695.00; video $615.00 Rental: $70.00 Preview: free

Dramatizes a typical situation in a unionized company—a violation of a contract between management and labor. Illustrates the 4 main steps to be followed in the grievance procedure.

628. Case of Insubordination
Roundtable Films, Inc 16mm film or videocassette color 20 min
Purchase: $425.00 Rental: $85.00 Preview: $30.00
Languages: English, French

One incident as perceived by 4 people: an employee, a supervisor, a witness, and an arbitrator. Essentially a simulation requiring active learner involvement in case about disciplinary and grievance procedures. Can also be used for perception, communication, or conflict resolution training.

629. Handling Health and Safety Grievances
NPL, Inc 16mm film 75 min
Purchase: $750.00 Rental: $75.00 Other cost factors: instructor's and learner's printed materials

Consists of 13 exercises and discusses the proper way to handle health and safety grievances. Addresses why they arise, how to deal with them, and working with procedures and rules. Emphasizes settling them at the earliest possible step. Suggested for 5 hours.

630. Scenes from the Workplace
National Audiovisual Center   1975   16mm film or videocassette   color   23 min
Purchase: film $146.75; video $110.25

Illustrates different grievances and how they are handled through 8 situations taking place in various types of public employment. Assists in developing understanding and skill for processing grievances. Teaches how to distinguish between complaints and grievances, identify the real grievances, and determine remedies.

631. Supervisor's Responsibility for Discovering and Adjusting Grievances
Continental Film Productions   slides or filmstrip and audiocassette   12 min
Purchase: filmstrip $105.00; slides $125.00

Pictures realistic conditions leading to grievances and what the supervisor can do to correct them. Supervisor Training Series.

Supervisor's Role in Preventing Grievances and Arbitration. For complete citation, *see* SUPERVISION.

632. Waldenville Jogger
National Audiovisual Center   1980   16mm film or videocassette   color   39 min
Purchase: film $267.25; video $75.00   Rental: $30.00

Portrays a grievance hearing between an employer and a union. Dramatization offers insight into the attitudes of each side and the preparation they made before meeting at the table. Open ending designed to prompt discussion. Shows how a grievance hearing is conducted and how an arbitrator referees the proceedings. Out of Conflict—Accord Series.

GROOMING

633. Good Grooming
National Audiovisual Center   1977   16mm film   28 min   learner's print materials
Purchase: $162.50   Rental: $12.50

Explores why well-groomed people are more likely to get jobs, keep jobs, and earn promotions. Uses vignettes, songs, and animation to offer tips on essential personal care skills that often spell success. You in Public Service Series.

634. Good Hygiene and Grooming Practices
National Educational Media, Inc   104 slides or filmstrip and audiocassette   11 min
Purchase: filmstrip $90.00–$95.00; slides $115.00

Teaches proper grooming and hygiene practices. Illustrates their importance to an employee's job performance and personal health. Stressing the role of good grooming in nonverbal communication, program encourages employees to take a personal interest in their outward appearance.

635. Personal Grooming and Hygiene
National Educational Media, Inc   1979   16mm film or super 8mm or videocassette   color   11 min   instructor's print materials; learner's print materials
Purchase: $330.00   Rental: 5-day $80.00; 3-day $70.00
Languages: English, French, Spanish

Illustrates the importance of proper personal hygiene to 5 working men and women. Detailed information on bathing, care of teeth, use of deodorants, perfumes, and cosmetics. Encourages employees to dress appropriately and to take a personal interest in their outward appearance. For all employees—men and women.

636. What Do We Look Like to Others
Barr Films   1973   16mm film or videocassette   color   11 min
Purchase: $190.00   Rental: $20.00   Preview: free

Reveals through 7 different office situations how important maintaining good personal appearance and attitudes are. Includes conduct and personal habits.

637. Your Personal Appearance
National Educational Media, Inc   1977   16mm film or super 8mm or videocassette   color   10 min   instructor's print materials; learner's print materials
Purchase: $320.00   Rental: 5-day $80.00; 3-day $70.00   Preview: free
Languages: English, Spanish, Japanese

Emphasizes that customers or business associates gain their impression of the company and the people with whom they will do business in the first seconds of contact. Includes how to dress appropriately for the time, place, and business at hand. Illustrates timeless principles of dress that are usable regardless of fashion or fad.

GROUP PROCESS
See also DECISION MAKING/PROBLEM SOLVING

Achieving Group Effectiveness. For complete citation, *see* TEAM BUILDING.

Decision-Making Process. For complete citation, *see* DECISION MAKING/PROBLEM SOLVING.

Employee Involvement: Issues and Concerns. For complete citation, *see* TEAM BUILDING.

638. Group Dynamics: GroupThink
CRM/McGraw-Hill Films   1973   16mm film or videocassette   color   22 min
Purchase: $425.00   Rental: $95.00   Preview: free

Portrays group decision making as it becomes groupthink, the process by which groups generate bad organizational decisions as the solidarity value takes precedence. Dr. Irving Janis highlights the symptoms of groupthink and points out how effective leadership can prevent such situations.

Group Leadership. For complete citation, *see* LEADERSHIP.

Managing in a Crisis. For complete citation, *see* DECISION MAKING/PROBLEM SOLVING.

Meeting in Progress. For complete citation, *see* MEETING MANAGEMENT.

Meeting Leading. For complete citation, *see* MEETING MANAGEMENT.

639. New Truck Dilemma
BNA Communications, Inc 1965 16mm film or videocassette color 23 min
Purchase: $435.00 Rental: 5-day $150.00; 3-day $105.00 Preview: $35.00
Languages: English, Spanish
Proposes using "group decision making" as the best way to involve people and get understanding and commitment for decisions. Norman R.F. Maier sets up a case situation in which managers can role play a problem of fairness and gain insight into the emotions, feelings, and attitudes that cause employees to accept or reject management decisions.

640. Team Building
CRM/McGraw-Hill Films 1983 16mm film or videocassette color 28 min instructor's print materials
Purchase: $595.00 Rental: $95.00 Preview: free
Identifies ways to work more effectively in groups responsible for making decisions and laying plans. Shows typical pitfalls common in group situations.

HANDICAPPED

641. Access America
National Audiovisual Center 1976 16mm film color 13 min
Purchase: $75.50
Good design solutions which provide handicapped access at minimal cost are depicted in a variety of settings. Enumerates difficulties of handicapped persons, particularly wheelchair bound, in maneuvering in their environment.

642. Learning about Disabled Co-Workers
National Audiovisual Center 1977 9 slide sets with 11 audiocassettes instructor's print materials; learner's print materials
Purchase: $275.00 Other cost factors: individual sets also priced separately
Designed to help prepare workers for the entry of a handicapped person into their work environment. The information presented in this series will help promote effective interaction among co-workers. Includes sound-slide sets on specific disabilities such as hearing impaired, mentally retarded, cerebral palsied, and physically handicapped.

643. Successful Supervision of Handicapped Employees
National Audiovisual Center 1977 328 color slides and 8 audiocassettes instructor's print materials; learner's print materials
Purchase: $80.25
Demonstrates supervisory practices and procedures that promote the efforts of selection and advancement of qualified handicapped individuals in the federal government and in private industry.

644. Walk Awhile...in My Shoes
National Film Board of Canada 1983 16mm film or videocassette color 27 min
Purchase: film $500.00; video $300.00 Rental: $100.0 Preview: $40.00
Looks at the world of mobility through the eyes of the disabled. Intended to sensitize the viewer to problems of the handicapped. Shows how the world is geared to the needs of the average person, not for the handicapped.

645. Working on Working
National Audiovisual Center 1979 16mm film or videocassette color 29 min
Purchase: film $250.00; video $65.00 Rental: $25.00
Urges acceptance of disabled employees for what they can do. Shows barriers faced by disabled: skeptical employers, reluctant teachers, and peers.

HEALTH

646. Addictions, Compulsions and Alternative Highs
Barr Films 16mm film or videocassette 23 min
Purchase: $490.00 Rental: 5-day $100.00 Preview: 2-day &50.00
Interviews explore a range of addictions and compulsions such as alcoholism, drug addiction, obesity, and compulsive gambling. Medical experts and former addicts are frank and revealing, pointing out that alternatives exist for such destructive habits. Useful in substance abuse and wellness training programs.

647. Ashes to Ashes
BNA Communications, Inc 1972 16mm film or videocassette color 24 min instructor's print materials
Purchase: $485.00 Rental: 5-day $130.00; 3-day $95.00 Preview: $30.00
Shows the impact of respiratory diseases on an organization's costs and an individual's health. Addresses practical means of dealing with colds, allergies, and emphysema. Strong focus on the importance of stopping smoking and how to do it. Project Health Series, no. 5.

648. Choice
Cally Curtis Company 16mm film or videocassette color 29 min meeting guide

Purchase: film $550.00; video $525.00   Rental: $130.00   Preview: $40.00

A comprehensive overview about health, self-fulfillment, and an individual's role in choice-making his/her own life. Key points are accept responsibility for one's own health, success, and happiness, and accept the fact that choice is possible.

649. Coping with Life on the Run
MTI Teleprograms, Inc   1977   16mm film   color   27 min
Purchase: $495.00   Rental: $100.00

Dr. George Sheehan explains why a good state of physical fitness is essential for coping with everyday challenges in business and industry. Emphasizes several key points in the development of a fitness program. Suggests that physical fitness leads to more productive performance in daily jobs and a higher level of self-confidence.

650. Dynamics of Fitness: The Body in Action
Ibis Media   240 slides and 3 audiocassettes   instructor's print materials

Defines fitness and reviews its 5 basic components: weight, strength, endurance, flexibility, and cardiovascular fitness. Examines roles of training and diet to good health.

651. Fat of the Land
BNA Communications, Inc   1972   16mm film or videocassette   color   26 min   instructor's print materials
Purchase: $475.00   Rental: 5-day $150.00; 3-day $105.00   Preview: $35.00

Understanding nutrition and learning how to eat right helps employees lose weight and keep it off.

652. For the Sake of Your Heart
Ibis Media   188 slides and 3 audiocassettes
Purchase: $215.00

Identifies 7 risk factors of heart disease. Reviews methods of heart disease prevention and treatment. Stresses the positive role of diet, exercise, and life-style habits.

653. Game Plan for Survival
MTI Teleprograms, Inc   1977   16mm film or videocassette   color   22 min
Purchase: film $435.00; video $395.00   Rental: $65.00   Preview: free

Dr. George Sheehan, Dr. Kenneth Cooper, and other physical fitness experts point out that fitness programs offer benefits such as improved productivity, reduced stress, reduction of lost-time days, lowered medical costs, and increased motivation and morale.

654. Gift of Energy
BNA Communications, Inc   1972   16mm film or videocassette   color   26 min   learner's print materials
Purchase: $475.00   Rental: 5-day $150.00; 3-day $105.00   Preview: $35.00

Focuses on the how and why of physical fitness. Shows physical fitness programs designed to fit every age and fitness category. Dr. Kenneth H. Cooper shows what aerobic exercises are and how they work on the body. Project Health Series, no. 3.

655. Health & Lifestyle: Positive Approaches to Well-Being
Spectrum Films   16mm film or videocassette   color   28 min
Purchase: $485.00   Rental: $65.00   Preview: $35.00

Guide to stress management, nutrition, weight control, exercise, and the psychology of dependence. Blends colorful images of real-world people and places with expert opinion and incisive host dialog.

656. Health Maintenance Organizations
National Audiovisual Center   1979   5 16mm films or videocassettes   color   12–28 min ea
Purchase: film $484.75; video $375.00   Rental: $125.00

An in-depth look at Health Maintenance Organizations (HMOs) and their current and potential impact. "A Closer Look" explores HMOs cost-effectiveness and the emphasis on health and preventive medicine. "Physicians Take a Second Look" cites advantages. "The Worker's View" offers advantages from the union point of view. "HMO's Mean Business" covers broad spectrum of implications from various perspectives. Hosted by Martin Agronsky.

657. Healthy Heart
BNA Communications, Inc   1972   16mm film or videocassette   color   27 min
Purchase: $525.00   Rental: 5-day $150.00; 3-day $105.00   Preview: $35.00

Advice of 7 distinguished physicians on what a heart attack is like and how blood pressure, smoking, and heredity contribute to heart attacks. Also gives a common-sense approach to exercise with advice on a prudent diet—measures to take to help prevent a heart attack. Project Health Series, no. 1.

658. Life Habits
American Hospital Association   126 slides and audiocassette or videocassette   color   17 min   instructor's print materials
Purchase: $100.00   Preview: $50.00

Intended to stimulate self-awareness of the importance (and difference) life habits make. Emphasizes the responsibility for health as well as information about the implications of various life style habits. For self or group study.

659. Medi$ense
Tylie Jones   16mm film or videocassette   color   20 min   instructor's print materials
Purchase: film $400.00; video $325.00   Rental: $100.00   Preview: $25.00

Documents the spiraling costs of health care. Indicates what individuals can do and outlines their responsibility. Intended to focus employee attention on the magnitude and complexity of health cost inflation.

660. Planning and Implementing a Personal Fitness Program
American Management Associations   6 audiocassettes   learner's print materials

Purchase: $145.00   Other cost factors: AMA members $135.00; discounts available for bulk orders of materials

Helps determine present fitness level and then designs a fitness program by incorporating exercise into a daily life-style. Includes getting the most from a program, evaluating exercise equipment, dealing with stress, and a sensible approach to nutrition and weight control.

661. Pressure Principle
BNA Communications, Inc   1972   16mm film or videocassette   color   25 min   instructor's print materials
Purchase: $525.00   Rental: 5-day $150.00; 3-day $105.00   Preview: $35.00

Reveals how the organizational structure creates or prevents many emotional problems. Explains human behavior patterns and why their success or failure may depend to a great extent on the type of job they hold. Identifies factors that create emotional problems. Project Health Series, no. 7.

662. What Is Your Health Hazard Risk?
Ibis Media   229 slides and 3 audiocassettes   learner's print materials
Purchase: $215.00

Uses quiz format to help viewers assess their current health in terms of fitness, nutrition, stress, and life-style. Suggests better health habits for physical and mental well-being.

663. When You Need Help: Understanding Your Own Mental Health
Ibis Media   240 slides and 3 audiocassettes   learner's print materials

Helps viewers distinguish between normal problems and serious mental illness. Provides approach to select right therapy and therapist. Discusses what to expect from therapeutic process.

664. Your Health, and Aging
Washington Film Company   1983   16mm film or videocassette   color   22 min
Purchase: film $595.00; video $545.00   Rental: $135.00   Preview: $40.00

Features a wellness approach to aging, explaining what happens to the body during the aging process and how to compensate for the changes, particularly the physiological aspects. Intended for use in preparing older employees for retirement.

HUMAN RELATIONS
See INTERPERSONAL RELATIONS

INFLATION
See also ECONOMIC CONDITIONS

665. Inflation
Phoenix Films, Inc   1975   16mm film or videocassette   color   54 min
Purchase: film $750.00; video $450.00   Rental: $65.00

Paul Samuelson describes the far-reaching consequences of inflation. Gives views of economists, corporate business politi-

cians, workers, and consumers. Provides the basic knowledge necessary to any attempt to control the inflationary spiral and revitalize the economy.

666. Inflation—On Prices and Wages and Running Amok
National Audiovisual Center   1973   16mm film or videocassette   color   18 min
Purchase: $104.50   Rental: $12.50

Explains what inflation is, how it affects us, and what can or cannot be done about it. Examines the price structures and forces which work to curb or temper the dangerous consequences of an uncontrolled inflationary spiral.

667. Inflation—One Company Fights the Battle
Phoenix Films, Inc   1975   16mm film or videocassette   color   14 min
Purchase: film $265.00; video $175.00   Rental: $25.00

Points out that whether the economic unit is a 2 billion dollar-a-year business, like Georgia Pacific Paper Company, or a modest household, like that of a Georgia Pacific employee and his family, everyone is caught up in the same alarming spirit of inflation. Narrated by Frank Reynolds.

668. What Is Inflation?
Phoenix Films, Inc   1975   16mm film or videocassette   color   13 min
Purchase: film $225.00; video $150.00   Rental: $25.00

Simple explanation of the various types of inflation beginning on the general level, with a definition of the classical model on inflation and the options open to government in dealing with it. Reconstructs the specific political, social, and natural factors which have given rise to the new economic phenomenon of "Stagflation."

INFORMATION SYSTEMS

669. Decision Making: Alternatives and Information
Barr Films   16mm film or videocassette   color   17 min
Purchase: $415.00   Rental: $100.00   Preview: $50.00

Describes how to expand alternatives and gather relevant information about each. Stresses the importance of then being open to new alternatives that evolve from the information assembled. Companion film to *Decision Making: Values and Goals*, and *Decision Making: Outcomes and Action*.

670. Gathering Good Information: "Get 'Em Up, Scout"
BNA Communications, Inc   1975   16mm film or videocassette   color   26 min   instructor's print materials
Purchase: $550.00   Rental: 5-day $150.00; 3-day $105.00   Preview: $35.00

Emphasizes bottom-line consequences of information and its costs, plus practical ways to use the idea, "Don't learn what you don't need." Dr. David K. Berlo discusses importance of information as a basis for decision making, informal leadership, authority and control vs. influence and status, and upward communication flow.

671. Goya Effect
Roundtable Films, Inc   16mm film or videocassette   color   24 min
Purchase: $400.00   Rental: $85.00   Preview: $30.00

Portrayal shows the need for a manager to retain personal knowledge of day-to-day problems and not rely solely on formal information systems. Demonstrates where to spend time for the most promising results yet remain aware of and sensitive to needs of employees. Intended for managers and supervisors.

672. Information Processing
CRM/McGraw-Hill Films   16mm film   color   29 min
Purchase: film $465.00; video $350.00   Rental: $45.00

Uses a cocktail party to illustrate the basic principles and ramifications of human information processing. Shows the methods which people use to receive, store, and then retrieve information as it is needed.

Information Processing and the Computer: A Survey. For complete citation, *see* COMPUTERS.

673. Legal Research
BNA Communications, Inc   1979   10 slide sets and audiocassettes   10–16 min ea
Purchase: $750.00 ($100.00 ea)

Teaches the use of legal materials—legal dictionaries and encyclopedias; legal periodicals and indexes; court reports; case digests; federal, state, and local legislation; and sources of administrative law and legislative history. Can be utilized by individuals for point-of-use instruction or in the classroom for group viewing.

Management by Exception. For complete citation, *see* MANAGEMENT.

674. "Mixed Model" Strategy for Changing Medical Centers
Development Digest   audiocassette
Purchase: $13.75

The way a medical center is organized helps determine the relative effectiveness in research, education, patient care, and administration. Martin Weisbord describes an approach used to measure the differences among medical centers and how they use information.

Out of Work. For complete citation, *see* INTERVIEWING.

Protection of Proprietary Information. For complete citation, *see* SECURITY.

INSTRUCTION AND INSTRUCTIONAL METHODS
See also TRAINING AND DEVELOPMENT

675. Class of Your Own
BNA Communications, Inc   16mm film   color   26 min
Purchase: $485.00   Rental: 5-day $150.00; 3-day $105.00   Preview: $35.00

Practical demonstration of effective teaching techniques. Shows preparing the lesson, using the question and answer technique, arranging teaching steps in logical sequence, using the chalk board, and making on-the-spot revisions as well as using time properly. Methods are illustrated in the classroom and on the job.

Coaching for Results. For complete citation, *see* TRAINING AND DEVELOPMENT.

676. Conducting Human Relations Workshops
Affective House   1977   6 audiocassettes
Purchase: $69.50

Covers 5 major human relations subject areas: trust, values clarification, self-awareness, self-defeating behavior, and life planning. Each presents theory background and sequenced exercises. Gives guidelines on how to introduce and process the exercises. Intended for the trainer.

677. Development and Management of Instructional Systems
Aerospace Education Foundation   1976   4 videocassettes   varying lengths   instructor's print materials; learner's print materials
Purchase: $949.25

Intended to bring to supervisors and managers the current concepts and philosophies in instructional systems development and management. Includes planning instructional systems, development, administration, and evaluation. Recommended as a 40-hour program.

Development of a Slide-Tape Instructional Presentation. For complete citation, *see* AUDIOVISUAL PRODUCTION.

Don't Just Tell Them...Show Them. For complete citation, *see* AUDIOVISUAL TECHNIQUES.

678. Dynamic Classroom
Resources for Education and Management, Inc   5 filmstrips or slides and audiocassettes or videocassettes or filmstrip cartridges   12–14 min ea   instructor's print materials
Purchase: video $305.00 ($75.00 ea); filmstrips $280.00 ($64.00 ea); filmstrip cartridges $425.00 ($85.00 ea); slides $295.00 ($67.00 ea)   Rental: $20.00

Describes participative classroom techniques in terms of strengths and weaknesses. Gives instructions on designing learning exercises, covering traditional and contemporary methods. Includes modules on learner-controlled instruction, case studies and the incident process, simulation through role playing, management and business games, and in-baskets and action mazes. Companion to *Elements of Effective Teaching* but includes more advanced techniques.

679. Elements of Effective Teaching
Resources for Education and Management, Inc   5 filmstrips or slides and audiocassettes or videocassettes or filmstrip cartridges   10–19 min ea   instructor's print materials
Purchase: video $305.00 ($75.00 ea); filmstrips $280.00 ($64.00 ea); filmstrip cartridges $425.00 ($85.00 ea); slides $295.00 ($67.00 ea)   Preview: $20.00

Focuses on classroom techniques. Modules include setting up classroom arrangements, planning classroom time, using visual aids and teaching materials, and handling problems.

680. ERIC: It's that Easy
National Audiovisual Center   1978   videocassette color   15 min
Purchase: $55.00

The Educational Resources Information Center (ERIC) encompasses a network of decentralized clearinghouses for educational literature and research. Describes ERIC, its various resources, and its application for research efforts. ERIC provides descriptions of exemplary programs, reports of research and development efforts, documents, and related materials useful in the design of more effective programs.

681. Evaluating Instructional Materials
Association for Educational Communications and Technology   1981   filmstrip and audiocassette   color   10 min
Purchase: $25.95

Suggests processes that lead to the best selection of AV materials. Provides set of criteria for previewing and suggests how to make cost effective decisions.

Good Beginning. For complete citation, *see* ORIENTATION.

Good Start. For complete citation, *see* ORIENTATION.

682. How to Teach Grown-Ups
Practical Management Associates, Inc   12 audiocassettes   instructor's print materials; learner's print materials
Purchase: $175.00; $250.00 for 3 learners

Focuses on how adult learners are different and how to use participative and experiential methods. Covers lesson planning and objectives, instructional aids, one-to-one instruction, and testing. Approach advocated is learner-centered. Intended for trainers and instructors of adult groups. Suggested for 8 sessions of 3-4 hours each.

683. Journey into Self
Learning Resources Corporation   16mm film   b/w 47 min
Purchase: $375.00   Rental: $85.00

Documentary of an intensive basic encounter group led by Carl Rogers and Richard Farson. Intended for those interested in encounter group phenomena and those who merely want to understand themselves and others better.

Malcolm Knowles—In an In-Depth Interview with Steve Becker. For complete citation, *see* TRAINING AND DEVELOPMENT.

684. Pattern for Instruction
Roundtable Films, Inc   1960   16mm film or videocassette   color   21 min
Purchase: $525.00   Rental: $100.00   Preview: $30.00
Languages: Danish, Dutch, English, French, Spanish, Swedish

Illustrates a 4-step instruction method: prepare, present, try-out, and follow-up. Relates the essentials of learning to the basics of instructing. Creates an understanding of the learning process and shows what motivates people to learn. Intended for supervisors and trainers.

685. Producing Better Learning
Resources for Education and Management, Inc   3 videocassettes or slides and audiocassettes or filmstrips or filmstrip cartridges   color   6 min ea instructor's print materials
Purchase: video $158.00 ($65.00 ea); filmstrips $110.00 ($45.00 ea); filmstrip cartridges $210.00 ($75.00 ea); slides $125.00 ($48.00 ea)

Provides a short course in fundamental teaching theory and practice. Modules include learner centered approach, keys to produce better learning (feedback, involvement, and accountability), and techniques for integrating these keys into the learning situation.

686. Programmed Learning
BNA Communications, Inc   16mm film or videocassette   color   33 min   instructor's print materials; transparencies
Purchase: $550.00   Rental: 5-day $150.00; 3-day $105.00   Preview: $35.00

Presents the philosophy, practicalities, and some of the hardware of a system that introduces a learning package through which individuals work at their own pace making responses to various stimuli until they can show what they have learned. Offers benefits of individual approach quality control because it shows what students are learning and makes better use of staff and better allocation of time to the needs of the individual.

687. Psychology of Learning
Learning Consultants, Inc   audiocassette   50 min
Purchase: $15.95

Identifies the factors that inhibit and those that enhance the learning process in school-based learning and in adult and lifelong learning. Emphasizes the importance of feedback.

688. Reality Practice: Theory and Skills of Role Playing Methods
Development Publications   6 audiocassettes learner's print materials
Purchase: $70.00   Other cost factors: nonprofit organizations $60.00

Instructs how to set up and lead role-playing activities in all kinds of training programs. Designed by Ronald Lippitt, Peggy Lippitt, and George Sproule.

689. Relating Learning Theory to Behavior Change in Organizations
Development Digest   audiocassette
Purchase: $13.75

Describes stimulus-response, cognitive, and social-emotional learning theories. Analyzes their relevance to changing individual behavior in organizations, stressing the popular aspects of each. Discusses the significance of "learning how to learn" at the organizational level.

690. Robert Mager: An In-Depth Interview with Steve Becker
Learncom, Inc   1979   6 audiocassettes
Purchase: $180.00

Robert Mager pioneered many instructional technology techniques and procedures that have become standard practice among trainers. Interview explores the design, development, and implementation of instruction as well as his innovative ideas on high quality instruction.

691. "Session I"
EFM Films   16mm film or videocassette   color   11 min   instructor's print materials; posters
Purchase: $395.00   Rental: $120.00   Preview: $40.00

Modifies schoolroom ideas employees bring to training programs by showing them that they can't get full benefit from an adult learning situation if they use adolescent learning skills. Gives trainees a clear understanding of what their challenges are in a training situation and gives them the tools they need to make training pay off.

692. Techniques for Teaching Consultants and the Organizational Aspects of "Psychological Climate"
Development Digest   audiocassette
Purchase: $13.75

Describes and demonstrates a training procedure for personnel people and for consultants.

Train the Trainer. For complete citation, *see* TRAINING AND DEVELOPMENT.

693. Training in Autonomy and Initiative
Development Digest   audiocassette
Purchase: $13.75

Describes a laboratory approach to training in autonomy and the taking of initiative. Roger Harrison discusses the way the experience is structured and conducted, the results it achieves, and the circumstances under which it will improve upon or detract from a program.

You Can Surpass Yourself. For complete citation, *see* TRAINING AND DEVELOPMENT.

You'll Soon Get the Hang of It. For complete citation, *see* TRAINING AND DEVELOPMENT.

INTERNATIONAL BUSINESS

694. Adventures in the China Trade
National Audiovisual Center   1981   16mm film or videocassette   color   28 min
Purchase: film $240.00; video $105.00   Rental: $50.00

Introduces the unique economic, political, and social history of China, its new economic thrust for self-sufficiency, the specific products and services sought, and common mistakes and misperceptions that can impede business negotiations. Offers commentary from economic advisors and corporate executives who know business with China firsthand.

695. China Trader
AMACOM   12 audiocassettes   12 hrs   booklet
Purchase: $300.00   Other cost factors: AMA members: $255.00

Presents potential, challenges, opportunities, and politics of commercial exchange with China. Julian Sobin interviews 25 experienced "China Hands" who share their strategies, insights, and mistakes.

696. Doing Business in China
National Audiovisual Center   1979   16mm film or videocassette   color   45 min
Purchase: film $287.00; video $148.00   Rental: $35.00   Preview: $35.00

Juanita Kreps introduces a roundtable discussion moderated by William Clarke, director of the China Division, with 3 American businesspeople who have been doing business in China. Through their experiences one gets a feel for what this marketing venture might mean to a business.

697. E Is for Export
National Audiovisual Center   1978   16mm film or videocassette   color   16 min
Purchase: film $102.00; video $88.00   Rental: $25.00

Shows how a small manufacturer can get into exporting through the experiences of a typical small company. Describes steps to successful entry. Export Development Series.

698. Export Opportunity
National Audiovisual Center   1978   16mm film or videocassette   color   16 min
Purchase: film $102.00; video $88.00   Rental: $25.00

Designed to motivate small firms with marketable products to consider exporting. Uses 3 small manufacturers to illustrate how similar firms can successfully export. Export Development Series.

Focus on Results. For complete citation, *see* MANAGEMENT.

699. Information Please—Getting the Facts on Foreign Markets
National Audiovisual Center   1979   16mm film or videocassette   color   14 min
Purchase: film $89.25; video $88.00

Shows how marketing information published by the Commerce Department is gathered, evaluated, and ultimately used. Helpful to those planning a sound exporting strategy.

700. Leiden Connection
National Audiovisual Center   1978   16mm film or videocassette   color   20 min
Purchase: film $127.00; video $88.00   Rental: $25.00

Shows how a computer matching service brings together American sellers and foreign buyers and helps 4 small businesses to streamline their exporting efforts.

Made in Japan. For complete citation, *see* MANAGEMENT.

701. Multinational Corporation
BNA Communications, Inc   1971   16mm film or videocassette   color   32 min
Purchase: $385.00   Rental: 5-day $150.00; 3-day $105.00   Preview: $35.00

Discusses the nature and future potential of multinational corporations. Explores management strategies for multinational business operations and examines how the development of multinational business structures is likely to proceed in the future. Managing Discontinuity Series, no. 7.

702. Showroom to the World
National Audiovisual Center   1978   16mm film or videocassette   color   6 min
Purchase: $38.25   Rental: $25.00   Preview: $25.00

Explains what a US Trade Center is and what it does. These centers offer American businesses a place to exhibit their products in coordinated marketing expositions. Gives a look at these centers in New York, Paris, and Stockholm. Describes how one company has success in utilizing this marketing service. Export Development Series.

703. Two Factories
LCA Video/Films   16mm film or videocassette   color   22 min   learner's print materials
Purchase: $375.00   Rental: $70.00   Preview: $30.00

Explores the American view of one's job as a means to an end vs. the Japanese view of the job being an extension of personal life. Encourages productivity, changes in attitudes, increased management-labor communication, and quality control. Intended to stimulate both managers and employees on all levels to examine the issues.

704. Yen for Harmony: Japanese Managers Try Their Style in North America
Document Associates   1976   16mm film or videocassette   color   26 min
Purchase: $400.00   Rental: $45.00

Investigates the aspects of Japanese management which affect productivity in organizations. Participatory management, consensus decision making, and lifetime employment are basics of the Japanese system. An inside look at the Panasonic Plant in Japan shows the system in action. Looks at the pros and cons of Western application in sequences with YKK Zipper and Japan Airlines.

INTERPERSONAL RELATIONS
See also CUSTOMER RELATIONS

705. Advanced TASC—Higher Levels in Transactional Analysis
Instructional Dynamics, Inc   audiocassette   learner's print materials
Purchase: $49.50

Focuses on transactional analysis (TA) in educational, clinical, or industrial settings. For laypeople or practitioners who have gone through TASC or introductory courses in TA. Designed for groups of 6 to 15; booklets are reusable. About 6 hours.

706. As Others See Us
Salenger Educational Media   1980   16mm film or videocassette   color   10 min   instructor's print materials
Purchase: $410.00   Rental: $125.00

Animated film illustrates the concept of the Johari Window to address problems managers face when their self-image differs from images others have of them. Intends to show how interpersonal relationships improve when self-image and images held by others are in closer harmony. Includes Johari graphic.

707. Behaviour Game
International Film Bureau, Inc   16mm film or videocassette   color   8 min
Purchase: $175.00   Rental: 5-day $25.00; 3-day $18.75   Preview: free

British production uses humor to illustrate the contagious nature of both positive and negative behavior when working with others. Shows that we constantly use behavior as a basis for judging others.

708. Business Courtesy
National Educational Media, Inc   16mm film or videocassette   color   12 min
Purchase: $399.00   Rental: 5-day $100; 3-day $90.00

Shows both incorrect and correct approaches to business courtesy in vignettes from business, retail, and service settings. Emphasizes the importance of punctuality, patient listening, and useful phrases.

709. Communicating Empathy
University Associates   1980   2 audiocassettes   learner's print materials
Purchase: $44.95

Accurate empathic understanding is an interpersonal skill associated with perception, communication, and sensitivity to the feelings and experience of others. Intended to develop empathic communication skills.

710. Coping Effectively with Difficult People
Lansford Publishing Company, Inc   6 audiocassettes   learner's print materials
Purchase: $149.95

Outlines methods for coping with 7 specific types of difficult behavior: indecisive, unresponsive, over-agreeable, hostile-aggressive, complaining, "all-knowing," and negativistic. Emphasis is on coping with rather than changing such people.

Dealing with the Unexpected. For complete citation, *see* COMMUNICATION.

711. Effective Interpersonal Relationships
University Associates   4 audiocassettes   instructor's print materials
Purchase: $54.95

Ten-session learning program provides an educational experience for people who want to further their personal growth. Formerly *Encountertapes for Personal Growth Groups.*

712. Employee and Team Development
University Associates   1976   4 audiocassettes instructor's print materials
Purchase: $54.95

Focuses on basic interpersonal skills required in the work environment: self-expression, active listening, ownership of feelings, problem solving, decision making, and feedback. Formerly *Encountertapes for Employee and Team Development.*

Employee Motivation: The Role of the Supervisor. For complete citation, *see* MOTIVATION.

Energy Carol. For complete citation, *see* CHANGE.

Face-to-Face Payoff: Dynamics of the Interview. For complete citation, *see* INTERVIEWING.

713. Farewell to Birdie McKeever
BNA Communications, Inc   16mm film   b/w   26 min
Purchase: $250.00   Rental: 5-day $130.00; 3-day $105.00   Preview: $35.00

Light treatment makes many striking points about human relations, perception, and feedback. Useful to study topics such as selling, communicating negative information, and utilization of personnel. Meeting opener.

Good Morning, Mister Roberts. For complete citation, *see* SUPERVISION.

Helping: A Growing Dimension of Management. For complete citation, *see* COUNSELING.

714. Inner Man Steps Out
Didactic Systems, Inc   16mm film or videocassette   b/w   35 min   instructor's print materials
Purchase: $150.00   Rental: $35.00   Preview: $15.00

Portrayal of a supervisor who has trouble getting along with others and himself. Animation shows how "inner selves" exist within everyone, representing their need for security and importance. Intended to deepen self-awareness and understanding.

Interpersonal Communication. For complete citation, *see* COMMUNICATION.

Intrapersonal Communication. For complete citation, *see* COMMUNICATION.

715. Johari Teleo-Vue
Teleometrics International   1978   60 slides and audiocassette   30 min   instructor's print materials
Purchase: $150.00   Preview: $15.00

Presents a step-by-step overview of the Johari model of interpersonal processes. Offers an analysis of interpersonal styles and suggests designs for behavioral change. Useful for group or individual study.

716. Managing Your Strengths
General Motors Corporation   videocassette instructor's print materials
Purchase: $500.00

Focuses on understanding relationships between self and others better and relating awareness of self, others, and job in a managerial role. Designed for line and staff managers who supervise other managers. Suggested to be used in conjunction with Elias H. Porter's personal strength assessment system.

717. On the Job
Thompson-Mitchell and Associates   1974   20 audiocassettes   instructor's print materials; learner's print materials
Purchase: $249.00

Identifies the interpersonal skills needed by young people to handle the situations that research has shown cause the most trouble in the first 30 to 90 days on the job. Covers troublesome areas that can lead to misunderstanding, conflict, quitting, or being fired. Includes 6 discussion tapes with a total of 18 critical-incident dramatizations. World of Work Series.

718. Person-to-Person Relationships
National Audiovisual Center   1977   16mm film   color   28 min   workbook
Purchase: $162.00   Rental: $12.50

Explores skills and attitudes that aid people in getting along well with others in one-to-one situations. You in Public Service Series.

719. Personnel Relations in Management
S&L Communications, Inc   1981   videocassette   color   27 min
Purchase: $90.00   Rental: $40.00   Other cost factors: SLCI members $60.00 (rental $30.00); personal relations survey instruments $4.00 ea

Explains a useful model of interpersonal relations called the Johari Window. Lecture by Maitland Huffman describes the use of the personnel relations survey that gives scores indicating one's personal style of communication.

Spinnolio. For complete citation, *see* ASSERTIVENESS.

Supervisor and Interpersonal Relations. For complete citation, *see* SUPERVISION.

720. Supervisor Training in Human Relations
American Learning Systems, Inc   8 filmstrips and audiocassettes or slides and audiocassettes or filmstrip cartridges or videocassettes   instructor's print materials; learner's print materials

Purchase: video $1,200.00; filmstrip $795.00; slides $1,000.00 Rental: $250.00 Preview: free

Discusses the role of supervisors and their responsibilities in the field of human relations as a representative of both management and employees. Shows how supervisors can use policies to work for them as effective human relations tools. Addresses specifics such as employee induction and training, grievances, discipline, placement, and cooperation.

Supervisor's Job. For complete citation, *see* SUPERVISION.

Taking Charge—The Manager Film. For complete citation, *see* SUPERVISION.

Transactional Analysis: A Tool for More Effective Interpersonal Relationships. For complete citation, *see* TRANSACTIONAL ANALYSIS.

What You Are Is... For complete citation, *see* COMMUNICATION.

What You Are Is Where You Were When. For complete citation, *see* COMMUNICATION.

721. What You Are Isn't Necessarily What You Will Be...
Twentieth Century-Fox Video, Inc 1977 16mm film or videocassette color 60 min instructor's print materials; book
Purchase: film $925.00; video $500.00 Rental: film $200.00; video $160.00 Preview: film $75.00; video $50.00

Describes how significant emotional events can change our behavioral patterns. Compares generations—the traditionalists and rejectionists—by contrasting their definitions of success and approaches to solving problems. Presentation by Morris Massey. Companion film to *What You Are Is What You Were When.*

722. When You're Smilin'
LCA Video/Films 1983 16mm film or videocassette 6 min instructor's print materials
Purchase: $250.00 Rental: $50.00 Preview: $25.00

Underscores the value of a positive outlook for employees at all levels, particularly those with public and customer contact. Points out that smiling is good for personal and business health.

723. Who Did What to Whom? —II
Research Press 16mm film or videocassette color 20 min instructor's print materials
Purchase: $325.00 Rental: $50.00

Focuses on the practical importance of good interpersonal relations. Offers basic principles of human behavior and practice in recognizing and correcting applications of these principles in work situations. Features Robert F. Mager. Based on 1972 classic training film also produced by Robert F. Mager.

724. Winning
Learning Dynamics 12 audiocassettes 30 min ea learner's print materials
Purchase: $126.00

Practical approach to understanding one's self, building rewarding relationships and developing one's human potential. Focuses on the dynamic personality systems, life scripts, manipulative games, and transactional analysis—as well as how to deal with problem personalities. Offers ways to use these skills in dealing with conflict, social control, competition, and rapid change.

725. "Working Together"
LCA Video/Films 1982 16mm film or videocassette color 15 min instructor's print materials; learner's print materials
Purchase: $350.00 Rental: $100.00 Preview: $50.00

Dramatizes 5 familiar office situations that are targets for good-natured gags. Humorous but practical approach. Australian production. Funny Business Series.

INTERVIEWING
See also COUNSELING

726. Appraisal & Career Counseling Interviews
AMACOM audiocassette 45 min instructor's print materials
Purchase: $30.00 Other cost factors: AMA members $25.50

A problem-solving approach to performance evaluation. Don Faber offers narration and dramatizations focused on job effectiveness, linking company goals and career goals, periodic check-ups, and new career directions. Emphasizes techniques of assessing employee talents. Productive Interviewing Series.

Appraising Performance: An Interview Skills Course. For complete citation, *see* PERFORMANCE APPRAISAL.

727. Art of Interviewing
Lansford Publishing Company, Inc 4 audiocassettes instructor's print materials
Purchase: $119.95

Lectures describe interviewing principles and techniques essential for information-gathering, appraisal, discipline, counseling, employment, and persuasive interviews. Covers interview structure, openings and closings, and questioning techniques.

Conducting Lawful Interviews: Guidelines for Non-Discriminatory Hiring Practices. For complete citation, *see* EQUAL EMPLOYMENT OPPORTUNITY.

Counsel Interview. For complete citation, *see* COUNSELING.

Discipline Interview. For complete citation, *see* DISCIPLINE.

728. Dynamics of Job Interviewing
Instructional Dynamics, Inc　8 audiocassettes　4½ hrs　guide
Purchase: $69.95 (series I $19.95; series II $34.95; series III $19.95)

Designed to give a job seeker knowledge about the job interview, information to help project "saleable" skills, and real-life examples of techniques on how to handle fear. Series I: "Reducing Stage Fright in the Interview." Series II: "The Face to Face Encounter." Series III: "Confessions of Interviewers."

729. Effective Interviewing Skills
Training by Design　4 audiocassettes　learner's print materials
Purchase: $95.00

Broadly focused on basics of interviewing such as setting objectives, using nondirect questioning techniques, analyzing information gaps, setting a positive climate, and communicating effectively. Brings out control and legal considerations for the interviewer.

730. Employment Interview
R. Fischer Olson & Associates, Inc　1978 videocassette　60 min　instructor's print materials; learner's print materials
Purchase: $1,000.00 (for 10 learners)　Preview: $95.00

Major focus is on the skills of interviewing—in particular, selection. Shows how to prepare for the interview, avoid traps, and ask questions to ease communication.

731. Exit Interview
AMACOM　audiocassette　45 min　learner's print materials
Purchase: $30.00　Other cost factors: AMA members $25.50

Major focus is on how to make exit interviews productive and to pinpoint reasons valuable people leave. John R. Hinrichs uses dramatizations to illustrate the interview.

732. Face-to-Face Payoff: Dynamics of the Interview
Creative Media　1975　16mm film or videocassette　color　28 min
Purchase: $475.00　Rental: $90.00　Preview: $30.00

Practical help in developing interviewing and interpersonal skills. Vignettes illustrate problem situations then show the correct way to deal with the problem. Features Joe Batten. Related case study in *Is It All Over—The Termination Interview.*

Fair Warning. For complete citation, *see* DISCIPLINE.

733. Getting a Job
Thompson-Mitchell and Associates　1974　12 audiocassettes　instructor's print materials; learner's print materials
Purchase: $149.00

Outlines the skills needed for job interviewing and filling out application forms. Explains how to contact job interviewers and agencies, make a good impression, and handle difficult ques-

tions. Includes 3 discussion tapes with a total of 9 critical-incident dramatizations. World of Work Series.

Hiring High Performers. For complete citation, *see* EMPLOYEE SELECTION AND PLACEMENT.

734. How to Interview Effectively
American Management Associations　6 audiocassettes　learner's print materials
Purchase: $145.00　Other cost factors: AMA members $135.00; discounts available for bulk orders of materials

Covers role of interviewing and includes the process and psychology of interviewing, the responsibilities of the interviewer, and the 4 basic types of interviews: appraisal, discipline, employment, and exit. Case study interviews are given to practice new techniques.

How's It Going? For complete citation, *see* PERFORMANCE APPRAISAL.

I'd Like a Word with You. For complete citation, *see* DISCIPLINE.

735. I'd Rather Not Say
Roundtable Films, Inc　1971　16mm film or videocassette　color　30 min
Purchase: $450.00　Rental: $85.00　Preview: $30.00

Highlights the fact that managers largely depend on what people are willing to tell them as a basis for decisions. Applies Kurt Lewin's Force Field Analysis to the interviewing situation and shows how forces that restrain open communication can be removed so information essential to decision making may be obtained. Provides techniques for upgrading the quality and quantity of information obtained verbally from other people.

Information Interview. For complete citation, *see* COMMUNICATION.

Interview. For complete citation, *see* EQUAL EMPLOYMENT OPPORTUNITY.

736. Interview Film
Barr Films　1977　16mm film or videocassette　color　21 min
Purchase: $430.00　Rental: $100.00　Preview: $25.00

Trains interviewers to select the best prospects for job openings in an organization. Shows how to screen employment applications and link a potential employee's skills, experience, educational background, attitudes, and personal appearance to the requirements of the available job.

737. Interviewing Skills
National Audiovisual Center　1977　16mm film or videocassette　color　28 min　learner's print materials
Purchase: $162.50　Rental: $12.50

Discusses how to obtain the right information at the right time. Encourages interviewer to know where to start and how to ask questions. Animated. You in Public Service Series.

738. Interviewing Skills and Techniques for Management
AMR International, Inc   6 audiocassettes   learner's print materials
Purchase: $295.00   Other cost factors: extra workbooks $25.00

Provides a range of techniques and guidelines to consider before, during, and after the conducting of an interview. Indicates what not to do and highlights what to do and how to do it. Covers the range of interviewing situations that confront managers. Includes discussions and portrayals to show typical interview situations.

739. Interviewing Skills
Resources for Education and Management, Inc   6 audiocassettes   11–14 min ea   instructor's print materials
Purchase: $75.00   Preview: $10.00

Dramatized interviews include mix of strong and weak points to illustrate general principles and techniques. Gives stop signals to encourage discussion points.

740. Interviewing Skills
Resources for Education and Management, Inc 1979   6 filmstrips or slides and audiocassettes or videocassettes or filmstrip cartridges   7–9 min ea instructor's print materials
Purchase: video $320.00 ($70.00 ea); filmstrips $295.00 ($58.00 ea); filmstrip cartridges $510.00 ($85.00 ea); slides $310.00 ($60.00 ea)

Presents the basic principles and skills to apply to 5 types of interviews: employment, counseling, disciplinary, appraisal, and exit. Initial module outlines general principles and effective procedures. Designed for new or prospective supervisors and managers.

741. Interviewing: The Key to Better Employees
Continental Film Productions 1979   slides or filmstrip and audiocassette   17 min   instructor's print materials; learner's print materials
Purchase: filmstrip $75.00; slides $95.00

Presents how to prepare and conduct interviews and how to evaluate job applications and applicant skills, capabilities, and attitudes. Offers guidelines regarding hiring practices. Uses dramatization. Intended for managers.

Is It All Over—The Termination Interview. For complete citation, *see* DISMISSAL.

742. Job Interview Pro Bowl
Centron Films   16mm film   color   19½ min
Purchase: $420.00

The job interview is treated as a spectator sport, complete with play-by-play commentary by 2 sportscasters. Shows the development of the interview from both the point of view of the applicant and the interviewer. Applicant explains how she prepared and what she expects to accomplish. Company representative describes what he will be watching for and details the specific skills and traits upon which job applicants are rated.

743. Man Hunt
Xicom-Video Arts 1974   16mm film or videocassette   color   31 min

Purchase: $625.00   Rental: $100.00   Preview: $35.00

Illustrates the major faults managers make in selection interviews. Shows how important it is to prepare, to draw the candidate out, and to ask direct, probing questions. Features John Cleese.

744. Management Guide to Successful Recruiting and Interviewing
Science Research Associates 1980   2 audiocassettes   2 hrs   instructor's print materials; learner's print materials; transparencies
Purchase: seminar format $430.00; self-study format $95.00

Illustrates how to develop a realistic job analysis, use recruiting sources, review applicant responses, conduct an effective interview, and notify candidates when final selection is made. Gives special attention to questioning techniques and recruiting with nondiscriminatory selection techniques. Offered in seminar format for groups of 10 and as self-study for individuals.

745. Matchmaking
Andragogy Press 1981 audiocassette   instructor's print materials; learner's print materials; transparencies
Purchase: $385.00

Regards the interview process as a 2-party exchange in which both parties need to get useful information in order to make a good long-term relationship. Suggests strategies that establish a climate which encourages an open and honest exchange of information. Does not explore EEO issues, the skill of updating job descriptions, or the skill of screening applications. Useful for those who counsel problem employees, guide career development, or appraise worker performance.

746. McGraw-Hill Course in Effective Interviewing
CRM/McGraw-Hill Films 1973 audiocassette   45 min   learner's print materials; book
Purchase: $42.50

Illustrates the effective use of today's best recommended interviewing techniques. Dramatizes with real-life situations not only the mechanics involved but the even more important task of interpreting results of the interview. Includes R. Fear's book *The Evaluation Interview*.

747. Out of Work
Manpower Education Institute 1975   10 videocassettes   color   29 min ea
Purchase: $1,000.00   Rental: $250.00

Intended to help people cope with the crisis of unemployment. Based on the premise that the solution to the problem of unemployment lies in a mix of activity of government agencies, business, membership organizations, and individuals. What is essential is that the person facing the problems of unemployment has access to information. Features dramatization and interviews.

Performance Appraisal Interview. For complete citation, *see* PERFORMANCE APPRAISAL.

Plant Shutdown. For complete citation, *see* CONFLICT AND CONFLICT MANAGEMENT.

748. Plug Us In
Manpower Education Institute   16mm film or videocassette   color   20 min
Purchase: $450.00   Rental: $75.00   Preview: $50.00

Depicts interviews and then shows how they could be improved. Presents job interview encounters faced by older workers. Prepares older job seekers to be assertive, self-confident, and to project a positive image. Explores the classic problems faced in job interviews and prepares interviewees to diplomatically deal with the myths about older workers.

Problem—Employee Interview. For complete citation, *see* DISCIPLINE.

Select the Best. For complete citation, *see* EMPLOYEE SELECTION AND PLACEMENT.

749. Selection Interview
AMACOM   audiocassette   60 min   learner's print materials
Purchase: $30.00   Other cost factors: AMA members $25.50

Provides a guide to interviewing potential employees. Excerpts from 5 diverse selection interviews and an illustrated guide for employment specialists and line managers. Shows how to spot and hire people who will stay and deliver top performance. Features Raymond Valentine. Productive Interviewing Series.

Selection Interview: Hiring without Regrets. For complete citation, *see* EMPLOYEE SELECTION AND PLACEMENT.

Selection Interviewing. For complete citation, *see* EMPLOYEE SELECTION AND PLACEMENT.

750. Selection Interviewing Program
Drake Beam Morin   1976   6 audiocassettes instructor's print materials; learner's print materials
Purchase: $295.00

Presents discussion of the skills needed for each kind of selection interview. Includes how to practice interviews, conduct them, interpret what is said, and make hiring decisions. Gives attention to getting the applicant to open up and estabishing the best interview climate. Features John D. Drake's Hypothesis Method. Four audiocassettes are for the learner; 2 are for the trainer. Intended for experienced supervisors. Suggested for a one-day program.

751. Tell Me about Yourself
Roundtable Films, Inc   1978   16mm film or videocassette   color   27 min
Purchase: $525.00   Rental: $100.00   Preview: $30.00
Languages: English, Japanese, Norwegian, Spanish, Swedish

Reviews the entire employment interview process. Demonstrates questioning techniques that help with common interviewing problems like probing for negatives, maintaining control, and handling moments of silence. Demonstrates the interview process of this interviewer as she attempts to achieve her interview objectives.

JOB SATISFACTION

Common Sense Motivation. For complete citation, *see* MOTIVATION.

752. Has Job Enrichment Been Oversold?
Development Digest   audiocassette
Purchase: $13.75

Emanuel Weintraub reviews results from an extensive survey of female workers in the soft goods industry showing that the economic package and working conditions are significantly more important than job enrichment.

Increasing Worker Satisfaction and Productivity. For complete citation, *see* PRODUCTIVITY.

753. It's Up to You
Salenger Educational Media   1980   16mm film or videocassette   color   instructor's print materials; learner's print materials
Purchase: $455.00   Rental: $125.00   Preview: $35.00

Teaches the skills people need to help them take charge of their jobs and lives successfully. Proposes that job satisfaction is primarily the employee's responsibility. Identifies several strategies to help people become involved in a positive way in people, the job, and the organization. Identifies the role of the manager in helping his/her employees grow and develop.

754. Joy of Achievement
Salenger Educational Media   1977   16mm film or videocassette   color   14 min   instructor's print materials
Purchase: $410.00   Rental: $125.00   Preview: $35.00

Shows opportunities and satisfactions derived from achievement. Proposes to stimulate pride in work, improve morale, and increase productivity. Depicts span of age and physical condition in work and living circumstances. Intended for all employees.

755. Spirit of Professionalism
Vantage Communications, Inc   1973   16mm film or videocassette   color   14 min
Purchase: $550.00   Rental: $125.00   Preview: $40.00

Explores the idea of professionalism as a state of mind regardless of a person's title or line of work. Part 1 offers an overview of professionalism and the power to move people. Part 2 shows how professionalism requires self-confidence, as illustrated by a tugboat captain who faces large responsibilities. Part 3 shows professionalism as an idea that can give meaning to a person's life.

LABOR RELATIONS
See ARBITRATION AND LABOR RELATIONS

LABOR UNIONS

756. Achievement and Challenge
American Federation of Labor and Congress of Industrial Organizations 1981 16mm film or videocassette or filmstrip color 12 min
Rental: $5.00

Reviews the history of unions in the US. Includes historic photographs and lively music with a voice-over narration.

757. Check-Off: The Only Way to Go
American Federation of Labor and Congress of Industrial Organizations 1980 16mm
film color 13 min
Rental: $5.00

Tells how to establish a COPE voluntary political check-off program and why it is important to every worker.

758. '88 Close the Gate
American Federation of Labor and Congress of Industrial Organizations 1980 16mm
film color 16 min
Rental: $5.00

Documents 12-week strike by United Steelworkers of America against a Virginia shipyard. Shows Union Local 8888 action and the police power in a right-to-work state.

759. Faces of a Union
American Federation of Labor and Congress of Industrial Organizations 1980 16mm
film color 28 min
Rental: $5.00

Details how democratic union functions by showing the United Steelworkers of America efforts. Shows activities of a union member's life on the job, processing grievances, bargaining, picketing, and attending classes.

760. Hobbs Act
American Federation of Labor and Congress of Industrial Organizations 1981 16mm film color 6 min
Rental: $5.00

Tells how picket line violence is adequately covered by state and local laws when it occurs. Produced to combat the Right-to-Work Committee's drive to amend the Hobbs Act, making strike-related violence a federal crime.

761. If You Don't Come in Sunday—Don't Come in Monday
Manpower Education Institute 1976 16mm film or videocassette color 58 min
Purchase: $825.00 Rental: $75.00

History of the American worker and the growth of the union movement traced through historical film footage, photographs, and documents. Produced for the United States Bicentennial. Narrated by Alexander Scourby.

762. Labor Unions: A Question of Violence
Carousel Films, Inc 1976 16mm film or videocassette color 15 min

Purchase: film $300.00; video $225.00 Rental: $35.00

Documents the confrontation between a successful, independent, nonunion building contractor in Philadelphia and the construction union. His fight to preserve his open shop precipitates violent union action.

763. Management and Unionism
Van De Water Associates, Inc 1978 4 videocassettes 30 min ea instructor's print materials
Purchase: $1,980.00 ($495.00 ea) Rental: $300.00 ($75.00 ea) Preview: $100.00

Presents the legal positions of management, unions, and employees. Focuses on unionism from the management viewpoint, avoiding unionization and nonunion campaigning. Produced by John Van de Water.

764. Reflections: George Meany
National Audiovisual Center 1979 16mm film or videocassette color 52 min
Purchase: film $450.00; video $95.00 Rental: $35.00

Biography of George Meany and labor unions. Combines in-depth interviews with Meany and others with documentary footage.

765. Texas Rally on the Prevailing Wage Law
American Federation of Labor and Congress of Industrial Organizations 1979 16mm
film color 12 min
Rental: $5.00

Records the march on Austin, Texas, with militant union members singing "Solidarity" and chanting "Kill that bill," to repeal the state wage law in 1979.

766. Time of Challenge
American Federation of Labor and Congress of Industrial Organizations 1981 16mm
film color 27 min
Rental: $5.00

Commemorates the 100th anniversary of the founding of the labor federation. Combines a look at the past with a look at unions today using photographs and historic film footage portraying the founding of the AFL in 1881 and 1886, early union leaders, and strikes which played a part in the long struggle for economic and social justice. Through interviews, reveals how union members today feel about their unions and the problems they face in the 1980s.

767. Union at Work
Films, Inc 1973 16mm film or videocassette color 25 min
Purchase: film $425.00; video $215.00

Portrays wide diversity of activities characterizing an effective labor union.

768. Working without Unions
Thompson-Mitchell and Associates 1978 16mm film or videocassette color 15 min instructor's print materials

Purchase: $495.00   Rental: $150.00   Preview: $35.00

Designed for management training, employee orientation, or company campaigns against unionization. Surfaces management concerns about unions through a portrayal of 2 friends on opposite sides of the issue of unionization.

LANGUAGE
See also COMMUNICATION; WRITING

769. Bergen Evans Vocabulary Program
Singer Management Institute   10 filmstrips and 5 audiocassettes   learner's print materials
Purchase: $139.50

Gives correct pronunciation of each word and hundreds of derivatives. Words are properly used, spelled, defined, and illustrated. Over 500 words are presented.

770. Business Vocabulary
Prentice Hall Media   9 filmstrips and audiocassettes   program guide
Purchase: $299.00

Presents a foundation of useful words and phrases in diverse areas such as accounting, purchasing, data processing, customer service, and sales. Includes technical and financial terms and abbreviations. Useful for new workers unfamiliar with business terms.

771. Interview
LCA Video/Films   16mm film or videocassette   color   5 min
Purchase: $175.00   Rental: $60.00   Preview: $30.00

Demonstrates the importance of language and communication with a jazz musician in an incomprehensible encounter with a radio interviewer. Animated.

772. Word Power Success Program
Tape Rental Library   1975   3 audiocassettes   60 min ea   learner's print materials
Purchase: $39.95

Focuses on vocabulary, pronunciation, voice training, and writing "tips" to develop both speaking and writing skills. Includes exercises for vocabulary recall. For use as group or self-study.

773. Wordcraft 1
Singer Management Institute   1981   6 filmstrips and 3 audiocassettes   learner's print materials
Purchase: $97.50

Intended to increase vocabulary so businesspeople can communicate more effectively. Gives definitions, correct spelling, and usage. Twenty lessons present 300 new words which are seen and heard in the context of short narratives. Thirty lessons present.

774. Wordcraft 2
Singer Management Institute   1981   4 filmstrips and 2 audiocassettes   learner's print materials
Purchase: $65.95

Intended to increase vocabulary so businesspeople can communicate more effectively. Gives definitions, correct spelling, and usage. Twenty lessons present 200 new words which are seen and heard in the context of short narratives.

775. Wordcraft 3
Singer Management Institute   1971   4 filmstrips and 2 audiocassettes   learner's print materials
Purchase: $65.95

Intended to increase vocabulary so businesspeople can communicate more effectively. Gives definitions, correct spelling, and usage. Twenty lessons present 200 new words which are seen and heard in the context of short narratives.

LEADERSHIP

776. Bennis on Leaders
AMACOM   5 audiocassettes   3¾ hrs   learner's print materials
Purchase: $125.00   Other cost factors: AMA members $110.00

Practical and theory-based presentation by Warren Bennis. Intended for present and aspiring leaders.

777. Case Studies in Leadership
Salenger Educational Media   16mm film or videocassette   color   18 min   instructor's print materials; learner's print materials; poster
Purchase: $455.00   Rental: $125.00   Preview: $35.00

Two dramatized cases illustrate different leadership styles. The Schmidt-Tannenbaum model is used to suggest that the most effective style is one contingent upon 3 factors that comprise every leadership situation: (1) forces within the leader, (2) forces within those being led, and (3) forces within the situation. Intended for managers or supervisors. Formerly titled *Doctor, Lawyer, Merchant, Chief: Case Studies in Leadership.*

778. Cave
CRM/McGraw-Hill Films   16mm film or videocassette   color   10 min
Purchase: $250.00   Rental: $75.00   Preview: free
Languages: English, Spanish

Classic parable about illusion and reality. Animated with narration by Orson Wells. Illustrates that leadership's role is to discover reality, help others to see it, and effect change.

779. Challenge of Leadership
BNA Communications, Inc   1961   16mm film or videocassette   color   16 min   booklet
Purchase: $250.00   Rental: 5-day $150.00; 3-day $105.00   Preview: $35.00

Shows how 5 men stranded on island cope with their situation. Illustrates how to identify, analyze, and use leadership qualities. Useful for supervisors in terms of teamwork, relationships, and authority. Modern Management Series.

780. Follow the Leader
Didactic Systems, Inc   16mm film or videocassette   color   11 min   discussion guide

Purchase: $190.00   Rental: $45.00   Preview: $15.00

Analyzes problems, pitfalls, and barriers facing the would-be leader or newly appointed supervisor. Identifies essential leadership skills. Useful for new managers.

781. Four Dimension Leadership

Learning Dynamics   1975   12 audiocassettes   30–45 min ea   instructor's print materials; learner's print materials
Purchase: $800.00 (for 10 learners)   Rental: $50.00   Preview: $250.00   Other cost factors: when rented, printed materials are extra at $195.00 per learner

Focuses on key leadership skills, particularly those in communication and decision making. Includes styles of leadership, motivation, communication, negotiating, and managing change. Units on dealing with problem people and resolving conflicts. Intended for experienced managers. Suggested for a 3-day program.

782. Group Leadership

Lansford Publishing Company, Inc   4 audiocassettes   30 min ea   instructor's print materials
Purchase: $109.95

Lectures discuss leadership, perspectives, styles of leadership, variables of leadership, effectiveness, leadership functions, and performances.

In Charge! For complete citation, *see* POWER AND AUTHORITY.

783. Leadership

Lansford Publishing Company, Inc   60 slides and audiocassette   learner's print materials
Purchase: $245.95

A concise survey of modern leadership insights and their applications in a wide variety of different settings. Covers theory, style, and fundamentals.

784. Leadership and Motivation: The Influence Process

Management Resources, Inc   5 audiocassettes   instructor's print materials; learner's print materials
Purchase: $65.00

Practical guide for supervisors and managers which includes developing personal power, applying leadership to work situations, communicating and motivating, counseling marginal employees, and understanding and managing change. Suggested for small group study.

785. Leadership

Resources for Education and Management, Inc   1972   3 filmstrips or slides and audiocassettes or videocassettes or filmstrip cartridges   15–18 min ea   instructor's print materials
Purchase: video $245.00 ($95.00); filmstrips $220.00 ($75.00 ea); filmstrip cartridges $255.00 ($85.00 ea); slides $235.00 ($80.00 ea)

Examines the traits of leadership and how they are acquired then applies sound leadership skills to a variety of on-the-job situations. Uses participative techniques with the audio-visual presentation.

786. Leadership: Style or Circumstance?

CRM/McGraw-Hill Films   1975   16mm film or videocassette   color   30 min
Purchase: $560.00   Rental: $95.00   Preview: free

Outspoken interviews by presidents of large corporations convey to managers and supervisors the essential importance of matching leadership style to a given situation. Shows need to blend an effective mixture of task-orientation and relating style to any given project. Features Fred E. Fiedler.

787. Managing through Leadership & Communications

Edupac, Inc   2 audiocassettes   instructor's print materials; learner's print materials
Purchase: $60.00

Offers specific techniques to better understand the terms leadership and communications. Principal areas are managing and doing activities, communications, delegation of activity, and planning. For group or individual study.

788. New Leadership Styles: Towards Human and Economic Development

Document Associates   1978   16mm film or videocassette   color   26 min
Purchase: $400.00   Rental: $45.00

What is the role of the manager in modern organizations? What qualities are essential for effective leadership? What is the impact of flexible leadership on motivation and productivity? Uses Michael Maccoby's gamesmanship concept to scrutinize innovative leadership styles. Demonstrates the effectiveness of treating each worker as a person with unique values, needs, and motivations. Promotes "industrial democracy" to maximize human potential and increase productivity.

789. Psychology of Winning

Singer Management Institute   6 audiocassettes   progress guide
Purchase: $63.95

Overview of a leader's 10 outstanding qualities. Highlights principles of thought and action that lead to the top. Stresses importance of a winning attitude, clearly defined goals and purposes, taking control of your life, practicing—and winning—mentally, and total communication in walking, talking, looking, listening, and reacting.

Sand Castle. For complete citation, *see* TEAM BUILDING.

790. Styles of Leadership

Roundtable Films, Inc   16mm film or videocassette   color   decision game
Purchase: $525.00   Rental: $100.00   Preview: $100.00
Languages: Dutch, English, French, German, Japanese, Norwegian, Spanish, Swedish

New version demonstrates 4 leadership styles: tells, joins, sells, consults. Decision to take on a new project is implemented by 4 different leaders. Advantages and disadvantages of each style are shown. Shows how to evaluate any given situation and choose an appropriate leadership style.

791. What Successful Leaders Do—And Don't Do
Organization Development Consultants   2
audiocassettes   113 min   learner's print materials
Purchase: $29.95

Offers a guide to better, stronger, more effective leadership in organizations. Points out how to evaluate credentials vs. accomplishments and experience vs. results in others.

LIABILITY

792. Customer Claims
American Learning Systems, Inc   1981   filmstrip or slides and audiocassettes or videocassette or filmstrip cartridge   12 min   instructor's print materials
Purchase: video $150.00; other formats
$125.00   Preview: free

Suggests procedures for handling claims related to accidents and injuries which may have occurred at the place of business. Includes customer claims for damage to personal property and claims of product liability.

793. Product Liability and the Reasonably Safe Product
Society of Manufacturing Engineers   1979
videocassette   color   55 min
Purchase: nonmember $260.00; member
$230.00   Rental: nonmember $50.00; member
$45.00

Stresses the avoidance of product liability suits and rising insurance rates through designing for safety from the start. Assists management in understanding the definitions of defects, warnings, and disclaimers to give them an understanding of what today's legal system demands in product safety. Features A. Weinstein.

LISTENING
See also COMMUNICATION

794. Are You Listening?
Didactic Systems, Inc   16mm film   b/w   12½ min
instructor's print materials
Purchase: $140.00   Rental: $35.00   Preview:
$15.00

Provides foundation for understanding and accepting the concept of effective listening. Five major causes of nonlistening are discussed with a look at their effects. Prompts self-assessment and open discussion of nonlistening habits.

795. Art of Listening
Classroom World Productions   4 audiocassettes
Purchase: $27.50

Presentation stresses importance of listening as well as how to improve present listening ability. Remembering what was heard, effect of emotions, and possibility of hidden meanings are highlighted.

796. Creative Listening
Edupac, Inc   2 audiocassettes   instructor's print materials; learner's print materials
Purchase: $60.00

Presents good listening techniques with narration, dialog, and dramatic readings that show good and bad listening techniques.

797. How to Improve Listening Skills
Singer Management Institute   40 slides and 2 audiocassettes   instructor's print materials; learner's print materials
Purchase: $195.00   Other cost factors: discounts available for bulk orders of materials

Addresses the skill of listening actively as a part of the management process. Offers guidelines for listening effectiveness and observing nonverbal communication.

798. Jones-Mohr Listening Test
University Associates   1976   audiocassette instructor's print materials; learner's print materials
Purchase: $44.95

A listening test that provides immediate feedback, demonstrates the need for listening improvements, and motivates learners to work on listening skills. Can fit into many training designs since listening is a core skill of interpersonal relations.

799. Language: Key to Human Understanding
Audio-Forum   audiocassette   50 min
Purchase: $10.95

Stresses importance of nonevaluative listening in personal and business communication. Features S.I. Hayakawa.

800. Listen and Be Listened To
American Management Associations   6
audiocassettes   learner's print materials
Purchase: $145.00   Other cost factors: AMA members $135.00; discounts available for bulk orders of materials

Intended to help managers assess their listening skills through a series of tests, including the Sperry Profile Quizzes, break bad listening habits, and develop their ability to understand and retain information.

801. Listen for Success
Training by Design   4 audiocassettes   learner's print materials
Purchase: $95.00

Builds listening skills and offers strategies for listening improvement. Includes active listening, reading language, and use of feedback.

802. Listen, Please
BNA Communications, Inc   1959   16mm film or videocassette   color   12 min   booklet
Purchase: $250.00   Rental: 5-day $150.00; 3-day
$105.00   Preview: $35.00
Languages: English, French, Portuguese, Spanish

Portrays how to develop more effective listening skills through commitment and practice. Modern Management Series, no. 5.

803. Listen to Communicate
CRM/McGraw-Hill Films   1980   16mm film or videocassette   color   40 min   learner's print materials; 6 audiocassettes
Purchase: $1,495.00   Preview: free

Shows how active listening aids good communication by deepening the ability to interpret hidden meanings in business discussions. Provides practical techniques for improving and tuning employee listening skills. A multimedia package that integrates print, audio, and audiovisual components. Suggested for full- or half-day scheduling. Printed materials include pre- and posttests.

804. Listen Your Way to Success
AMACOM   3 audiocassettes   learner's print materials
Purchase: $85.00   Other cost factors: AMA members $72.25

Presents fundamentals, practical tips, a test, and an exercise in the skill of listening. Relates listening skills to support, conflict resolution, advance and progress, and authority.

805. Listening
Roundtable Films, Inc   16mm film or videocassette   color   14 min
Purchase: $350.00   Rental: $75.00   Preview: $30.00

Through a case study a manager is shown that his inability to listen impairs his department's effectiveness. Identifies the central causes of poor listening and what can be done to overcome them. Shows how to evaluate and improve listening habits.

806. Listening: A Key to Problem Solving
PCI   1979   16mm film   color   22 min
Purchase: $390.00   Rental: $55.00

Points out listening techniques to reduce problems, improve working relationships, and increase productivity. Shows how well listening occurs in a true-to-life management situation. Dramatization with narration and commentary by Joseph Campanella.

807. Listening for Results
Roundtable Films, Inc   1981   16mm film or videocassette   color   10 min
Purchase: $350.00   Rental: $85.00   Preview: $30.00

Dramatizes the direct link between listening effectiveness and productivity. Demonstrates several common causes of poor listening and how problems could have been avoided through proper listening. Presents 6 rules for developing sound listening habits.

808. Listening Makes a Difference
Salenger Educational Media   1978   16mm film or videocassette   color   7 min
Purchase: $350.00   Rental: $125.00   Preview: $35.00

Demonstrates the importance of active listening through several vignettes illustrating interactions between retail sales personnel and customers.

809. Listening on the Job
Addison-Wesley Publishing Company, Inc   3 audiocassettes   instructor's print materials; learner's print materials
Purchase: $245.00

A practical approach to a recurring problem in business and industry: oral communication—not in conveying information, but in receiving information.

810. Listening—The Problem Solver
Barr Films   16mm film or videocassette   color   20 min
Purchase: $495.00   Rental: $100.00   Preview: $50.00

Reviews basic listening skills and then focuses on 3 distinct yet equally important kinds of listening: critical, creative, and sympathetic. Useful for management communication and listening skills, training and personal development programs. Follow-up to *You're Not Listening*.

811. Many Hear—Some Listen
Centron Films   1975   16mm film   color   12 min
Purchase: $220.00

Examines several listening styles and makes the point that effective communication involves the listener as well as the speaker.

812. Power of Listening
CRM/McGraw-Hill Films   1978   16mm film or videocassette   color   26 min   instructor's print materials; learner's print materials
Purchase: $560.00   Rental: $95.00   Preview: free

Examines role of listening in the communications process from a variety of viewpoints, placing particular emphasis on spotting and correcting major blocks to effective listening. Shows that good listening is a skill that can be taught and why this skill is so important. Demonstrates a workshop conducted by Anthony Alessandra. Focus is on a variety of exercises to dissect, examine, practice, and improve upon communication patterns in daily organizational life.

813. Strategies for Effective Listening
Xerox Learning Systems   1978   3 audiocassettes   4 hrs   instructor's print materials; learner's print materials
Purchase: $125.00 plus learner's materials

Audiocassettes guide interactive program focused on the listening skills essential for 2-way communication. Topics highlighted include why listening is important, active listening, interactive listening, and listening strategies. Program is adaptable in the use of its presentations, group discussions, and self-study exercises.

814. You're Not Listening
Barr Films   16mm film or videocassette   color   20 min
Purchase: $425.00   Rental: $100.00   Preview: $50.00

Presents 7 techniques for improving listening skills, using humorous vignettes to effectively identify poor listening habits. Outlines how to overcome those bad habits for a less stressful, more productive life.

LOSS PREVENTION

815. Burglary Loss Prevention
American Learning Systems, Inc 1981 filmstrip or slides and audiocassette or videocassette or filmstrip cartridge 12 min instructor's print materials Purchase: video $150.00; other formats $125.00 Preview: free

Trains business personnel in the prevention of burglaries. Also discusses what persons should do if they find their places of business have been broken into. Includes advice about securing the facility, keeping information about the facility confidential, and how to react should there be an illegal entry.

816. Cargo Security
National Audiovisual Center 1978 2 16mm films Purchase: $145.00

Explores problems involved in bulk cargo shipping, including loss and theft.

817. Check Cashing
American Learning Systems, Inc 1981 filmstrip or slides and audiocassette or videocassette or filmstrip cartridge 12 min instructor's print materials Purchase: video $150.00; other formats $125.00 Preview: free

Offers guidelines to follow in the acceptance of checks. Covers definition of checks, what the risk factors are, policies and procedures to follow in addition to individual company's procedures, and examining and evaluating checks.

818. Checks: What to Cash
BNA Communications, Inc 1972 16mm film or videocassette color 16 min Purchase: $275.00 Rental: 5-day $150.00; 3-day $105.00 Preview: $35.00

Illustrates the 4 general conditions that must be met before cashing a check, then gives 12 situations where the viewer must decide whether to cash a check or refer it to a manager. Loss Prevention Series.

819. Checks: When to Cash
BNA Communications, Inc 16mm film or videocassette color 16 min Purchase: $275.00 Rental: 5-day $150.00; 3-day $105.00 Preview: $35.00

Reviews conditions for cashing a check and tricks used by check swindlers. Shows transactions where a check-cashing swindler may or may not be involved, exposing several different schemes and how to deal with them. Loss Prevention Series.

820. Crime: I Gave at the Office
National Audiovisual Center 1977 videocassette color 13 min Purchase: $88.00

A tongue-in-cheek approach is used to encourage awareness of common institutional crimes and offer suggestions for prevention. Intended for employees of health care facilities.

821. Currency Protection
American Learning Systems, Inc 1981 videocassette or filmstrip cartridge or filmstrip or slides and audiocassette 12 min instructor's print materials Purchase: video $150.00; other formats $125.00 Preview: free

Gives advice on how to handle money, security measures to take in storing it, and how to guard against "till tap" thefts—all measures to prevent loss due to mistakes and theft by fraud or diversion.

Employee Inaccuracy Elimination. For complete citation, *see* EMPLOYEE PERFORMANCE.

Games People Play: Currency and Check Schemes. For complete citation, *see* FRAUD.

822. Handling Checks
National Educational Media, Inc 1975 16mm film or videocassette color 10 min instructor's print materials; learner's print materials Purchase: $270.00 Rental: 5-day $80.00; 3-day $70.00 Languages: English, Spanish

Short situations are portrayed to demonstrate how to handle checks, identify bad checks, correct amounts and dates, validate signatures, and forestall fraud. Emphasis throughout is on customer courtesy. Suggests standards and procedures for check handling. For employees who deal with customers.

823. Handling Credit Cards
National Educational Media, Inc 1975 16mm film or super 8mm or videocassette color 10 min instructor's print materials; learner's print materials Purchase: $270.00 Rental: 5-day $80.00; 3-day $70.00 Languages: English, Spanish

Provides essential training for completing a credit card transaction to protect the organization's interests yet maintain a cordial relationship with customers. Shows an effective routine procedure for reducing risks. Stresses good customer relations practices throughout the validation procedure. Can be used to prevent carelessness in validating credit cards and to ensure proper procedures are followed when dealing with invalid or stolen credit cards.

824. Handling Money
National Educational Media, Inc 1974 16mm film or super 8mm or videocassette color 14 min instructor's print materials; learner's print materials Purchase: $330.00 Rental: 5-day $80.00; 3-day $70.00 Languages: English, Spanish

Illustrates the proper and safe methods of handling money. Dramatizes principles through real-life situations showing where mistakes most often occur. Suggests careful handling of money while being courteous to all customers.

825. Inside Story
National Audiovisual Center   16mm film or videocassette   color   15 min
Purchase: $87.00   Rental: $12.50

Illustrates steps which can be taken to limit or prevent pilferage by plant employees. Reveals that an old, trusted employee can be guilty.

826. Introduction to Crime Prevention
MTI Teleprograms, Inc   1974   16mm film or videocassette   color   23 min   guide
Purchase: film $345.00; video $310.00   Rental: 5-day $60.00

Shows the major changes required to implement crime prevention strategy and methods. Covers wide range of criminal opportunities and methods, particularly burglary. Detailed information on locks, lights, doors, and windows.

827. Know Exactly What to Do
MTI Teleprograms, Inc   1978   16mm film or videocassette   color   15 min   learner's print materials
Purchase: film $410.00; video $375.00   Rental: $80.00

Designed to provide basic instruction for employees of financial institutions on procedures to follow in case they are involved in a robbery. Includes instructions on how to act in a robbery, handle a note, and activate several types of alarms. Stresses the importance of obtaining an immediate and accurate description of the robber and protecting fingerprints.

828. Look in Time
Dartnell   16mm film or videocassette   color   15 min
Purchase: $425.00   Rental: $120.00   Preview: free

Depicts the many techniques used by the potential shoplifter, as they would be seen by employees. Shows how easily goods can be stolen and how pilferage can be prevented when employees are alert. Pinpoints how to recognize certain elements of behavior which identify potential shoplifters and prevent them from pilfering. Dramatizes typical retail situations.

829. Loss Control Auditing
American Learning Systems, Inc   1981   2 filmstrips or slides with audiocassettes or videocassettes or filmstrip cartridges   12 min ea   instructor's print materials
Purchase: $250.00   Preview: free

Proposes an overall audit program to enable owners and managers to determine areas of potential loss. Advocates this as a fundamental part of any loss prevention effort.

830. Loss Prevention Orientation
American Learning Systems, Inc   1981   filmstrip or slides and audiocassette or videocassette or filmstrip cartridge   12 min   instructor's print materials
Purchase: video $150.00; other formats $125.00   Preview: free

Includes rules, controls, and procedures designed to build an effective defense against all possible methods which cause loss.

831. $9+ $1=$20: Shortchanged
BNA Communications, Inc   1972   16mm film or videocassette   color   27 min
Purchase: $525.00   Rental: 5-day $150.00; 3-day $105.00   Preview: $35.00

Shows how to deal effectively with shortchange artists without losing money or offending honest customers. Exposes the methods shortchange artists use. Loss Prevention Series.

832. Pilferage
American Learning Systems, Inc   1981   videocassette or filmstrip or filmstrip cartridge or slide and audiocassette   12 min   instructor's print materials
Purchase: $150.00   Preview: free

Points out that theft of merchandise, services, supplies, or time by employees is possibly the greatest of hazards to the place of business—because it is destruction from within. Discusses the position of the company and its policies in regard to theft by employees.

833. Pilferage Protection
American Learning Systems, Inc   1981   videocassette or filmstrips or filmstrip cartridge or slides and audiocassette   12 min ea   instructor's print materials
Purchase: video $125.00; slides $125.00; filmstrips $95.00; filmstrip cartridges $95.00   Preview: free

Points out that the success of any pilferage protection program depends on the amount of effort management expends on it. Stresses use of controls to reduce the opportunity for employee theft. Intended for managers and supervisors.

834. Pilferage Reaction
American Learning Systems, Inc   1981   videocassette or filmstrip or filmstrip cartridge or slides and audiocassette   12 min   instructor's print materials
Purchase: video $150.00; other formats $125.00

Shows methods of detection and investigation of employee theft incidents. Gives guidelines in handling suspected or known internal theft matters and the employees who are involved in such matters. Intended for managers and supervisors.

Plan for Security. For complete citation, *see* SECURITY.

835. Preventing Employee Theft
National Educational Media, Inc   1972   16mm film of super 8mm or videocassette   color   12 min   instructor's print materials; learner's print materials
Purchase: $365.00   Rental: 5-day $90.00; 3-day $80.00
Languages: English, French, Spanish, Japanese

Gives guidelines to help all responsible people in an organization prevent employee theft. Provides insight into the methods and motivations of the would-be thief. Presents a simple and direct program of management action which will reduce embezzlement and pilferage: illustrates 4 essential principles for preventing employee pilferage and embezzlement, reduce temptation, limit opportunity, establish controls, and communicate the importance of teamwork in preventing employee theft.

836. Robbery Prevention
American Learning Systems, Inc 1981 filmstrip or slides and audiocassette or videocassette or filmstrip cartridges 12 min instructor's print materials
Purchase: video $150.00; other formats $125.00 Preview: free

Stresses the importance of all concerned being alert and suspicious, handling and storing money properly, and entering and leaving the place of business cautiously as necessary measures to prevent robberies.

837. Robbery Reaction
American Learning Systems, Inc 1981 filmstrip or slides and audiocassette or videocassette or filmstrip cartridge 12 min instructor's print materials
Purchase: $150.00 Preview: free

Gives advice to possible victims should a robbery occur: be calm, do not resist, obey the robber, be observant, collect and protect the evidence, and cooperate with the police and courts in the prosecution of the robbers.

838. Shoplifting
American Learning Systems, Inc 1981 filmstrip or slides and audiocassette or videocassette or filmstrip cartridge 12 min instructor's print materials
Purchase: video $150.00; other formats $125.00 Preview: free

Addresses theft of store merchandise, a common problem to all retailers from the smallest store to the largest. Discusses the necessary prevention and security measures to take as the best defense.

839. Signed, Sealed, and Delivered
National Audiovisual Center 1978 16mm film color 10 min
Purchase: $58.00

Designed for those who are involved in or affected by the shipment of cargo by truck, train, or plane. Establishes the fact that cargo loss is a major problem in the US, affecting us all. Cargo Security Series.

840. Stop the Shoplifter
Classroom World Productions 4 audiocassettes
Purchase: $27.50

Describes the many methods shoplifters use. Shows how to stop shoplifters and associated crooks without personal risk and without exposing the employer to lawsuits.

841. Supervisor's Role in Preventing Employee Pilferage and Theft
Bureau of Business Practice 16mm film or videocassette color 20 min
Purchase: $425.00 Rental: $95.00 Preview: $45.00

Dramatized situations illustrate how actions can actually encourage employees to steal company property. Shows consequences of a casual attitude toward supplies and equipment and how valuable company products may be viewed as cost-free commodities. Identifies conditions that encourage "borrowing."

842. Victim
National Audiovisual Center 1978 16mm film color 15 min
Purchase: $87.00

Presents an anatomy of a railcar theft. Explains the ramifications to the railroad, the shipper, the manufacturer, and ultimately the consumer in higher prices. Cargo Security Series.

843. Waste Loss Prevention
American Learning Systems, Inc 1981 filmstrip or slides and audiocassette or videocassette or filmstrip cartridge 12 min instructor's print materials
Purchase: video $150.00; other formats $125.00 Preview: free

Shows that prevention of loss due to damage and waste of an employer's merchandise, supplies, equipment, and property is a part of every employee's obligation to the employer.

MANAGEMENT

Acquiring, Merging and Selling Companies. For complete citation, *see* BUSINESS ENVIRONMENT.

844. Banking Managerial Skills
Resources for Education and Management, Inc slides and 5 audiocassettes or 5 filmstrips or 5 filmstrip cartridges color 9–11 min ea instructor's print materials
Purchase: filmstrips $280.00 ($64.00 ea); filmstrip cartridges $425.00 ($85.00 ea); slides $295.00 ($67.00 ea)

Deals with essential managerial skills in banking setting. Modules include effective management skills, organizing and planning skills, decision-making skills, leadership, and perception. Combines audiovisual reinforcement of key issues with realistic in-basket exercises. Suggested for a one- or 2-day workshop for new or prospective bank managers.

845. Basic Business Psychology
American Management Associations 6 audiocassettes 10 hrs learner's print materials
Purchase: $145.00 Other cost factors: AMA members $135.00; discounts available for bulk orders of materials

Job-related psychological principles are described in lectures by successful managers. These principles are applied to selecting employees, training, problem solving, motivation, conflict, and communication.

846. Behavioral Aspects of Management: Introduction and Applications
Lansford Publishing Company, Inc 60 slides and audiocassette instructor's print materials
Purchase: $295.95

Deals with the essentials of the modern behavioral aspects of management. Includes historical perspective, major theories, alternative management styles, practical implications, and applications. Written materials include lecture notebook and references.

847. Beyond Theory Y: The Contingency Approach to Management
Salenger Educational Media   16mm film or videocassette   color   14 min   instructor's print materials; learner's print materials; posters
Purchase: $435.00   Rental: 5-day $125.00   Preview: $35.00

Describes both bureaucratic and participative management styles. The contingency approach offered is that selection of the best organizational structure depends on the nature of the job and the nature of the people involved.

848. Building a Management Philosophy
Audio-Forum   audiocassette   29 min
Purchase: $10.95

Discusses establishing a personal managerial philosophy through a manager's own ideas, beliefs, and opinions.

849. Business Law: Contracts
Bruno Associates   audiocassettes   instructor's print materials
Purchase: $12.95

Lecture presentation covers basic contract concepts, the nature of the contract agreement, types of considerations to be included, statute frauds, third party rights, and breach of contract.

850. Competitive Spirit
Xicom-Video Arts   16mm film   color   29 min
Purchase: $530.00   Rental: $100.00   Preview: $35.00

Exposes one of best known but least discussed problems in corporate management, that of status-seeking, empire-building, and inter-departmental politics. John Cleese's humor and the insights of Antony Jay are intended to prompt managers and executives to some introspection. British production.

Computer Basics for Management. For complete citation, *see* COMPUTERS.

851. Concepts of Management
Classroom World Productions   4 audiocassettes
Purchase: $27.50

Brief, broad-brush approach to management. Addresses 3 levels of direction: management, administrative, and supervisory. Includes coping with human nature, self-development for promotion, missed management opportunities, and obtaining rewards from work.

852. Creative Management: A Key to the Kingdom
PCI   16mm film   color   23 min
Purchase: $390.00   Rental: $55.00

Advocates building an atmosphere that encourages creativity and enhances sound decision making. Emphasizes the benefits of creative management and reveals steps managers can use to develop their own creative potential.

853. Drucker on Management
AMACOM   8 audiocassettes   45 min ea   guide
Purchase: $200.00   Other cost factors: AMA members $175.00

Practical and incisive perspective on management issues from Peter Drucker. Reveals the perspective of a manager in controlling chaos, juggling conflicting demands, making decisions, crossing established lines of communication, and decision making.

854. Effective Management Program
BNA Communications, Inc   40 audiocassettes   12 min ea
Purchase: $400.00 ($100.00 per series; $12.00 ea)

Translates behavioral science concepts into practical, usable management methods. Each series consists of 10 cassettes. Series 1: Managing Individuals Effectively. Series 2: Achieving Group Effectiveness. Series 3: Developing Personal Effectiveness. Series 4: Leadership Guide.

855. Effective Office Worker
Resources for Education and Management, Inc   5 filmstrips or slides and audiocassettes or videocassettes or filmstrip cartridges   8–10 min ea   instructor's print materials
Purchase: video $305.00 ($75.00 ea); filmstrips $280.00 ($64.00 ea); filmstrip cartridges $425.00 ($85.00 ea); slides $295.00 ($67.00 ea)   Preview: $20.00

Modules cover the role of the office worker, managing time and the job, making the boss look good, and improving communication skills. Offers specific tips on planning and organizing work, increasing communicating skills, and improving interpersonal relations. Intended for office managers and supervisors.

856. Effective Organization
BNA Communications, Inc   6 audiocassettes   30 min ea
Purchase: $72.00 ($12.00 ea)

Saul Gellerman introduces and builds on the ideas presented in the Effective Organization Series and provides added insight into the work of behavioral science practitioners. Covers assessing management potential, management by participation, pay for performance, making human resources productive, team building, and confronting conflict.

857. Eight Steps toward Excellence
Applied Management Science, Inc   8 videocassettes   color   30 min ea   instructor's print materials; learner's print materials
Purchase: $9,500.00   Rental: $170.00 per learner   Preview: free

Covers scope of managerial responsibilities: problem solving, creativity, leadership, meeting management, troubleshooting, and people problem solving. Intended for supervisors and managers.

Enterprise I. For complete citation, *see* BUSINESS ENVIRONMENT.

858. Evolving Models of Organizational Behavior
Audio-Forum   audiocassette   27 min
Purchase: $10.95

Presents 4 different approaches to working with people in organizations: autocratic, custodial, supportive, and collegial. Presented by Keith Davis.

859. Executive Management Workshop
Creative Universal, Inc 1977 audiocassettes
instructor's print materials; learner's print materials;
transparencies
Purchase: $1,995.00 (for 10 learners) Preview:
$20.00

Identifies management styles and responsibilities, the skills
managers need, and how they operate. Includes planning and
organizing, time management, communication, and problem
solving. Suggested as a 30-hour program in 10 3-hour sessions.

860. Executive Skills
MBO, Inc 12 audiocassettes 30 min ea
Purchase: $196.00
Languages: English, Spanish

George S. Odiorne gives functional and developmental approach to management by objectives (MBO), a results-centered
system of management. Designed for top and middle managers
to provide an understanding of the management skills needed to
do their jobs and to manage subordinate managers. Includes
real versus apparent effectiveness, managerial style, goal setting,
problem solving, performance appraisal, and motivation.

861. Five 'M's
International Film Bureau, Inc 16mm film or
videocassette color 25 min
Purchase: $495.00 Rental: 5-day $67.00; 3-day
$50.00 Preview: free

Money, Margins, Market potential, and Management data are
the 'M's discussed by 4 managers. Stresses the importance for
managers to face, coordinate, and review the real issues of a
business. Effort and resources must be effectively coordinated
or developed. Finance for Managers Series.

**Focus on Ethics: The Role of Values in Decision-
Making.** For complete citation, *see* ETHICS AND
VALUES.

862. Focus on Results
BNA Communications, Inc 1973 16mm film or
videocassette color 20 min instructor's print
materials; learner's print materials
Purchase: $535.00 Rental: 5-day $150.00; 3-day
$105.00 Preview: $35.00

Dramatization of a newly formed subsidiary of a British
multinational corporation facing typical challenges. Gives insight into international business operations and delves deeply
into strategic, managerial, and operational decision making,
forecasting, and measuring performance. Focus on Management Series, no. 1.

863. Focus on Tomorrow
BNA Communications, Inc 1968 16mm film or
videocassette color 21 min
Purchase: $525.00 Rental: 5-day $150.00; 3-day
$105.00 Preview: $35.00
Languages: English, Dutch, German, Portuguese,
Spanish, Swedish

Dramatization of managerial decisions in relation to risk-
taking, long-range planning, problem solving and decision
making, and allocation of resources between new vs. existing

products. Features Peter Drucker. Effective Executive Series,
no. 33.

Four Dimension Leadership. For complete citation,
see LEADERSHIP.

864. Four Essential Managerial Skills
Management Resources, Inc 7 audiocassettes
instructor's print materials; learner's print materials
Purchase: $275.00

Focuses on practical managerial functions of planning, budgeting, scheduling work, and maintaining standards. Printed
materials include application workbooks and tests for which a
scoring and feedback service is provided. One cassette provides
5 dramatized case studies specialized by type of management
such as government, manufacturing, and bank health. Intended
for individual or group study.

865. Fundamentals of Management and Supervision
Applied Management Institute, Inc audiocassettes
Purchase: $65.00

A taped one-day seminar by John R. Van de Water. Starts with
an analysis of planning, organizing, staffing, directing, and
controlling. Then introduces practical communication skills,
personal time management, delegation methods, creative problem solving, job enrichment techniques, and the importance of
values and ethical standard in the professional management
decision-making process.

866. How Do You Manage?
LCA Video/Films 1982 16mm film or
videocassette color 19 min instructor's print
materials; learner's print materials
Purchase: $350.00 Rental: $70.00 Preview:
$35.00

Portrays 3 department managers who examine their performances and begin to strengthen their skills in leadership,
delegation, and risk-taking. Humorous but practical. Australian
production. Funny Business Series.

867. How Not to Succeed in Business
Phoenix Films, Inc 1977 16mm film or
videocassette color 10 min
Purchase: film $195.00; video $135.00 Rental:
$20.00

Demonstrates the meaning of Parkinson's Law: Work expands
to fill the time available for its own completion. Shows how
many hands make heavy work. Shows how activities can
expand and multiply in every conceivable business situation.

868. How Successful Managers Manage
Edupac, Inc 7 audiocassettes instructor's print
materials; learner's print materials
Purchase: $295.00

Focuses on people and behavior skills through simulated job
situations. Shows decision making as an organizational process
and gives problem-solving techniques. Offers methods to give
employees balanced leadership. Seventh cassette includes 5
dramatized case studies from one of several areas: manufacturing, banking, insurance, health care, government, or service.
For group or individual study. Recommended time is 15 hours.

869. How to Be an Effective Middle Manager
American Management Associations   6 audiocassettes   learner's print materials
Purchase: $145.00   Other cost factors: AMA members $135.00; discounts available for bulk orders of materials

Recognizes that middle managers face unique problems and opportunities because of their position in the organization. Helps modify accepted management principles. Offers tools and techniques for decision making, managing relationships, influencing peers, being a catalyst, and delegating appropriately. Addresses the needs of the manager between upper management and personnel and production problems.

870. "How to" Drucker
AMACOM   4 audiocassettes   60 min   learner's print materials
Purchase: $130.00   Other cost factors: AMA members $110.00

Peter Drucker offers a practicing manager's day-to-day guide. Includes people relationships (staffing, peers, promoting and development), self-development, effective tools, and the future. Intended for new or experienced managers and supervisors.

871. How to Fail in Managing without Really Trying
Salenger Educational Media   1974   16mm film or videocassette   color   32 min   instructor's print materials; learner's print materials
Purchase: $495.00   Rental: $125.00   Preview: $35.00

Intended to improve understanding of the functions of the managerial role. Harold Koontz describes 13 key failures in the art of delegation and presents 20 common management pitfalls. Points up subtleties involved in effective management.

872. How to Manage the Boss
BNA Communications, Inc   1977   16mm film or videocassette   color   24 min   instructor's print materials
Purchase: $560.00   Rental: 5-day $150.00; 3-day $105.00   Preview: $35.00
Languages: English, Spanish, French

Dramatization provides Peter Drucker an opportunity to describe the importance of the relationship of managers with the boss. He points out what to do and what not to do. Stresses why it is essential to understand that the boss is a human being and must be treated as such. Manager and the Organization Series, no. 1.

873. How to Manage: The Process Approach and Henri Fayol
Salenger Educational Media   1982   16mm film or videocassette   color   14 min   instructor's print materials
Purchase: $475.00   Rental: $125.00   Preview: $35.00

Explains Fayol's system of management theory. Explores 5 functions or processes of management: planning, organizing, directing, coordinating, and controlling. Shows how managers can use this approach to aid them in becoming more effective.

874. Human Side of Management
Resources for Education and Management, Inc   4 filmstrips or slides and audiocassettes or videocassettes or filmstrip cartridges   9–14 min ea   instructor's print materials
Purchase: video $280.00 ($85.00 ea); filmstrips $235.00 ($69.00 ea); film cartridges $340.00 ($85.00 ea); slides $255.00 ($73.00 ea)

Presents overview of popular human behavior theory related to working with and supervising people. Emphasizes positive steps managers can use to influence on-the-job behavior. Intended for first-line supervisors.

If—For Anyone Who Makes Excuses. For complete citation, *see* COMMUNICATION.

875. If Japan Can—Why Can't We?
Films, Inc   1980   16mm film or videocassette   color   78 min
Purchase: film $1,050.00; video $695.00   Rental: $125.00   Preview: free

Reports on current projects designed to employ Japanese methods in American business such as the highly effective practice of giving workers a greater degree of participation and responsibility in the manufacture of quality products.

876. Importance of People
Audio-Forum   audiocassette   22 min
Purchase: $10.95

A consideration of the importance of people in modern management including topics such as human relations, horizontal promotion, and leadership.

877. Improving Managerial Skills
Resources for Education and Management, Inc   5 filmstrips or slides and audiocassettes or videocassettes or filmstrip cartridge   11–15 min ea   instructor's print materials
Purchase: video $305.00 ($75.00 ea); filmstrips $280.00 ($64.00 ea); filmstrip cartridge $425.00 ($85.00 ea); slides $295.00 ($67.00 ea)

Presents the basics of managing: overview, organizing and planning, decision making, motivation, and perception. Includes techniques for self-assessment of managerial skills.

878. Intergovernmental Management—The Task Ahead
National Audiovisual Center   1975   16mm film or videocassete   color   30 min
Purchase: $174.00   Rental: $12.50

Proposes developing policy options and strategies for strengthening the management capability of state and local governments through review of state and local management needs.

879. Introduction to Business and Small Business Management
Lansford Publishing Company, Inc   5 audiocassettes   instructor's print materials; transparencies
Purchase: $1,659.95

Learning modules include forms of business organization, finance, break-even and cost-volume profit analysis. Principles and concepts of management build a base for those interested in starting a business.

I've Got a Woman Boss. For complete citation, *see* WOMEN.

Jamestown Story: Improved Human Relations Can Change a Community. For complete citation, *see* BUSINESS ENVIRONMENT.

880. Joe Batten on Management
Creative Media   6 audiocassettes   1 hr ea
Purchase: $109.45

Series of dramatized and humorous situations with old-time radio actors sharing the fundamentals of Joe Batten's book *Tough-Minded Management*. Includes techniques of profitability, motivation, communication, setting goals and objectives, growing and stretching by building on strengths, a personal self-improvement program, and establishing a productivity climate.

881. Kaiser Corporation's Exempt Merit Increase Program
Development Digest   audiocassette
Purchase: $13.75

Arthur A. Handy, Jr. describes Kaiser's program: general principles, specifics of design, and ways to involve managers in ownership of the program.

882. Made in Japan
MTI Teleprograms, Inc   1982   2 16mm films or videocassettes   color   16 min and 20 min
Purchase: part 1 film $290.00; part 2 film $360.00; part 1 video $160.00; part 2 video $200.00   Rental: $25.00   Preview: free

Provides an in-depth look at the education, traditions, history, and culture that have shaped the Japanese success story. Explores attitudes and opinions of workers and top management through interviews. Concludes by citing how US industries like Ford and Westinghouse are already profiting by adapting some progressive Japanese techniques, many of which were originally American innovations. Part I: "Cultural Influences"; Part II "Business Practices."

883. Making Management Less Complex and More Fun—With Better Results
Lansford Publishing Company, Inc   4 audiocassettes   instructor's print materials; learner's print materials
Purchase: $109.95

Covers achievement thinking, management by objectives, feedback, positive reinforcement, communication, and evaluation. Intended for self-study by managers.

884. Man the Manager
Thompson-Mitchell and Associates   16mm film or videocassette   color   12 min   learner's print materials
Purchase: $195.00   Rental: $45.00   Preview: $15.00

Animated portrayal traces vital aspects of the management process as it deals with solutions of specific problems. Highlights how a manager can best use a growing list of resources to get things done.

885. Man the Manager Case Histories
Thompson-Mitchell and Associates   16mm film or videocassette   b/w   7 min   learner's print materials
Purchase: $80.00   Rental: $20.00   Preview: $15.00

Shows the consequences of ignoring basic managerial principles through 3 case histories. One concerns need for clear objectives, one the knowledge and experience of others, and one the importance of understanding the underlying causes of conflict.

886. Manage Your Way to Personal Success
Chamber of Commerce of the United States   6 audiocassettes   45–50 min ea   study guide
Purchase: $65.00

Offers hundreds of guidelines to achieve success in business, reorder personal life, and improve interpersonal relations. Stresses importance of understanding one's own potential, the need for sharpening personal skills, the art of harmonious motivation and the job, and responsibility of success. Intended for new or experienced managers.

887. Management
Lansford Publishing Company, Inc   60 slides and audiocassettes   learner's print materials
Purchase: $245.95

Deals with the essentials of the modern behavioral aspects of management. Includes historical perspective, major theories of human behavior, alternative management styles, and practical implications and applications.

888. Management by Example
BNA Communications, Inc   1969   16mm film or videocassette   color   24 min
Purchase: $525.00   Rental: 5-day $150.00; 3-day $105.00   Preview: $35.00

Introduces tough-minded management which involves human relations, the warmth and understanding of others' motives as well as their need for significance. Joe Batten illustrates his philosophy and discusses the 10 basics of management. Useful to center on discussing such themes as management philosophy, managerial ethics, authority, decision making, and management by objectives. Tough-minded Management Series, no. 1.

889. Management by Exception
Edupac, Inc   3 audiocassettes   learner's print materials
Purchase: $60.00

Emphasizes the importance of an information reporting system to pinpoint exceptions from realistic goals or forecasts. The reason for the variance is determined and that makes an appropriate response possible.

890. Management by Participation
BNA Communications, Inc   1971   16mm film or videocassette   color   30 min
Purchase: $550.00   Rental: 5-day $150.00; 3-day $105.00   Preview: $35.00
Languages: Arabic, English, French, Spanish

Management by participation is defined and discussed in terms of company cost, support from labor unions, employees, supervisors, and effects on productivity. Dramatic episodes illustrate how participatory management can be utilized in various types of companies. Saul Gellerman and Alfred Marrow examine the management by participation system instituted at Harwood Companies, Inc. Effective Organization Series, no. 2.

891. Management Discussions
Practical Management Associates, Inc   13 audiocassettes   30–45 min ea
Purchase: $200.00 ($18.00 ea)

Practical, nontheoretical views of many functions and problems managers face every day. Focus is on managing within the organization, leadership, principles of management, and current issues. Some cassettes are lectures; others are panel discussions. For group or self-study.

892. Management of Work
Resources for Education and Management, Inc   5 filmstrips or slides and audiocassettes or videocassettes or filmstrip cartridges   9–12 min ea instructor's print materials
Purchase: video $305.00 ($75.00 ea); filmstrips $280.00 ($64.00 ea); filmstrip cartridges $425.00 ($85.00 ea); slides $295.00 ($67.00 ea)   Preview: $20.00

Focuses on key management skills of planning, organizing and directing, and controlling after defining managers and their functions.

893. Management: Principles and Concepts
Lansford Publishing Company, Inc   1979   60 slides and 2 audiocassettes   instructor's print materials; learner's print materials
Purchase: $295.00

Deals with modern management concepts and principles at an introductory level. Broad approach to definition, background, organizational principles, and the functions of planning and managing.

894. Management Productivity
CRM/McGraw-Hill Films   1980   4 sets slides and audiocassettes   15 min ea   instructor's print materials; learner's print materials; transparencies
Purchase: $800.00 (for 20 participants)   Preview: free

Describes basic management and supervisory skills. Includes setting operational goals and objectives, effective delegation, problem solving, and the challenge of discipline. Intended for experienced or inexperienced managers and supervisors.

895. Management Techniques for Women
Science Research Associates   6 audiocassettes learner's print materials
Purchase: $245.00

Covers human behavior, human relations, communication, time management, and management techniques for women. Highlights motivation, performance appraisal, interviewing new employees, the new and temporary employee, and decision making and problem solving.

896. Management Training
BNA Communications, Inc   1971   16mm film or videocassette   color   24 min
Purchase: $525.00   Rental: 5-day $150.00; 3-day $105.00   Preview: $35.00
Languages: English, Portuguese

Points out the need for an organization to assess its management training program and analyze the needs and improvements required. Presents a case study of a company operating under management by objectives that experiences a key problem resulting from a failure to identify training needs. Management by Objectives Series, no. 5.

897. Manager and the Law
National Educational Media, Inc   1975   16mm film or videocassette   color   19 min   instructor's print materials; learner's print materials
Purchase: $399.00   Rental: 5-day $90.00; 3-day $80.00
Languages: English, Spanish

Introduces legal aspects of management. Gives typical examples of business situations with legal implications and 6 guidelines for avoiding legal problems in business. Illustrates the essential principles for coping with today's growing maze of laws and regulations. A lawyer/host describes how to use an attorney effectively. Features Norman Alden.

898. Managerial Control
National Educational Media, Inc   1981   16mm film or super 8mm or videocassette   color   instructor's print materials; learner's print materials
Purchase: $525.00   Rental: 5-day $125.00; 3-day $115.00
Languages: English, Spanish

Reveals how simple control procedures help supervisors and managers keep their operations within budget and on schedule without losing sight of their goals. Describes a 3-step approach to establishing and maintaining control. Points are illustrated with 3 episodes showing how lack of a meaningful control system eliminates the benefits of an otherwise well-executed plan, then shows how appropriate use of control techniques affect a plan.

899. Managerial Planning, Organizing, and Controlling
Training by Design   4 audiocassettes   4 hrs learner's print materials
Purchase: $95.00

Gives forms and levels of planning, fundamental concepts of organizing, effects of centralization/decentralization, ways to coordinate activity, matrix organization, and task forces and the essential role of control. Self-instructional.

900. Managerial Skills
Resources for Education and Management, Inc   5 filmstrips or slides and audiocassettes or filmstrip cartridges   8–12 min ea   instructor's print materials
Purchase: filmstrips $280.00 ($64.00 ea); filmstrip cartridges $425.00 ($85.00 ea); slides $295.00 ($67.00 ea); audiocassettes $65.00

Identifies essential managerial skills or organizing, decision making, and leadership. Organizing and perception modules utilize in-basket exercises from the text. Relates perception to the work environment, and provides examples of both accurate and poor perception. The text *Problems in Supervision* by Cabot L. Jaffee is available for an additional fee.

901. Managerial Skills for New and Prospective Managers

American Management Associations   6 audiocassettes   learner's print materials
Purchase: $145.00   Other cost factors: AMA members $135.00

Seeks to answer typical questions new managers have about their roles and responsibilities. Presents basic management skills and builds self-confidence. Includes basic managerial functions such as planning, delegation, time management, and control techniques.

902. Managing in the Year 2000

Creative Universal, Inc   77 slides and audiocassette
Purchase: $100.00

Highlights motivation, management by objectives, human relations, scientific and commodity issues. Intended for managers interested in trends in human performance and planning for the work force of tomorrow.

Managing Innovation and Growth. For complete citation, *see* TECHNOLOGY.

Managing the Knowledge Worker. For complete citation, *see* PERSONNEL MANAGEMENT.

903. Men Who Are Working with Women in Management

Martha Stuart Communications, Inc   1974   16mm film or videocassette or audiocassette   color   29 min
Purchase: film $450.00; video $300.00; audio $30.00   Rental: film $65.00; video $50.00

Shows a group of male executives at AT&T exploring the changes in their personal and corporate awareness brought about by their women colleagues. They discuss the differences in attitude reflected by language and the awkwardness of changes in their own life styles at home and at work required by women's new status. Tells how these men have coped with training, advancing, advising, and criticizing women. Are You Listening? Series.

904. Mondragon Experiment

Films, Inc   16mm film or videocassette   color   50 min
Purchase: film $860.00; video $430.00   Rental: $75.00   Preview: free

Examines a blend of capitalism and the highest degree of worker involvement in Mondragon, Spain, with its more than 80 factories ranging from iron foundries and shipyards to printing works and sawmills. All of these factories have had extraordinary worker participation for 25 years and are the most efficient factories in Spain.

905. National Managerial Test

Roundtable Films, Inc   16mm film or videocassette   b/w or color   60 min   learner's print materials
Purchase: $475.00   Rental: $125.00   Preview: $30.00

Intended to identify managerial strengths and weaknesses, monitor improvement, and establish goals for growth. Programed test presents 12 multiple choice questions—10 about dramatic episodes and 2 involving open-ended cases.

906. Objective-Focused Management

AMACOM   6 audiocassettes   60 min ea   learner's print materials
Purchase: $125.00   Other cost factors: AMA members $106.25

Presents the changes likely to take place in the next 10 years and points out the adaptations managers will need to make. Identifies the strategies required to cope with these changes and succeed. Features George Odiorne.

907. One Minute Manager

Twentieth Century-Fox Video, Inc   videocassette   color   50 min   book
Purchase: $950.00   Rental: $160.00   Preview: $90.00

Offers time-efficient management techniques: one-minute goals, one-minute praising, and one-minute reprimands. Routine practice of 3 simple steps aims at good performance, good results, and good feelings. Features Ken Blanchard, author of the book by the same name.

908. People in Management

Phoenix-BFA Films and Video, Inc   1976   16mm film   color   18 min
Purchase: $350.00   Rental: $53.00   Preview: free

Follows daily activities of several men and women at all stages of management from a trainee to a president of a large corporation. Shows their interactions with other people, their reflections on how they started their careers in management, what they like and dislike about their work, and what they see for themselves in the future.

909. Performance-Based Management

Organization Development Consultants   2 audiocassettes   3 hrs   learner's print materials
Purchase: $45.00

Emphasizes how to prioritize responsibilities, develop realistic plans, and improve decision-making capabilities. Suggests how to remove obstacles, reduce or eliminate conflict, and measure and gain from one's achievements. Includes a Self-Appraisal Inventory.

910. Peter Principle

Films, Inc   16mm film or videocassette   color   25 min
Purchase: film $520.00; video $260.00   Rental: $60.00   Preview: free

Examines the implications of Laurence J. Peter's theory for the individual and the organization. The dangers for the individual are stress diseases and an unbalanced homelife. The dangers for the organization are incompetence and inefficiency.

911. Peter Principle: Why Things Always Go Wrong
Salenger Educational Media   1975   16mm film or
videocassette   color   31 min   instructor's print
materials; learner's print materials; posters
Purchase: $495.00   Rental: $125.00   Preview:
$35.00

Shows the need for careful placement and management and
supervisory training to avoid the Peter Principle: employees will
rise to their level of incompetence. Prompts self-awareness of
personal level of competency. Includes competency analysis
tests for learners. Features Laurence J. Peter, author of *The
Peter Principle*.

912. Principles and Concepts of Management: An Introduction
Lansford Publishing Company, Inc   audiocassette
instructor's print materials; transparencies
Purchase: $295.00

Covers fundamental principles and concepts of management
oriented towards the formal aspects of management contrasted
with informal or behavioral aspects. Overview of early management scholars and practitioners such as Fayol and Taylor and
Gantt, as well as to more recent writers in the so-called
management process school.

913. Profile of a Manager
National Educational Media, Inc   1977   16mm film
or super 8mm or videocassette   14 min
instructor's print materials; learner's print materials
Purchase: $475.00   Rental: 5-day $115.00; 3-day
$105.00
Languages: English, Japanese, Spanish

Shows people problems that come to new and experienced
managers: creating a team in spite of conflicting personalities,
changing relationships with former peers, answering a dissatisfied boss, facing an emotional decision, and confronting a crisis.
Focuses on the attitudinal side of management, emphasizing the
need for continuing training in basic management skills.
Valuable orientation for managers.

914. Project Management
AMR International, Inc   6 audiocassettes   learner's
print materials
Purchase: $375.00

Emphasizes the strategic aspects of project management, systems for project management, and specific techniques to use.
Discusses organizational structures for projects and the behavioral aspects for managing projects. Features material by John
E. Mulvaney.

915. Psychology of Employee-Management Relations
Audio-Forum   audiocassette   20 min
Purchase: $10.95

Discusses psychological management versus autocratic management in relation to employee motivation and employee dynamics. Features Roger M. Bellows.

Secretary as Manager. For complete citation, *see*
SECRETARIAL SKILLS.

916. Self-Discovery for the Manager
AMACOM   3 audiocassettes

Purchase: $59.95   Other cost factors: AMA members
$49.95

Enables managers to understand self-perception and the perception of others about them. Then points out ways to come across
as a productive, successful manager. Features Mortimer R.
Feinberg.

917. Skills of the Executive
American Management Associations   1982   5
audiocassettes   learner's print materials
Purchase: $135.00   Other cost factors: AMA
members $121.50

Interviews with Peter F. Drucker about making the full use of
executive initiative to break through barriers and make positive
contributions. Focuses on making decisions right and effective,
job relationships, leadership, and careers.

918. Step in the Right Direction
National Audiovisual Center   1970   16mm
film   color   13 min
Purchase: $75.50   Rental: $12.50

Dramatizes importance of merchandise control in retail stores
and illustrates some control procedures and techniques.

919. Strategy of the Achiever
Vantage Communications, Inc   1978   16mm film or
videocassette   color   27 min
Purchase: $475.00

Shows the importance of smooth teamwork, individual performance, and the pursuit of excellence. Dramatization of a racing
yacht demonstrates the skipper's use of good management
techniques as he gets his people involved in solving a problem,
draws out their best ideas, and reinforces their good efforts
every step of the way.

920. Successful Management the Expert's Way
AMACOM   5 audiocassettes   60 min ea   booklet
Purchase: $125.00   Other cost factors: AMA
members $106.25

Synthesis and digest of management "greats." Appley, Bennis,
Hayes, Drucker, the Likerts, and Mintzberg are featured.

921. Ten Management Subjects
Van De Water Associates, Inc   1974   10
audiocassettes   45 min ea   learner's print materials
Purchase: $200.00

Broad coverage of management principles for experienced
managers. Includes communication, motivational factors, use of
time, rational problem solving, creativity, managing by goals
and results, management strategy, and union organizing. Suggested as a 10-hour program for group or self-study.

922. Texas Instruments' Success Sharing Program
Development Digest   audiocassette
Purchase: $13.75

Describes in detail Texas Instruments, Inc: the organization,
the philosophy of management, the People Asset Effectiveness
Program and its link with their success sharing program.

923. Theory X and Theory Y: The Work of Douglas McGregor, Part I, Description
BNA Communications, Inc 1969 16mm film or videocassette color 25 min instructor's print materials
Purchase: $535.00 Rental: 5-day $150.00; 3-day $105.00 Preview: $35.00
Languages: English, French, Portuguese, Spanish

Contrasts traditional management theory with the new behavioral science approach to management. Richard Beckhard and Warren Bennis interpret and explain McGregor's findings in layman's terms. Motivation and Productivity Series, no. 5.

924. Theory X and Theory Y: The Work of Douglas McGregor, Part II, Application
BNA Communications, Inc 1969 16mm film or videocassette color 25 min instructor's print materials
Purchase: $535.00 Rental: 5-day $150.00; 3-day $105.00 Preview: $35.00
Languages: English, French, Portuguese, Spanish

Presents applications of Douglas McGregor's behavioral science findings to managerial situations. Shows how "self-fulfilling prophecy" can determine how others will behave toward you, the best way to develop trust among your people, and why a change in managerial assumptions is more important than a change in tactics. Richard Beckhard, Warren Bennis, and John Paul Jones give examples of how Theory Y is used successfully in different organizations. Motivation and Productivity Series, no. 6.

925. Theory X and Theory Y: Two Sets of Assumptions in Management
Salenger Educational Media 1974 16mm film or videocassette color 10 min instructor's print materials; learner's print materials
Purchase: $395.00 Rental: $125.00 Preview: $35.00

Introduces 2 different sets of assumptions about human behavior as identified by Douglas McGregor. Clarifies the contrasting management styles that result from adopting one or the other of these sets of assumptions. Indicates the relationship between management style and employee response. Provides managers with an increased awareness and appreciation of their own styles and the implications that their styles have on their current and/or future effectiveness as managers.

To Be a Winner, Back Your Winners. For complete citation, *see* COMMUNICATION.

926. Tools and Skills of Management
Classroom World Productions 4 audiocassettes
Purchase: $27.50

General overview of management aspects important to new managers. Emphasizes the significance of relationships with employees and understanding their feelings. Highlights art of delegation, decision-making process, time management, and selection and training employees.

927. Try to See It My Way
Xicom-Video Arts 1977 16mm film or videocassette color 28 min
Purchase: $530.00 Rental: $100.00 Preview: $35.00

Attacks principle area of inefficiency and time-wasting: management of the manager's own office. Portrays how wrong attitudes of a boss and secretary take their office partnership to the brink of breakdown. A third party shows what went wrong. Features John Cleese and Adrienne Posta. Companion film to *We Can Work It Out.* Secretary and Her Boss Series, no. 1.

928. Turning Management On
Exec-U-Service Associates 1971–1973 10 videocassettes color 50–60 min ea instructor's print materials
Purchase: $9,250.00 ($925.00 ea) Preview: free

Focuses on key concepts and skills related to such subjects as improving meetings, understanding and managing inter-departmental conflict, organizational change, the role of middle managers in organizational planning, management use of budgets and motivation, and decision making. Introduces key concepts and tools through discussion techniques. Generates participative experiences rather than passive viewing. Each videocassette serves as the resource base for a 3-hour program.

929. Type Z: An Alternative Management Style
Twentieth Century-Fox Video, Inc 1981 16mm film or videocassette color 95 min
Purchase: film $1,195.00; video $750.00 Rental: film $200.00; video $160.00 Preview: free

Presents 5 years of research work on Japanese and American management done by Dr. William G. Ouchi. He discovered and identified type Z, a new style emerging in the US, successfully blending both systems. Type Z firms have greater productivity, higher employee morale, and a successful quality of work life. Shows historical and sociological view of organizational development in Japan and US with new insight into employer-employee relations, power structures, and the growing concern for quality work environments.

Understanding Behavior in Organizations: How I Feel Is What I Do. For complete citation, *see* ORGANIZATIONAL CHANGE AND DEVELOPMENT.

930. Unorganized Manager
Xicom-Video Arts 1983 2 16mm films or videocassettes color 25 min ea instructor's print materials
Purchase: $650.00 ea Rental: $120.00 ea Preview: $40.00 ea

Follows disorganized manager through an ordinary day showing time-wasting blunders. Each error is then corrected, showing how to manage each day, set priorities, deflect distractions, and organize others. Features John Cleese.

Using Managerial Authority. For complete citation, *see* POWER AND AUTHORITY.

931. We Can Work It Out
Xicom-Video Arts 1977 16mm film or videocassette color 28 min instructor's print materials
Purchase: $530.00 Rental: $100.00 Preview: $35.00

Deals with the management of a manager's office. Shows through several enactments the consequences of ignoring the proper techniques and procedures. Stresses the importance of a boss and secretary as a team instead of as 2 individuals doing separate jobs. Companion film to *Try to See It My Way*. Secretary and Her Boss Series, no. 2.

932. What Can I Contribute?
BNA Communications, Inc   1968   16mm film or videocassette   color   23 min
Purchase: $525.00   Rental: 5-day $150.00; 3-day $105.00   Preview: $35.00
Languages: Dutch, English, French, German, Portuguese, Spanish, Swedish

Dramatization with Peter Drucker advising company about effective use of staff, teamwork, communication, planning, and introducing change. The Effective Executive, no. 2.

933. When Commitments Aren't Met
Creative Media   1979   16mm film or videocassette   color   10 min   instructor's print materials
Purchase: $250.00   Rental: $60.00   Preview: $20.00

Dramatization shows how essential the employee's internal commitment is to make and meet verbal commitments. A supervisor, with the help of a manager, learns how to use an "expective" vs. directive style of management to motivate employee's commitment.

934. Winning with Leadership Skills
American Management Associations   6 audiocassettes   learner's print materials
Purchase: $145.00   Other cost factors: AMA members $135.00; discounts available for bulk orders of materials

Shows how to analyze problems with subordinates and modify management styles into leadership patterns that get results. Comprehensive coverage.

Woman as Effective Executive. For complete citation, *see* WOMEN.

Women in Management. For complete citation, *see* WOMEN.

Women in Management: Opportunity or Tokenism? For complete citation, *see* WOMEN.

Women in Middle Management. For complete citation, *see* WOMEN.

Women in the Work Force: A Manager's Role. For complete citation, *see* WOMEN.

935. You Can Manage and Motivate
Singer Management Institute   4 audiocassettes instructor's print materials
Purchase: $60.00   Preview: $15.00

Useful to help new managers solve problems creatively, manage time effectively, and communicate with employees through recognitions. Strong emphasis on motivation.

MANAGEMENT BY OBJECTIVES

936. Colt—A Case History
BNA Communications, Inc   1970   16mm film or videocassette   color   25 min
Purchase: $495.00   Rental: 5-day $150.00; 3-day $105.00   Preview: $35.00

Presents the process of introducing management by objectives in a medium-sized British company. Analyzes strengths and weaknesses after 2½ years and shows how the system was simplified and modified. Management by Objectives Series, no. 6.

Defining the Manager's Job. For complete citation, *see* GOALS AND GOAL SETTING.

Executive Skills. For complete citation, *see* MANAGEMENT.

Flight Plan. For complete citation, *see* PLANNING.

937. How to Get Organized—MBO for Individuals
MOR Associates   4 videocassettes   color   30–60 min ea   instructor's print materials; learner's print materials
Purchase: $995.00   Rental: $250.00   Preview: $95.00

Edited version of a live seminar conducted by George Morrisey. Covers introduction to management by objectives, determining key results areas, the decision matrix, and setting objectives and action plans. Four separate modules suggested for 2-hour sessions each.

938. How to Manage by Objectives
MBO, Inc   1975   4 16mm films or videocassettes   color   15 min ea   instructor's print materials; learner's print materials
Purchase: $1,295.00 (includes single copy of learner's workbook)   Rental: film only $184.00   Preview: $73.00   Other cost factors: additional learner's workbooks at $32.00 ea

Presents an MBO system to introduce management development methods. Emphasizes 2 stages: management by anticipation and management by commitment. Shows how program audits fit into an MBO system. Features George Odiorne. Suggested for a 2-day seminar.

939. How to Manage by Results
American Media, Inc   1978   2 16mm films or super 8mm or videocassettes   color   22 min ea   instructor's print materials; learner's print materials
Purchase: $840.00   Rental: $170.00   Preview: $45.00

In the first film, Dale McConkey shows through dramatizations what it takes to make management by objectives (MBO) really work in an organization. Then, in film 2, he explains a 3-step practical application: preparation, writing, and action. Useful to prepare employees for the introduction of MBO into an organization.

940. Integrating MBO into Your Management Development Program
Development Digest   audiocassette
Purchase: $13.75

George S. Odiorne presents ways to integrate management by objectives (MBO) into management development programs. An overview of the MBO system related to a total system of management development.

941. Interaction between MBO and OD Efforts
Development Digest   audiocassette
Purchase: $13.75

Discusses 3 basic questions: Which comes first, management by objectives (MBO) or organization development (OD)? Is an OD philosophy critical to the success of an OD effort? Is an effective MBO program critical to sustaining an OD effort?

942. Introduction to Management by Objectives and Results
MOR Associates   audiocassette
Purchase: $10.00

Provides a general overview by George Morrisey of the key issues covered in the MOR approach.

943. MBO and Performance Appraisal
Thompson-Mitchell and Associates   3 16mm films or videocassettes   color   15–20 min ea
Purchase: $752.00 ($294.00 ea)   Rental: $110.00   Preview: free

Focuses on the interrelationship of management and labor in a management by objectives program. Three modules—"What is MBO?," "Development Objectives," and "Performance Appraisal"—show how to apply MBO in planning, controlling, career development, and performance appraisal.

944. MBO for Operating Managers
MBO, Inc   1978   123 slides and audiocassette learner's print materials
Purchase: $275.00 (for 20 listeners)   Preview: $58.00

Major focus is on management roles, scheduling, situation analysis, objectives and strategies, planning and budgeting, evaluation, and monitoring. Intended for experienced managers. Suggested for a 4- to 6-hour program.

945. Management by Objectives
AMACOM   6 audiocassettes   60 min ea   learner's print materials
Purchase: $95.00   Other cost factors: AMA members $85.00

Discusses how to establish relevant, measurable objectives, increase productivity and profits through individual involvement, evaluate performance, avoid the common pitfalls of implementing MBO, and use MBO techniques to increase motivation.

946. Management by Objectives and Results
Schrello Associates   6 audiocassettes   learner's print materials
Purchase: $295.00

Emphasizes how to manage day-to-day activities in order to achieve the results wanted. Includes establishing objectives,

setting priorities, identifying indicators to measure progress, develop teamwork, and taking corrective action when needed.

947. Management by Objectives and Results Overview
Addison-Wesley Publishing Company, Inc   1973   audiocassette
Purchase: $15.95

Brief but comprehensive description of management by objectives and its results, principles, and application. Intended for use with George W. Morrisey's book *Management by Objectives and Results*. Useful for group or self-study.

948. Management by Objectives and Results Self-Teaching Audiocassette Kit
Addison-Wesley Publishing Company, Inc   1975   6 audiocassettes   learner's print materials
Purchase: $85.00

Helps managers take a large and complex job and break it down into manageable units. Places particular emphasis on identifying indicators of effectiveness, establishing realistic and measurable objectives, preparing action plans for achieving those objectives, and taking corrective measures to keep objectives and action plans directed toward the results wanted.

949. Management by Objectives and Results Video Tape Overview
Addison-Wesley Publishing Company, Inc   1974   videocassette   30 min
Purchase: $300.00   Preview: $25.00

Brief description of *Management by Objectives and Results* by George M. Morrisey.

950. Management by Objectives
BNA Communications, Inc   1971   16mm film or videocassette   color   30 min
Purchase: $525.00   Rental: 5-day $150.00; 3-day $105.00   Preview: $35.00
Languages: English, Portuguese, Spanish

Illustrates what management by objectives is and is not. Outlines top management's responsibilities for goal setting and stresses the actions top executives must take to step up a management development plan to meet goals set. Shows how to bring together the organization's need for growth and profit and the individual's need to contribute.

951. Management by Objectives
BNA Communications, Inc   3 audiocassettes   40 min ea
Purchase: $36.00 ($12.00)

Peter F. Drucker and John Humble exchange ideas on management and issues. Addresses how to evaluate management potential and accomplishment. Explores the myths and realities of participative management. Offers ideas on the management of the nonprofit organization.

952. Management by Objectives
CRM/McGraw-Hill Films   2 16mm films or videocassettes   color   13–14 min ea
Purchase: $752.25 ($295.00 ea)   Rental: $75.00 ea   Preview: free

Animated presentations that present the philosophy and implementation of management by objectives (MBO), offer precise guidelines for well-written objectives, and illustrate MBO in action through techniques of performance appraisal.

953. Management by Objectives
Lansford Publishing Company, Inc   1981   60 slides and audiocassette   learner's print materials
Purchase: $255.95

Underlines the fundamental concepts and philosophy of management by objectives (MBO) with its emphasis on self-determination and self-motivation of employees. Designed to give students and trainees an authentic feel for MBO, a good grasp of its basic concepts, realistic awareness of its pitfalls, and skills in implementation.

954. Management by Objectives
Penton/IPC Education Division   3 audiocassettes learner's print materials
Purchase: $60.00

Offers instructions on how to establish objectives, set standards for measuring performance, and conduct measurements to determine progress.

955. Management by Objectives
Resources for Education and Management, Inc   3 filmstrips or slides and audiocassettes or videocassettes or filmstrip cartridges   8–10 min ea instructor's print materials
Purchase: video $245.00 ($95.00 ea); filmstrips $220.00 ($75.00 ea); filmstrip cartridges $255.00 ($85.00 ea); slides $235.00 ($80.00 ea)   Preview: $20.00

Designed for all levels of management in any organization implementing or seeking to improve a management by objectives (MBO) program. Includes modules introducing the parts of MBO, goal setting, and the steps to install MBO.

Managerial Game Plan. For complete citation, *see* TEAM BUILDING.

956. Managing by Objectives
AMR International, Inc   8 audiocassettes
Purchase: $350.00

Presents the management by objectives system addressing 9 key questions. Includes how to select the most critical components of MBO, to identify indicators of effectiveness, and to develop objectives and action plans.

957. Managing by Objectives
American Management Associations   6 audiocassettes   learner's print materials
Purchase: $145.00   Other cost factors: AMA members $135.00

Describes how to organize efforts at every level of the organization toward the achievement of common objectives. Shows middle managers how they fit into a management by objectives system. Emphasizes importance of objectives, individual involvement, performance evaluation, and motivation.

958. Managing the Nonprofit Organization
MBO, Inc   6 audiocassettes   30 min ea   manual

Purchase: $98.00
Designed for top-level and middle management of nonprofit organizations. Shows skills they need to improve their organizations. Suggests a 2-stage management by objectives systems (anticipation and commitment).

959. OD to MBO or MBO to OD: Does It Make a Difference?
Development Digest   audiocassette
Purchase: $13.75

Distinguishes differences between MBO and OD in theory and practice. Proposes a model for getting results through people that transcend the conventional definitions yet synthesizes the concepts.

960. Recipe for Results: Making Management by Objectives Work
Creative Media   1976   16mm film or super 8mm or videocassette   color   32 min   instructor's print materials
Purchase: $475.00   Rental: $90.00   Preview: $30.00

Offers practical help in designing and implementing a management by objectives system. Step-by-step development of key areas include brainstorming and identifying key result areas, gathering input and obtaining staff involvement and commitment, writing simple, direct objectives, planning and developing an operation strategy to meet established objectives, and measuring and controlling progress to ensure that objectives are being met. Features Joe Batten.

961. Training by Objectives
MBO, Inc   6 audiocassettes   30 min ea   learner's print materials
Purchase: $98.00

Applies management by objectives to the training function and describes the importance of training in economic terms. Presents the central objective of training as changing behavior and offers a variety of approaches to do that. Presents the full range of trainer responsibilities: identifying needs, training techniques, evaluation of training effectiveness. Features George Odiorne.

Women and MORe—Winning Techniques for Goal Setting. For complete citation, *see* GOALS AND GOAL SETTING.

MANAGEMENT DEVELOPMENT

962. Assessing Management Potential
BNA Communications, Inc   1971   16mm film or videocassette   33 min
Purchase: $550.00   Rental: 5-day $150.00; 3-day $105.00   Preview: $35.00
Languages: English, Spanish

A lecture by Douglas Bray describes how to identify management potential within the organization. Career planning helps an organization provide for personnel contingencies. Covers promotion policy and practice, managerial selection, career counseling, and how to tell personnel they are not qualified for promotion. Intended for middle management and above. Effective Organization Series, no. 1.

963. Executive Development and Training Issues— Government and Industry
National Audiovisual Center 1976 3
videocassettes color 19–22 min ea instructor's print materials
Purchase: $281.00 (part 1 $101.00; part 2 $101.00; part 3 $79.50)

Government and industry officials discuss executive development, training programs, and mobility. They cite general principles and specific examples and point out that development is long term and immediate payoff is rare.

Integrating MBO into Your Management Development Program. For complete citation, *see* MANAGEMENT BY OBJECTIVES.

964. Management Development: A Top Executive's View
Development Digest audiocassette
Purchase: $13.75

Describes the systems approach employed by KLM for management development, management by objectives, and organization development.

Management Development for Organizational Development. For complete citation, *see* ORGANIZATIONAL CHANGE AND DEVELOPMENT.

965. Manager as Entrepreneur
BNA Communications, Inc 1971 16mm film or videocassette color 31 min instructor's print materials
Purchase: $385.00 Rental: 5-day $150.00; 3-day $105.00 Preview: $35.00

Discusses the managerial staffing required by showing one way for managers to view themselves. Suggests that assuming the role of an entrepeneur stimulates managers to respond positively and imaginatively to demands as well as to think and behave in ways that support innovation and continuing self-renewal. Managing Discontinuity Series, no. 9.

966. Manager under Pressure
Xicom-Video Arts 1977 16mm film or videocassette color 17 min instructor's print materials; learner's print materials
Purchase: $390.00 Rental: $100.00 Preview: $35.00

Examines the plight of a typical manager caught in a pressure squeeze. Analyzes the dynamics of pressure situations and emphasizes that pressure is unavoidable and normal. Shows manager confronted with intense personal and professional conflicts who analyzes alternatives and solutions available to him. Points out that times of puzzlement and pain, if explored properly, are times for gaining perspective and learning about ourselves. Animation with video "slice of life" situations.

967. Manager Wanted
Roundtable Films, Inc 16mm film or videocassette color 28 min
Purchase: $425.00 Rental: $85.00 Preview: $30.00

Develops around a situation which occurs when a junior executive feels he is not ready to take over a more senior position. Shows that management must be prepared to create the right atmosphere and must accept responsibility for the development of subordinates as well as setting them an example. Outlines essential requirements for effective managerial training and the importance of delegation.

968. Role of Management Education in Management Development
Development Digest audiocassette
Purchase: $13.75

Distinguishes between education, training, and management development. Discusses the integration of teaching models into a composite designed especially for specific management development objectives. Analyzes factors which complicate training for international management and discusses appropriate education processes.

969. Thank God It's Friday
International Film Bureau, Inc 16mm film or videocassette color 25 min instructor's print materials
Purchase: $495.00 Rental: 5-day $67.00; 3-day $50.00

Dramatizes the current managerial development problems of 2 brothers in their respective companies. Designed to prompt managers to begin discussion on self-development and to prompt organizations to identify and start appropriate activities which encourage and support managers who take positive action to forward their own self-development.

MANAGEMENT TECHNIQUES

970. Advanced Management Techniques for Women
Science Research Associates 6 audiocassettes learner's print materials
Purchase: $95.00 Other cost factors: additional workbooks $5.00 ea

Program focuses on motivation, performance appraisal, interviewing new employees, the new employee and the temporary worker, decision making, and problem solving. A practical approach.

971. Applied Management Series
Organizational Dynamics 1980 4 films or videocassettes 11–18 min ea instructor's print materials; learner's print materials
Purchase: $4,800.00 ($1,200.00 ea) Preview: free Other cost factors: additional learner materials

Four separate units—the lecture portion of a 4-day workshop—include performance review, managing time, managing conflict, and decision making/problem solving. Emphasizes working with subordinates and within a systematic review process. Includes case studies and exercises. One-day workshops suggested for each unit. Intended for managers.

972. Basics of Management
AMACOM 3 audiocassettes 3 hrs learner's print materials

Purchase: $69.95   Other cost factors: AMA members $59.45

Nontechnical presentation of the most essential management concepts. Covers planning, organizing, directing, controlling, communicating, decision making, and motivating. Intended for new or experienced managers; useful for self-study. Features Roy A. Lindberg. AMA Management Basics Series.

973. Building Basic Management Skills
Lansford Publishing Company, Inc   4 audiocassettes   instructor's print materials; learner's print materials
Purchase: $119.95

Examines 3 major management problems: determining what must be done, how this can be shared appropriately with those who will do it, and how group effort can equal more than the sum of the individual contributions.

974. Compleat Manager: What Works When
Research Press   11 audiocassettes
Purchase: $150.00

Intended for supervisors and executives who seek to maximize people, products, and profits. Dr. Alan C. Filley presents a wide range of techniques from decision making and problem solving to time management.

975. Complete Management Course
Lansford Publishing Company, Inc   5 audiocassettes   instructor's print materials; learner's print materials
Purchase: $2,395.00

An introductory course in management. Focus is on the modern behavioral aspects of management but also includes traditional and modern quantitative approaches.

Developing Personal Effectiveness. For complete citation, *see* CAREER PLANNING AND DEVELOPMENT.

976. Executive Seminars in Sound
Nation's Business   8 audiocassettes
Purchase: $100.00   Preview: free

Dramatizations of work situations that show skill areas needed by managers. Emphasizes communication, time management, decisive thinking, delegating, organization and planning, working with others, and strategizing for success.

977. Face-to-Face Management
Creative Media   4 audiocassettes   2 hrs
Purchase: $59.50

Joe Batten presents principles and suggests practical application of good management techniques. Discussion includes a broad definition of success, leadership and management, managing the strengths and not the weaknesses of others, and managing through "vulnerability."

978. How to Work with Your Fellow Managers
BNA Communications, Inc   1977   16mm film or videocassette   color   21 min   instructor's print materials
Purchase: $560.00   Rental: 5-day $150.00; 3-day $105.00   Preview: $35.00

Languages: English, French, Spanish

Peter Drucker shows how to eliminate frictions with peers and gain the cooperation needed. Dramatization shows situation where information is needed but impossible to obtain because a manager lacks acceptance, understanding, and respect from his fellow managers. Intended for new and experienced managers. Manager and the Organization Series, no. 2.

MANAGERIAL GRID

Grid Approach to Conflict Solving. For complete citation, *see* CONFLICT AND CONFLICT MANAGEMENT.

979. How to Improve Your Management Style—And How the Managerial Grid Can Help
AMACOM   3 audiocassettes
Purchase: $85.00   Other cost factors: AMA members $72.25

Robert R. Blake and Jane S. Mouton offer the managerial grid to managers to help them discover the kind of managers they are and what the ideal manager is. Materials include a personal assessment test.

980. Managerial Grid in Action
BNA Communications, Inc   1974   16mm film or videocassette   color   33 min
Purchase: $550.00   Rental: 5-day $150.00; 3-day $105.00   Preview: $35.00
Languages: English, Spanish

Explains the managerial grid approach to management. The managerial grid allows the manager to become aware of leadership style and the results it produces, then to select the most effective style of management. Features Robert R. Blake and Jane S. Mouton. Managerial Grid Series, no. 1.

981. Styles of Management
S&L Communications, Inc   1981   videocassette   color   43 min
Purchase: $100.00   Rental: $45.00   Other cost factors: SLCI members $75.00 (rental $30.00); styles of management inventory instrument $4.00 ea

Explains the managerial grid and its implications for effective management. Lecture by Maitland Huffman describes the use of a styles of management inventory that gives scores indicating one's personal style of management.

MANPOWER PLANNING
See PRODUCTIVITY

MARKETING

982. Basics of Marketing Management
AMACOM   3 audiocassettes   3 hrs   learner's print materials
Purchase: $69.95   Other cost factors: AMA members $59.45

Practical primer on the marketing function in an organization. Describes the processes of marketing research (collecting the data) and activating marketing strategies for new and old products. Features Houston Elam and Norton Paley. AMA Management Basics Series.

983. Five Greatest Marketing Blunders of the Century
Audio-Forum   audiocassette   84 min
Purchase: $11.95

Describes how errors in calculation figured in the experiences of 5 large companies as they had to abandon products with substantial market research, promotional effort, and money investments. Reveals problems they faced and how they dealt with them.

984. Fundamentals of Marketing
Penton/IPC Education Division   3 audiocassettes
learner's print materials
Purchase: $60.00

Examines how to satisfy customers' needs and maximize profits through the manipulation of marketing elements.

985. "I Don't Care What You Call It, Marketing or Selling!"
BNA Communications, Inc   1972   16mm film or videocassette   color   24 min
Purchase: $540.00   Rental: 5-day $150.00; 3-day $105.00   Preview: $35.00

Portrayal of a company losing a key customer and how its managers devise a comprehensive new marketing program to remedy the situation. Helps clarify marketing as related to and distinct from other functions. Companion film to *What Business Are You Really In?* Management Practice Series B, Marketing, Part I.

986. Marketing for Non-Profit Organizations
Lansford Publishing Company, Inc   3 audiocassettes
Purchase: $79.95

Explains why and how price, product, and promotion may be used by public sector organizations to make their activities more effective.

987. This is a Recorded Message
National Film Board of Canada   16mm film   color   10 min
Purchase: $200.00   Rental: $40.00   Preview: free

Advertising's visual appeal has been developed into such a persuasive force that it shapes the desires, the needs, and, to a large degree, even the lives of modern-age people. Film brings out the conflict between the illusion and reality.

988. Tomorrow's Customers
BNA Communications, Inc   1971   16mm film or videocassette   color   34 min
Purchase: $385.00   Rental: 5-day $150.00; 3-day $105.00   Preview: $35.00

Stresses importance of innovative marketing in long-range planning, reviewing strategies, and making changes in this period of rapidly shifting trends, tastes, and demands. Elizabeth Hall, Vermont Royster, and Peter Drucker discuss innovative marketing. Changes in the composition and structure of the market, particularly the values and expectations of the individu-al and industrial customers, are overlooked by many managers. Managing Discontinuity Series, no. 1.

989. What Business Are You Really In?
BNA Communications, Inc   1972   16mm film or videocassette   color   34 min
Purchase: $260.00   Rental: 5-day $150.00; 3-day $105.00   Preview: $35.00

Points out responsibility of management in the marketing area. Makes a distinction between consumers and customers and between marketing and sales. Features Theodore Levitt and John Humble. Companion film to *"I Don't Care What You Call It. Marketing or Selling!"* Management Practice Series B, Marketings, Part II. Management Practice Series B, Marketings, Part II. Management Practice Series B, Marketings, Part II. Management Practice Series B, Marketings, Part II.Management Practice Series B, Marketings, Part II. Management Management Practice Series Management Practice Series B, Marketings, Part II. Marnagement Practice Series Management Practice Series

MATH

990. Arithmetic Refresher
HBJ Media Systems Corporation   1981   6 slide/audiocassette presentations (3 audiocassettes)
instructor's print materials; learner's print materials
Purchase: $1,875.00

Shows typical addition, subtraction, multiplication, and division skills; performing arithmetic operations with fractions, decimals, and percentages. Helpful to increase speed, accuracy, and confidence in performing basic computations. Intended for any employee in need of improved computational skills. Suggested for 10–16 hours.

991. Basic Mathematics
HBJ Media Systems Corporation   1981   64 slide/audiocassette presentations   instructor's print materials; learner's print materials
Purchase: $17,855.00

Offers a comprehensive program in arithmetic skills and problem solving. Includes addition and subtraction, multiplication and division, fractions and mixed numbers, decimals, percents, and ratio and proportion. Suggested for 100–120 hours.

992. Business Math Skills
Prentice Hall Media   1981   7 filmstrips and audiocassettes   program guide
Purchase: $245.00

Presents practical mathematics required by different units within an organization. Each module emphasizes skill-building and application of specific skills: simple interest, compound interest, discounts and commissions, payroll, depreciation, retail computations, and inventory control.

993. Interest and Present Value
HBJ Media Systems Corporation   1981   6 slide/audiocassette presentations   instructor's print materials; learner's print materials
Purchase: $1,785.00

Shows how to calculate interest, bank discounts, and present value. Suggested for 10–12 hours.

994. Math Solution
AMACOM   6 audiocassettes   60 min ea   learner's print materials
Purchase: $109.95

Focuses on business math, providing step-by-step techniques for improving problem-solving skills and progressively developing basic math competency. Designed to reduce the time-consuming and debilitating effects of math anxiety and open listeners to more effective learning as well as to increase proficiency and accuracy in basic arithmetic skills. Includes lectures, group discussions and dialog, question and answer sessions, and written exercises.

MEETING MANAGEMENT
See also PRESENTATIONS

Communicating Successfully. For complete citation, *see* PRESENTATIONS.

995. Communicating Successfully, Meetings
Time-Life Video   1973   16mm film or videocassette   color   25 min
Purchase: film $550.00; video $400.00   Rental: $55.00   Preview: free

Dramatizes problems that may arise in a typical meeting and gives possible solutions. Shows how to conduct meetings for positive results. Features Robert Morse. Book and audiocassette available separately.

Communication Skills for Managers. For complete citation, *see* COMMUNICATION.

996. Conference Leading Skills
Resources for Education and Management, Inc   3 filmstrips or slides and audiocassettes or videocassettes or filmstrip cartridges   13–18 min ea   instructor's print materials
Purchase: video $245.00 ($95.00 ea); filmstrip $220.00 ($75.00 ea); filmstrip cartridges $225.00 ($85.00 ea); slides $235.00 ($80.00 ea)   Preview: $20.00

Covers basic principles of effective conference leadership with particular emphasis on the planning and organizing steps necessary. Includes how to maximize conference resources and capitalize on group dynamics through participation.

Effective Speaking for Managers. For complete citation, *see* PRESENTATIONS.

997. How to Conduct a Meeting
Centron Films   1979   16mm film   color   18 min
Purchase: $385.00

Dramatization reveals rules of parliamentary procedure, the roles and functions of the group officers, and the importance of adhering to the agenda of business. Examines basic procedures which include presenting committee reports, making motions and amendments, conducting debate and voting, and nominat-ing and electing candidates for positions. Intended for those who conduct meetings through parliamentary procedure.

998. How to Hold a Meeting
Creative Media   1977   16mm film or videocassette   color   30 min
Purchase: $450.00   Rental: 3-day $85.00   Preview: 3-day $25.00

Practical information on how to conduct an effective meeting by having a purpose, reducing tension, increasing participation, having a caring attitude, being ready to deal with almost anything, and leaving the meeting with a plan of action.

999. How to Run Productive Meetings
American Management Associations   6 audiocassettes   learner's print materials
Purchase: $145.00   Other cost factors: AMA members $135.00; discounts available for bulk orders of materials

Managers who can consistently get results from meetings recover their investment of time and salaries. Comprehensive, practical cassettes cover questioning techniques to guide and control meetings, use of visual aids, outlines to keep meeting on track, and listening skills. Also deals with how to control problem members and channel their efforts into productive contributions.

1000. Meeting in Progress
Roundtable Films, Inc   1970   16mm film or videocassette   color   40 min   learner's print materials
Purchase: $550.00   Rental: $125.00   Preview: $30.00
Languages: Danish, Dutch, English, French, German, Japanese, Spanish, Swedish

Shows techniques essential for effective conference leadership and meeting management. Shows how to effectively deal with 12 critical points typical of any meeting, including keeping people on the subject, what to do when challenged, and determining the amount of agreement required. Takes conference leaders through a typical problem-solving conference demonstrating ways to deal with situations crucial to the success of a meeting. Includes stop action points and alternative choices.

1001. Meeting Leading
Professional Development, Inc   1976   2 16mm film or videocassette   color   34 min ea   instructor's print materials; learner's print materials
Purchase: films $1,450.00 ($750.00 ea); video $1,250.00 ($650.00 ea)   Rental: film $195.00; video $175.00   Preview: $75.00

Addresses everything from mechanics, preparations, and objectives to group dynamics and a resulting action plan. The first film covers preparation of the facility and environment psychological preparation—planning for impact and control. The second deals with the conduct and management of the meeting, handling problem participants, and use of leadership techniques.

1002. Meetings, Bloody Meetings
Xicom-Video Arts   1976   16mm film or videocassette   color   30 min

Purchase: $625.00   Rental: $100.00   Preview: $35.00

Points out disciplines and techniques that are available for making meetings shorter, more productive, and more satisfying. Portrays 5 meetings that fail through typical faults. Features John Cleese.

1003. Take the Chair

BNA Communications, Inc   1973   16mm film or videocassette   color   28 min
Purchase: $510.00   Rental: 5-day $150.00; 3-day $105.00   Preview: $35.00

Shows tried and tested methods, actions, and techniques to effectively conduct or participate in a meeting. Dramatizes details and actions that spell the difference between a meeting's success or failure yet are often deceptively simple.

MEMORY

1004. How to Get What Ya Want with What Ya Got

General Cassette Corporation   6 audiocassettes
Purchase: $49.50

Cavett Robert offers 6 guides for success and ways to improve memory. Merlyn Cundiff presents how to communicate effectively through use of "body language."

1005. How to Improve Your Memory

AMACOM   6 audiocassettes   1 hr ea   learner's print materials
Purchase: $145.00   Other cost factors: AMA members $135.00; discounts for bulk orders of materials

Presents general learning principles and specific mnemonic devices showing how to choose techniques to fit particular memory problems. Good memory helps organize thinking and improve manager effectiveness.

1006. Memory

CRM/McGraw-Hill Films   1980   16mm film or videocassette   color   30 min   instructor's print materials
Purchase: $560.00   Rental: $95.00   Preview: free

Concentrates on improvement of long-term memories, illustrating a variety of very effective methods of categorizing and referencing memories in order to facilitate fast, efficient recall. Organization of information is shown to be the most important key, and lively examples from the past, present, and probable future drive this point home.

1007. Memory

Classroom World Productions   4 audiocassettes
Purchase: $27.50

Techniques for remembering different kinds of information to advance socially and in business.

1008. Memory Made Easy

AMACOM   3 audiocassettes   60 min ea
Purchase: $85.00   Other cost factors: AMA members $72.25

Presents memory tools and techniques for complex data—recall of numbers and names, dates, facts, and figures.

1009. Remembering Names and Faces

Roundtable Films, Inc   1978   16mm film or videocassette or 27 slides with audiocassette   color   17 min   instructor's print materials; learner's print materials
Purchase: $475.00   Rental: $85.00   Preview: $30.00
Languages: Dutch, English

Uses dramatization of a salesman forgetting a customer's name. Shows proven techniques for "storing" and "retrieving" names, based upon sound psychological concepts. Provides a 6-step method for recalling names. Printed materials provide name recall practice with audiocassette, slides, and exercises using pre- and posttests.

1010. Thanks for the Memory

LCA Video/Films   1982   16mm film or videocassette   18 min   instructor's print materials; learner's print materials
Purchase: $350.00   Rental: $70.00   Preview: $35.00

Dramatizes a salesman who learns a few key memory techniques. Humorous but practical approach. Australian production. Funny Business Series.

MENTAL HEALTH
See HEALTH

METRIC
See WEIGHTS AND MEASURES

MINORITY EMPLOYMENT
See EQUAL EMPLOYMENT OPPORTUNITY

MOTIVATION

Are You Earning the Right to Manage Others? For complete citation, *see* SUPERVISION.

1011. Art of Motivation

Thompson-Mitchell and Associates   1974   16mm film or videocassette   color   10 min
Purchase: $195.00   Rental: $25.00

Stresses the importance of motivation in relation to productivity. Illustrates Theory X, Theory Y, and Herzberg's Theories with numerous portrayals and graphics. Aim is to strengthen middle management's ability to handle personnel more effectively.

1012. Behavioral Approach to Management

Lansford Publishing Company, Inc   4 audiocassettes   instructor's print materials
Purchase: $99.95

Covers positive motivational techniques for improving behavior of people on the job. Based on modern behavioral psychology.

1013. Common Sense Motivation
Roundtable Films, Inc 1981 16mm film color 12 min
Purchase: $400.00 Rental: $75.00 Preview: $30.00

Dramatization surfaces sources of job satisfaction and a checklist of management skills that motivate employees. The application and value of motivation is shown as a supervisory skill.

Communication and Motivation. For complete citation, *see* COMMUNICATION.

1014. Employee Motivation and Organizational Behavior
Lansford Publishing Company, Inc 5 audiocassettes instructor's print materials; learner's print materials
Purchase: $149.00

Overview of several aspects including work performance and job satisfaction, understanding and inducing motivation, and the psychological contract at work.

1015. Employee Motivation: The Role of the Supervisor
Audio-Forum audiocassette 22 min
Purchase: $10.95

Roger Bellows discusses the supervisor's role in interpersonal on-the-job relationships.

1016. Face-to-Face Motivation
Creative Media 4 audiocassettes
Purchase: $45.00

Joe Batten presents his ideas of how employees can become self-motivating through self-awareness.

1017. Gellerman on Motivation and Productivity
University Associates 1971 2 audiocassettes learner's print materials
Purchase: $49.95

Explores motivational techniques as related to work experiences and productivity problems. A conversation featuring Saul W. Gellerman with Dr. Manny Kay and experienced managers and supervisors relating their dealing with down time, absenteeism, dissatisfaction with pay, and other employee grievances.

1018. Go-Giver
American Media, Inc 1980 16mm film 30 min
Purchase: $550.00 Rental: $110.00 Preview: $35.00

Dramatization of a middle-level manager in a publishing company who sees himself as a real "go-getter." He will not be effective motivating others until he learns "go-giver" techniques that work in the office and at home.

1019. Habit of Winning
Cally Curtis Company 16mm film or videocassette color 28 min instructor's print materials
Purchase: film $525.00; video $500.00 Rental: $130.00 Preview: $40.00

Jerry Kramer and 6 former professional football players who are now in business discuss how Vince Lombardi's teachings and motivational techniques helped them achieve business success.

1020. Human Nature and Organizational Realities
BNA Communications, Inc 1967 16mm film or videocassette color 29 min
Purchase: $535.00 Rental: 5-day $150.00; 3-day $105.00 Preview: $35.00
Languages: Dutch, English, French, Portuguese, Spanish

Chris Argyris illustrates and explains how jobs can be designed to motivate individuals at lower levels of responsibility. Motivation can reduce apathy and provide paths to change and responsibility. Motivation and Productivity Series, no. 7.

1021. Human Relations and Motivation
Applied Management Science, Inc 1968 10 videocassettes color 30 min ea instructor's print materials; learner's print materials
Purchase: $9,500.00 Rental: $170.00 per learner Preview: free

Shows how any behavior is the result of a person's attempt to satisfy needs. Demonstrates how supervisors can channel the efforts of employees to satisfy more of their needs on the job, making employees more productive and more satisfied. Helps supervisors and managers see how to use meaningful, nonmonetary incentives to unleash the full potential of their employees.

1022. Incentive Awards—A Positive Force in Personnel Administration
National Audiovisual Center 1976 80 slides and audiocassette 35 min
Purchase: $31.50

Incentive awards are to motivate employees and to recognize their accomplishments. Describes the kinds of awards available through the Federal Incentive Awards Program, along with the basic criteria for submission. Useful for first-line supervisors.

1023. Incentive Awards: Management's Prerogative—Management's Obligation
National Audiovisual Center 1979 80 slides and audiocassette 15 min
Purchase: $31.50

Describes the Federal Incentive Awards Program for employee recognition, a program required in federal departments and agencies.

1024. It's a Matter of Pride
Salenger Educational Media 1975 16mm film or videocassette 17 min instructor's print materials; learner's print materials
Purchase: $410.00 Rental: $125.00 Preview: $35.00

Advocates the value of pride and self-satisfaction as a motivator. Humorous vignettes show the rewards of having pride in one's work. Useful for groups where quality, service, and productivity are important.

1025. Job Enrichment
Resources for Education and Management, Inc
1970   4 filmstrips or slides and audiocassettes or
videocassettes or filmstrip cartridges   10–13 min
instructor's print materials
Purchase: video $280.00 ($85.00 ea); filmstrips
$255.00 ($69.00 ea); filmstrip cartridges $340.00
($85.00 ea); slides $270.00 ($73.00 ea)

Introduces job enrichment as a way of overcoming poor
performance and attitude problems. Shows how to enrich jobs
and how to handle some common job enrichment problems.
Examines motivational factors and symptoms of the need for
job enrichment.

1026. Job Enrichment
Salenger Educational Media   16mm film or
videocassette   color   14 min   instructor's print
materials; learner's print materials; posters
Purchase: $455.00   Rental: $125.00   Preview:
$35.00

Designed to help managers and supervisors understand what
job enrichment is and how and when it can be used to motivate
people. Explores job enlargement, job satisfaction, and job
motivation. Defines job enrichment as a technique of job
design.

1027. Job Enrichment in Action
BNA Communications, Inc   1969   16mm film or
videocassette   color   21 min
Purchase: $535.00   Rental: 5-day $150.00; 3-day
$105.00   Preview: $35.00
Languages: Dutch, English, Portuguese, French

A dramatized case shows an approach to introduce or install a
job enrichment program. Dan Hertzberg comments on some
common problems and pitfalls found in job enrichment.
Motivation to Work Series, no. 3.

**1028. Job Enrichment: Managerial Milestone a
Myth?**
Salenger Educational Media   1974   16mm film or
videocassette   color   14 min   instructor's print
materials; learner's print materials; posters
Purchase: $425.00   Rental: $100.00   Preview:
$35.00

Deals with job enrichment as a technique of job design. The
contingency approach is when job enrichment fits the nature of
the technology it is being applied to and the nature of the
person working on that technology. Only then will it lead to
high organizational performance and to high worker motivation.

1029. Jumping for the Jellybeans
Films, Inc   16mm film or videocassette   color   25
min
Purchase: film $520.00; video $260.00   Rental:
$60.00   Preview: free

Explores Fred Herzberg's widely accepted theories on job
enrichment and the nature of the motivation to work. Motivation comes primarily from what people actually do at work and
does not rest solely on salary and working conditions. It is
based on ability and the opportunity given to use that ability,
which leads to the concept of "job enrichment" and the

importance of designing jobs that enable a person to learn and
grow.

**Kaiser Corporation's Exempt Merit Increase Pro-
gram.** For complete citation, *see* MANAGEMENT.

**1030. Keep Reaching: The Power of High Expecta-
tions**
Creative Media   1977   16mm film or
videocassette   color   30 min   instructor's print
materials
Purchase: English $495.00; Spanish $485.00   Rental:
$110.00   Preview: $30.00   Other cost factors:
learner's printed materials

Dramatization of a husband and father who finds that high
expectations influence the results he gets from himself and
others. Synthesizes Joe Batten's research and application of
motivation tools and concepts. Focuses on developing effective
motivation skills and increasing self-awareness. Learner's printed materials, separately priced, include self-discovery hand-
books—one for managers and supervisors and one for general
audiences.

1031. Kita, or, What Have You Done for Me Lately?
BNA Communications, Inc   1977   16mm film or
videocassette   color   24 min   instructor's print
materials
Purchase: $535.00   Rental: 5-day $150.00; 3-day
$105.00   Preview: $35.00
Languages: Dutch, English, French, Spanish,
Portuguese

Series of vignettes reveals typical employee reaction to a
manager's use of hygiene factors (as described by Herzberg) and
motivation. Addresses supervisory responsibility for motivation
of employees and emphasizes that motivation comes from
within. Motivation to Work Series, no. 2.

1032. Managing Motivation
Salenger Educational Media   1981   16mm film or
videocassette   color   10½ min   instructor's print
materials; learner's print materials
Purchase: $410.00   Rental: $125.00   Preview:
$35.00

Tells managers/supervisors how productivity can be increased
through increased motivation. Defines and illustrates 3 factors
important to motivation: providing desirable rewards, creating
expectations of success, and maintaining open communication.

**1033. Maslow's Hierarchy of Needs: Almost Every-
thing You Ever Wanted to Know about Motivating
People**
Salenger Educational Media   1975   16mm film or
videocassette   color   15 min   instructor's print
materials; learner's print materials
Purchase: $455.00   Rental: $125.00   Preview:
$35.00

Presents Abraham Maslow's theory of human motivation—the
hierarchy of needs theory. Explores human motivation as it
applies to work situations. Increases awareness of people's
needs and understanding of the factors involved in satisfying
those needs.

1034. Modern Meaning of Efficiency
BNA Communications, Inc 1969 16mm film or videocassette color 27 min
Purchase: $535.00 Rental: 5-day $150.00; 3-day $105.00 Preview: $35.00
Languages: Dutch, English, French, Portuguese, Spanish

Illustrates the results of job oversimplification and outlines an effective approach to motivation in today's changing world. Features Frederick Herzberg. Motivation to Work Series, no. 1.

Motivating Employees: Understanding Legal Requirements. For complete citation, *see* EQUAL EMPLOYMENT OPPORTUNITY.

1035. Motivating for Profit
Edupac, Inc 2 audiocassettes instructor's print materials; learner's print materials
Purchase: $75.00

Identifies applications of motivational principles and the importance of motivation to profitable operations.

1036. Motivating for Profit
Management Resources, Inc 2 audiocassettes instructor's print materials; learner's print materials
Purchase: $75.00

Pinpoints the importance of motivation to profitable operations. Identifies 5 needs that motivate people, 5 "satisfiers" and "dissatisfiers" that affect job performance, and 7 systems of personal values that motivate. Explores applications of motivational principles.

1037. Motivation and Supervision
Bureau of Business Practice 16mm film or videocassette color 20 min
Purchase: $425.00 Rental: $95.00 Preview: $45.00

Illustrates the motivational fundamentals every supervisor must know in order to raise morale, strengthen control, and increase productivity. Deals with profit robbing problems—low productivity, high turnover, chronic absenteeism, habitual tardiness, and general lack of job interest.

1038. Motivation & Discipline
Practical Management Associates, Inc 6 audiocassettes 4½ hrs
Purchase: $125.00

Discusses the relation of motivation and performance and the responsibility of the supervisor. Addresses discipline of unmotivated employees and the pitfalls in working to correct unmotivated employees.

1039. Motivation for Managers
Classroom World Productions 4 audiocassettes
Purchase: $27.50

Emphasizes the importance of understanding motivation and setting goals for one's self and others. Addresses the unmotivated employee, reading attitudes, the gentle art of persuasion, and the responsibilities of authority.

1040. Motivation in Perspective
BNA Communications, Inc 1969 16mm film or videocassette color 22 min
Purchase: $285.00 Rental: 5-day $150.00; 3-day $105.00 Preview: $35.00
Languages: English, Spanish

Summarizes and contrasts predominant ideas and theories in the management of motivation. Concluding the series, Saul Gellerman ties all the concepts of earlier films together. Motivation and Productivity Series, no. 9.

1041. Motivation: It's Not Just the Money
Document Associates 1977 16mm film or videocassette color 26 min
Purchase: $400.00 Rental: $45.00

Examines factors that contribute to satisfaction and productivity. Looks at the Volvo automobile plant where an innovative approach to manufacturing was established to better meet the needs of employees. Improvements added variety, challenge, responsibility, and interest to work; decreased conflict; and led to greater productivity. Discusses the far-reaching ideas of Abraham Maslow and Douglas McGregor.

1042. Motivation: Making It Happen
CRM/McGraw-Hill Films 16mm film or videocassette color 12½ min
Purchase: $295.00 Rental: $75.00 Preview: free

Tells the story of Ernie who has never had any musical training yet is able to organize and direct the company band because he believes in himself and motivates others to do the same. Animated. Meeting starter.

1043. Motivation, Organization Development, and Individual Career Achievement
Development Digest audiocassette
Purchase: $13.75

Reviews McClelland's need for achievement, power, and affiliation and what these concepts mean in an organizational setting. Features R.D. Brynildsen.

1044. Motivation & Supervision
Bureau of Business Practice 16mm film or videocassette color 20 min
Purchase: $425.00 Rental: $95.00 Preview: $45.00

Dramatizes typical situations that help supervisors develop a stronger ability to motivate people to their fullest potential. Shows the mistakes supervisors make which lead to low production, high turnover, and general lack of job interest. Explains how to avoid these mistakes. Portrays typical supervisors in ordinary shop scenes.

1045. Motivation through Job Enrichment
BNA Communications, Inc 1967 16mm film or videocassette color 28 min
Purchase: $535.00 Rental: 5-day $150.00; 3-day $105.00 Preview: $35.00
Languages: Dutch, English, French, Portuguese, Spanish

Emphasizes that motivation is found only in the job itself, in the opportunity to satisfy the human need for accomplishment. Frederick Hertzberg discusses and illustrates his famous "Motivation-Hygiene Theory." He advocates job enrichment—the deliberate enlargement of a job's responsibility, scope, and challenge. Motivation and Productivity Series, no. 2.

1046. Motivation through the Work Itself
Development Digest   audiocassette
Purchase: $13.75

Suggests job enrichment, a well-established way to motivate employees with results far beyond such secondary motivators as job enlargement, job rotation, and job simplification.

1047. Moving and the Stuck
Goodmeasure, Inc   1980   slides and audiocassette
13 min   instructor's print materials
Purchase: $425.00   Rental: $125.00

Employees who are "moving" are those who are productive and motivated. Those who are "stuck" are neither. Graphics show how job situations affect aspirations, self-confidence, morale, and effort and illustrates how opportunity shapes career potential leaving some people out, causing them to become "stuck." Companion to *Getting Them Moving*. P/QWL Series, no. 3.

1048. New Look at Motivation
CRM/McGraw-Hill Films   16mm film or videocassette   color   32 min
Purchase: $560.00   Rental: $95.00   Preview: free

Examines the impact of employee desires for affiliation, power, and achievement on performance. Identifies personality types and the most suitable methods of motivating each type. Proposes that self-motivation based on individual needs fulfillment is the most lasting and effective form of motivation. Features David McClelland.

1049. Pay for Performance
BNA Communications, Inc   1971   16mm film or videocassette   color   31 min
Purchase: $550.00   Rental: 5-day $150.00; 3-day $105.00   Preview: $35.00
Languages: English, Spanish

Shows how open communication about pay policies can result in the better use of pay as a motivator in support of nonfinancial incentives. Stresses replacing performance appraisal programs with goal setting. Uses dramatic episodes. Features Emanuel Kay and Saul Gellerman. Effective Organization Series, no. 3.

1050. People Factor: The Hawthorne Studies for Today's Managers
Salenger Educational Media   1976   16mm film   11 min   instructor's print materials; learner's print materials
Purchase: $425.00   Rental: $125.00   Preview: $35.00

Reviews the experiments of the classic Hawthorne studies of 1920 including some original motion picture footage. Clarifies the principles that evolved from the studies and reveals their present day managerial applications. The studies form the basis of the humanistic approach used in management today.

Productivity: Getting Your Employees to Care. For complete citation, *see* PRODUCTIVITY.

Psychology of Employee-Management Relations. For complete citation, *see* MANAGEMENT.

1051. Putting the Motivation Back into Work
AMACOM   3 audiocassettes
Purchase: $80.00   Other cost factors: AMA members $65.00

Discusses how to design jobs with built-in motivators, ways to work with negative feedback—what you can do to set things "right" and how to provide immediate, direct feedback so that you can stay on top of what's really happening in your department. Features Robert N. Ford.

1052. Self-Motivated Achiever
BNA Communications, Inc   1967   16mm film or videocassette   color   27 min
Purchase: $535.00   Rental: 5-day $150.00; 3-day $105.00   Preview: $35.00
Languages: Dutch, English, Spanish

Discusses the self-motivated achiever and gives several pointers on how to manage this individual effectively. Focuses on how to identify self-motivated people in the organization and manage them successfully. Utilizes dramatizations and David McClelland's research on achievement motives. Motivation and Productivity Series, no. 3.

1053. Something to Work For
Roundtable Films, Inc   1966   16mm film or videocassette   color   30 min
Purchase: $425.00   Rental: $85.00   Preview: $30.00
Languages: Danish, Dutch, English, French, German, Japanese, Norwegian, Portuguese, Spanish, Swedish

Dramatizes the need for high, clear expectations, open communication, and encouragement in reaching common goals. Contrasts the attempts of 2 managers to motivate their people. Identifies motivational approaches and how to expand a worker's self-image. Shows why some people respond positively and others negatively to attempts to "motivate" them.

1054. Strategy for Productive Behavior
BNA Communications, Inc   1969   16mm film or videocassette   color   20 min
Purchase: $285.00   Rental: 5-day $150.00; 3-day $105.00   Preview: $35.00
Languages: English, Spanish

Introduces concepts such as the role of behavioral science in management and organization and motivation as a force in employee satisfaction and productivity. Features Saul Gellerman. An introduction to the series. Motivation and Productivity Series, no. 1.

1055. Supervisor—Motivating through Insight
National Educational Media, Inc   1971   16mm film or super 8mm or videocassette   color   11 min   instructor's print materials; learner's print materials
Purchase: $365.00   Rental: 5-day $90.00; 3-day $80.00
Languages: English, French, Greek, Japanese, Spanish

Provides insight into employee psychology, the way motivation works, and the keys to achieve it. Based on theories of Maslow and Herzberg, uses chess game metaphor to counter old myths about job needs and to reveal a dignified approach to employee motivation. Role play demonstrations give further insight into the emotional needs of both workers and supervisors.

1056. This Matter of Motivation
Dartnell 13 16mm films or videocassettes color film 28 min; cases 3–5 min instructor's print materials
Purchase: film $545.00; case studies $125.00 ea Rental: film $165.00; case studies $60.00 ea Preview: film $45.00; case study $20.00

Presents Frederick Herzberg's techniques as applied to personnel problems in basic film. Other films are brief case studies that pose a typical behavioral problem such as absenteeism, low productivity, sour employees, and rumor mills. Intended for managers and supervisory personnel.

1057. Twelve Minutes a Day
Goodmeasure, Inc 1980 slides and audiocassette 13 min instructor's print materials
Purchase: $425.00 Rental: $125.00

Presents the new skills needed by managers of the new work force. Uses graphics to illustrate practical action steps that can help managers solve important workplace problems by motivation and managing employees better. Gives special attention to women, minorities, and older employees. P/QWL Series, no. 6.

1058. Understanding Motivation
BNA Communications, Inc 1967 16mm film or videocassette color 29 min
Purchase: $535.00 Rental: 5-day $150.00; 3-day $105.00 Preview: $35.00
Languages: Dutch, English, French, Spanish

Saul Gellerman gives tips on how to diagnose specific problems and take action that gets at root causes instead of symptoms. He outlines 3 broad prescriptions that often have a positive motivational effect. Motivation and Productivity Series, no. 4.

1059. What Really Motivates People?
American Media, Inc 16mm film or videocassette color 15 min
Purchase: $395.00 Rental: $85.00 Preview: $30.00

Illustrates the factors that have the greatest influence upon an employee's motivation and are directly within the manager's control. Focuses on 4 key "motivators" and job satisfiers, what really motivates people, and how to use these elements to increase productivity.

Will to Work. For complete citation, *see* SUPERVISION.

You Can Manage and Motivate. For complete citation, *see* MANAGEMENT.

MULTINATIONAL CORPORATIONS
See INTERNATIONAL BUSINESS

NEGOTIATION
See also ARBITRATION AND LABOR RELATIONS; CONFLICT AND CONFLICT MANAGEMENT; GRIEVANCE

1060. Art of Negotiating
Dartnell 16mm film color 29 min
Purchase: $575.00 Rental: $135.00 Preview: $45.00

Seeks to remove fears of negotiating and provide a clear understanding of the negotiation process. Focuses on the "win-win" style of negotiating that meets the needs of both sides. Shows real-life situations.

1061. Art of Negotiating
Negotiation Institute, Inc 1977 12 videocassettes color instructor's print materials; learner's print materials; 4 books
Purchase: 180-day license $1,750.00; 90-day license $875.00 Preview: $100.00 per learner for materials

Edited 2-day seminar with comprehensive coverage of personal and business skills used in negotiating situations. Covers setting climate for negotiating, preparing for negotiating, effective communicating, overcoming barriers, and negotiating philosophies. Learner fee includes *Negotiation Manual*, a comprehensive 500-page manual with negotiating strategies, counterstrategies, checklists, preparation charts, and tools.

1062. Art of Negotiating
Negotiation Institute, Inc 1977 12 audiocassettes learner's print materials; 3 books
Purchase: $295.00

Fundamentals of negotiating and its state-of-the-art. Both offensive and defensive strategies are discussed in terms of specific techniques. Cassettes were taped at Gerard Nierenberg seminar; includes how to neutralize surprises, build the climate, open alternatives, and sustain a negotiated success. Intended for self-study.

At the Table. For complete citation, *see* ARBITRATION AND LABOR RELATIONS.

1063. Effective Negotiating: Tactics and Countermeasures that Work for Training Directors
Development Digest audiocassette
Purchase: $13.75

Examines techniques for negotiating more effectively. Points out overlooked power in individuals and how to use it. Discusses the relevance of both deadlines and deadlocks. Describes 5 modes of negotiation. Presented by Chester L. Karrass.

1064. Engineering of Agreement
Roundtable Films, Inc 1978 16mm film or videocassette 21 min
Purchase: $495.00 Rental: $100.00 Preview: $30.00

Demonstrates successful directive and nondirective questioning techniques basic to obtaining cooperation, winning acceptance, or selling products. Includes a special section to help viewers practice techniques. Updated version.

1065. Everyone's a Negotiator
Twentieth Century-Fox Video, Inc 1980 16mm film or videocassette color 70 min instructor's print materials
Purchase: film $945.00; video $600.00 Rental: film $200.00; video $160.00 Preview: free

Herb Cohen illustrates the 3 crucial factors for successful negotiations: information, organizational pressure and time, and power. He indicates it as an ongoing communication process that can be analyzed, predicted, and understood.

Harmonics of Conflict. For complete citation, *see* CONFLICT AND CONFLICT MANAGEMENT.

1066. Negotiating Leverage
AMR International, Inc 1981 16 audiocassettes learner's print materials
Purchase: $395.00

Uses interviews and interpretive narration by Edward C. Caprielian. Presents strategies and skills based on the tested use of power and psychological principles in negotiations. Focuses primarily on getting leverage through negotiating. Comprehensive.

1067. Negotiating Successfully
Time-Life Video 1975 6 16mm films or videocassettes color 25 min ea learner's print materials
Purchase: film $2,995.00; video $2,500.00 Rental: $200.00 Preview: free

Explains the basic principles of interaction and the complex ways in which they work. Examines the problems from both sides of the negotiation table: buyer and seller, management and employee. Offers specific techniques for each of 4 stages of negotiating. Stresses that negotiations should be thoroughly satisfying and the result should be a mutually beneficial arrangement. Features Chester L. Karrass.

1068. Persuasive Negotiating
Twentieth Century-Fox Video, Inc 16mm film or videocassette color 60 min instructor's print materials; book
Purchase: film $875.00; video $500.00 Rental: film $200.00; video $160.00 Preview: film $75.00; video $50.00

Compares 2 distinct styles of negotiating—the competitive "win-lose" typical of adversary relationships vs. the collaborative "win-win" style, where needs of both parties are met. Exposes tactics often used to take advantage of the unsuspecting. Herb Cohen shows how to identify and satisfy mutual needs. Companion film to *Everyone's a Negotiator*.

1069. Practical Negotiating Skills
Applied Management Institute, Inc audiocassettes
Purchase: $65.00

Identifies the basics of negotiating, negotiating behavior, the use of power, and strategies and tactics. Cassettes of a one-day seminar conducted by Robert J. Laser.

Through Conflict to Negotiation. For complete citation, *see* CONFLICT AND CONFLICT MANAGEMENT.

Waldenville II. For complete citation, *see* ARBITRATION AND LABOR RELATIONS.

NONVERBAL COMMUNICATION
See also COMMUNICATION

1070. Communication by Voice and Action
Centron Films 1979 16mm film color 14 min
Purchase: $305.00

Illustrates through short dramatizations how important nonverbal communication is in transmitting the meaning of messages. Deals with interpersonal and public address situations. Blends basic theories and techniques for speech delivery.

1071. Communication: The Nonverbal Agenda
CRM/McGraw-Hill Films 1975 16mm film or videocassette color 30 min
Purchase: $560.00 Rental: $95.00 Preview: free

Intended to show managers how to constructively use both nonverbal and verbal communication in instructions. Dramatizations illustrate theories of Dr. Albert Mehrabian. Intended to alert viewers to the constant interpersonal flow of nonverbal communication.

How to Get What Ya Want with What Ya Got. For complete citation, *see* MEMORY.

1072. Non-Verbal Communication
Creative Media 3 audiocassettes
Purchase: $28.00

Revised edition presents Dorothy Shaffer discussing how to interpret "body language."

1073. Non-Verbal Communication
Salenger Educational Media 1979 16mm film or videocassette color 17 min instructor's print materials; learner's print materials; book
Purchase: $455.00 Rental: $125.00 Preview: $35.00

Intended to help employees become more aware of the nonverbal messages others send and more conscious of the messages they send. Illustrates how nonverbal messages reveal our attitudes and feelings.

1074. Nonverbal Communication and Interaction
Lansford Publishing Company, Inc audiocassette instructor's print materials; learner's print materials; transparencies
Purchase: $209.95

Introduces the fundamentals of nonverbal communication. Includes body motion, the language of distance and environment, and tactile and written communication.

OFFICE MANAGEMENT
See MANAGEMENT

OFFICE SKILLS
See CLERICAL SKILLS

ORGANIZATIONAL CHANGE AND DEVELOPMENT
See also CHANGE

1075. Basic Concepts and Practices of Organization Development
Development Digest 1980 10 audiocassettes 1 hr ea learner's print materials
Purchase: $169.50 Preview: $50.00

Organization development theory together with its application in changing an organization through interventions. Describes 4 ways to diagnose an organization and key dimensions of its culture. Intended for experienced managers; suggested for individual or group study.

Bob Knowlton Story. For complete citation, *see* COMMUNICATION.

Building More Effective Teams: The Organization Development (O.D.) Approach. For complete citation, *see* TEAM BUILDING.

1076. Changing Organizations: Designing for People and Purpose
Document Associates 1978 16mm film or videocassette color 26 min
Purchase: $400.00 Rental: $45.00

Illustrates theories of organizational structure and how they seek to ensure high productivity and employee satisfaction. Jay Lorsch offers his contingency theory: the task-organization-people fit model. General Foods and Hanover Trust Company show this model in action.

1077. Chris Argyris on Organization Predictions/ Prescriptions
AMACOM 4 audiocassettes 4 hrs booklet
Purchase: $100.00 Other cost factors: AMA members $85.00

Chris Argyris discusses principles for success, organizational change, handling conflict, and communication from his broad background and expertise in management.

1078. Client as Theorist: An Approach to Individual and Organization Development
Development Digest audiocassette
Purchase: $13.75

Discusses the basic model underlying Lee Bolman's cognitive approach: do "X" in situation "S" to achieve goal "G." Explains use of this process to assess goals, assumptions, strategies, and outcomes of client groups. Urges organizational development practitioners and clients to be more explicit with their theories.

Concept of Organizational Climate. For complete citation, *see* PERSONNEL MANAGEMENT.

1079. Concepts and Theories of Organization Development
Development Digest 4 audiocassettes
Purchase: $63.00

Presents dimensions of organizational development presented by W. Warner Burke. Interactive cassette poses questions to listener that foster understanding and application. Especially useful for those taking part in organizational change for the first time.

Confrontation, Search and Coping. For complete citation, *see* CONFLICT AND CONFLICT MANAGEMENT.

1080. Consulting Process in Action Skill-Development Kit
Learning Resources Corporation 6 audiocassettes learner's print materials
Purchase: $190.00

Ronald and Gordon Lippitt dialog in this self-study kit for groups or individuals working on skills development. Includes practice module and exercises. Covers discovering the need for help, establishing credibility, formulating a contract, identifying the problem and potential for change, goals and planning, follow-up support, and motivation and commitment.

Coping with Change. For complete citation, *see* CHANGE.

1081. Do-It-Yourself Organization Diagnosis
Practical Management Associates, Inc audiocassette learner's print materials
Purchase: $28.00

Self-study program on the organization-analysis technique in which numerical values are assigned to each action of authority and control. In comparing the organization's analysis with ideal ranges, the organization's ailments will surface.

1082. Frontiers of OD: Three Views
Development Digest 2 audiocassettes
Purchase: $27.50

Emphasizes the significance of persons and their values in organizational development efforts. Suresh Srivastva, Stanley M. Herman, and Sheldon A. Davis give their viewpoints from academic and industry stances.

Fully Functioning Organization. For complete citation, *see* ETHICS AND VALUES.

1083. Gestalt Orientation to Organization Development
Development Digest audiocassette
Purchase: $13.75

Stanley M. Herman applies Gestalt principles to organizational change and shows how it has helped to revitalize organizations.

1084. Growth Stages of Organizations
BNA Communications, Inc 1969 16mm film or videocassette color 31 min
Purchase: $525.00 Rental: 5-day $150.00; 3-day $105.00 Preview: $35.00

Delves into causes of interdepartment strife and explores marketing, physical and financial resources, productivity, human resources, innovation and creativity, profitability, and social responsibility. Dr. Gordon Lippitt introduces the concept of organization renewal and the 6 stages of organization growth. Organization Renewal Series, no. 1.

1085. How Organization Renewal Works
BNA Communications, Inc   1969   16mm film or videocassette   color   27 min   guide
Purchase: $525.00   Rental: 5-day $150.00; 3-day $105.00   Preview: $35.00

Gordon Lippitt discusses who should take the lead in organization renewal and how to obtain the support of top management. He stresses the role of the "internal consultant," illustrates how to organize task forces, details the elements of teamwork, clarifies roles, describes traps to avoid, and discusses contributions vs. total commitment. Organization Renewal Series, no. 5.

How to Make the Organization Work for You. For complete citation, *see* CAREER PLANNING AND DEVELOPMENT.

1086. Initiating Planned Change in Health Care Systems
Development Digest   audiocassette
Purchase: $13.75

Describes the causal factors within health care organizations which require change efforts that are different from those used in other organizations. Suggests changes for improving the effectiveness of consultants to health care systems.

1087. Innovative Organization
BNA Communications, Inc   1971   16mm film or videocassette   color   35 min
Purchase: $385.00   Rental: 5-day $150.00; 3-day $105.00   Preview: $35.00

An interview with Peter Drucker and John Humble who discuss the innovative process in organizations. They discuss the establishment of balance between emphasis on authority-obedience and creativity-interdependence, hierarchical or "free form" structure, efficiency and effectiveness, and information flow. Characteristics of the organization of the future are suggested. Managing Discontinuity Series, no. 8.

1088. Integrating Disrupted Work Relationships: An Action Design for a Critical Intervention
Development Digest   audiocassette
Purchase: $13.75

Robert T. Golembiewski and Stokes Carrigan present an approach which will help managers and consultants humanely and constructively handle forced reductions in the organizational work force.

1089. Integrating Organizational Specialists into School Districts
Development Digest   audiocassette
Purchase: $13.75

Since organizational development is not likely to last long without internal supervisors, 2 consultants describe how they have integrated OD specialists into an educational organization.

Interaction between MBO and OD Efforts. For complete citation, *see* MANAGEMENT BY OBJECTIVES.

1090. Interface between Quality of Work Life and Organizational Development
Development Digest   3 audiocassettes
Purchase: $53.25

Through several points of view, quality of work life (QWL) is examined in terms of its similarities, differences, and connections with organization development (OD). Considers both social and organizational change.

1091. Interventions in Organization Development
Development Digest   audiocassette
Purchase: $13.75

W. Warner Burke presents a range of interventions in organizational development (OD) criteria for intervention as a part of OD and the appropriateness of training as intervention.

1092. Job Enrichment as a Catalyst for Other OD Functions
Development Digest   audiocassette
Purchase: $13.75

Reviews major problems confronting organizations and shows the effects job enrichment can have on them through one organization's approach. Suggests steps in redesigning jobs. Details difficulties encountered in changing jobs and organizational structure.

Leonard Nadler—An In-Depth Interview with Steve Becker. For complete citation, *see* TRAINING AND DEVELOPMENT.

1093. Line Management Approach to Organization Development
Development Digest   audiocassette
Purchase: $13.75

Describes and discusses an OD program at the H.G. Heinz Company that operates through line managers, using their power and terms to convert fear of new programs into excitement and acceptance.

1094. Management Development for Organizational Development
Development Digest   audiocassette
Purchase: $13.75

Describes programs for developing individual managers' relationships to the organization. Presents examples of what organizations do to maximize their growth through planned individual development. Features Benjamin B. Tregoe.

Management of Change. For complete citation, *see* CHANGE.

Managing Change. For complete citation, *see* CHANGE.

Managing for Creativity in Organizations: Problems and Issues in Training and OD. For complete citation, *see* CREATIVITY.

Matter of Survival. For complete citation, *see* COMPUTERS.

1095. More We Are Together
International Film Bureau, Inc 1979 16mm film or videocassette color 21 min
Purchase: $450.00 Rental: 5-day $60.00; 3-day $45.00 Preview: free

Illustrates the attitude of senior, middle, and junior managers in 2 companies toward proposed changes in organizational style and procedures. Dramatizes one company's attempts to reorganize. Setbacks result from failure to inform, consult, and involve management at all levels. Practical Participation Series.

Motivation, Organization Development, and Individual Career Achievement. For complete citation, *see* MOTIVATION.

OD to MBO or MBO to OD: Does It Make a Difference? For complete citation, *see* MANAGEMENT BY OBJECTIVES.

1096. OD: Other Dimensions—Does this Path Have a Heart?
Development Digest audiocassette
Purchase: $13.75

Robert Tannenbaum puts a new dimension on organization development as he relates stories of the Sufi masters to find relationships.

1097. Organization Development
Resources for Education and Management, Inc 4 filmstrips or slides and audiocassettes or videocassettes or film cartridges 12–17 min ea instructor's print materials
Purchase: video $280.00 ($85.00 ea); filmstrips $255.00 ($69.00 ea); film cartridges $340.00 ($85.00 ea); slides $270.00 ($73.00 ea) Preview: $20.00

Presents an overview for human resource developers of the concepts of organization development (OD) and how it coincides with management development. Can also be used to inform middle and lower management levels on what OD is and how it works. Illustrates approaches and techniques for implementation.

1098. Organization Development Overview
Addison-Wesley Publishing Company, Inc 1973 audiocassette 50 min
Purchase: $15.00

Jack N. Fordyce tells what OD is, what it does, how it works, and how it can affect your organization. Covers the practical interests and typical questions of most managers.

1099. Organization Image Process
Development Digest audiocassette
Purchase: $13.75

Describes the organizational image process, a simple technique for gathering, evaluating, feeding back results, and, based on these results, formulating an action plan similar to an MBO approach. The process generates a high level of activity and has become a popular organizational development intervention.

Organizing for Productivity. For complete citation, *see* PRODUCTIVITY.

Overmanagement. For complete citation, *see* CHANGE.

1100. Pairing of Internal and External OD Consultants
Development Digest 2 audiocassettes
Purchase: $35.50

Sheldon Davis and Herbert Shepard propose that pairing organization development consultants provides distinct advantages not available when working alone. Audiocassette Library on Organizational Development Series.

1101. Parallel Organization: Experience with the New Structural Intervention in General Motors
Development Digest audiocassette
Purchase: $15.75

Provides information on the origin of the parallel organization, the method of setting goals in relation to where they were and where they wanted to be, the projects, and the results achieved.

Peter Principle. For complete citation, *see* MANAGEMENT.

1102. Physical Setting, the Organization, and the Social System: How OD Practitioners Can Improve the Interaction
Development Digest audiocassette
Purchase: $15.75

Focuses on the wasted energy which results from the bad fit between an organization and its people, the organization and its physical setting, and the people and their physical settings. Recommends organization development practitioners improve operations by reducing this waste. Suggests 6 dimensions to examine when working with these problems.

1103. Practice of Organization Development: What Do You Do When You Do OD?
Development Digest 6 audiocassettes
Purchase: $106.50

Discusses W. Warner Burke's approach to organization development: contact, diagnosis, feedback, and intervention. Illustrates 4 methods of diagnosis, 2 feedback activities, and 6 categories of OD interventions. Uses "programmed divided-attention learning" format which enables user to listen while doing other tasks and then answer questions to check understanding. Audiocassette Library on Organization Development Series.

1104. Practice Theories in Organization Development
Development Digest audiocassette
Purchase: $13.75

Peter B. Vaill discusses the models on which OD practitioners base their work. Recommends the use of action research to develop and implement programs simultaneously.

1105. Putting It All Together—Organization
National Audiovisual Center 1973 16mm film or videocassette color 22 min
Purchase: film $127.50; video $100.00

Describes the concepts of organization, the tools for organizing, and the impact of good organization. Putting It All Together Series.

1106. Putting It All Together—Policies
National Audiovisual Center 1973 16mm film or videocassette color 16 min
Purchase: film $92.50; video $79.25

Shows how an organization conscientiously chooses, after careful analysis, to channel its activities in one direction rather than another. Demonstrates how articulating such policies can avoid needless conflict. Putting It All Together Series.

1107. Relocation: A Corporate Decision
Lansford Publishing Company, Inc audiocassette learner's print materials; game
Purchase: $59.95

Presents the full range of pressures involved in a business, the city it plans to leave, and the city it intends to relocate in. Presents the decisions that must be made and deals with single-perspective problems that arise.

1108. Research and the Change Process
Development Digest audiocassette
Purchase: $13.75

Focuses on the use of research results as an organization development (OD) intervention at General Motors. Describes research into the causes of absenteeism and the feeding back of results as part of the OD program. Also presents examples using research as an OD intervention in medium and long-time frames. Concludes with the theory underlying action research and its use in a generalized model of change.

1109. Role for the OD Practitioner in the Organization's Strategic Planning Process
Development Digest audiocassette
Purchase: $15.75

Peter B. Vaill maintains that organizational development (OD) interventions can and should play an important part in the process of setting the basic shape and direction of the organization. Describes the evolving literature on behavioral aspects of strategizing and ways a management team can improve its strategic thinking. Focuses on the relationship of an organization to its environment.

1110. Socio-Technical Systems: An Intervention Strategy
Development Digest audiocassette
Purchase: $13.75

Provides an 8-step strategy for making structural interventions based on an agriculture experiment. Discusses its application in detail.

1111. Some Guidelines for Tomorrow's OD
Development Digest audiocassette
Purchase: $13.75

Claims the philosophy on which many organization development practices are based should be questioned. Features Robert T. Golembiewski.

Team Building. For complete citation, *see* TEAM BUILDING.

1112. Techniques or Values: An Emerging Controversy among OD Practitioners
Development Digest 2 audiocassettes
Purchase: $35.50

Presents issues in the growing controversy in Organization Development (OD) between an emphasis on technology versus an emphasis on values. Explore such questions as: Are current OD consulting practices the way of the future? Will smoothing and refining practice transform consultants into superhumans? Have OD practitioners become organizational flunkies who have sold their souls for the organization's gold?

1113. Three-Factor Model of Organizational Behavior
Development Digest audiocassette
Purchase: $13.75

Claims there have been few attempts since the work of Kurt Lewin to provide a comprehensive structure of the variables that account for organizational behavior. Suggests grouping variables into 3 clusters. Describes the actions taken and the results achieved when this approach was applied to an industrial client.

1114. Tools and Strategies for Organization Diagnosis and Intervention
Development Digest audiocassette
Purchase: $13.75

Traces the study of organizations from the earliest concepts through current ones. Examines data collection and strategies for databased interventions. Reviews the elements in work-oriented, databased projects. Focuses on how to diagnose organizational issues and problems.

1115. "TORI" Community Experience as an Organizational Change Intervention
Development Digest audiocassette
Purchase: $13.75

The TORI experience develops more open and personal relationships among people as opposed to closed and role-related behavior. Features Jack R. Gibb.

1116. Understanding Behavior in Organizations: How I Feel Is What I Do
Document Associates 1977 16mm film or videocassette color 26 min
Purchase: $400.00 Rental: $45.00

Demonstrates that a knowledge of human behavior can help in designing more effective organizations. Significant concepts in psychoanalytic theory are analyzed in terms of their applicability to corporate settings. Harry Levinson defines certain human needs which organizations must understand and fulfill in order to better design jobs and foster employee commitment. Emphasizes how managers can become more effective through a greater sensitivity to other's feelings and needs.

1117. Up the Organization
Time-Life Video 1973 videocassette color 30 min
Purchase: $150.00 Rental: $35.00

Robert Townsend, who wrote the book *Up the Organization*, gives his very personal views on such topics as the chief executive, personnel department, management consultants, computers, the public relations department, and "Getting In and Getting On."

1118. Use of Models as a Normative OD Intervention
Development Digest   audiocassette
Purchase: $13.75

Jay Hall and Thomas E. DeGrazia describe high-to-low contents as well as process approaches to OD interventions. Analyzes a case study on the basis of Argyris's criteria and the content/process approach. Discusses the use of popular models as interventions to find out what is going on in an organization.

1119. Women in Organizations: Change Agent Skills
Development Digest   audiocassette
Purchase: $13.75

Rosabeth Moss Kanter suggests ways change agents' skills may be refined and modified in 3 areas—knowledge, interaction, and system diagnosis. Suggests changes in organizational structures which will reduce discrimination.

ORIENTATION
See also TRAINING AND DEVELOPMENT

1120. All Employee Training
Butler Learning Systems   552 slides and audiocassettes   instructor's print materials; learner's print materials
Purchase: $2,595.00 plus $10.00 per learner   Preview: free

Presents 7 30-minute sessions on topics such as communication, human relations, working with a supervisor, a sense of service, and the importance of safety. Intended for orientation or retraining at all levels.

Catching On. For complete citation, *see* TRAINING AND DEVELOPMENT.

1121. Good Beginning
BNA Communications, Inc   1963   16mm film or videocassette   color   13 min   learner's print materials
Purchase: $250.00   Rental: 5-day $150.00; 3-day $105.00   Preview: $35.00
Languages: Portuguese, Spanish

Dramatization showing right and wrong ways to indoctrinate new employees. Illustrates the problems of the new worker and employee attitudes. Modern Management Series, no. 3.

1122. Good Start
Dartnell   16mm film or videocassette   color   15 min   instructor's print materials; learner's print materials
Purchase: $425.00   Rental: $95.00

Presents simple formula to guide supervisors who orient new employees in their work units. Formula includes good preparation, using an effective "buddy" system, and knowing when and how to "let go" after training.

1123. Language of Work
Thompson-Mitchell and Associates   1974   15 audiocassettes   instructor's print materials; learner's print materials; transparencies
Purchase: $199.00

Explains basics of working for new workers: following instructions; answering phones; taking messages; what an invoice, packing slip, and purchase order are; what a business is; how it operates; the role of unions; and the basic rules of safety. Includes 3 discussion tapes with 9 critical-incident dramatizations. Useful for employees with low reading skills. World of Work Series.

1124. Orientation: Attitude, Appearance, Approach
CRM/McGraw-Hill Films   16mm film or videocassette   color   12 min
Purchase: $295.00   Rental: $75.00   Preview: free

Dramatizes the importance of attitude, appearance, approach, and active listening skills. Shows an imperiled sales career jeopardized by a poor orientation in terms of attitude, appearance, and approach.

1125. Supervisor's Responsibility for Induction and Job Instruction
Continental Film Productions   slides or filmstrip and audiocassette   12 min
Purchase: filmstrip $105.00; slides $125.00

Treats the induction of the new employee in the job in a systematic and organized manner. Supervisor Training Series.

1126. Welcome Aboard!
Roundtable Films, Inc   16mm film or videocassette   color   21 min   instructor's print materials; learner's print materials; poster
Purchase: $495.00   Rental: $100.00   Preview: $30.00
Languages: English, French, Norwegian, Spanish

Shows the importance of an orientation program to strengthen job induction, reduce turnover, and improve productivity. Portrays young supervisor insensitive to needs of new employees—until he is one. Identifies the factors to include in an orientation program.

1127. Where Do I Fit In?
Manpower Education Institute   1979   16mm film or videocassette   color   15 min
Purchase: $275.00   Rental: $50.00   Preview: $50.00

Addresses the needs of a young person on a first job. Covers getting along with the boss, handling discrimination, punctuality, meeting deadlines, and dress requirements.

1128. Work Environment
Singer Management Institute   14 filmstrips and cassettes
Purchase: $29.50 ea   Preview: $15.00

Gives inexperienced employees an overview of factors that make up the job environment: physical requirements, stress conditions and competition, work settings and schedules, and jobs that involve working with people, objects or machinery, ideas or data.

PAY PRACTICES

1129. Day's Work—A Day's Pay
American Federation of Labor and Congress of
Industrial Organizations   1979   16mm
film   color   20 min
Rental: $5.00

Takes a brief look at the history of prevailing wage legislation,
why it was enacted, and how it protects workers and local
contractors bidding on federal contracts.

1130. Handling Employee Questions about Pay
AMACOM   audiocassette   60 min   booklet
Purchase: $30.00   Other cost factors: AMA members
$25.00

A guide to managers who must talk about money with
employees. Gives techniques that address questions that are
confronting, that turn complaints around, and that get management's point across clearly.

1131. Research and Development in Flexible Compensation: TRW's New Program
Development Digest   audiocassette
Purchase: $13.75

Eugene K. Hamilton points out flexible compensation is
inevitable if the concepts from behavioral science are followed.
Describes in detail the design of the TRW program and the way
it was initiated. Discusses criticism of the program and plans for
modification.

PERCEPTION

1132. Brain Power
LCA Video/Films   1983   16mm film or
videocassette   color   11 min
Purchase: $350.00   Rental: $70.00   Preview:
$35.00

Involves learners with mental challenges and visual brain
teasers to prepare them for an upcoming meeting. Solutions
reveal key principles of perception: recognition, interpretation,
and expectation. Designed to shape meeting sessions into active,
alert interchanges. Draws from Karl Albrecht's book and
features John Houseman.

Case of Insubordination. For complete citation, *see*
GRIEVANCE.

1133. Drawing Conclusions Is a Tricky Art
Centron Films   1975   16mm film or
videocassette   color   13 min
Purchase: $235.00

Describes a 3-step process for observing, interpreting or assuming, and concluding. Presents humorous examples of what
might happen if we operated on a literal basis without making
assumptions. Includes segments of a 2-party conversation, one
without sound track to prompt viewers to assume and one with
soundtrack to check accuracy of assumptions made.

1134. Eye of the Beholder
BNA Communications, Inc   1953   16mm film   b/w
or color   26 min
Purchase: 16mm b/w $425.00; 16mm "moodcolor"
$475.00   Rental: 5-day $130.00; 3-day
$105.00   Preview: $35.00
Languages: English, Dutch, French, Portuguese,
Spanish

Film classic designed to develop a greater awareness of the
pitfalls of subjective analysis and the need for objectivity and
careful evaluation of facts.

Farewell to Birdie McKeever. For complete citation,
see INTERPERSONAL RELATIONS.

1135. Perception
CRM/McGraw-Hill Films   1979   16mm film or
videocassette   color   27 min
Purchase: $560.00   Rental: $95.00   Preview: free

Shows how perception is an individual and subjective means of
viewing reality influenced by our social upbringings and culture
as well as media. Vignettes in business as well as social settings
depict the consequences of individuals perceiving situations
differently. Points out that with effort and self-awareness it is
possible to minimize the negative effects of the subjectivity of
people's perceptions.

1136. Perception: Key to Effective Management Communication
CRM/McGraw-Hill Films   1981   16mm film and
audiocassettes or videocassette   color   47 min
instructor's print materials; learner's print materials
Purchase: $1,495.00   Preview: free

Alerts managers and employees to the importance of shared
perceptions for effective relationships and communications.
Dramatizes how to correct or resolve problem areas resulting
from unconscious misperceptions about one's self, co-workers,
or the work environment. Multimedia package that integrates
print, audio, and audiovisual components. Suggested for full- or
half-day scheduling.

1137. Perception: The Tragedy of the Friendly Breakfast
Salenger Educational Media   16mm film or
videocassette   color   6 min   instructor's print
materials
Purchase: $210.00   Rental: $80.00   Preview:
$35.00

Brief look at different perceptual sets as they are revealed in
dramatic snip of life and death. Stresses importance of knowing
one's own perceptions and keeping communication channels
open. Dramatization of death at an otherwise friendly breakfast.

Self-Discovery for the Manager. For complete
citation, *see* MANAGEMENT.

1138. Sky's the Limit
LCA Video/Films   1981   2 videocassettes   color   30
min and 26 min   instructor's print materials
Purchase: $995.00   Rental: $200.00   Preview:
$100.00

Presents Wayne Dyer and his philosophy of the "no-limit" person, one who is free of self-determined limitations. Argues that behavior patterns and old thinking habits can change once a person decides to alter them.

1139. Way I See It
Roundtable Films, Inc 1965 16mm film or videocassette color 23 min learner's print materials
Purchase: $400.00 Rental: $85.00 Preview: $30.00

Shows the importance of setting goals, defining objectives, and establishing review points. Dramatization follows a young supervisor whose point of view changes as his position changes. Useful to illustrate how differences in perception can influence job performance and on-the-job conflicts.

PERFORMANCE APPRAISAL
See also EMPLOYEE PERFORMANCE

Appraisal & Career Counseling Interviews. For complete citation, *see* INTERVIEWING.

1140. Appraisal Interview
BNA Communications, Inc 1972 16mm film or videocassette color 28 min
Purchase: $485.00 Rental: 5-day $150.00; 3-day $105.00 Preview: $35.00

Explores the concept of objective appraisal of job performance based on previously agreed targets and the essential role of the interview. Reveals how to establish rapport, show commitment, and use specific questioning techniques. Emphasizes joint solutions and goal setting. Interviewing Series, no. 1.

1141. Appraisals in Action
Professional Development, Inc 1975 4 16mm films or videocassettes color 30 min ea instructor's print materials; learner's print materials
Purchase: films $2,940.00 ($650.00 ea); video $2,450.00 ($495.00 ea) Rental: films $750.00–$1,500.00; video $895.00–$1,950.00 Preview: 30-min highlights program free

An overall approach to the appraisal process—training employees how to prepare for and conduct performance appraisals and why a systematic system is important. Strong section on developmental planning with those supervised. Dramatized enactments demonstrate specific steps and interpersonal skills needed. How to document personnel actions for third-party review is also covered.

1142. Appraising People
Organization Development Consultants audiocassette 40 min
Purchase: $15.95

Explains how successful managers appraise themselves and others and offers 8 steps to improving performance. Practical tips include how to avoid rewarding mediocrity.

1143. Appraising Performance: An Interview Skills Course
University Associates 1976 2 audiocassettes instructor's print materials; learner's print materials
Purchase: $44.95

Taped demonstration interviews plus commentary illustrate methods and skills needed to communicate appraisal of employee work performance. Typical appraisal situations clarify interviewing objectives and offer a framework to practice skills. Learner roleplay, feedback, small-group discussion, and self-assessment foster on-the-job application. Designed to cover 6 3-hour sessions. Book to accompany course, *Appraisal Interview: Three Basic Approaches,* must be purchased separately.

1144. Conducting Performance Appraisals
Training by Design 4 audiocassettes learner's print materials
Purchase: $95.00

Offers a step-by-step orientation to appraisals and establishing corresponding standards of performance. Gives key steps for evaluating all performers: the exceptional, the satisfactory, and the poor. Suggests 8 guidelines for successful performance appraisals.

Critic. For complete citation, *see* COMMUNICATION.

Discipline Interview. For complete citation, *see* DISCIPLINE.

1145. Evaluating Performance
Organization Development Consultants audiocassette 43 min
Purchase: $11.95

Details a systematic approach to evaluating performance. Includes profiling management skills and self-appraisal. Highlights how to negotiate honest and reasonable expectations.

1146. Eye of the Supervisor
National Educational Media, Inc 1971 16mm film or super 8mm or videocassette color 12 min instructor's print materials; learner's print materials
Purchase: $385.00 Rental: 5-day $90.00; 2-day $80.00 Preview: free
Languages: English, French, German, Japanese, Portuguese

Designed to assist managers and supervisors in their task of reviewing and evaluating employee behavior and performance. Stresses collecting and evaluating information before acting and emphasizes the need for an "open eye"—open to positive as well as negative information.

1147. How Am I Doing?
Xicom-Video Arts 1977 16mm film or videocassette color 26 min booklet
Purchase: $625.00 Rental: $100.00 Preview: $35.00

John Cleese demonstrates the catastrophic consequences of ignoring the techniques and misunderstanding the purpose of staff appraisal. Intended to make working managers aware of the most frequent and damaging errors of appraisal reviews and to introduce them to the basic principles, techniques, and psychology of appraisal interviewing.

1148. How Supervisors Should Appraise Employee Performance

Bureau of Business Practice   1979   16mm film   color   23 min
Purchase: $425.00   Rental: $95.00   Preview: $49.00

Shows supervisors how to use appraisals to reduce turnover and uncover employee discontent. Enactments show how to interview, analyze, and evaluate employees to spot persons who need additional training, pick out those with special potential, and find those with skills and attitudes to fill more demanding jobs.

1149. How to Evaluate Performance and Assess Potential

American Management Associations   6 audiocassettes   learner's print materials
Purchase: $145.00   Other cost factors: AMA members $135.00; discounts available for bulk orders of materials

Helps supervisors develop a review system that ensures employees have clear expectations, useful feedback, and open lines of communication. Cassettes, supplemented by role-playing activities and exercises, show how appraisal process can be used as a management tool. Specific steps are covered.

1150. How to Install a Tough-Minded Performance Appraisal System

Creative Media   audiocassette   34 min
Purchase: $7.95

Presents ways to uncover hidden strengths and build rapport through positive performance appraisals.

1151. How's It Going?

Didactic Systems, Inc   16mm film   b/w   11 min   instructor's print materials
Purchase: $130.00   Rental: $25.00   Preview: $15.00

Evaluation of job performance can be difficult and sensitive. Four cases show ways to create a favorable interview climate, the importance of 2-way communication, the need for a plan of action and how it can be blocked, and how to conduct the interview so both parties gain.

MBO and Performance Appraisal. For complete citation, *see* MANAGEMENT BY OBJECTIVES.

1152. Nuts and Bolts of Performance Appraisal

Creative Media   1973   16mm film or super 8mm or videocassette   color   32 min   instructor's print materials
Purchase: $475.00   Rental: $90.00   Preview: $30.00
Languages: English, Spanish

Provides managers with a step-by-step procedure to improve performance appraisals. Gives 5 rules and 7 tools needed to effectively plan and conduct any performance appraisal. Shows practical examples for planning and conducting successful, results-oriented performance appraisals. Intended for new and experienced managers and supervisors.

1153. Performance and Potential Review

BNA Communications, Inc   1970   16mm film or videocassette   color   21 min
Purchase: $525.00   Rental: 5-day $150.00; 3-day $105.00   Preview: $35.00
Languages: English, Portuguese, Spanish

Portrays how to use performance reviews to follow up on managers' progress toward previously agreed upon goals. Reviews should not only provide an opportunity for discussion and appraisal, but should act as a means of reviewing a manager's potential for new responsibilities. British production. Companion film to *Defining the Manager's Job.* Management by Objectives Series, no. 4.

1154. Performance Appraisal

Resources for Education and Management, Inc   3 filmstrips or slides and audiocassettes or videocassettes or filmstrip cartridges   8–9 min ea   instructor's print materials
Purchase: video $245.00 ($95.00 ea); filmstrips $220.00 ($75.00 ea); filmstrip cartridges $255.00 ($85.00 ea); slides $235.00 ($80.00 ea)

Discusses why performance appraisal is critical and shows it as an important and effective management tool. Presents what to appraise and procedures to use in setting up and implementing an effective system. Suggested for a one-day training session for supervisors and managers.

1155. Performance Appraisal: A Program for Improving Productivity

WMI Corporation   1981   3 videocassettes and 2 audiocassettes   3 hrs
Purchase: $1,000.00   Other cost factors: administrator's kit ($750.00) and learner's printed materials

Emphasizes practical skills and procedures for performance measures, job standards, reviews, and action planning. Video, audio, and printed materials are closely integrated. Suggested for 1–1½ day program.

1156. Performance Appraisal for Managers

Time-Life Video   7 videocassettes   color   30 min ea   instructor's print materials
Purchase: $3,950.00   Rental: $500.00   Preview: free

Sequential portrayals show 3 manager-staff conferences: goal setting, coaching, and evaluating. Identifies many issues and problems a manager faces in making employee evaluations. Practical applications of the principles of goal setting, effective communicating, coaching, and motivating self-development. For group or self-study.

1157. Performance Appraisal Interview

Advance Learning Systems   1978   videocassette   color   30 min   instructor's print materials; learner's print materials
Purchase: $1,045.00   Preview: $95.00

Examines the appraisal interview—the boss's assessment of it and the employee's reaction to it. Emphasizes assessment in terms of specific goals and an active approach to appraisal rather than a pro forma attitude. Suggested for a 2–4 hour program.

1158. Performance Appraisal Process
General Motors Corporation 1983 videocassette
color 30 min instructor's print materials; learner's
print materials
Purchase: $650.00

For organizations interested in implementing, revising, or
improving an appraisal system. Includes performance planning,
appraisal cycle, sample forms, and system design. Separate
package available including only the appraisal interview segment.

1159. Performance Appraisal: The Human Dynamics
CRM/McGraw-Hill Films 1979 16mm film or
videocassette color 28 min instructor's print
materials; learner's print materials
Purchase: $560.00 Rental: $95.00 Preview: free

Traditional appraisal methods rely heavily on subjective and
unilateral judgments by supervisors. This results in friction and
resentment. Alternative techniques use interpersonal skills to
create open dialogs so appraisals become rewarding and regen-
erative feedback sessions for both parties. Two industrial
examples provide application of the principles.

1160. Performance Counseling and Appraisal
Management Decision Systems, Inc 1980 4 16mm
films or videocassettes plus slides and
audiocassettes color 30 min ea instructor's print
materials; learner's print materials
Purchase: $5,900.00 Preview: free

Demonstrates a supervisor counseling an employee showing an
overview of the process, how to set performance objectives,
performance counseling, and appraisal. Presents basic concepts
and techniques. Urges plan for applying these skills on the job.

1161. Performance Review
Dialogue Systems, Inc videocassette color 45 min
instructor's print materials; learner's print materials
Purchase: $750.00 Rental: $225.00

Five vignettes show the importance of planning and of being
direct and honest. Shows techniques of keeping a meeting on
track and dealing with unexpected reactions. Offers a model for
reaching mutually agreed-upon goals.

1162. Performance Reviews that Build Commitment
Professional Development, Inc 1971 6 16mm films
or videocassettes color 30 min ea instructor's
print materials; learner's print materials
Purchase: films $3,575.00 ($595.00 ea); video
$2,800.00 ($495.00 ea) Rental: films $575.00
($195.00); video $500.00 ($145.00 ea)

ws how a supervisor and an employee, working together, can
develop performance yardsticks and commitment. Illustrates
how job descriptions, performance standards, specific objectives, goals, and career development plans are all inter-related.
Highlights importance of supportive coaching. Dramatization
shows step-by-step process.

1163. Performance Standards and Specific Objectives
Development Digest audiocassette
Purchase: $13.75

Reviews some dysfunctional aspects of performance appraisal.
Combines setting objectives with establishing performance

standards to improve performance appraisal. Richard Guyon
describes the steps in the process.

1164. Skill and Effort Rating
Maynard Management Institute 16mm
film color 12 min
Purchase: $360.00 Rental: $40.00

Explains principles of leveling method in performance rating.
Shows shop and office scenes to illustrate "indicators" used in
setting top and bottom of rating scale.

1165. Where Are You? Where Are You Going?
Roundtable Films, Inc 1978 16mm film or
videocassette color 24 min
Purchase: $525.00 Rental: $100.00 Preview:
$30.00 Other cost factors: participants workbook
Languages: Dutch, English, Norwegian, Swedish

Dramatization demonstrates a model performance appraisal
from the preparatory stage through the conclusion of the
interview. Shows key stages of interview. Suggests techniques to
put employees at ease, probe for problem areas, critique
performance, and set objectives.

Where Do I Go from Here? For complete citation,
see CAREER PLANNING AND DEVELOPMENT.

1166. Who Wants to Play God?
American Media, Inc 1980 16mm film or super
8mm or videocassette color 20 min
Purchase: $475.00 Rental: $95.00 Preview:
$30.00

Simulated work situations demonstrate a 3-part system for
performance reviews. This system avoids supervisors who "play
God by judging a person's worth," thus causing resentment and
resistance. Presents a participatory approach between supervisor and subordinate, each taking responsibility. A step-by-step
procedure can improve performance appraisals and can increase
motivation, productivity, and morale.

1167. You're Coming Along Fine
Roundtable Films, Inc 1968 16mm film or
videocassette b/w and color
Purchase: $450.00 Rental: $100.00 Preview:
$30.00 Other cost factors: manager's guidebook
Languages: Dutch, English, French, German,
Norwegian, Swedish

Shows how to make appraisals vital and useful tools. Reveals
how managers can get trapped between bolstering an employee's ego and giving accurate judgments to superiors. Dramatization emphasizes the importance of establishing mutually shared
objectives and giving honest feedback toward the realization of
goals.

PERFORMANCE FEEDBACK AND POSITIVE REINFORCEMENT
See BEHAVIOR MODIFICATION

PERFORMANCE REVIEW
See PERFORMANCE APPRAISAL

PERSONAL GROWTH
See also CHANGE

Building a Climate for Individual Growth. For complete citation, *see* PERSONNEL MANAGEMENT.

1168. Caterpillar and the Wild Animals
American Educational Films   16mm film or videocassette   color   7 min   learner's print materials
Purchase: $170.00   Rental: $25.00
Introduces a creature who gets by on bluff, who claims he is somebody he isn't, and who is finally exposed. Includes values, the limits of blowing your own horn, and the necessity of matching actions with reality.

1169. Dr. Denis Waitley Series
American Salesmasters, Inc   1980   6 16mm films or videocassettes   color   25–30 min ea   instructor's print materials
Purchase: $3,300.00   Rental: $1,500.00
Offers presentations by Denis Waitley on personal improvement, self-esteem, stress, attitude, issues of control, and how to handle and respond to a crisis. General theme is one of encouragement for personal and professional development.

1170. Great Ideas
Nightingale-Conant Corporation   6 audiocassettes
Purchase: $40.00
Offers ideas about enhancing personal image, communicating clearly and effectively, persuading others, avoiding discouragement, and maintaining abundant energy, drive, and enthusiasm. Features Earl Nightingale.

1171. Joshua and the Shadow
CRM/McGraw-Hill Films   1977   16mm film or videocassette   color   9½ min
Purchase: $225.00   Rental: $75.00   Preview: free
Animated, nonnarrated story shows Joshua afraid of his own shadow when he discovers light can control it. Shadows are problems and anxieties, and light is our own understanding. Provides a brief introduction to human nature and development. Useful as meeting opener or discussion starter. Joshua Trilogy Series.

Journey into Self. For complete citation, *see* INSTRUCTION AND INSTRUCTIONAL METHODS.

Lead the Field. For complete citation, *see* DECISION MAKING/PROBLEM SOLVING.

1172. Men under Siege: Life with the Modern Woman
MTI Teleprograms, Inc   16mm film or videocassette   color   33 min
Purchase: film $470.00; video $300.00   Rental: $50.00   Preview: $50.00
Draws portraits of Americans struggling to define new roles for men and women, told in their own words. Explores men's attitudes toward themselves and their jobs, toward women who compete with them on equal terms, and toward wives whose earning capacity may exceed their own.

1173. Non-Traditional Approaches to Human Potential Development
Development Digest   audiocassette
Purchase: $13.75
Briefly reviews 6 nontraditional ways of expanding human potential. Examines current training techniques which use each.

1174. Practical Self Management
MOR Associates   2 audiocassettes   learner's print materials
Purchase: $35.00
Stresses the personal and organizational benefits to be gained from identifying payoff areas, goals, and actions.

Thank God It's Friday. For complete citation, *see* MANAGEMENT DEVELOPMENT.

1175. Unused Keys to Success
Organization Development Consultants   audiocassette   20 min
Purchase: $10.00
Cites 10 most fundamental, yet often neglected keys to success. Identifies principles used by the nation's most prominent executives. Intended for persons who are sidetracked from meeting their potential.

What Have You Done for Yourself Lately? For complete citation, *see* CAREER PLANNING AND DEVELOPMENT.

1176. What Is Success?
Organization Development Consultants   audiocassette   53 min
Purchase: $12.95
Helps one identify one's personal definition of success, then reach it. Offers clues of what to do and not do to achieve personal success.

1177. You
Cally Curtis Company   16mm film or videocassette   color   4 min
Purchase: film $225.00; video $200.00   Rental: $75.00   Preview: $40.00
Stars a baby, a dog, and the legs of 2 adults. Shows natural enthusiasm, an excitement for new things, a joy for life, and the ability to rebound after a fall. Along the way, day to day problems dampen enthusiasm and positive outlook. Useful for meeting or discussion starter.

1178. You, Yourself, Incorporated
BNA Communications, Inc   1965   16mm film or videocassette   color   24 min   instructor's print materials
Purchase: $450.00   Rental: 5-day $150.00; 3-day $105.00   Preview: $35.00
Languages: English, Portuguese, Spanish
Joe Powell uses anecdotes, advice, and humor to spark interest in self-development. Useful for a "kick-off" that urges extra

effort or shedding of lethargy. Urges seizing opportunities for growth. Joe Powell Film, no. 5.

1179. Your Self-Concept and Your Job
Singer Management Institute   4 filmstrips and audiocassettes
Purchase: $29.50   Rental: $15.00

Shows how self-concept affects job performance. Builds skills of self-appraisal in terms of responsibility and being liked. Intended for employees with little work experience.

PERSONNEL MANAGEMENT

Assessing Management Potential. For complete citation, *see* MANAGEMENT DEVELOPMENT.

1180. Basics of Personnel Management
AMACOM   4 audiocassettes   4 hrs   learner's print materials
Purchase: $79.95   Other cost factors: AMA members $67.95

Discusses methods and techniques to recruit and select qualified people, recognize training needs of each individual, conduct performance appraisals, open up communication, maintain employee files, deal with labor unions, and implement fair wage and salary practices. Intended to apply in large or small companies. Useful when creating a personnel department. AMA Management Basics Series.

1181. Behavioral Sciences
MBO, Inc   12 audiocassettes   6 hrs   instructor's print materials
Purchase: $184.00

An overview of behavioral sciences as applied to the management of human resources. George Odiorne covers subjects such as managing human behavior, small groups, leadership, organization development and organization planning, motivation, communication, discipline, and decision making. Intended for managers at all levels.

1182. Building a Climate for Individual Growth
BNA Communications, Inc   1969   16mm film or videocassette   color   24 min
Purchase: $525.00   Rental: $150.00   Preview: $35.00
Languages: English, Spanish

Discusses 6 stages of psychological growth together with the ways an organization can stimulate or thwart it at each stage. Frederick Hertzberg offers management techniques designed to control "psychologically dying" employees.

1183. Come Work with Us
Filmasters, Inc   1977   16mm film   color   19 min
Purchase: $175.00   Rental: $35.00

Intended for personnel managers, managers, and supervisory personnel. Urges them to apply reasonable criteria in regard to providing employment opportunity for individuals with physical or mental limitations. Uses 6 work place settings to illustrate possibilities.

1184. Concept of Organizational Climate
Audio-Forum audiocassette   20 min
Purchase: $10.95

Discusses how individual personalities and job requirements interact to produce a climate significant to both the individual and to the organization.

1185. Confidence Game
Educational Resources Foundation   1976   3 16mm films or videocassettes and 3 audiocassettes   color   20 min (films and video); 30 min (audiocassettes)   instructor's print materials; learner's print materials
Purchase: film $1,500.00 ($575.00 ea); video $1,275.00   Rental: $375.00 ($125.00 ea)   Preview: $30.00 ($10.00 ea)   Other cost factors: printed materials priced separately

Designed to increase cooperation, confidence, and competence in middle management, first-line supervisors, and office staff. Dramatization shows typical company. Emphasizes affirmative action, making employees more promotable, and team building. Helps employees see the value of and the best path to personal growth. Points out the relationship between the organization's success and the future of the employees.

1186. Controlling Costs for Profit
Edupac, Inc   2 audiocassettes   instructor's print materials; learner's print materials
Purchase: $75.00

Helps managers identify ways of eliminating work and make methods and procedures more cost effective. Tells ways to control the costs of machine operations, materials handling, and quality control. Identifies dangers of overstaffing, costs of absenteeism and how to reduce them, and the kinds of employee training needed to control costs.

Correct Way of Correcting. For complete citation, *see* DISCIPLINE.

1187. The Dryden File
Motivision, Ltd   16mm film or videocassette   color   27½ min   instructor's print materials
Purchase: $475.00   Preview: $25.00
Languages: English, French

Dramatizes how troubled employee's actions make the supervisor discover it's not his job to diagnose alcohol, drug, or other personal problems. Shows a better way to help a person avoid dismissal and become productive again.

1188. ECS: A Supervisor's Alternative
National Audiovisual Center   1981   16mm film or videocassette   color   27 min
Purchase: film $235.00; video $65.00   Rental: $25.00

Presents a case study that deals with declining employee performance resulting from personal problems. Points out the role of the supervisor as helping employees recognize the effect of personal problems on job performance.

Handling "Problem Employees": How to Take Corrective Action. For complete citation, *see* DISCIPLINE.

1189. How Supervisors Can Reduce Turnover
Bureau of Business Practice   16mm film or videocassette   color   20 min
Purchase: $425.00   Rental: $95.00   Preview: $49.00

Designed to help supervisors build a more stable and valuable work unit with higher productivity. Techniques to turn around potentially valuable employees and yield benefits to both employee and company. Reveals effective alternatives to letting workers go.

1190. How to Control People Costs
Organization Development Consultants
audiocassette   60 min
Purchase: $13.95

Stresses increasing productivity by controlling people costs, such as conflict, compensation plans, bonus systems, seniority, poor performers, and underemployment.

"How to" Drucker. For complete citation, *see* MANAGEMENT.

1191. How to Get the Most Out of Marginal Employees
Bureau of Business Practice   1979   16mm film or videocassette   color   22 min
Purchase: $425.00   Rental: $95.00   Preview: $49.00

Dramatized situations illustrate the problems marginal employees create in the work place: poor general morale, bottlenecks, and lower production quality. Presents the 5 most common causes of marginal performance and the ways to handle each one. Offers tips, techniques, and a test to cull employees with solvable problems.

Human Side of Supervision. For complete citation, *see* SUPERVISION.

1192. Judging People
Roundtable Films, Inc   1962   16mm film   b/w   23 min
Purchase: $200.00   Rental: $75.00   Preview: $30.00
Languages: Dutch, English, Norwegian, Spanish, Swedish

Presents practical techniques for supervisors and managers to reach accurate estimates of ability, personality, intelligence, and potential. Shows techniques to gather information and evaluate opinions.

1193. Leading the Way in Human Resource Management
AMACOM   4 audiocassettes   60 min ea   learner's print materials
Purchase: $100.00   Other cost factors: AMA members $85.00

Broad approach to managing personnel resources from forecasting needs, projecting losses, identifying training needs, and taking surveys and samples. Attention is given to productivity and performance levels, sound placement, and recognizing leaders.

1194. Making Human Resources Productive
BNA Communications, Inc   1971   16mm film or videocassette   color   33 min
Purchase: $550.00   Rental: 5-day $150.00; 3-day $105.00   Preview: $35.00

Stresses the concept that the aim of job enrichment is not merely to provide satisfaction but also to make the organization more efficient. Presents 2 case studies to illustrate the pitfalls involved and the need for 2-way communication at all times. M. Scott Myers provides commentary on the principles involved. Effective Organization Series, no. 4.

1195. Management of Field Sales
American Management Associations   6 audiocassettes   workbook
Purchase: $145.00   Other cost factors: AMA members $135.00

Helps those who manage field sales staff to identify potential and motivate and train those who have it. Includes compensation plan to stimulate more sales.

1196. Management of Human Assets
BNA Communications, Inc   1969   16mm film or videocassette   color   25 min
Purchase: $535.00   Rental: 5-day $150.00; 3-day $105.00   Preview: $35.00
Languages: Dutch, English, Portuguese, French, Spanish

Explains 4 scales for rating management styles, particularly "System 4" which can enable organizations to cut costs and increase productivity simultaneously. Identifies the 3 basic principles that support the system and explains how to rate an organization according to prevailing management system and style. Features Rensis Likert.

1197. Management Profiling: A Disparity Model for Developing Motivation for Change
Development Digest   audiocassette
Purchase: $13.75

Presents an approach to induce behavioral change based on the belief that individuals will change when they recognize disparity between actual and desired behavior. Introduces a questionnaire based on the Likert scale that identifies actual and desired behavior. Features William G. Dyer.

1198. Managing the Knowledge Worker
BNA Communications, Inc   1981   16mm film or videocassette   color   23 min   instructor's print materials; learner's print materials
Purchase: $630.00   Rental: $245.00

Addresses the importance for managers to understand and cope with expert professional or semiprofessional subordinates who may know more about their specialty than the supervisor does. Emphasizes the supervisor's job to challenge the knowledge workers, make use of their capabilities, and give them responsibility. Asserts the knowledge worker has the responsibility to educate the supervisors and make them more effective. Features Peter Drucker. Managing for Tomorrow Series, no. 1.

Matchmaking. For complete citation, *see* INTERVIEWING.

1199. New Employees and the New Customers
BNA Communications, Inc 1981 16mm film or videocassette color 20 min instructor's print materials; learner's print materials
Purchase: $630.00 Rental: $245.00

Shows how the changing makeup of our population and changing expectations affect both employment policy and marketing strategy. Features Peter Drucker. Managing for Tomorrow Series, no. 3.

1200. Orientation and the Hiring Process
American Management Associations 6 audiocassettes learner's print materials
Purchase: $145.00 Other cost factors: AMA members $135.00; discounts available for bulk orders of materials

Shows how to create a positive relationship with an employee—from selection through all phases of his/her employment. Includes selecting the best candidate for a job, orientation, building job enthusiasm and keeping it high, reducing costly turnover.

1201. Personnel Administration by Objectives
MBO, Inc 6 audiocassettes 30 min ea learner's print materials
Purchase: $98.00

Takes a fresh look at how to manage a personnel department effectively. Proposes new methods for managing employment, compensation, and training functions. George Odiorne discusses how to develop personnel programs for managing professional humanpower and for managing minorities, measuring the effectiveness of personnel administration, and goal setting for personnel managers.

1202. Planning Your Manpower Needs
Development Digest audiocassette
Purchase: $13.75

Reviews the concepts of human resource accounting as they apply to planning departments. Discusses recruitment planning for various corporate settings. Delineates problems and advantages of in-house transfers. Advocates in-house development of personnel.

1203. Promotion and Transfer
BNA Communications, Inc 16mm film or videocassette or videodisc color 14 min learner's print materials
Purchase: $630.00 Rental: 5-day $246.00; 3-day $201.00 Preview: $132.00

Depicts what and what not to say or do when a female wants to be promoted or transferred to a job you don't think is "woman's work." Identifies the real reasons you can justify or deny a promotion or transfer: job performance and merit determined by objective criteria and equal treatment. Participant's manual presents several exercises on equal treatment, training and wages, preinterview planning, and working conditions. Fair Employment Practice Training Program, no. 2.

1204. Staffing for Strength
BNA Communications, Inc 1968 16mm film or videocassette color 25 min
Purchase: $525.00 Rental: 5-day $125.00; 3-day $105.00 Preview: $35.00
Languages: Dutch, English, French, German, Spanish, Swedish

Illustrates the difficulties in personality vs. staffing decisions, tolerating the "no" man, encouraging staff growth, and assessing the performance of subordinates. In dramatization Peter Drucker shows how to use the strengths of individual managers wisely as he dispels numerous management myths. Effective Executive Series, no. 5.

Supervisor and OJT. For complete citation, *see* SUPERVISION.

1205. Survey of Laws Affecting Personnel Management
S&L Communications, Inc videocassette color 43 min
Purchase: $100.00 Rental: $45.00 Other cost factors: SLCI members: purchase $75.00; rental $30.00

Covers a variety of laws concerning personnel management including age discrimination, equal pay, vocational rehabilitation, veterans readjustment, nondiscrimination, labor/relations, and fair labor standards. Ben F. Foster explains who administers each law, remedies employees may seek, and exemptions and gives examples of how the law works.

1206. To Meet a Need
Motivision, Ltd 16mm film or videocassette color 9 min
Purchase: $237.00 Rental: $25.00

Useful for top level management presentations that propose, begin, or promote an existing employee assistance program.

1207. Troubled Employee
Dartnell 16mm film color 25 min instructor's print materials
Purchase: $495.00 Rental: $135.00

Presents recommended approach to handling employee job performance problems when the cause is off-job circumstances, such as substance abuse, financial problems, or marital difficulties. Requires sensitivity and legal considerations.

PHYSICAL FITNESS
See HEALTH

PLANNING

1208. "All I Want to Know Is, What's in It for Me?"
BNA Communications, Inc 1972 16mm film or videocassette color 23 min
Purchase: $540.00 Rental: 5-day $150.00; 3-day $105.00 Preview: $35.00

Reveals why many long-range planning programs fail. Focuses on the need for situation analysis, realistic objectives, strategies, commitment by the chief officer, involvement of managers, and the other essentials required to make such a program successful. Companion film to *Invent Your Own Future.* Management Practice Series C, Long-Range Planning, Part 1.

Business Plan—For Small Businessmen. For complete citation, *see* SMALL BUSINESS MANAGEMENT.

1209. Challenge over the Atlantic
Vantage Communications, Inc   1979   16mm film or videocassette   color   14 min
Purchase: $325.00   Rental: $75.00   Preview: $25.00

Documents Double Eagle II balloon flight to illustrate achieving difficult objectives through teamwork, positive thinking, and meticulous preparation. Useful to prepare work group facing tough challenge.

1210. Corporate Planning I
AMR International, Inc   16 audiocassettes
Purchase: $385.00

Experts present topics such as human behavior and the planning process, characteristics of good plans and planners, zero-based budgeting, capital controls, and planning in an inflationary environment.

1211. Corporate Planning II
AMR International, Inc   1981   10 audiocassettes
learner's print materials
Purchase: $350.00

Ten planners share their practical expertise in coping with increasing demands for strategic corporate planning. Includes bracket budgeting, financial planning, the planner and chief executive officer, and budget preparation for performance evaluation.

1212. Critical Path in Use
Roundtable Films, Inc   16mm film or videocassette   b/w   28 min
Purchase: $295.00   Rental: $75.00   Preview: $30.00

Traces a project from planning to completion and reveals how the critical path analysis concept can be applied at all levels of management. Encourages thinking, personal commitment, and a free flow of information by all participants in a project. British production.

1213. Flight Plan
National Educational Media, Inc   1974   16mm film or super 8mm or videocassette   color   14 min
instructor's print materials; learner's print materials
Purchase: $490.00   Rental: 5-day $90.00; 3-day $80.00   Preview: free
Languages: English, French, German, Greek, Japanese, Spanish

A successful manager illustrates the elements of planning to an inexperienced manager by comparing the risks of management with the risks of flying a plane. Analogy shows the critical need for planning. Introduces tools for immediate application of good planning principles. Includes principles of management by objectives. Intended for new and experienced managers.

1214. Focus the Future
BNA Communications, Inc   1971   16mm film or videocassette   color   27 min
Purchase: $595.00   Rental: 5-day $150.00; 3-day $105.00   Preview: $35.00
Languages: English, Portuguese, Spanish

Dramatization illustrates how and why an organization must look ahead to see how the future might affect today's decisions. Illustrates why long-term objectives are needed, what they should consist of, who should handle them, and how a total systems approach aids management. Management by Objectives Series, no. 1.

1215. Fundamentals of Planning
Penton/IPC Education Division   3 audiocassettes
learner's print materials
Purchase: $60.00

Provides a detailed expansion of each step in long- and short-range planning: becoming aware of opportunities, establishing objectives, defining all premises, determining alternative courses—evaluating and selecting them, formulating derivative plans, and implementing the plans.

1216. The "How" of Strategic Planning
AMACOM   4 audiocassettes   1 hr ea   learner's print materials; manual
Purchase: $120.00   Other cost factors: AMA members $102.00

Dr. George A. Steiner provides conceptual models for large, medium, and small companies and gives practical methods for managers who are more interested in applications and results than in theories. Covers uses for strategic planning situation audit, creating strategic plan, tools and techniques for decision making, network of aims and risks, evaluating strategies, and time scheduling.

1217. How to Plan
Management Programs   1977   audiocassettes
learner's print materials
Purchase: $750.00 per participant

Offers practical sequence for developing a planning system. Stresses the importance of planning, reasons for failure, and how to improve the planning process used. Suggested for a 4-hour program in group or self-study structure. For experienced managers.

1218. How to Plan, Organize, and Implement Work
Educational Resources Foundation   1977   16mm film or videocassette   color   24 min
Purchase: $450.00   Rental: $65.00   Preview: $15.00   Other cost factors: leader's guide $4.00; student guide $2.50

Deals with the specifics of how to plan work, organize resources, and implement plans. Introduces terms such as process analysis and short interval scheduling. Tied to common practical problems.

1219. Invent Your Own Future
BNA Communications, Inc   1972   16mm film or videocassette   color   33 min
Purchase: $260.00   Rental: 5-day $150.00; 3-day $105.00   Preview: $35.00

Covers elements of strategic planning, target determination, and the intuition's role in long-range planning. Discusses the need for flexibility, anticipating crises, and how to give every manager "a piece of the action." Features George A. Steiner and John Humble. Companion film to "*All I Want to Know Is, What's in It for Me?*" Management Practice Series C, Long-Range Planning, Part II.

1220. It'll Be O.K. on the Day
Video Arts, Inc   1975   16mm film or videocassette   color   28 min   instructor's print materials; booklet
Purchase: $530.00   Rental: $100.00   Preview: $35.00

Dramatization illustrates the wrong way to plan and produce an exhibition show and the right way to plan with objectives, tasks, key dates, and one person in charge. Also shows critical path and network analysis and project management principles.

Managerial Planning, Organizing, and Controlling.
For complete citation, *see* MANAGEMENT.

New Guide for Starting Your Own Small Business.
For complete citation, *see* SMALL BUSINESS MANAGEMENT.

1221. PERT
Lansford Publishing Company, Inc   1981   60 slides and audiocassette
Purchase: $255.00

Program Evaluation and Review Technique (PERT) is a planning and control tool for managers. Presents the history and use of PERT and Critical Path Method (CPM), illustrating its documentation. Presents sequential problems for group use including plotting charts with time scales, network planning, dealing with breakdown, balancing time and cost, and using PERT with the computer.

1222. Planning and Goal Setting, Time-Waste or Management Tool?
BNA Communications, Inc   1977   16mm film or videocassette   color   22 min   instructor's print materials
Purchase: $560.00   Rental: 5-day $150.00; 3-day $105.00   Preview: $35.00
Languages: English, French, Spanish

Reveals some of the fallacies in long-range planning but advocates planning and goal setting as important for large and small organizations. Intended for managers. Manager and the Organization Series, no. 4.

Planning Your Manpower Needs.
For complete citation, *see* PERSONNEL MANAGEMENT.

1223. Putting It All Together—Action Plans
National Audiovisual Center   1973   16mm film or videocassette   color   26 min
Purchase: film $150.75; video $100.00

Illustrates how definable steps in a chosen strategy are put into the work stream of an organization. Examines 2 new activities for their fiscal and humanpower applications. Putting It All Together Series.

1224. Putting It All Together—Concept of Strategy
National Audiovisual Center   1973   16mm film or videocassette   color   25 min
Purchase: film $145.00; video $100.00

Shows how alternative means may be devised to achieve objectives. Describes ways of developing priorities among the strategies. Putting It All Together Series.

1225. Putting It All Together—Introduction to Planning
National Audiovisual Center   1973   16mm film or videocassette   color   12 min
Purchase: film $69.50; video $79.25

Points out consequences of the absence of planning and indicates the necessity for a rational approach to planning. Putting It All Together Series.

1226. Putting It All Together—It All Depends
National Audiovisual Center   1973   16mm film or videocassette   color   18 min
Purchase: film $104.50; video $79.25

Stresses the importance of understanding the situation before setting objectives or committing resources when planning. Provides guidance for structuring an analysis of the situation to make it useful in decision making. Putting It All Together Series.

1227. Putting It All Together—Pitfalls of Planning
National Audiovisual Center   1973   16mm film or videocassette   color   29 min
Purchase: film $168.25; video $100.00

Discusses 7 of the most critical reasons why planning fails and offers suggestions to prevent this. Putting It All Together Series.

1228. Putting It All Together—Planning
National Audiovisual Center   1973   16mm film or videocassette   color   57 min
Purchase: film $330.50; video $151.25

Presents the principles of management. Emphasizes the differences between management activities and technical activities. Presents the concepts as a system of management in which planning is stressed. Putting It All Together Series.

1229. Putting It All Together—Values in Planning
National Audiovisual Center   1973   16mm film or videocassette   color   14 min
Purchase: film $81.25; video $79.25

Demonstrates the value of a visible system of beliefs and assumptions in the management of a school system. Provides a discussion of the basic issues involved in the management of a school system. Putting It All Together Series.

Work Planning and Scheduling for Supervisors.
For complete citation, *see* SCHEDULING.

POWER AND AUTHORITY

1230. Effective Uses of Power and Authority
CRM/McGraw-Hill Films   1979   16mm film or videocassette   color   32 min   instructor's print

materials; learner's print materials
Purchase: $560.00   Rental: $95.00   Preview: free

Scenes from a power and influence seminar illustrate the best ways managers can use their power and share it with subordinates. Dr. Stan Charnofsky gives a general framework of the use of power in interpersonal relationships to generate or resolve conflict. Acknowledges trend toward involving employees in organizational decision making and goal setting. CRM Management Development Series.

1231. In Charge!
Cally Curtis Company   16mm film or videocassette   color   14 min
Purchase: film $400.00; video $375.00   Rental: $100.00   Preview: $40.00

Position power comes with a title but personal power is the key to leadership. Suggested for management and supervisory training programs.

1232. Machiavelli: On Power
Salenger Educational Media   16mm film or videocassette   color   29 min   instructor's print materials
Purchase: $495.00   Rental: $125.00   Preview: $35.00

Introduces arguments for and against the exercise of raw power by individuals in leadership positions. Presents Niccolo Machiavelli's ideas on the characteristics of an effective leader as reflected in his book *The Prince*. Open-ended to promote discussion about the different kinds and uses of "power" and their relevance to the organization. Asks if Machiavelli's ideas describe the world as it really is or if he merely supplies a superficial rationale to opportunists and dictators.

1233. Power Laboratory
Development Digest   audiocassette
Purchase: $13.75

Barry I. Oshry describes a training laboratory in which the power dimension can be highlighted, experimented with, and examined more carefully, especially in terms of use and misuse of power in organizational settings.

1234. Powerlessness Corrupts
Goodmeasure, Inc   1980   slides and audiocassette   13 min   instructor's print materials
Purchase: $425.00   Rental: $125.00

Power, defined as the capacity to mobilize resources, helps employees get cooperation, information, and respect. Powerless managers can unintentionally turn into rules-minded petty tyrants, thus stifling their employees. Addresses particularly the question of women and minorities and offers insights into what it takes to grow as a leader in an organization. Uses graphics. Companion to *Turning on the Power*. P/QWL Series, no. 5.

1235. Turning on the Power
Goodmeasure, Inc   1980   slides and audiocassette   13 min   instructor's print materials
Purchase: $425.00   Rental: $125.00

Shows how to develop a strategy to recognize and use the power potential already in a job to accomplish more and benefit both individual and organization. Addresses how to design jobs for discretion, visibility, and relevance to cutting edge problems— plus creating access to senior contacts, peer networks, and developing subordinates. Companion to *Powerlessness Corrupts*. P/QWL Series, no. 4.

1236. Using Managerial Authority
American Management Associations   1974   6 audiocassettes   60 min ea   learner's print materials
Purchase: $145.00   Other cost factors: AMA members $135.00; discounts available for bulk orders of materials

Presents the nature and use of modern managerial authority, the various types of authority, and how to extend influence and use authority to complement and support other managerial skills as well as increase effectiveness. Considers the use of authority in discipline and control, what erodes authority, and the unprofessional uses of authority.

PRESENTATIONS
See also COMMUNICATION; MEETING MANAGEMENT

1237. Aids to Speaking
Centron Films   16mm film   color   15 min   instructor's print materials
Purchase: $325.00

Appropriate use of the microphone, lectern, and visual aids greatly improves the effectiveness of public speakers. Dramatized examples show improper use of these tools and the consequences. Practical, detailed, and valuable guidelines are given to help those responsible for public presentations. Particularly useful for the new and nervous.

1238. The Anatomy of a Presentation
Roundtable Films, Inc   16mm film or super 8mm film or videocassette   color   30 min   instructor's print materials
Purchase: $450.00   Rental: $85.00   Preview: $30.00

Dramatization of junior executive substituting for senior executive at the last minute. Shows how to make an effective oral presentation to a group by showing how to help select proper visual aids, collect data, and organize the presentation. He learns how to analyze the needs of the audience, the importance of preparation, and the guidelines that make such a presentation easier and more effective. Intended for managerial and technical personnel who must present reports, ideas, and proposals.

1239. Applause!
Cally Curtis Company   1976   16mm film or videocassette   color   26 min
Purchase: film $550.00; video $525.00   Rental: $130.00   Preview: $40.00

Intended for those inexperienced in public speaking. Georgette McGregor presents 7 steps leading to self-confident presentations. Stresses the importance of studying speech and organizing thoughts.

1240. Building Confidence for Public Speaking
Instructional Dynamics, Inc 1979 audiocassette
learner's print materials
Purchase: $15.45

Includes how to prepare the topic, decide how best to appeal to the audience, handle a hostile audience, shorten a speech at the last minute, and appeal to an uninterested audience. Intended for the person who becomes tense and nervous when doing a public presentation.

Can We Please Have That the Right Way Round?
For complete citation, *see* AUDIOVISUAL TECHNIQUES.

Communicate What You Think. For complete citation, *see* COMMUNICATION.

1241. Communicating Successfully
Time-Life Video 1973 3 16mm films or
videocassettes and audiocassettes color 25 min ea
learner's print materials
Purchase: film $1,500.00 ($500.00 ea); video
$1,095.00 ($400.00 ea) Rental: $150.00 ea Preview:
free

Three units: *How to Make a More Effective Speech, How to Give a More Persuasive Presentation*, and *How to Conduct a More Productive Meeting*. First focuses on techniques for preparing, organizing, and delivering a speech. Second deals with being persuasive as a speaker and use of audiovisuals. Third shows how to conduct meetings to bring positive results. All are dramatizations.

1242. Communicating with a Group
Roundtable Films, Inc 16mm film or
videocassette color 23 min
Purchase: $400.00 Rental: $85.00 Preview:
$30.00

Illustrates the skills and techniques required for an effective presentation. Shows a good trainer handling many of the problems faced by anyone engaged in group communications such as nonparticipation and heckling.

Communication by Voice and Action. For complete citation, *see* NONVERBAL COMMUNICATION.

Communication Skills for Managers. For complete citation, *see* COMMUNICATION.

1243. Compleat Speaker
Nightingale-Conant Corporation 6 audiocassettes
learner's print materials
Purchase: $63.95 Preview: $15.00

Earl Nightingale presents 20 lessons that cover all facets of speech making. Covers various types of speeches, audiovisual aids, motivating an audience, and radio and TV interviews. Designed for self-study. Used by Toastmasters International.

1244. Effective Speaking
Resources for Education and Management, Inc 1971
6 filmstrips or slides and audiocassettes or
videocassettes or filmstrip cartridges 12–16 min ea
instructor's print materials

Purchase: video $320.00 ($70.00 ea); filmstrips
$295.00 ($58.00 ea); filmstrip cartridges $510.00
($85.00 ea); slides $310.00 ($60.00 ea)

Presents a step-by-step approach to successful public speaking. Examines the entire speech-making process from planning and writing to actual delivery. Includes the use of visual aids, basic conference leading, and oral presentation skills. Intended for supervisors and managers.

1245. Effective Speaking for Managers
AMACOM 4 audiocassettes 40–54 min ea guide
Purchase: $85.00 Other cost factors: AMA members
$72.25

Proposes that the ability to express an idea is often as important as the idea itself and that effective speaking can be learned. Includes techniques for platform speeches, one-to-one speeches, and conducting meetings. Tips on impromptu talks, humor, and telephone communication.

Effective Visual Presentations. For complete citation, *see* AUDIOVISUAL TECHNIQUES.

1246. Executive's Shortcut Course to Speech Improvement
Bureau of Business Practice 12 audiocassettes 30
min ea learner's print materials
Purchase: $69.00 Preview: free

Emphasizes use of intonation as a tool. Gives tips on extemporaneous presentations with clear ideas.

1247. Floor Is Yours
BNA Communications, Inc 1972 16mm film or
videocassette color 27 min instructor's print
materials
Purchase: $535.00 Rental: 5-day $150.00; 3-day
$105.00 Preview: $35.00

For those who give talks or reports inside or outside the organization. Shows how to set the objective, plan an effective presentation, prepare materials, and rehearse and practice delivery.

1248. How Not to Exhibit Yourself
Video Arts, Inc 1974 16mm film and audiocassette
or videocassette color 30 min learner's print
materials
Purchase: $550.00 Rental: $100.00 Preview:
$35.00

Humorous dramatization of a briefing session for those who staff booths at trade exhibitions. Illustrates exhibition techniques and discipline essential for clear projection of company image. Audiocassette offers supplementary material.

1249. How to Be a Successful Public Speaker
AMACOM 1974 6 audiocassettes 6 hrs
instructor's print materials; learner's print materials
Purchase: $130.00 Other cost factors: discounts
available for bulk orders of materials

Describes and illustrates practical skills needed to deliver a successful presentation. Focuses on the importance of a personal approach and making a personal plan for improving presentation skills. Pretest and posttest available. Designed for self-study or group instruction.

1250. How to Keep from Talking to Yourself
Practical Management Associates, Inc   audiocassette
learner's print materials
Purchase: $28.00

Based on research of audience retention from a variety of
lecture/speech-type meetings. Covers where to use visual aids,
what turns an audience on or off, assuring attention and interest
without "gimmicks," and how to put across a message effectively.

Impact of Visuals on the Speechmaking Process. For
complete citation, *see* AUDIOVISUAL
TECHNIQUES.

1251. Making Your Case
Xicom-Video Arts   1982   16mm film or
videocassette   color   26 in   instructor's print
materials; learner's print materials
Purchase: $625.00   Rental: $120.00   Preview:
$40.00

Illustrates typical errors of first-time presenters in dream
sequence. Coach shows value of preparation for confidence and
importance of clear messages for audiences. Suggests secrets for
smooth delivery. Features John Cleese.

1252. Meeting Kit #5: "Playing to Win"
Vantage Communications, Inc   1980   16mm film
and slides and audiocassette   color   9 min
instructor's print materials; learner's print materials
Purchase: $450.00   Preview: $30.00

Guidelines on how to plan a meeting and speak more effectively. Covers the use of slides, audio equipment, quotations, and
films. Useful for group or self-study by managers and supervisors.

1253. Opening Speech
International Film Bureau, Inc   16mm film or
videocassette   color   8 min
Purchase: film $85.00; video $100.00   Rental:
$9.00

Animation of a difficult welcome speech with a master of
ceremonies and a rebellious microphone. Concludes with "welcome" in 25 languages.

1254. Our Featured Speaker
General Motors Corporation   16mm film or
videocassette   color   30 min   instructor's print
materials
Purchase: film $750.00; video $600.00   Preview: film
$60.00; video $40.00

Portrays a presentation that reveals 65 faults commonly made
by speakers, repeats with the mistakes labeled, then with them
corrected. Highlights 6 key areas of speaker concern.

1255. Planning Your Speech
Centron Films   1980   16mm film or
videocassette   color   13 min
Purchase: $275.00   Rental: $55.00   Preview:
$55.00

Illustrates how to design and structure an effective speech.
Quotes selections from famous speeches to demonstrate the
function and form of the introduction, the main point and its

supporting points, and the conclusion. Visuals and narration
emphasize the importance of a strong outline and the need to
use language appropriate to the situation and the audience.

1256. Presentation Planning Skills
Singer Management Institute   audiocassette
learner's print materials
Purchase: $24.99   Preview: $15.00

Shows how to develop confidence, how to be professional, and
how to design, develop, and give effective presentations.
Includes how to use audiovisual supports and do a presentation
evaluation.

1257. Reporting and Briefing
Centron Films   16mm film   color   15½ min
Purchase: $335.00

Good and poor techniques in reporting are vividly contrasted.
Shows how clarity, accuracy, and interest can be achieved
through logical organization of the material; specific examples
and illustrations; appropriate humor; and proper use of visual
aids. Replaces *Reporting and Explaining.*

1258. So You're Going on Camera?
A.N.A. Audio Visual Committee   videocassette   color
14 min
Purchase: $85.00

Designed for people getting ready to appear on tape or film.
Includes tips for projecting one's self well and emphasizes the
need for practice. Discusses personal and technical factors
influencing the image projected and how effectively the message
comes across.

Speaking Effectively...To One or One Thousand. For
complete citation, *see* COMMUNICATION.

1259. Stage Fright
Centron Films   1979   16mm film   color   13 min
Purchase: $280.00

Helps those confronted with giving a speech by dramatizing an
individual in that situation. Introduces specific techniques that
any speaker can use successfully to control and harness stage
fright.

1260. Unaccustomed as They Are
BNA Communications, Inc   1971   16mm film or
videocassette   color   33 min
Purchase: $450.00   Rental: 5-day $150.00; 3-day
$105.00   Preview: $35.00
Languages: English, Spanish

Shows how to speak effectively whether reporting to top
management or addressing a local business group. Approach
includes selecting the audience and theme, collecting and
organizing ideas, using humor and trigger words—everything
necessary to sell ideas, get known, and quoted. Compares
examples of effective and ineffective speeches. Joe Powell Films,
no. 4.

Visual Aids. For complete citation, *see*
AUDIOVISUAL TECHNIQUES.

1261. Voice, Vocabulary and Delivery
Classroom World Productions   audiocassettes

Purchase: $27.50

Basics of public speaking: bad habits, diction, word selection, pacing, and pronunciation.

1262. Who Me? Make a Presentation

EFM Films   1980   16mm film or videocassette   color   15 min   instructor's print materials; learner's print materials
Purchase: $425.00   Rental: $120.00   Preview: $40.00 (can apply to purchase)

Uses dramatization that reinforces critical planning and delivery steps with humorous cuts that demonstrate what not to do. Shows how to gain, hold, and persuade an audience with a natural, personal style. Printed materials include pre- and posttest and 5 speech planners addressing specific considerations.

1263. You Can Conduct Better Meetings and Speak with Confidence

Singer Management Institute   4 audiocassettes instructor's print materials
Purchase: $60.00   Rental: $15.00

Shows how to improve speaking skills for meetings and presentations. Urges using preparation, participation, and personalization to give better speeches and presentations. Shows importance of feedback and how to get it.

PROBLEM SOLVING
See DECISION MAKING/PROBLEM SOLVING

PRODUCTIVITY
See also EMPLOYEE PERFORMANCE

1264. America Works When America Works

Films, Inc   1981   16mm film or videocassette   color   78 min
Purchase: film $1,050.00; video $695.00   Rental: $125.00   Preview: free

Examines the deficiencies of a human resources system that has failed to keep up with industrial change. Skills phased out of the economy leave a growing residue of unemployed while new enterprises are short of skilled workers. Unlike other western nations, America has no unified human resources policy. Our greatest resource—labor—is virtually ignored.

Approaches to Organizational Behavior Modification (OBM). For complete citation, *see* BEHAVIOR MODIFICATION.

Career Development: A Plan for All Seasons. For complete citation, *see* CAREER PLANNING AND DEVELOPMENT.

1265. Challenge of Productivity

BNA Communications, Inc   1981   16mm film or videocassette   color   20 min   instructor's print materials; learner's print materials
Purchase: $650.00   Rental: $245.00

Shows why increasing productivity will become even more important in the future and that productivity requires constant attention and hard work. Suggests that employee suggestion groups (quality circles) can be an important factor in the results. Features Peter Drucker. Managing for Tomorrow Series, no. 4.

Disassemble the Assembly Line to Increase Production. For complete citation, *see* WORK.

End of Mechanism. For complete citation, *see* TECHNOLOGY.

Gellerman on Motivation and Productivity. For complete citation, *see* MOTIVATION.

1266. Goldbricking

Xerox Education Publications   1979   16mm film or videocassette   color   12 min
Purchase: film $250.00; video $155.00   Rental: $28.00

In this dramatization, coworkers unearth a variety of tactics to avoid work at all costs. This becomes contagious even to management levels. Useful for all employees to open communication on this issue.

1267. Increasing Productivity

National Educational Media, Inc   1973   16mm film or videocassette   color   14 min   instructor's print materials; learner's print materials
Purchase: $399.00   Rental: 5-day $90.00; 3-day $80.00   Preview: $60.00
Languages: English, French, Japanese, Spanish

Basic premise is that increasing productivity is every manager's responsibility. Demonstrates that productivity can be managed, changes can be initiated, and innovations can be accomplished. Details the responsibilities for change that managers must assume: initiative for change, accurate measurement, involvement of others, and leadership in increasing productivity.

1268. Increasing Worker Satisfaction and Productivity

Development Digest   audiocassette
Purchase: $13.75

Explores a range of opinions on the effectiveness of job security, pay, and incentives for building worker satisfaction and productivity.

Japan Inc. Lessons for North America. For complete citation, *see* BUSINESS ENVIRONMENT.

Job Enrichment: Managerial Milestone a Myth? For complete citation, *see* MOTIVATION.

Learning the Principles of MTM. For complete citation, *see* EMPLOYEE PERFORMANCE.

Listening for Results. For complete citation, *see* LISTENING.

MTM for Better Methods and Fair Standards. For complete citation, *see* EMPLOYEE PERFORMANCE.

1269. Organizing for Productivity
Goodmeasure, Inc   1980   slides and audiocassette   13 min   instructor's print materials
Purchase: $425.00   Rental: $125.00

Graphics show how to improve organizational effectiveness including setting new career directions, reassigning work, and building "parallel organizations"—new cross-hierarchical problem-solving systems. P/QWL Series, no. 7.

1270. People Factor in Our Productivity Improvement
Society of Manufacturing Engineers   1980   videocassette   color   35 min
Purchase: $190.00   Rental: $45.00   Other cost factors: SME members $160.00 (rental $40.00)

Explains steps to take to remove the institutionalized impediments to improved productivity. Advocates a focus on specific projects rather than psychological generalities.

1271. Personal Productivity
Organization Development Consultants   audiocassette   58 min
Purchase: $13.95

Reveals how to identify one's own strengths and use them to the best advantage. Deals with problem solving and bringing out the best of one's self and others at work. Focuses on being a better worker and manager.

1272. Personal Productivity, The Key to Success
Management Decision Systems, Inc   16mm film   color   25 min   instructor's print materials; learner's print materials
Purchase: $475.00   Rental: $125.00

Introduces the concept and its importance. Emphasizes working smarter, not harder. Focuses on long-term personal goal setting, interpersonal relations and communications, task and time management, and health maintenance. Part of the larger training package that includes case studies and participant exercises.

1273. Perspective on Productivity
Development Digest   audiocassette
Purchase: $14.00

Summarizes 50 years of study on productivity. Discussion covers costs associated with turnover, job satisfaction as an index of productivity, meaningful work, and the central role of play.

Planning Tomorrow's Methods Today. For complete citation, *see* EMPLOYEE PERFORMANCE.

1274. Production-Minded Management
Resources for Education and Management, Inc   4 videocassettes or slides and audiocassette or filmstrips or filmstrip cartridges   color   11–13 min ea   instructor's print materials
Purchase: video $280.00 ($85.00 ea); filmstrips $255.00 ($69.00 ea); filmstrip cartridges $340.00 ($85.00 ea); slides $270.00 ($73.00 ea)   Rental: $20.00

Views efficient production as goal management. Examines production in relation to inflation and small things that erode productivity. Explores ways of improving and changing attitudes about productivity.

Productive Person: A Choice Awareness Workshop. For complete citation, *see* DECISION MAKING/ PROBLEM SOLVING.

1275. Productivity and the Self-Fulfilling Prophecy: The Pygmalion Effect
CRM/McGraw-Hill Films   1974   16mm film or videocassette   color   28 min   instructor's print materials; learner's print materials
Purchase: $560.00   Rental: $95.00   Preview: free

Illustrates, through dramatization and animation, how people tend to perform in accord with what is expected of them. Explores several examples of how the Pygmalion Effect—self-fulfilling prophecy—works. Points out importance of identifying negative Pygmalions and how to increase the influence of positive Pygmalions.

1276. Productivity Breakthroughs: Begin with Results Instead of Preparation
Society of Manufacturing Engineers   1980   videocassette   color   28 min
Purchase: $195.00   Rental: $45.00   Other cost factors: SME members $160.00 (rental $40.00)

Interview with Robert Schaffer explains how some managers wait for motivated workers, cooperative unions, and new equipment while others make dramatic productivity gains with resources available. Tells how to focus on even modest success.

1277. Productivity Challenge
LCA Video/Films   1982   4 videocassettes   color   30 min ea   instructor's print materials; learner's print materials
Purchase: lease $50–200 per month per person for 6 months

Dramatizations show skills in earning employee commitment, controlling absenteeism, improving employee performance, and applying corrective discipline. Suggested for a 2-day program or 4 modules of 4 hours each. Two versions available: union or nonunion organization.

1278. Productivity Challenge in the Decade of the 80's
Society of Manufacturing Engineers   1980   videocassette   color   43 min
Purchase: $260.00   Rental: $50.00   Other cost factors: SME members $230.00 (rental $45.00)

Discusses the attitudes of both manager and worker, excessive regulation, and the lack of cooperation between government and industry. Proposes a return to a sense of national spirit, unity, and pride in order to effectively deal with lagging productivity.

1279. Productivity Film
LCA Video/Films   16mm film or videocassette   6 min   instructor's print materials
Purchase: $195.00   Rental: $50.00   Preview: $25.00

Reviews reasons for declining American productivity. Clarifies the relationship between productivity and quality of work life.

1280. Productivity: Getting Your Employees to Care
AMACOM 4 audiocassettes 60 min ea learner's print materials
Purchase: $99.95 Other cost factors: AMA members $84.95

Shows how motivational research is now being used successfully to increase productivity in private and public organizations and union and nonunion shops across the country. Reviews the motivational research done by Maslow, McGregor, Likert, and other authorities. Gives examples of principles in action in business, industry, education, and government. Offers summary of 18 proven ways to improve productivity.

1281. Productivity Payoff
LCA Video/Films 1982 videocassettes color 45 min instructor's print materials; learner's print materials
Purchase: $450.00 Preview: $50.00

Designed for managers and first-line supervisors. Available in 3 versions: business, government, and nonmanagement. Builds understanding of what productivity means, how it affects employee lives on and off the job, why it is important to improve it, and how it pays off. Suggested for 6-hour session.

1282. Productivity: The Key to America's Future
Chamber of Commerce of the United States 79 slides and audiocassette 20 min script
Purchase: $37.50

Analyzes current decline in US productivity that has alarmed business people, economists, politicians, and labor leaders alike. Explanation of the causes of the decline, the effects on business and individuals, and the steps that must be taken to reverse the trend.

Strategy for Productive Behavior. For complete citation, *see* MOTIVATION.

Supervising for Productivity. For complete citation, *see* SUPERVISION.

1283. Supervisor's Guide to Boosting Productivity
American Management Associations 6 audiocassettes workbook
Purchase: $145.00 Other cost factors: AMA members $135.00

Covers key ways to increase productivity: effective planning, time management, skillful direction of work unit, understanding people, and building the will to work. Discusses performance development techniques, conducting interviews and meetings productively, and introducing change. Includes CPM, PERT, and budgets for productivity.

1284. Supervisor's Role in Increasing Productivity
Bureau of Business Practice 1980 16mm film or videocassette color 20 min
Purchase: $425.00 Rental: $95.00 Preview: $45.00

Shows supervisors how to develop positive job attitudes, stimulate pride in their work, and train workers to catch and correct mistakes. Reveals causes of poor productivity and how to eliminate them.

1285. What Makes Japan Work
Hartley Film Foundation 1983 16mm film or videocassette color 11 min
Purchase: $250.00 Rental: $50.00

Surfaces the deeper meaning of the relationship of productivity to worker philosophy. Three Japanese workers demonstrate an attitude that definitely influences the quality of their work. The meditative state of mind is explained and demonstrated by Alan Watts.

Work Sampling Technique. For complete citation, *see* EMPLOYEE PERFORMANCE.

PROFIT
See FINANCIAL MANAGEMENT

PUBLIC RELATIONS
See CUSTOMER RELATIONS

PUBLIC SPEAKING
See PRESENTATIONS

QUALITY CIRCLES
See also TEAM BUILDING

Action-Oriented Problem Solving. For complete citation, *see* DECISION MAKING/PROBLEM SOLVING.

Challenge of Productivity. For complete citation, *see* PRODUCTIVITY.

1286. Extra Care Story: A Quality Circle Case Study
Films, Inc 1981 16mm film or videocassette color 34 min
Purchase: film $680.00; video $550.00 Rental: $90.00

Details the Quality Circle program at a Johnson & Johnson facility from introduction to implementation. Shows how line personnel participate creatively in the manufacturing process. Depicts the successful outcomes of this particular Quality Circles application.

1287. Implementing Quality Circles
BNA Communications, Inc 1980 400 slides and 8 audiocassettes or videocassette 10 min ea instructor's print materials; learner's print materials
Purchase: $640.00 Other cost factors: introductory kit $110.00

Emphasis is on teamwork, problem identification, problem solving, and idea presentation. Two separate programs are available: one for manufacturing companies and one for non-manufacturing organizations. Includes background on quality circles as well as techniques to build them within the organization. Intended to train quality circle facilitators, leaders, and members. Suggested for weekly one-hour sessions.

1288. Quality Circle Training Kit
Lansford Publishing Company, Inc   501 slides and 8 audiocassettes   instructor's print materials; learner's print materials
Purchase: $950.00

Quality circles use employees as group problem solvers to correct procedures and prevent future problems. Materials allow an organization to set up its own quality circle program.

1289. Quality Circles—First Year in Review
Society of Manufacturing Engineers   1980 videocassette   color
Purchase: $260.00   Rental: $50.00

Use of quality circles in a company for one year added to worker morale and productivity improvement. Offers a guideline to review a program or to learn from someone else's application. Advocates that management should listen to as well as direct the work force.

1290. Quality Control Circles: A Lasting Impact?
Twentieth Century-Fox Video, Inc   videocassette color   70 min   instructor's print materials; learner's print materials; book
Purchase: $680.00   Rental: $160.00   Preview: $50.00

Discusses the applicability of Japanese managerial practices to the west. Outlines the human element in Japanese productivity and the assumptions which underlie this humanistic approach. Offers suggestions for American firms who are contemplating, or struggling with, the implementation of Japanese managerial practices. Features Bob Cole.

1291. What This Country Needs
Films, Inc   1981   16mm film or videocassette   color   30 min
Purchase: film $550.00; video $275.00   Rental: $60.00

Discusses the problems of worker-management relationships, the implications of changing worker attitudes, and the need for management to provide motivation. Offers a provocative look at one of our nation's major concerns—the declining growth rate of productivity. Gives several examples of working smarter not harder, of offering good working conditions, and of using incentives and adapting quality circle concepts.

QUALITY CONTROL

1292. Quality Control
Society of Manufacturing Engineers   13 videocassettes   color   60 min ea
Purchase: $3,790.00 ($335.00 ea)   Rental: $940.00 ($85.00 ea)   Other cost factors: learner's study guide $34.00; textbook $28.50

Gives guidelines for performing a practical and complete review of a quality control program. Offers sound principles and points out how to identify and correct problem areas. Explains sampling plans, control charts, and tolerance specifications. Features Sanford B. Thayer.

Quality Control Circles: A Lasting Impact? For complete citation, *see* QUALITY CIRCLES.

1293. Quality Insurance
ROA Films   1982   6 videocassettes   1 hr ea instructor's print materials
Purchase: $5,100.00 ($850.00 ea)   Preview: $75.00

Demonstrates operating quality assurance programs under actual working conditions in several industries. Includes measuring and calibrations, testing, quality assurance documentation, and international standards. Intended for engineers, forepersons, accountants, inspectors, purchasing agents, and other personnel engaged in manufacturing, production, or construction where quality of output is important.

1294. Quality Planning
Society of Manufacturing Engineers   1977   10 videocassettes   color   60 min
Purchase: $2,950.00 ($335.00 ea)   Rental: $725.00 ($85.00 ea)

Examines the design, organization, and technical aspects of a successful cost-effective quality program. Explores quality control in actual situations. Intended for quality control and production managers. Lecture presentations.

1295. Supervisor's Role in Quality Control
Bureau of Business Practice   16mm film or videocassette   color   20 min
Purchase: $425.00   Rental: $95.00   Preview: $45.00

Dramatizations show how to develop positive job attitudes in workers, stimulate an employee's pride in good work, develop cooperation between quality control and production personnel, and train workers to accept quality as the key to consumer confidence.

READING

1296. Effective Reading, Self-Taught
Xerox Learning Systems   1980   4 audiocassettes learner's print materials
Purchase: $95.00

Instructs how to read faster and improve comprehension. Indicates techniques for adapting to different types of reading material. Useful for self-instruction. Suggested for 8–12 hours.

1297. Managerial Reading Training Program
Creative Curriculum, Inc   51 slides and special equipment   learner's print materials
Purchase: $529.00 (includes reader simulator)

Uses sequence of exercises to promote improved reading efficiency. Can be used by employees at any level either as self-study or group learning situation. Producer's reader simulator displays slides at various speeds.

Read Your Way Up. For complete citation, *see* COMMUNICATION.

1298. Reading
HBJ Media Systems Corporation 1981 10 slide/
audiocassette presentations (34 audiocassettes)
instructor's print materials; learner's print materials
Purchase: $15,715.00

Offers a systematic skills approach to reading improvement.
Shows how to apply 10 fundamental reading comprehension
skills to understand the meaning of written materials. Suggested
for 90–100 hours.

1299. Reading Efficiency System
Time-Life Video 1979 12 videocassettes color 30
min ea instructor's print materials; learner's print
materials
Purchase: $3,950.00 Rental: $1,250.00 Preview:
free

Aims at developing 4 basic skills of reading efficiency: comprehension skills, critical thought skills, vocabulary skills, and rate
improvement skills. Printed materials include exercises in each
skill area. Intended for group or self-study. Features Bill Cosby.

1300. Reading Plus
AMACOM 1979 6 audiocassettes instructor's
print materials; learner's print materials; 3 books
Purchase: $115.00 Other cost factors: AMA
members $97.50

Gives techniques for reading, understanding, and remembering.
Includes work with vocabulary, handling paperwork, skimming, and scanning. Suggested for a 20-hour program.

**1301. Reading/Plus: Speed, Learning and Retention
for Managers**
AMACOM 6 audiocassettes 30 min ea learner's
print materials; 3 books
Purchase: $115.00 Other cost factors: AMA
members $97.75

Presents a key to speed reading, greater comprehension, and
positive habits. Offers memory improvement techniques. Printed materials include practice readings, charts and diagrams, and
tests.

1302. Speed Learning
Learn, Inc 1977 9 16mm films or
videocassettes color 30 min ea
Purchase: $3,900.00 Rental: $1,200.00 Preview:
$35.00 Other cost factors: learner's print materials
$45.00; 4 audiocassettes $99.95; instructor's print
materials $75.00

Presents a series of skills to develop a pattern of reading
organization, comprehension, retention, recall, and rate improvement. Shows how to handle printed information more
rapidly and efficiently. Includes skimming, scanning, study
reading, and surveying. Reveals how to separate fact from
fiction, handle decision making with confidence, and how to
better manage time. Includes pre- and posttest measurements.
For group or self-study.

1303. Speed Learning
Penton/IPC Education Division 3 audiocassettes
learner's print materials
Purchase: $89.95

Presents how to decide quickly whether material is important,
improve concentration and retention, establish a clear purpose
for each piece of reading, and shift gears and read at different
speeds for different types of materials.

1304. Speed Reading
Time-Life Video 1974 8 videocassettes color 30
min ea learner's print materials
Purchase: $3,950.00 Rental: $500.00 Preview:
free

Demonstrates techniques to improve reading speed and retention. Emphasizes the art of skimming, improved study habits,
and an enlarged vocabulary. Print materials closely correlated
with videocassettes. Includes paced reading, eye exercises, and
comprehension and retention drills. Features Dick Cavett.

RECORDS AND RECORD KEEPING

1305. Audio Aid to OSHA Recordkeeping (Revised)
National Audiovisual Center 1978 audiocassette
24 min instructor's print materials; learner's print
materials
Purchase: $11.00

AN OSHA produced cassette to clarify record keeping forms
required in safety and health problem areas. Discusses how
properly kept forms enable a company to chart work safety
progress over a given time period.

1306. Basic Record Keeping
National Audiovisual Center 1977 16mm film or
videocassette color 28 min learner's print
materials
Purchase: film $162.50; video $110.25 Rental:
$12.50

Illustrates the need for efficient record keeping. Includes record
keeping principles, methods for classifying information, and tips
for proper maintenance of records. You in Public Service Series.

1307. Filing and Retrieval
HBJ Media Systems Corporation 1981 9 slides/
audiocassette presentations instructor's print
materials; learner's print materials
Purchase: $2,680.00

Includes principles of records management, selection and use of
basic equipment and supplies, and how to establish and
maintain alphabetical, numerical, geographic and subject-entry
filing systems. Intended for those who keep and use files.
Suggested for 18–25 hours.

1308. Language of Business
National Audiovisual Center 16mm film or
videocassette color 15 min
Purchase: $87.00 Rental: $12.50

Dramatizes the need for being able to analyze facts and problem
areas in a business so that decisions can be made. Shows the
value of records in business management.

Notes, Reports, and Communications. For complete
citation, *see* SECURITY.

1309. People, Not Paper
National Audiovisual Center 1977 16mm film or videocassette color 18 min
Purchase: film $115.00; video $88.00 Rental: $25.00

Paul Duke narrates this documentary on the impact of federal paperwork. Illustrations and examples drawn from the work of the 2-year Commission on Federal Paperwork are used to demonstrate steps to take in reducing the problem.

1310. Record Keeping
HBJ Media Systems Corporation 1981 6 slide/ audiocassette presentations instructor's print materials; learner's print materials
Purchase: $1,785.00

Shows the preparation and maintenance of petty cash vouchers, expense reports, and routine office records. Suggested for 12–14 hours.

1311. Records Management
Educational Resources Foundation 1971 5 16mm films or videocassettes color 15–18 min ea
Purchase: $325.00 ea Rental: $50.00 ea Preview: $15.00 ea Other cost factors: student guide $7.00

Provides the information necessary for establishing and maintaining a proper and effective records management system for business. Useful to orient employees to the need for the comprehensive, planned records system. Produced in cooperation with the Association of Records Managers and Administrators (ARMA).

Typing Medical Forms and Reports. For complete citation, *see* TYPEWRITING.

RECRUITMENT
See EMPLOYEE SELECTION AND PLACEMENT

RETIREMENT

1312. Forever Young
LCA Video/Films 1982 16mm film or videocassette color 58 min instructor's print materials
Purchase: $750.00 Rental: $120.00 Preview: $60.00

Prompts viewers to look forward to retirement years as 26 very active senior citizens are interviewed. They speak positively on all aspects of aging and retirement.

1313. More than Retirement
National Audiovisual Center 1981 16mm film or videocassette color 15 min
Purchase: film $130.00; video $55.00 Rental: $25.00

Focuses on 4 individuals far from retirement age who have suffered physical or emotional hardship and who—thanks to Social Security—have been able to maintain their independence and self-respect.

1314. Preretirement Planning—It Makes a Difference
National Audiovisual Center 1981 16mm film color 15 min
Purchase: film $130.00; video $55.00 Rental: $25.00

Advocates preretirement planning with emotional, geographical, and financial considerations. Offers advice from retirees.

1315. Ready or Not
Manpower Education Institute 6 16mm films or videocassettes color 15–20 min ea handbook
Purchase: depends on extent of program usage

Presents the challenges and options that face individuals approaching retirement age. Describes key areas of finances, legal affairs, health, leisure, and earning money. Handbook offers charts and workpages to give permanent record for planning. Useful for organizational preretirement programs.

1316. Toward Retirement
Washington Film Company 16mm film or videocassette color 14 min
Purchase: film $445.00; video $305.00 Rental: $95.00 Preview: $30.00

Designed for use as an introduction to a retirement planning course. Features interviews with successful retirees from all walks of life. Introduces the basics of retirement planning and emphasizes role crisis. Premises: early planning (5 to 7 years) is essential to a successful retirement, and planning is an individual function.

Your Health, and Aging. For complete citation, *see* HEALTH.

SAFETY

Audio Aid to OSHA Recordkeeping (Revised). For complete citation, *see* RECORDS AND RECORD KEEPING.

1317. Guide to Voluntary Compliance
National Audiovisual Center 1973 186 slides instructor's print materials
Purchase: $74.00

Program guide to develop a systematic self-inspection procedure for the correction of workplace deficiencies in accordance with Occupational Safety and Health Act Standards.

1318. Make Your Investigation Count
Educational Resources Foundation 16mm film or videocassette color 10 min instructor's print materials
Purchase: $260.00 Rental: $50.00 Preview: $15.00

Shows both the wrong way to do an investigation and the right way. Illustrates basics such as securing the area, taking care of the injured employee, doing the investigation immediately after the action occurs, looking for the real causes of the accident, and then making recommendations and changes to prevent future accidents. Intended for first-line industrial supervisors who have to do accident investigations.

1319. OSHA File—Cases and Compliance
Bureau of Business Practice 1973 16mm film or
videocassette color 20 min
Purchase: $425.00 Rental: $95.00 Preview:
$45.00

Briefs supervisors on the consequences of OSHA violations.
Court cases drawn from actual OSHA files show supervisors
the steps they must take to live up to the law.

**1320. Safety and the Supervisor: Positive Attitudes
Pay Off**
Bureau of Business Practice 16mm film or
videocassette color 21 min
Purchase: $425.00 Rental: $95.00 Preview:
$45.00

Shows supervisors how to make safety observance a company-
wide practice. Reveals the steps supervisors must take to reduce
lost-time injuries. Dramatizations show how to instill positive
safety attitudes, learn how to enforce the rules, outlaw the use
of risky tools, and prevent unsafe acts.

1321. Safety for Retailers
American Learning Systems, Inc 1981 2 filmstrips
or slides and audiocassettes or videocassettes or
filmstrip cartridges 12 min   instructor's print
materials
Purchase: $250.00 Preview: free

Addresses the proper attitude toward safety by employees.
Unsafe acts and omissions that cause injury to employees,
visitors, customers, and employer's property constitute business
losses.

1322. Simple Choice
Tylie Jones 16mm film or super 8mm film or
videocassette color 18 min
Purchase: $350.00 Rental: $100.00 Preview:
$25.00

Shows requirements for Occupational Safety and Health Administration compliance and the reasons for it. Discusses the
consequences of carelessness, ego gratification, and the belief
that rules are made for someone else.

**1323. 16 Leading Causes of OSHA Citations and
How to Avoid Them**
Bureau of Business Practice 16mm film or
videocassette color 20 min
Purchase: $425.00 Rental: $95.00 Preview:
$45.00

Shows supervisors how to correct unsafe conditions that may
exist in unexpected places. A camera tour of a typical plant
reveals unsuspected but common violations cited by compliance
officers during routine inspections.

1324. Supervisor's Safety Orientation Program
Bureau of Business Practice 2 audiocassettes
learner's print materials
Purchase: $25.00

Tells how the occupational safety law works, what an Occupational Safety and Health Administration inspection is like, how
to find and eliminate the hazards.

1325. Unplanned
National Film Board of Canada 1983 16mm film
or videocassette color 20 min   instructor's print
materials
Purchase: film $410.00; video $300.00 Rental:
$100.00 Preview: $40.00

Illustrates 2 basic accident prevention tenets—multiple causes
and different causes for an accident and injury. Intended to
stimulate discussion at the managerial and supervisory levels.

1326. Wheelchair
Dartnell 16mm film or videocassette color 15
min
Purchase: $425.00 Rental: $95.00

A foundation on which to build a safety program by changing
attitudes toward safety. Not a "how to" film but a "why" and
"what's in it for me? " film. British film.

1327. You and Office Safety
Xerox Education Publications 16mm film or
videocassette color 8½ min
Purchase: film $225.00; video $130.00 Rental:
$28.00 Preview: free

Using visual hyperbole and laughter, this humorous, fast-paced
film illustrates how easy it is to avoid many common office
accidents. Shows how safety in the office can be assured by
using a little common sense, by thinking ahead, and by
considering the consequences of one's actions.

SCHEDULING

**1328. Roadmap to Less Effort—The Flow Process
Chart**
National Audiovisual Center 1973 16mm
film color 15 min
Purchase: $87.00

Illustrates the use, preparation, and analysis of the flow process
chart, a device for the solution of work efficiency problems.

1329. Scheduling for Profit
Management Resources, Inc 1976 2
audiocassettes   instructor's print materials; learner's
print materials
Purchase: $75.00

Identifies the basic steps in scheduling work. Describes kinds of
projects that require network analysis techniques of scheduling.
Details short interval scheduling for routine work.

Time Study Methods. For complete citation, *see*
TIME MANAGEMENT.

1330. Work Planning and Scheduling for Supervisors
Training by Design 2 audiocassettes   learner's
print materials
Purchase: $95.00

Identifies the differences between planning and scheduling
work. Offers an 8-step planning process, critical path concept,
and how to establish controls. Suggests how to analyze
performance gaps to improve future planning and performance.

SECRETARIAL SKILLS
See also DICTATION; TYPEWRITING

1331. Business Writing Skills for Secretaries
Training by Design   4 audiocassettes
Purchase: $95.00

Details writing effective business letters—grammar, punctuation, and sentence construction, as well as general writing skills. Includes report writing and composing effective correspondence.

Desk Set. For complete citation, *see* COMMUNICATION.

1332. Guide for Executive Secretaries and Administrative Assistants
American Management Associations   6 audiocassettes
learner's print materials
Purchase: $145.00 Other cost factors: AMA members $135.00; discounts available for bulk orders of materials

Intended to upgrade performance of executive secretaries or administrative assistants. Emphasizes using judgment and initiative to sort out and handle increased responsibilities, get things done through others, control time wasters, communicate effectively, handle crises, and solve problems consistent with personal management style.

1333. Mail and Telephone
HBJ Media Systems Corporation   1981   6 slide/audiocassette presentations   instructor's print materials; learner's print materials
Purchase: $1,815.00

Gives instruction in the efficient processing of mail and telephone messages. Includes skills for processing incoming and outgoing mail and techniques for receiving, recording, and delivering phone messages. Intended for receptionists, secretaries, and others who handle office communications. Suggested for 10–12 hours.

1334. Professional Skills for Secretaries
Time-Life Video   4 videocassettes   color   30 min ea   instructor's print materials; learner's print materials
Purchase: $3,950.00   Rental: $500.00   Preview: free

Vignettes and interviews portray typical actions and problems of office workers. Explores role of today's secretary. Gives guidelines to take stock of their own aptitudes and abilities. Demonstrates good organizational skills and interpersonal abilities needed. Addresses the office of the future and its need for secretaries.

1335. Secretarial Practice
Educational Research Associates   6 audiocassettes
Purchase: $133.40

General overview of all aspects of the job of a secretary, looking at the requirements, duties, and qualifications. Intended as an introduction.

1336. Secretary as Manager
Training by Design   4 audiocassettes   instructor's print materials; learner's print materials

Purchase: $95.00   Rental: $15.00

Designed to help secretaries upgrade their managerial skills and to improve their working relationships with their bosses. Emphasizes time management, effective interpersonal relationships, and public relations. Discusses how to approach the job professionally and efficiently.

1337. Secretary in a Changing World
Teaching Aids, Inc   4 filmstrips and audiocassettes   color   instructor's print materials
Purchase: $87.00

Presents communications explosion and its impact on society through charting recent developments in office equipment and computer technology. Takes a look at the vital role secretaries play in the professional world. Career possibilities in business, medicine, law, science, government, engineering, and communications are explored. Focuses on the essential attributes of a top secretary. Revised Edition.

1338. Techniques of Machine Transcription
Thompson-Mitchell and Associates   filmstrips or slides and audiocassettes
Purchase: filmstrip $60.00; slides $100.00

Describes brands of transcription equipment, types of media used; machine parts, operation art of efficient transcription, how to produce first-time mailable copy, and helpful hints for effective transcription.

1339. Travel and Conference Arrangements
HBJ Media Systems Corporation   1981   8 slide/audiocassette presentations   instructor's print materials; learner's print materials
Purchase: $2,380.00

Gives step-by-step procedures to implement every phase of business travel. Includes how to plan for the manager's business travel, make airline reservations, secure hotel accommodations, see that the office runs smoothly in the manager's absence, and many related skills. Intended for secretaries, adminstrative assistants, and others who assist in arranging business trips and conferences. Suggested for 14–16 hours.

What Is a Word Processor? For complete citation, *see* COMPUTERS.

SECURITY
See also CRIME PREVENTION

1340. Achieving Computer Security
American Management Associations   6 audiocassettes   learner's print materials
Purchase: $145.00   Other cost factors: AMA members $135.00; discounts available for bulk orders of materials

Step-by-step instructions to protect organizational assets with audit and control procedures. Emphasizes use of controls available now and preparing for future security problems. Includes specifics such as auditing distributive systems, preventing errors in integrated systems, security in time-sharing systems, and disaster planning for EDP systems.

1341. Alarm Systems
American Learning Systems, Inc   1981   2 filmstrips or slides and audiocassettes or videocassettes or filmstrip cartridge   12 min ea   instructor's print materials
Purchase: video $250.00; other formats $150.00   Preview: free

Discusses in nontechnical language the methods of electronically defending a facility from illegal intrusion and procedures to be followed in use of alarm systems. Familiarized owners or managers of places of business with electronic equipment used to provide facility's security. Intended for managers and supervisors.

1342. The Anatomy of Terrorism
MTI Teleprograms, Inc   1975   2 16mm films   28 min and 25 min   learner's print materials
Purchase: $450.00   Rental: $125.00
Languages: *Personal and Family Security* also available in Spanish.

A restricted, multimedia executive protection training program. *Executive Decision* develops awareness and security consciousness by top management and illustrates key attitudes and practices that must be developed. *Personal and Family Security* adds specific security details for the executive and family, building on the dramatization in the first film.

1343. Basic Security Surveys
MTI Teleprograms, Inc   16mm film or videocassette   color   25 min   instructor's print materials
Purchase: film $355.00; video $320.00   Rental: $60.00

Covers objectives and techniques in making a security survey—assessing opportunities for a crime to be committed in a specific location. Examples include small retail operation, tavern, and warehouse.

1344. Bomb Search Procedures
MTI Teleprograms, Inc   16mm film or videocassette   color   16 min
Purchase: film $165.00; video $150.00   Preview: free

Shows in detail the establishment of search teams and functions of the team. Includes what to look for, where to look, and how to use standard search equipment and marking materials. Designed for security, safety management, and operation personnel.

1345. Bomb Threat! Plan, Don't Panic
MTI Teleprograms, Inc   16mm film or videocassette   color   15 min
Purchase: $325.00   Rental: $70.00   Preview: free
Languages: English, Spanish

Shows the steps to take when faced with a bomb threat. Details how to get information from the threat itself, report it to authorities, and conduct the search and evacuate the building. Intended for all employee levels.

1346. Bomb Threats
American Learning Systems, Inc   1981   filmstrip or slides and audiocassette or videocassette or filmstrip cartridge   12 min   instructor's print materials
Purchase: video $150.00; other formats $125.00   Preview: free

Discusses how to handle threats received by a place of business that an explosive device has been placed within the facility. Continues with the preparation of the management staff and training of employees to put these procedures into effect.

1347. Handling Telephone Bomb Threats
MTI Teleprograms, Inc   slides and audiocassettes   instructor's print materials; learner's print materials
Purchase: $115.00

Designed to train switchboard operators and others who might receive telephone bomb threat calls. Details what information to write down, how to ask the right questions, how to recognize a caller's significant speech patterns and characteristics, and how to record all information.

1348. Notes, Reports, and Communications
MTI Teleprograms, Inc   1977   slides and audiocassette or filmstrip cartridge   14 min
Purchase: English $175.00; Spanish $195.00   Rental: $35.00
Languages: English, Spanish

Deals with how security officers report incidents occurring during a watch. Shows careful observation and accurate and detailed note taking as the critical factors in writing up good reports. Dramatizes sample situations for learners to respond to. Professional Security Training Series, no. 3.

1349. Plan for Security
MTI Teleprograms, Inc   1977   filmstrip cartridge or slides and audiocassette   12 min
Purchase: English $130.00; Spanish $145.00   Rental: $35.00
Languages: English, Spanish

Explores security as an organized approach to preventing loss of assets. Shows how security works, what its tools are, and how the security officer's attitude and skills make him/her the most important part of the security operation. Professional Security Training Series, no. 1B.

1350. Planning for Bomb Threats
MTI Teleprograms, Inc   filmstrip and audiocassettes   16 min
Purchase: $150.00   Rental: $35.00

Covers the nature of bomb threats, search and evacuation procedures, bomb threat communications, and bomb recognition and handling. Intended to train security personnel, supervisors, and management in developing plans for effectively handling bomb threats.

1351. Postmark: Terror
MTI Teleprograms, Inc   16mm film or videocassette   color   15 min   poster
Purchase: $325.00   Rental: $50.00

Deals with all aspects of package bombs. Provides definitions and diagrams of letter and package bombs, and shows how to recognize these devices and what to do with suspected material.

Helps develop proper awareness and attitudes that could save lives.

1352. Professional Patrol
MTI Teleprograms, Inc 1977 slides and audiocassette or filmstrip cartridge 14 min
Purchase: English $175.00; Spanish $195.00 Rental: $35.00
Languages: English, Spanish

Stresses the importance of the routine patrol. Covers the functions of patrol tactics, different patrol requirements, and decision making. Professional Security Training Series, no. 2.

1353. Protection of Proprietary Information
MTI Teleprograms, Inc 1980 16mm film or videocassette or slides and audiocassette color 22–30 min instructor's print materials; learner's print materials
Purchase: film $695.00; video $650.00 Rental: $165.00 Preview: $95.00

Intended for managers and employees at all levels to stress the need for protection of company information. Emphasizes company policies and procedures, gossip, the press, classification and duplication of sensitive materials, controlling access, and procedures with vendors. Suggested for 1½ hour program.

1354. Public Relations in Security
MTI Teleprograms, Inc 1977 slides and audiocassette or filmstrip cartridge 12 min
Purchase: English $130.00; Spanish $145.00 Rental: $35.00
Languages: English, Spanish

Demonstrates why dealing with people effectively is such a critical part of being a successful security officer. Shows the importance of courtesy, good manners, tact, and personal deportment in dealing with the public. Uses examples relevant to the security officer's daily routine. Professional Security Training Series, no. 1C.

1355. Robbery by Kidnapping and Extortion
American Learning Systems, Inc 1981 2 filmstrips or slides and audiocassettes or videocassettes or filmstrip cartridge 12 min ea instructor's print materials
Purchase: video $250.00; other formats $150.00 Preview: free

Trains the business executive in methods of kidnap and extortion preparedness and prevention. Suggests procedures to establish for the prevention of kidnapping and preparation for such an eventuality. Intended for managers and supervisors.

1356. Security and the Law
MTI Teleprograms, Inc 1977 slides and audiocassette or filmstrip cartridge 14 min
Purchase: $175.00 Rental: $35.00

Discusses the extent and types of authority legally held by private security officers. Shows how the interplay of personal moral decisions, company policies, and the law affect each decision made by a security officer. Explains probable cause, laws of arrest, discretionary authority, and law enforcement coordination. Professional Security Training Series, no. 4.

1357. Security Story
MTI Teleprograms, Inc 1977 slides and audiocassette or filmstrip cartridge 12 min
Purchase: English $130.00; Spanish $145.00 Rental: $35.00
Languages: English, Spanish

Presents a brief history of the development of private security in America. Shows today's security professional in his/her role as a protector of assets. Demonstrates tools of modern-day security and emphasizes the importance of training employees to use these tools. Professional Security Training Series, no. 1A.

1358. Security Surveys in Manufacturing
MTI Teleprograms, Inc 1974 16mm film or videocassette color 11 min instructor's print materials
Purchase: $210.00 Rental: $45.00 Preview: free

Deals with a clothing manufacturer's security/crime prevention plan. Survey uncovers weaknesses in entrances, windows, alarms, and internal procedures.

1359. Surviving Hostage Situations
MTI Teleprograms, Inc 1975 16mm film or videocassette color 25 min
Purchase: film $695.00; video $625.00 Rental: $125.00 Preview: free

Presents a filmed case history told by a victim who is assisted by an expert from his company. Shows each phase of the kidnap situation and how to deal with the problems in each—whether it be the trauma of the initial capture or the extreme boredom of long term captivity.

SEXUAL HARASSMENT

1360. Power Pinch
Goodmeasure, Inc 1981 16mm film or videocassette color 28 min instructor's print materials
Purchase: film $595.00; video $535.00 Rental: $150.00 Preview: $95.00

Trains managers to deal effectively with incidents of sexual harassment within the organization. Sensitized employees to their own responsibility for keeping the workplace free from sexual harassment. Demonstrates commitment to the control and prevention of sexual harassment. Useful for employees at all levels.

1361. Preventing Sexual Harassment
BNA Communications, Inc 1980 16mm film or videocassette or videodisc color 25 min instructor's print materials; learner's print materials
Purchase: $630.00 Rental: $246.00 Preview: $132.00

Explores sexual harassment from innuendo to blatant attack. Points out management responsibilities and employee rights. Presents guidelines for dealing with incidents involving sexual harassment. Emphasizes the need to act promptly and properly should such an incident occur. Shows how practicing the principles of good management can protect a manager or supervisor against an unjustified charge of sexual harassment. Fair Employment Practice Training Program, no. 4.

1362. Sexual Harassment—A Threat to Your Profits
American Media, Inc 1982 16mm film color 20 min instructor's print materials; posters
Purchase: $585.00 Rental: $150.00 Preview: $30.00

Examines the devastating effects that sexual harassment can have on company productivity and profit from the obvious losses of court cases to the hidden effects of low morale and poor public relations. Printed materials include policy guidelines manual. Companion film to *Sexual Harassment—That's Not in My Job Description*. Intended for management.

1363. Sexual Harassment—That's Not in My Job Description
American Media, Inc 1982 16mm film color 20 min instructor's print materials; posters
Purchase: $495.00 Rental: $150.00 Preview: $30.00

Looks at all forms of sexual harassment. Addresses harassing behavior by men, women, nonemployees, and the work environment itself. Explores the sexual power struggles between individuals on the job. Offers suggestions to your employees on how to personally confront and handle harassing situations. Intended for employees. Companion film to *Sexual Harassment—A Threat to Your Profits*.

1364. Workplace Hustle
MTI Teleprograms, Inc 1980 16mm film or videocassette color 30 min instructor's print materials; learner's print materials
Purchase: $520.00 Rental: $18.50 Preview: free

Dramatizes on-the-job situations involving sexual pressures and evaluates the underlying emotional and social forces. Encourages men and women to talk candidly about their attitudes toward sexuality and the meaning of sexual equality. Suggests specific steps women should take if they become victims of sexual harassment. Narrated by Ed Asner.

SHORTHAND
See DICTATION

SMALL BUSINESS MANAGEMENT

1365. Business Plan—For Small Businessmen
National Audiovisual Center 1972 16mm film 15 min
Purchase: $87.00 Rental: $12.50

Basically a dialog between 2 men in small business. Dramatizes the need for and elements in a business plan as a management tool for successful business operation.

1366. Doing Business
Document Associates 1981 16mm film color 15 min
Purchase: $300.00 Rental: $30.00

A look at 3 small businesses exposes both the pleasures and problems. Shows the hard work involved in a small business and the rewards of being one's own boss.

1367. How to Start a Part-Time Consulting Business
Measurable Performance Systems audiocassette learner's print materials
Purchase: $29.95

Details 8 crucial steps individuals face when beginning consulting from scratch: identifying opportunities, building a reputation, skills building, action plan, pricing services, maintaining client relationships, and working with other consultants. Developed by Larry L. Nelson.

1368. It's Your Move
National Audiovisual Center 16mm film or videocassette color 13 min
Purchase: $75.50 Rental: $12.50

Informs small business owners faced with relocation problems because of urban renewal about help available through SBA and Urban Renewal Offices.

1369. New Guide for Starting Your Own Small Business
Instructional Dynamics, Inc audiocassette learner's print materials
Purchase: $18.00

Strategies and techniques to plan and launch a successful business. Printed materials include a do-it-yourself planning portfolio.

1370. Small Business Gets It All Together
Chamber of Commerce of the United States 80 slides and audiocassette
Purchase: $35.00

Shows how to be more effective in the small business movement. Demonstrates through experiences of local chambers, community leaders, and owners and operators of small businesses who have set up small business councils.

1371. Small Business Planning System
Instructional Dynamics, Inc audiocassette 2 books
Purchase: $18.00

Presents new facts, strategies, and techniques for those who want to plan and launch a successful business. Offers a definite and detailed plan of what to do to start a business—and 7 pitfalls to avoid.

SOCIETAL CHANGE

1372. Encounters with the Future
Nightingale-Conant Corporation 6 audiocassettes
Purchase: $65.00

Reveals changes, opportunities, and challenges to be expected in the future. Includes medical advances, cybernetics and communications, robotics, employment, education, social changes, family life, energy, space, technology, and international trends. Time frame is the next decade.

STATISTICS

1373. Descriptive Statistics
Lansford Publishing Company, Inc   40 slides and audiocassette   instructor's print materials; learner's print materials
Purchase: $179.95

Deals with frequency distributions, measures of central tendency, and measures of dispersion. Introductory level with emphasis on understanding of concepts with examples and applications.

1374. How to Lie with Statistics
Xicom-Video Arts   1974 and 1977   2 16mm films or videocassettes   12 min and 13 min
Purchase: $350.00 ea   Rental: $100.00 ea   Preview: $35.00 ea

Animated illustrations of manipulations of statistics with graphs and averages. *The Gee-Whiz Graph* is intended as basic numeracy training for managers, but it is useful at any age level in the organization. *The Average Chap* provides a layperson's guide to averages: what kinds of averages exist, how they are used, and how they are misused. Both are Tony Hart cartoons.

1375. Statistics
HBJ Media Systems Corporation   1981   4 slide/audiocassette presentations   instructor's print materials; learner's print materials
Purchase: $1,190.00

Practical introduction to arithmetic mean, median, and mode. Includes how to prepare and interpret a variety of graphic presentations commonly used in reports and documents. Intended for financial and accounting clerks, secretaries, and others whose duties require them to work with business reports and documents. Suggested for 6–8 hours.

1376. Statistics at a Glance
Media Guild   1972   videocassette   color   27 min
Purchase: $390.00   Rental: $35.00

Illustrates each statistical method with clear and sometimes humorous examples. Introduces elementary principles of descriptive statistics: frequency distributions, measures of central tendency, variability, and correlation.

STRESS AND STRESS MANAGEMENT

Alcohol, Drugs or Alternatives. For complete citation, *see* ALCOHOLISM.

1377. Burnout
Learning Consultants, Inc   4 audiocassettes   instructor's print materials; learner's print materials
Purchase: $115.00

Portrays typical burnout cases from today's stress-filled work environments. Cites burnout as a result of constant stress, coupled with a lack of independence or control. Explores how working structures can be more efficient and humane.

1378. Burnout
MTI Teleprograms, Inc   16mm film or videocassette   color   26 min   instructor's print materials; learner's print materials; manual
Purchase: film $460.00; video $415.00   Rental: $70.00   Preview: free

Identifies symptoms of burnout, a malady that results from prolonged, intense emotional involvement with other people's problems. Humorous touch opens up discussion of this sensitive subject. Intended for professionals in helping services.

1379. Burnout on the Job
Ibis Media   289 slides and 4 audiocassettes   instructor's print materials
Purchase: $239.00

Gives warning signs of job burnout and profiles high risk individuals. Analyzes total work environment and how it can be used to prevent burnout. Provides solutions for burnout victims, identifying realistic goals and possible support systems. Examines burnout prevention from employer's viewpoint.

1380. Coping with Personal and Professional Stress
S&L Communications, Inc   2 videocassettes   color   80 min
Purchase: $150.00   Rental: $40.00   Other cost factors: SLIC members $80.00 (rental $25.00)

Explains the sources of stress and how to develop practical ways of handling it. Using personal anecdotes, Steve Martin traces the causes of stress from childhood to old age and presents a 6-step approach to deal with stress more efficiently.

1381. Coping with Stress
AMACOM   1979   3 audiocassettes   90 min ea   instructor's print materials; learner's print materials
Purchase: $85.00; audiocassettes without materials $69.95   Other cost factors: AMA members $72.25; audiocassettes without materials $59.45

Identifies causes of stress and how to recognize it in individuals and in the organization. Interviews with John M. Ivancevich and Michael T. Matteson identify key stress points and describe the General Adaptation Syndrome, an explanation of the stress process. Printed materials include self-diagnostic tests.

1382. Coping with Stress
Learning Consultants, Inc   2 audiocassettes   50 min ea
Purchase: $29.95

Identifies the common sources of stress and how it can be dealt with in a mature and positive way.

1383. Depression—Blahs, Blues, and Better Days
American Educational Films   1974   16mm film or videocassette   color   18 min   learner's print materials
Purchase: $375.00   Rental: $50.00
Languages: Arabic, English

Deals positively with depression, showing how it can be recognized and overcome and what kinds of problems can lead to it. Intended for employers and their work force. Features Joseph Campanella.

1384. Heart Attack: Stress Prevention
Salenger Educational Media 1978 16mm film or videocassette color 19 min instructor's print materials
Purchase: $455.00 Rental: $80.00 Preview: $35.00

Shows the physical and psychological causes of heart attacks along with suggested ways to prevent them. Major problems are stress and life style. Proposes delegation as a way managers can cope with stress. Done with a light touch.

1385. How to Turn Off Stress
AMACOM audiocassette 1 hr learner's print materials
Purchase: $12.95 Other cost factors: AMA members $11.95

Presents 2 simple exercises to alleviate stress that require no special equipment and can be performed safely by almost everyone regardless of current endurance levels. Uses breath regulation and self-awareness through autogenic concentration.

1386. Lifestyle Management: Coping with Stress
American Learning Systems, Inc 1981 5 filmstrips or filmstrip cartridges or slides and audiocassettes or videocassettes 12–15 min ea instructor's print materials; learner's print materials
Purchase: video $750.00; slides $650.00; other formats $475.00 Preview: free

Identifies stress and its effects. Shows ways to adapt and adjust with stress release activities, sound personal and professional management, and psychological strategies. Seeks to build basic lifetime coping skills and constructive habits that improve on-the-job performance. Single audiocassette includes relaxation techniques.

1387. Living with Stress
Xerox Learning Systems 16mm film or videocassette color 22 min
Purchase: film $490.00; video $295.00 Rental: $28.00

Emphasizes that stress is a problem that each person must first understand and then deal with in an individual way. Looks at typical daily stress-producing situations.

1388. Living with Stress Successfully
Creative Media 4 audiocassettes
Purchase: $49.00

Ken Olson presents a practical approach to dealing with stress.

1389. Manage Your Stress
CRM/McGraw-Hill Films 1980 16mm film or videocassette color 55 min instructor's print materials; learner's print materials
Purchase: $1,495.00 Preview: free Other cost factors: audio $10.00

Provides both in-depth understanding of and practical how-to dealing with stress. Offers self-regulatory techniques for stress management. Explains what can be done immediately to relieve anxiety and shows how to continue a personal program of stress reduction. A multimedia package that integrates print, audio, and audiovisual components. Suggested for full- or half-day scheduling.

1390. Managing Stress
CRM/McGraw-Hill Films 1979 16mm film or videocassette color 33 min
Purchase: $575.00 Rental: $95.00 Preview: free

Explores the types of stress that are generated in individuals, in relationships, and in organizations. Animation and dramatized case study interviews show how stress can be curbed on the job and how it can be handled to actually increase productivity. Suggest methods of alleviating stress.

1391. Managing Stress, Anxiety, and Frustration
Ibis Media 1982 302 slides and 4 audiocassettes instructor's print materials
Purchase: $239.00

Defines different types of stress and the stress-prone occupations. Discusses the physiological basis for stress and its physical manifestations. Describes noneffective responses to stress and how to recognize them. Offers specific relaxation techniques.

1392. Managing Stress on the Job
Organization Development Consultants 2 audiocassettes 109 min learner's print materials
Purchase: $29.95

Explores how to get rid of stressors through a sequence of steps to stress management and a "Contract for Stress Reduction." Designed for those working in decision making, leadership positions. Includes a Job Stress Checklist.

Peter Principle. For complete citation, *see* MANAGEMENT.

Reckoning. For complete citation, *see* ECONOMIC CONDITIONS.

1393. Stress!
American Hospital Association 16mm film or videocassette or 39 slides and audiocassette color 15 min; slides and audio 5 min instructor's print materials; learner's print materials
Purchase: film $187.50; video $73.25–$81.25 Other cost factors: reduced rates for AHA members

Shows how to recognize personal stress symptoms and deal with life situations, pleasant and unpleasant, that can cause stress. Focuses on the reactions of one family to a series of common stress situations. Slides are cartoon style "advice to the stressful." For employees at all levels.

1394. Stress
Human Resources Development videocassette and 2 audiocassettes color 20 min instructor's print materials; learner's print materials
Purchase: $695.00 Preview: $125.00

Identifies what stress is, how it affects us, and what an organization can do about it. Based on the stress management program of Dr. Petur Gudjonsson. Audiocassettes include practical exercises and a detailed discussion on the manifestation and causes of stress and principles of stress management. Intended for employees at any level.

1395. Stress: A Personal Challenge
MTI Teleprograms, Inc   1980   16mm film or videocassette   color   30 min   instructor's print materials; learner's print materials
Purchase: film $470.00; video $300.00   Rental: $50.00   Preview: free

Uses narration, interviews, and a dramatization to show impact of stress and its emotional and physiological effects. Defines its causes and suggests techniques to deal with stress. Features Hans Selye.

1396. Stress: Are We Killing Ourselves?
MTI Teleprograms, Inc   1979   16mm film or videocassette   color   15 min
Purchase: $150.00

Explains the common warning signs of stress. Examines mounting medical evidence that links long-term stress with deadly diseases. Presents variety of stress-avoidance techniques along with the drawbacks of using drugs or alcohol to reduce symptoms of stress. Concludes with practical and life-saving suggestions.

1397. Stress Management
Videocenters   1979   5 videocassettes   30 min ea   instructor's print materials; learner's print materials
Purchase: $2,250.00 ($495.00 ea)   Rental: $250.00 ($65.00 ea)   Preview: $25.00

Describes specific skills needed to cope with stress and shows a stress workshop in session. Provides an introduction to stress management, the use of relaxation techniques and straight thinking along with assertiveness and time management as techniques to use. Video and audiocassettes cover the same material.

1398. Stress Management: A Positive Strategy
Time-Life Video   1982   5 videocassettes   color   30 min ea   instructor's print materials
Purchase: $3,950.00   Rental: $500.00   Preview: free   Other cost factors: participant's handbook $31.95

Shows how to identify personal stress ranges for effective functioning and how to reduce stress to increase productivity, enjoy better physical health, have more satisfying relationships, and experience a greater sense of well-being. Commentary and dramatic vignettes. Designed for managers at all levels.

1399. Stress Management: Wedding Daze
PCI   16mm film   color   29 min
Purchase: $300.00   Rental: $55.00

Dramatizes stressful situation and how different people deal with it. Identifies causes and effects of stress. Assists awareness of techniques and strategies for coping with stresses at work, home, and in everyday living. Features Jan Margolis.

1400. Stress Mess
Barr Films   16mm film or videocassette   color   25 min
Purchase: $515.00   Rental: $100.00   Preview: $50.00

Shows how to reduce and manage stress and how to identify the sources of stress. Suggests important time management techniques. Humorous dramatization to show the importance of setting priorities, delegating tasks, learning how to say no, and learning how to relax.

1401. Success Is a State of Mind
Singer Management Institute   6 audiocassettes   guide
Purchase: $62.50

Concerns dealing more effectively with emotions, managing time and money better, and dealing with stress creatively. Features Joyce Brothers.

1402. Success without Stress
AMACOM   2 audiocassettes
Purchase: $35.00   Other cost factors: AMA members $30.00

Presents simple, basic exercises combining the best and most successful highlights of yoga and meditation.

1403. Take Charge: Controlling the Stress Factor
Learncom, Inc   6 audiocassettes   learner's print materials
Purchase: $165.00   Preview: $15.00

Identifies sources of positive and negative stress and the early warning signals stress gives. Offers 3 practical techniques for controlling stress and how to buffer it by improving both life style and environment. Features Jan Margolis.

1404. Taking It in Stride: Positive Approaches to Stress Management
Spectrum Films   16mm film or videocassette   color   22 min
Purchase: $450.00   Rental: $65.00   Preview: $35.00

Vignettes focus on solutions to coping with stress. Balances training to adapt to stress with learning to uncomplicate personal lives. Addresses the challenge of how to manage stress productively.

1405. Tension Easers
Leadership Catalysts, Inc   1979   4 audiocassettes   instructor's print materials; learner's print materials
Purchase: $79.95

Describes how to manage daily stress and counter job burnout and costly mistakes. Offers exercises to reduce tension and manage stress effectively. For all employee levels for group or self-study.

1406. Tension Management and Relaxation
Learning Resources Corporation   4 audiocassettes   book
Purchase: $55.95

Presents an approach to a balanced way of living in a self-treatment package. Designed to relieve the stress and tension that affect physical and mental health.

1407. Understanding and Managing Stress
American Management Associations   6 audiocassettes   learner's print materials
Purchase: $145.00   Other cost factors: AMA members $135.00; discounts available for bulk orders of materials

Points out symptoms of on-the-job stress. Recommends that managers identify stress producing situations before they cause crises, lessen negative reactions, accommodate tension, and use positive stress to improve performance. Covers relaxation and meditation, biofeedback, and how to manage time. Highlights special situations that create stress such as mid-career crisis.

1408. Your Own Worst Enemy: Stress
CRM/McGraw-Hill Films 1976 16mm film or videocassette color 24 min
Purchase: $435.00 Rental: $75.00 Preview: free

Documents experiences of individuals who have suffered the debilitating effects of stress and have taken active steps against it. Proposes how to recognize it, cope with it, and make it work for instead of against an individual.

SUPERVISION

1409. Action-Oriented Supervision
Butler Learning Systems 558 slides and 7 audiocassettes instructor's print materials; learner's print materials
Purchase: $2,595.00 plus $75.00 per learner Preview: free

Focuses on skills and motivation factors for supervision. Begins with a learner's self-inventory and presents 40 problem-solving situations. Includes human relations, motivation, leadership, communication, supervising one's self, people, and the job itself.

1410. After All, You're the Supervisor
Roundtable Films, Inc 16mm film or videocassette color 20 min instructor's print materials
Purchase: $525.00 Rental: $100.00 Preview: $30.00

Dramatization reveals 17 essential supervisory activities in realistic settings. Shows the frustrations and the fulfillment inherent in the job and provides a role model to help new supervisors make the transition from nonsupervisory positions. A supervisor's handbook, *The Skillful Supervisor*, is keyed to the film but is priced separately.

1411. Are You Earning the Right to Manage Others?
BNA Communications, Inc 1967 16mm film or videocassette color 28 min learner's print materials
Purchase: $375.00 Rental: 5-day $150.00; 3-day $105.00 Preview: $35.00
Languages: English, Spanish, Portuguese

Dramatized portrayal with Bill Gove uses humor and examples to show supervisors an excellent way to get their people involved in their work and interested in improving their performance. Shows supportive vs autocratic supervision. Useful for supervisors.

1412. CRM/McGraw Hill Supervision Training Program
CRM/McGraw-Hill Films 15 16mm films or videocassettes color 3½–4 hrs ea instructor's print materials
Purchase: $940.00 ea Preview: free

Modules include basic supervisory skills, such as managing people, communicating, getting commitment, giving orders and instructions, assessing and coaching performance, improving employee work habits, delegating effectively, dealing with employee complaints and conflicts and response to controls, implementing change, using positive discipline, terminating an employee, and training trainers of supervisors. Each is from the supervisor's viewpoint. All modules are described in 50-minute video preview.

1413. Call Walsh
Motivision, Ltd 16mm film or videocassette color 23 min instructor's print materials
Purchase: $475.00 Rental: $25.00

Shows the problems a supervisor has with 2 employees (one male and one female) and how the supervisor is manipulated by each person hiding shortcomings in work performance. The supervisor learns how to handle a situation more objectively and to take advantage of the Employee Assistance Program.

1414. Case of the Missing Person
CRM/McGraw-Hill Films 1983 16mm film or videocassette color 15 min instructor's print materials
Purchase: $495.00 Rental: $75.00 Preview: free

Looks at how managers' expectations influence employees' performance. Case study of self-fulfilling prophecy in action. Focus is on productivity, interpersonal relations, and self-esteem.

1415. Developing Your Supervisory Skills
Training House, Inc 1979 5 audiocassettes instructor's print materials; learner's print materials
Purchase: $2,800.00 Preview: $252.00

Presents the supervisor's role, styles of management, motivation, communication, training/coaching, and time management. Suggested use is as 5 modules, each offered one day a week for 5 weeks, in workshop format. Uses self-study exercises and group discussion.

1416. Do You Think You Can Manage?
Xicom-Video Arts 1982 16mm film or videocassette color 26 min instructor's print materials; learner's print materials
Purchase: $625.00 Rental: $120.00 Preview: $40.00

Intended to prepare new supervisors for their first supervisory jobs. Portrayal shows typical new-person mistakes of promoted individual. Shows productive ways of handling volatile interpersonal situations, meetings, delegation, and discipline.

1417. Don't Just Sit There
Manpower Education Institute 16mm film or videocassette color 15 min
Purchase: $275.00 Rental: $50.00

Encourages supervisors of young workers to make certain that young people know their responsibilities and how they are to do their work and to assist them with their problems. Dramatization shows both the supervisors and workers doing their jobs.

1418. Duties of First-Line Supervisors
Practical Management Associates, Inc   audiocassette   learner's print materials
Purchase: $28.00

Describes first-line supervisory duties relevant to overseeing a particular kind of work. Useful to set performance standards, select and orient new supervisors, and upgrade management team work.

1419. Effective Supervision
Educational Resources Foundation   1971   10 videocassettes   instructor's print materials; learner's print materials
Purchase: $390.00 ea   Rental: $50.00 ea   Preview: $15.00 ea

Series designed for first-line plant supervisors aimed to result in high output and quality. Sessions cover supervision generally and, in particular, human relations, motivation, communication, training, turnover, leadership, work measurement, and work methods.

1420. Every Day Supervisory Skills
Resources for Education and Management, Inc   6 filmstrips or slides and audiocassettes or videocassettes or filmstrip cartridges   7–10 min ea instructor's print materials
Purchase: filmstrips $295.00 ($58.00 ea); filmstrip cartridges $510.00 ($85.00 ea); slides $320.00 ($70.00 ea)

Examines problems supervisors face in the course of the day. Includes modules on planning and organizing work, loyalty, conflict, employee appraisal, motivation, and report writing.

1421. Everything You've Always Wanted to Know about Supervision
American Media, Inc   1980   16mm film or super 8mm or videocassette   color   28 min
Purchase: $550.00   Rental: $110.00   Preview: $35.00

Dramatization of a young woman supervisor who learns how to plan, delegate, discipline, communicate, and motivate. Emphasizes essential skills of organizing and communicating in a business setting.

1422. Face-to-Face Human Relations & Communication
Practical Management Associates, Inc   1978   10 audiocassettes   instructor's print materials; learner's print materials
Purchase: $650.00 (for group of 5 people); $380.00 (for individual study by 10 people); $30.00 (individual module)

Includes modules that emphasize "people skills": the "people" side of supervision, satisfying human needs and job demands, assigning work and checking progress, correcting errors, straightening out rule violations, handling suggestions and complaints, giving recognition, introducing changes, building

self-sufficiency and creativity in subordinates, and releasing "peoplepower" in group meetings. Relies on interaction of audio and printed materials with exercises. Designed for group or self-study by new supervisors. Fundamentals of Supervision Series.

1423. Foreman's Part in Methods Improvement
Maynard Management Institute   16mm   film   color   18 min

Defines the foreperson's role in any effort to improve methods. Illustrates how better methods are applied to a job benefiting worker, company, and foreperson.

1424. Front Line Supervision
Advance Learning Systems   1978   4 videocassettes   10 min ea   instructor's print materials
Purchase: $1,980.00 ($495.00 ea)   Preview: $95.00

Presents dramatizations that show supervisors correcting employees or dealing with difficult problems. Includes 4 modules: safety, interdepartmental conflict, discipline, and absenteeism. Suggested for a 4–8 hour program.

Fundamentals of Management and Supervision. For complete citation, *see* MANAGEMENT.

1425. Good Morning, Mister Roberts
Sandy Corporation   1979   16mm film or videocassette   color   26 min   instructor's print materials
Purchase: $495.00   Rental: $100.00

Deals with changes in interpersonal relationships faced by a new supervisor. Illustrated with scenes from a new supervisor's experiences both at home and on the job. Includes several vignettes that clarify adjustment problems faced by minority supervisors. Describes problems faced because of age, sex, or color. Intended for new supervisors.

1426. Hot Potatoes: Learning Experiences
Roundtable Films, Inc   1981   15 audiocassettes   2½–3 min ea   instructor's print materials
Purchase: $295.00

Presents short, open-ended cases that present typical supervisory problems that call for listener response. Emphasizes application of supervisory techniques. Can be used in conjunction with other supervisory programs. Useful for new or less experienced supervisors.

1427. How Good Is a Good Guy?
Roundtable Films, Inc   1960   16mm film   color   21 min
Purchase: $375.00   Rental: $75.00   Preview: $30.00

Three typical cases of supervisory failure show why some supervisors' fear of losing the approval of their subordinates detracts from their effectiveness in giving direction and supervision. Helps supervisors to be more effective and confident and to develop disciplinary control. For the novice and lower-level supervisor.

How Supervisors Can Reduce Turnover. For complete citation, *see* PERSONNEL MANAGEMENT.

1428. How to Be an Effective Supervisor
American Management Associations 6
audiocassettes learner's print materials
Purchase: $145.00 Other cost factors: AMA
members $135.00; discounts available for bulk orders
of materials

Focuses on the tools and techniques of supervision, the human
relations skills needed to get the job done, and the methods of
integrating these tools and skills into a personal leadership style.
Techniques include how to orient, train, plan work, handle
grievances and difficult employees, maintain good union relations, formulate work unit goals, communicate, and make
decisions effectively.

1429. How to Give Orders
Bureau of Business Practice 1977 16mm film or
videocassette color 29 min
Purchase: $475.00 Rental: $95.00 Preview:
$49.00

Shows supervisors how to give clear, concise, and direct orders
and eliminate misunderstandings. Dramatizations show typical
errors in giving orders such as talking too fast, rambling, and
emphasizing negatives.

1430. Human Side of Supervision
Bureau of Business Practice 1982 16mm
film color 23 min
Purchase: $425.00 Rental: $95.00 Preview:
$49.00

Reveals typical ways that supervisors affect employee morale
and performance. In this dramatization, a manager mishandles
a situation, then shows techniques for managing workers
tactfully and skillfully.

1431. I Told 'Em Exactly How to Do It
Xicom-Video Arts 1974 16mm film or
videocassette color 11 min
Purchase: $350.00 Rental: $100.00 Preview:
$35.00

Humorous animated story about a foreman who treats his
subordinates as if they are unteachable morons and is then
surprised when they do not learn. Useful to prompt discussion
about communication and supervision.

1432. If You Want It Done Right
Roundtable Films, Inc 16mm film or
videocassette color 20 min learner's print
materials
Purchase: $495.00 Rental: $100.00 Preview:
$30.00
Languages: English, Spanish

Portrayal of how the correct techniques for assigning work are
essential to get a job done right the first time. Explains the
communication process involved and common errors made
during work assignments. Models the proper way work assignments should be planned and communicated. Has key discussion stops for involvement.

Implementing Staff Development. For complete
citation, *see* TRAINING AND DEVELOPMENT.

Inner Man Steps Out. For complete citation, *see*
INTERPERSONAL RELATIONS.

Instructions or Obstructions. For complete citation,
see COMMUNICATION.

1433. Job of Supervision
Practical Management Associates, Inc 6
audiocassettes 4½ hrs
Purchase: $125.00

Defines supervisor's job and suggests techniques for fulfilling
those responsibilities. Points out the difference between supervising and managing as well as the qualities of an outstanding
supervisor. Offers a 7-step problem prevention and problem-
solving guide. Taped seminar.

Leadership and Motivation: The Influence Process.
For complete citation, *see* LEADERSHIP.

1434. Making the Pieces Fit
Educational Resources Foundation 1976 16mm
film or videocassette color 28 min instructor's
print materials
Purchase: $450.00 ea Rental: $65.00 Preview:
$15.00 Other cost factors: student guide and
workbook $2.25 ea

Portrays the key role of a job site supervisor as he guides the
efforts of an on-site construction team. Offers insights on
leadership styles, communication, training, work planning,
scheduling, quality control, and individual motivation.

Management Productivity. For complete citation, *see*
MANAGEMENT.

Managing Your Strengths. For complete citation, *see*
INTERPERSONAL RELATIONS.

1435. Me and You
Roundtable Films, Inc 1980 16mm film or
videocassette color 12 min
Purchase: $400.00 Rental: $85.00 Preview:
$30.00

Raises the awareness of supervisors of the impact their attitudes
and behavior have on the performance and development of
employees. Illustrates Theory X and Theory Y assumptions in
dealing with their employees. Encourages supervisors to recognize and be sensitive to employees' individual differences and
needs. Animated.

1436. Modern Supervision
Applied Management Science, Inc 10
videocassettes color 30 min ea instructor's print
materials; learner's print materials
Purchase: $9,500.00 Rental: $170.00 per
learner Preview: free

Covers functions and activities inherent in any supervisory
position including delegation, communication, and performance
appraisals. The focus is on awareness and skill. Intended for
those up through the level of middle management. Suggested
for weekly sessions of 2½–3 hours each. Companion to *Modern
Supervisory Techniques*.

1437. Modern Supervisory Techniques
Applied Management Science, Inc   10
videocassettes   color   30 min ea   instructor's print
materials;   learner's print materials
Purchase: $9,500.00   Rental: $170.00 per
learner   Preview: free

Covers typical supervisory functions such as motivation, discipline, employee training and development, communication, and
planning. Suggested for weekly sessions of 2½–3 hours each.
Companion to *Modern Supervision.*

1438. New Supervisor
Resources for Education and Management, Inc   5
filmstrips or slides and audiocassettes or
videocassettes or film cartridges   9–11 min ea
instructor's print materials
Purchase: video $305.00 ($75.00 ea); filmstrips
$280.00 ($64.00 ea); film cartridges $425.00 ($85.00
ea); slides $295.00 ($67.00 ea)   Preview: $20.00

Covers those matters of immediate concern to a new supervisor.
Examines the new skills, relationships, and attitudes a new
supervisor must have to be successful. Includes communications, training and development of subordinates, job enrichment, motivation, and self-development.

1439. New Supervisor Audio Cassette Program
Resources for Education and Management, Inc   14
audiocassettes   learner's print materials
Purchase: $225.00   Rental: $25.00

Introduces various skills and techniques of managing and
supervising. Presents and analyzes many practical, real-life
situations illustrating such activities as delegating, communicating, planning, directing, and training. Intended for beginning
supervisors, refresher training, and for correction of "problem"
situations. Presented by Martin Broadwell and based on his
book *The New Supervisor.*

1440. Organizational Role of Supervisors
Practical Management Associates, Inc   1978   10
audiocassettes   instructor's print materials; learner's
print materials
Purchase: $550.00 (for groups of 5 people); $304.00
(for individual study by 10 people)

Emphasizes where the supervisor fits into the organization.
Discusses role in relation to the management team, other
supervisors, and as a head of a workgroup. Relies on interaction
of audio and printed materials with exercises. Designed for new
supervisors. Fundamentals of Supervision Series.

Performance Counseling and Appraisal. For complete
citation, *see* PERFORMANCE APPRAISAL.

1441. Planning, Organizing and Controlling, Part I
BNA Communications, Inc   1975   16mm film or
videocassette   color   23 min   instructor's print
materials;   learner's print materials
Purchase: $575.00   Rental: 5-day $150.00; 3-day
$105.00   Preview: $35.00
Languages: English, French

Points out common sources of contingencies or emergencies.
Delves into the dangers of preoccupation, illustrates the importance of patrolling, gives tips on budgeting time, discusses the

need for flexibility, and tells how to make critical decisions.
Uses dramatization. Intended for supervisors. Practice of
Supervision Program, no. 1.

1442. Planning, Organizing and Controlling, Part II
BNA Communications, Inc   1975   16mm film or
videocassette   color   23 min   instructor's print
materials;   learner's print materials
Purchase: $575.00   Rental: 5-day $150.00; 3-day
$105.00   Preview: $35.00
Languages: English, French

Uses dramatization to show how supervisors can prepare their
people to handle all sorts of contingencies and make correct
decisions in cases where instinctive reactions would cause
harmful results. Shows how to reinforce fundamentals, prevent
erosion of training, use rehearsals, motivate people to do dull or
tedious jobs, overcome the "there's nothing to do" situation,
schedule people, and work for balanced performance. Practice
of Supervision Program, no. 2.

1443. Planning, Organizing and Controlling, Part III
BNA Communications, Inc   1975   16mm film or
videocassette   color   21 min   instructor's print
materials;   learner's print materials
Purchase: $575.00   Rental: 5-day $150.00; 3-day
$105.00   Preview: $35.00
Languages: English, French

Uses dramatizations to center on the critical decision whether
the supervisor should intervene in a contingency and, if so,
when. Outlines active steps supervisors can take to keep
contingencies under control. Exposes the consequences of too
much or too little intervention. Shows how to enforce rules
employees are most likely to resist. Practice of Supervision
Program, no. 3.

1444. Practice of Supervising
Resources for Education and Management, Inc   10
audiocassettes   instructor's print materials; learner's
print materials
Purchase: $190.00   Preview: $25.00

Provides practical, useable information on such key subjects as
motivation, discipline, team building, and performance appraisal. Aimed at experienced supervisors who have never had
supervisory training or who need to be brought up to date with
current trends. For group or self-study.

Pre-Supervisory Training. For complete citation, *see*
TRAINING AND DEVELOPMENT.

1445. Problem Solving Skills for Supervisors
Training by Design   4 audiocassettes   4 hrs
learner's print materials
Purchase: $95.00

Outlines how to analyze performance problems, identify alternative actions to solve problems, develop action plans and
implement them, evaluate results. Includes techniques for group
problem solving. Self-instructional.

Productivity Challenge. For complete citation, *see*
PRODUCTIVITY.

1446. Results through People
NPL, Inc   16mm film or 345 slides and
audiocassette
Purchase: film $645.00; slides $450.00   Rental:
$50.00   Other cost factors: student packets $8.00 ea;
instructor packet $1.25

Emphasizes the development of sound relations with supervisors and the skills needed to lead others. Offers principles. Suggested for 4 hours and 42 minutes. Intended for supervisors.

1447. Selecting the Right Supervisor
Singer Management Institute   20 slides and 2
audiocassettes   learner's print materials;
transparencies
Purchase: $175.00

Defines the supervisor's 6 major responsibilities and points out the knowledge and skills to look for when selecting potential candidates. Addresses the problem of legally and effectively choosing supervisors and takes a look at the kind of training the new supervisor will need. Identifies how the supervisor affects subordinates' productivity and 5 areas for improved productivity. For anyone involved in selecting new supervisors.

1448. Short Course on Supervisory Functions
Lansford Publishing Company, Inc   5
audiocassettes   transparencies
Purchase: $289.95

Deals with solving supervisory problems. Provides minicases dealing with organizing for effective work, problems, and performance evaluation. Possible solutions are provided for each incident.

1449. Sounds of Supervision
Bureau of Business Practice   1982   audiocassettes
Purchase: $7.95 per month

Monthly audiocassettes that focus on specific supervisory skills. Each uses dramatizations and typical plant problems such as morale, absenteeism, training, delegation, and grievances.

Successful Supervision of Handicapped Employees.
For complete citation, *see* HANDICAPPED.

1450. Supervising and People Problems
Phoenix-BFA Films and Video, Inc   1982   16mm
film or videocassette   color   21 min
Purchase: film $495.00; video $375.00   Rental:
$50.00

Addresses the problems of personal conflicts intruding on the workplace. Discusses the difficulties in balancing personal problems and work and suggests 4 approaches that can help a supervisor resolve such difficulties: know when to intervene, empathize with the employee's problem, listen carefully, and maintain a balance between personal and professional involvement. Supervising for Results Series, no. 4.

1451. Supervising and the Organization
Phoenix-BFA Films and Video, Inc   1982   16mm
film or videocassette   color   12 min
Purchase: film $495.00; video $375.00   Rental:
$50.00

Explores supervisory skills needed to fit employees into new work situations. Illustrates key areas of expertise such as hiring, orienting, managing conflicts, and adapting. Supervising for Results Series, no. 2.

1452. Supervising for Productivity
Phoenix-BFA Films and Video, Inc   1982   16mm
film or videocassette   color   18 min
Purchase: film $495.00; video $375.00   Rental:
$50.00

Examines practical supervising techniques aimed at increasing productivity. Discusses facilitating communication, good leadership, increased motivation, and increased responsibility. Illustrated by actual work situations. Supervising for Results Series, no. 1.

1453. Supervising the Disadvantaged
Resources for Education and Management, Inc   5
filmstrips or slides and audiocassettes or
videocassettes or filmstrip cartridges   8-10 min ea
instructor's print materials
Purchase: video $305.00 ($75.00 ea); filmstrips
$280.00 ($64.00 ea); filmstrip cartridges $425.00
($85.00 ea); slides $295.00 ($67.00 ea)   Preview:
20.00

Offers techniques for interviewing, training, resolving conflict, and motivating the "hard core" unemployed worker. Discusses some basic differences in environment, background, education, and goals of disadvantaged workers which can cause problems in the work group.

1454. Supervisor and Interpersonal Relations
Resources for Education and Management, Inc   5
filmstrips or slides and audiocassettes or
videocassettes or filmstrip cartridges   11-13 min
ea   instructor's print materials
Purchase: video $305.00 ($75.00 ea); filmstrips
$280.00 ($64.00 ea); filmstrip cartridges $425.00
($85.00 ea): slides $295.00 ($67.00 ea)   Preview:
$20.00

Examines the supervisor's role in managing attitudes and interpersonal relations within the work group. Covers general problems of interpersonal conflict and how to reduce conflict in the organization through the supervisory position. Includes how to improve relationships between peers, attitudes toward subordinates, and supervision.

1455. Supervisor and OJT
Resources for Education and Management, Inc   1975
5 filmstrips or slides and audiocassettes or
videocassettes or filmstrip cartridges   9-15 min ea
instructor's print materials
Purchase: video $305.00 ($75.00 ea); filmstrips
$280.00 ($64.00 ea); filmstrip cartridges $425.00
($85.00 ea); slides $295.00 ($67.00 ea)

Deals with the supervisor's responsibility for on-the-job training. Presents a basic 3-step process for teaching specific skills or procedures. Offers guidelines for task analysis, writing training objectives, and evaluating training. Stresses better utilization of employees and training for upward mobility.

1456. Supervisor and the Supervisory Function
Lansford Publishing Company, Inc   4
audiocassettes

Purchase: $99.95

Examines the role of the supervisor in terms of important skills involved in directive and nondirective counseling, motivating employees, and leadership behavior in business, industry, and government.

1457. Supervisor as a Classroom Instructor

Resources for Education and Management, Inc 1970   6 filmstrips or slides and audiocassettes or videocassettes or filmstrip cartridges   10–12 min ea   instructor's print materials
Purchase: video $320.00 ($70.00); filmstrips $295.00 ($58.00 ea); filmstrip cartridges $510.00 ($85.00 ea); slides $310.00 ($60.00 ea)

Designed for supervisors who conduct classroom training sessions. Describes the teaching-learning process, effective communicating techniques in the classroom, preplanning and objectives, ways to help the learner learn and evaluate follow-up. Offers fundamental concepts and a practical approach.

Supervisor Training in Human Relations. For complete citation, *see* INTERPERSONAL RELATIONS.

1458. Supervisor Training Series

Continental Film Productions   1979   7 filmstrips and 7 audiocassettes or slides and 7 audiocassettes   10–15 min ea   instructor's print materials; learner's print materials
Purchase: filmstrips $700.00; slides $840.00

Presents supervisory skills and techniques, outlining the supervisor's job, the responsibility for interpreting policy, grievance handling, induction, and job training. Also focuses on how the supervisor represents management to employees and employees to management, promotion, and training of others. Learner's print materials include self-tests. Suggested for a 4–6 hour program.

1459. Supervisor's Job

Continental Film Productions   slides or filmstrip and audiocassette   12 min
Purchase: filmstrip $105.00; slides $125.00

Points out the important role that supervisors play in their companies and defines their responsibilities in the field of human relations. Supervisor Training Series.

1460. Supervisor's Responsibility for Interpreting Policy

Continental Film Productions   slides or filmstrip and audiocassette   12 min
Purchase: filmstrip $105.00; slides $125.00

Keynotes the supervisor's responsibility in the interpretation and application of company policies. Supervisor Training Series.

1461. Supervisor's Responsibility for Promoting Co-operation between Employees and Departments

Continental Film Productions   slides or filmstrip and audiocassette   12 min
Purchase: filmstrip $105.00; slides $125.00

Defines the vital need of ways of promoting cooperation at all levels of operation. Supervisor Training Series.

1462. Supervisor's Responsibility for Representing Management to Employees, and Employees to Management

Continental Film Productions   slides or filmstrip and audiocassette   12 min
Purchase: filmstrip $105.00; slides $125.00

Emphasizes the supervisor's responsibility for building better communications between management and employees. Supervisor Training Series.

Supervisor's Responsibility for Transfer, Promotion, and Training for Responsibility. For complete citation, *see* TRAINING AND DEVELOPMENT.

Supervisor's Role in Increasing Productivity. For complete citation, *see* PRODUCTIVITY.

Supervisor's Role in Preventing Employee Pilferage and Theft. For complete citation, *see* LOSS PREVENTION.

1463. Supervisor's Role in Preventing Grievances and Arbitration

Bureau of Business Practice   16mm film or videocassette   color   20 min
Purchase: $425.00   Rental: $95.00   Preview: $45.00

Dramatizations reveal how 4 common supervisory mistakes magnify minor disputes into heated confrontations. Shows how to correct mistakes without sacrificing employee discipline and keep conflicts from becoming grievances that embroil a company in expensive arbitration.

Supervisor's Role in Quality Control. For complete citation, *see* QUALITY CONTROL.

1464. Supervisor's Role in Simplifying Work Procedures

Bureau of Business Practice   1983   16mm film   color   20 min
Purchase: $475.00   Rental: $95.00   Preview: $49.00

Show supervisors the benefits of taking a careful look at work procedures, asking the purpose of each step and considering alternatives to existing ways of doing things. Details interviewing techniques, evaluation methods, investigative tactics, and corrective measures.

Supervisor's Role in Training New Employees. For complete citation, *see* TRAINING AND DEVELOPMENT.

1465. Supervisory Effectiveness

AMACOM   6 audiocassettes   learner's print materials
Purchase: $95.00   Other cost factors: AMA members $85.00

Sets supervisor's role within the organizational context. Deals with planning and organizing work, motivation, communication, and group management.

1466. Supervisory Grid
BNA Communications, Inc 1976 16mm film or videocassette color 26 min
Purchase: $550.00 Rental: 5-day $150.00; 3-day $105.00 Preview: $35.00 Other cost factors: learner's print materials

Discusses how to achieve personal growth through self-development, how to get and use feedback to advantage, and how to develop high performing teams.

1467. Supervisory Methods
International Training Consultants, Inc 12 16mm films or videocassettes color instructor's print materials; learner's print materials
Purchase: $7900.00 ($500.00–$750.00 ea) Rental: $150.00–$250.00 ea

Designed for first-line and middle managers. Includes modules on attendance, performance and workhabits, discipline and problems, complaints, motivation, appraisal and standards, goals and objectives, interviewing and selecting, and decision making and problem solving. Specifically directed to industrial, office, or health care fields.

1468. Supervisory Skills
American Learning Systems, Inc 25 filmstrips and audiocassettes or filmstrip cartridges 12 min ea
Purchase: $2,000.00 set ($80.00 ea) Preview: free

Covers basic functions of supervisors and gives special attention to the new supervisor and supervising the disadvantaged. Uses cartoon art to illustrate main points.

1469. Supervisory Skills
MBO, Inc 12 audiocassettes 30 min ea learner's print materials
Purchase: $196.00

Designed for first-level and middle managers of people and situations who serve as a vehicle for extending a goals-oriented management style down throughout the organization. Describes what to do, how to do it, and what not to do to become an effective supervisor. Topics include motivation, goal setting, increasing productivity, learning techniques, and time saving. Features George Odiorne.

1470. Supervisory Skills
Practical Management Associates, Inc 1978 10 audiocassettes instructor's print materials; learner's print materials
Purchase: $650.00 (for groups of 5 people); $380.00 (for individual study by 10 people); $30.00 (individual module)

Includes modules on what supervisors do, a practical approach to motivation, building 2-way communication, work planning and control, time management and delegation, leadership, training and orientation, decision making and problem solving, performance counseling, and diagnosing causes of low performance. Relies on interaction of audio and printed materials with exercises. Designed for group or self-study by new supervisors. Fundamentals of Supervision Series.

1471. Superisory Skills
Time-Life Video 1982 3 videocassettes 30 min ea instructor's print materials; learner's print materials
Purchase: $3,950.00 Rental: $500.00

Presents the function, role, key responsibilites, and skill requirements of a supervisor/first-level manager. Addresses the complex challenge of problem solving in typical supervisory situations. Intended to equip supervisors and first-level managers to understand their role and build needed skills. Print materials include evaluation tools.

1472. Supervisory Success
Training by Design 7 audiocassettes instructor's print materials; learner's print materials
Purchase: $95.00

Helps new supervisors make an effective changeover from nonsupervisory positions. Includes special emphasis on planning, communication, and human relations from a supervisory vantage point. Gives emphasis to working with the boss. Intended for group or self-study. One audiocassette is for instructor use.

1473. Taking Charge—The Manager Film
Southerby Productions, Inc 16mm film or videocassette color 25 min instructor's print materials; learner's print materials
Purchase: $550.00 Rental: $125.00 Preview: $50.00

Shows extreme examples of troubled employees and the results of delayed confrontation. Intended for managers who must recognize and identify symptoms at an early stage to avoid crises. Designed for corporate management level. Includes Employee Checklist for Managers.

Tell-Sell-Resolve. For complete citation, *see* COMMUNICATION.

Way I See It. For complete citation, *see* PERCEPTION.

1474. What Supervisors Can Do about Planning Time
Bureau of Business Practice 16mm film or videocassette 30 min
Purchase: $425.00 Rental: $95.00 Preview: $49.00

Dramatizations show how to delegate jobs, organize work, and increase planning and scheduling efficiency. Emphasizes how to discover mistakes and correct them and how to set priorities. Points out the futility of procrastination and other time-wasters.

1475. When Should You Call?
Motivision, Ltd 16mm film or videocassette color 13 min
Purchase: $237.00 Preview: $25.00

Demonstrates supervisor referral showing a supervisor who becomes the victim of an employee skilled at concealing the truth about his job performance. Edited from *Call Walsh.*

1476. Who's in Charge?
Xicom-Video Arts 1978 16mm film or videocassette color 23 min instructor's print materials; booklet
Purchase: $390.00 Rental: $100.00 Preview: $35.00

Dramatization of a newly appointed supervisor facing his first leadership crisis that combines 3 of the toughest and most frequent challenges a manager has to face: getting the group to do something they are opposed to, dealing with an open breach of discipline, and facing a direct attack on his authority. Illustrates both the wrong way and the right way of meeting these challenges.

1477. Why Didn't Somebody Tell Me?
BNA Communications, Inc 16mm film or videocassette color 23 min instructor's print materials; learner's print materials
Purchase: $550.00 Rental: 5-day $150.00; 3-day $105.00 Preview: $35.00

Shows supervisors how to tackle employee behavior problems that waste time and reduce productivity; how to tighten discipline where lax enforcement of rules has led to abuse of privileges; and how to improve communication with employees. Cooperation at work, distracting behavior, correcting fellow workers, and wasted time as a threat to job security are put into perspective. Reducing Wasted Time Program.

1478. Will to Work
Roundtable Films, Inc 16mm film or videocassette color 22 min
Purchase: $400.00 Rental: $75.00 Preview: $30.00

Dramatization shows a supervisor's responsibilities for morale: concern for the individual, fair discipline, self-control, impartiality, loyalty, and concern for the working group. Outlines the leadership qualities a supervisor must develop to successfully provide motivation for employees. Points out what negative actions affect low morale: insensitivity to employee's needs and being self-centered and inconsiderate. For new supervisors.

1479. Working with Troubled Employees
BNA Communications, Inc 1974 16mm film or videocassette color 32 min
Purchase: $550.00 Rental: 5-day $150.00; 3-day $105.00 Preview: $35.00

Harry Levinson illustrates 2 common forms of troubled behavior and shows how supervisors should deal with them. He points out the responsibility of supervisors and outlines 3 steps they can take to obtain a mutually satisfactory solution. Advanced Supervision Series, no. 2.

1480. You Gotta Face People
Continental Film Productions 16mm film or super 8mm or videocassette or slides and audiocassette or filmstrip cartridge color 14 min
Purchase: 16mm film $190.00; super 8mm $195.00; slides $95.00; filmstrip cartridge $95.00

Contrasts push-and-punishment leadership with motivate-and-management leadership. Explores everyday situations and reactions and makes suggestions for improving communications and attitudes. Suggests that management personnel should be properly trained before they can effectively supervise subordinates. Cartoon art.

1481. You—The Supervisor
Professional Development, Inc 1972 8 16mm film or videocassettes color 30 min ea instructor's print materials; learner's print materials
Purchase: film $4,950.00 ($650.00 ea); video $3,900.00 ($495.00 ea) Rental: film $1,750.00 ($195.00 ea); video $1,500.00 ($175.00 ea) Other cost factors: leader guides and participant guides

Geared to the needs and realities of the first line supervisor's working world. Emphasis is on providing guidelines for the specific tasks which are the core of the job. Basic principles are presented through portrayal of a supervisor with work, dealing with work planning and selecting, training, motivating, and developing employees. Suggested for an 8-week period or for a 2–3 day workshop.

TEAM BUILDING
See also QUALITY CIRCLES

1482. Achieving Group Effectiveness
BNA Communications, Inc 10 audiocassettes
Purchase: $100.00 ($12.00 ea)

Focuses on developing and managing a team. Includes developing departmental goals, handling conflict, managing change, and organizational renewal. Effective Management Program, series 2.

Action-Oriented Problem Solving. For complete citation, *see* DECISION MAKING/PROBLEM SOLVING.

Boss/Secretary. For complete citation, *see* COMMUNICATION.

1483. Building a Winning Team
Organization Development Consultants 4 audiocassettes 4 hrs learner's print materials
Purchase: $65.00

Offers techniques for management-level people who work as a team. Leads to effective, productive, and wise work habits through understanding one's own role, the role of the team, the job, and the organization. Includes a Personal Profile.

Building a Working Team: "Let's Get Engaged". For complete citation, *see* COMMUNICATION.

1484. Building More Effective Teams: The Organization Development (O.D.) Approach
Document Associates 1978 16mm film or videocassette color 26 min
Purchase: $425.00 Rental: $45.00

Documents Peter Block's work with the New York Board of Cooperative Educational Services. Demonstrates how to identify structures and relationships that hinder organizational growth and productivity and how to allocate the time and resources needed for change.

Challenge of Leadership. For complete citation, *see* LEADERSHIP.

Challenge over the Atlantic. For complete citation, *see* PLANNING.

Challenger: An Industrial Romance. For complete citation, *see* DECISION MAKING/PROBLEM SOLVING.

1485. Climb for the Top
Barr Films   16mm film or videocassette   color   15 min
Purchase: $290.00 lease   Rental: $100.00   Preview: $25.00

Shows the importance of teamwork in meeting a challenge of the ascent of Mt. McKinley. Illustrates how the challenges of business can be successfully met by combining the talents and energies of staff. Useful for team building.

Confronting Conflict. For complete citation, *see* CONFLICT AND CONFLICT MANAGEMENT.

1486. Effective Team Building
American Management Associations   6 audiocassettes   learner's print materials
Other cost factors: AMA members $135.00; discounts available for bulk orders

Team building efforts must identify and build on employee strengths, reduce conflicts and politicking, increase morale, and lower absenteeism. Focuses on the communication leadership process and how to develop an open atmosphere and form good one-to-one relationships. Includes how to motivate a team to use their creative potential and how to affect change in a team.

Employee and Team Development. For complete citation, *see* INTERPERSONAL RELATIONS.

1487. Employee Involvement: Issues and Concerns
LCA Video/Films   16mm film or videocassette   color   27 min   slides and audiocassette (15 min)
Purchase: $650.00   Preview: $50.00

Addresses problems in implementing employee involvement programs such as quality circles. Surfaces feelings that impede employee involvement and shows key role supervisors play. Serves as an idea starter for companies considering participative programs.

1488. Excel
American Management Associations   1972   16mm film and audiocassette or videocassette   color instructor's print materials; learner's print materials
Purchase: $4,250.00   Preview: available at AMA centers

Designed to improve support skills and build morale for work unit team. Aimed at both administrative and support staff, it covers communication skills, working with others, on-the-job changes, self-development, and working with different managerial styles. Suggested for 2½-day program.

1489. Individuality and Teamwork
BNA Communications, Inc   1969   16mm film or videocassette   color   27 min   learner's print materials
Purchase: $525.00   Rental: 5-day $150.00; 3-day $105.00   Preview: $35.00

Explains the "matrix organization" and how the individual can make contributions to group action by being themselves and playing a group member role. Accents teamwork, needs of the group, and group processes. Organization Renewal Series, no. 3.

1490. Managerial Game Plan
Professional Development, Inc   1975   5 16mm films or videocassettes   color   30 min ea   instructor's print materials; learner's print materials
Purchase: film $3,750.00 ($650.00 ea); video $2,850.00 ($495.00 ea)   Rental: film $795.00 ($495.00 ea); video $750.00 ($175.00 ea)   Preview: $95.00

Presents team building through the management by objectives process. Shows planning principles through analogies from pro football. Useful as a starter program when utilized as a planning tool to assist in needs analysis or to determine systematic steps to take in reaching a desired goal.

On the Right Course. For complete citation, *see* TRAINING AND DEVELOPMENT.

1491. Performance Circles: An American Alternative to Quality Circles
Measurable Performance Systems   audiocassette
Purchase: $19.95   Other cost factors: leader's guide and modular tape program $95.00

The performance circle system is primarily designed for team building of top and middle managers and secondly for first line supervisors. Performance in relation to productivity is emphasized rather than abstract theory. Leader's guide includes planning guide, productivity checklist, state-of-the-art modules, art work, rights to reproduce forms, and an annual subscription to the *Performance Circle Quarterly Newsletter*.

1492. Sand Castle
National Film Board of Canada   16mm film or videocassette   color   13 min
Purchase: film $235.00; video $175.00   Rental: $20.00   Preview: $20.00

Animation presents a group of creatures who have been shaped to do specific jobs in the construction of a sand castle. Illustrates the importance of leadership, teamwork, support systems, and the act of contributing. Useful to open a meeting, stimulate discussion, and reaffirm ideas about job identification, team building, and leadership.

1493. Setting the Right Climate
BNA Communications, Inc   16mm film or videocassette   color   22 min   learner's print materials
Purchase: $630.00   Rental: 5-day $150.00; 3-day $105.00   Preview: $35.00

Dramatizes what teamwork is, how to institute it, and how to assess the climate in which it can flourish. Presents a 6-point model for critiquing progress. Brings out the line manager's vital role as a paraprofessional trainer. Increasing Productivity and Efficiency Program, no. 2.

1494. Successful Teamwork
AMACOM   2 audiocassettes   60 min   booklet
Purchase: $45.00   Other cost factors: AMA members $38.25

Shows both secretaries and their bosses how to work together to establish open communications, a climate of success, and habits that lead to mutual advancement. Offers techniques that help manager/secretary teams handle criticism positively, level with each other, and build each other up instead of putting each other down.

Supervisor's Responsibility for Promoting Cooperation between Employees and Departments. For complete citation, *see* SUPERVISION.

1495. Team Building
BNA Communications, Inc   1971   16mm film or videocassette   color   30 min   instructor's print materials
Purchase: $550.00   Rental: 5-day $150.00; 3-day $105.00   Preview: $35.00

Presents the purpose and effects of team building as a procedure of organizational development through dramatization in an advertising company. Saul Gellerman and Sheldon Davis suggest methods to preserve the beneficial effects and extend team building further in an organization. Companion film to *Confronting Conflict*. Effective Organization Series, no. 6.

1496. Teamwork: A Film from the People's Republic of China
Salenger Educational Media   1983   16mm film or videocassette   color   11 min   instructor's print materials
Purchase: $275.00   Rental: $125.00   Preview: $35.00

Silent, animated film illustrates importance and possibilities for teamwork. Useful for initiating training in group dynamics, employee responsibility, and accomplishing organizational goals.

1497. Temporary Task Forces: A Humanistic Problem-Solving Structure
Development Digest   audiocassette
Purchase: $13.75

Temporary teams are necessary for effective organizations. Robert A. Luke describes the use of this organizational structure for member selection, interpersonal maintenance, and interfacing with other units.

1498. That's Not My Job
Roundtable Films, Inc   1967   16mm film or videocassette   color   26 min
Purchase: $400.00   Rental: $85.00   Preview: $30.00

Dramatizes the importance of teamwork in improving productivity and morale. Shows how a supervisor motivates an uncooperative employee to operate fully within the job's boundaries. Helps to shape positive attitudes in new employees.

1499. Tough-Minded Team Building
AMACOM   3 audiocassettes   60 min ea   booklet
Purchase: $85.00   Other cost factors: AMA members $72.50

Identifies ways to find and build on employee strengths and turn adversaries into teams. Suggests how to see work tasks as challenges and set goals. Features Joe and Hal Batten.

Try to See It My Way. For complete citation, *see* MANAGEMENT.

We Can Work It Out. For complete citation, *see* MANAGEMENT.

TECHNOLOGY
See also AUTOMATION

1500. Cave Man to Space Man
BNA Communications, Inc   1974   16mm film or videocassette   color   44 min   instructor's print materials
Purchase: $575.00   Rental: 5-day $150.00; 3-day $105.00   Preview: $35.00

Technological advances have changed the times and the nature of our world. Presentation by Joe Powell encourages people to keep pace with progress, thus increasing their own well-being as well as the profits and productivity of their organizations.

Coping with Technological Change. For complete citation, *see* CHANGE.

1501. Coping with Technology: Beyond Bureaucracy, Towards a New Democracy
Document Associates   16mm film   color   26 min
Purchase: $400.00   Rental: $45.00

Dr. Warren Bennis provides a provocative analysis of the impact of technology on human life. He discusses the inability of rigid, bureaucratic organizations to cope with rapid technological growth and suggest that new, more open and democratic forms must develop to keep pace with change. Robert Heilbroner and Buckminster Fuller comment on the prospects of humanity and organizations in the face of rapid technological progress.

Encounters with the Future. For complete citation, *see* SOCIETAL CHANGE.

1502. End of Mechanism
Development Digest   audiocassette
Purchase: $14.00

Discusses the beginning of the fall of technology from its previous plateau. Recommends the nation's focus on the quality of working life as the best means of assuring productivity increases. Features Ted Mills.

1503. Future of Technology
BNA Communications, Inc   1971   16mm film or videocassette   color   28 min
Purchase: $350.00   Rental: 5-day $150.00; 3-day $105.00   Preview: $35.00

Peter Drucker, Elizabeth Hall, and Charles DeCarlo assess the forces and trends likely to shape the future as they discuss the technological forces influencing managerial operations. Managing Discontinuity Series, no. 2.

1504. Future Shock
CRM/McGraw-Hill Films   16mm film or videocassette   color   42 min
Purchase: film $695.00; video $525.00   Rental: 2-week $80.00; 1-week $60.00

Presents possiblity of a future of unrestrained technology yet proposes we need not be victims of our own inventions if we control them. Orson Welles narrates.

1505. Managing Innovation and Growth
BNA Communications, Inc   1981   16mm film or videocassette   color   24 min   instructor's print materials; learner's print materials
Purchase: $630.00   Rental: $245.00

Shows the best way to initiate new technological projects and get approval from finance officers and budget committees. Stresses importance of project staging, predicting results, and anticipating financial returns. Features Peter Drucker. Managing for Tomorrow Series, no. 2.

1506. Other Way
Films, Inc   16mm film or videocassette   color   50 min
Purchase: film $800.00; video $400.00   Rental: $75.00   Preview: free

Warns that we must stress human requirements along with technical development. Speculates on the alternative to "bigger is better" philosophy. Raises the question of whether a humanistic use of modern technology would increase self-sufficiency and make work a more enjoyable experience. Features E.F. Schumacher.

Secretary in a Changing World. For complete citation, *see* SECRETARIAL SKILLS.

1507. Trigger Effect
Time-Life Video   1979   16mm film   color   52 min
Purchase: $750.00

Shows how we reached our present state of dependency on a complex technological network like the one that brought New York City to a standstill during the blackout.

TELEPHONE USAGE
See also COMMUNICATION

1508. Effective Telephone Calling
National Educational Media, Inc   16mm film or super 8mm or videocassette   color   13 min   instructor's print materials; learner's print materials
Purchase: $320.00   Rental: 5-day $80.00; 3-day $70.00
Languages: English, Spanish

Dramatizations illustrate procedures and techniques for courteous and effective calls. Companion film to *Telephone Manners*. Intended for everyone in an organization.

1509. Importance of You to Better Telephone Communications
Classroom World Productions   2 filmstrips and audiocassette
Purchase: filmstrips $60.00; audiocassette only $7.50

Includes how to handle telephone equipment properly, answer and place calls, screen callers, and take messages effectively.

Mail and Telephone. For complete citation, *see* SECRETARIAL SKILLS.

1510. Placing Telephone Calls
National Educational Media, Inc   filmstrip and audiocassette or slides   12 min
Purchase: filmstrip 16mm $95.00; filmstrip 35mm $90.00; slides $115.00   Other cost factors: study material kits (40 study guides and one leader's kit) $12.00

Illustrates a step-by-step procedure for buying and confirming appointments and orders: preplanning, identifying one's self, exploring for facts, and obtaining commitments. Companion to *Receiving Telephone Calls*.

1511. Receiving Telephone Calls
National Educational Media, Inc   slides or filmstrip
Purchase: filmstrip 35mm $90.00, filmstrip 16mm $95.00; slides $115.00   Other cost factors: study material kits (40 study guides and 1 leader's kit) $12.00

Emphasizes that the voice on the phone is the voice of the organization. Illustrates how to take clear, error-free messages, how to use common courtesy on every call, and how to deliver a message for maximum results.

1512. Telephone Basics for Business
National Educational Media, Inc   1980   3 16mm films or videocassettes or slides and audiocassettes   color   13 min ea   instructor's print materials; learner's print materials
Purchase: films or videocassettes $925.00; slides and audiocassettes $381.00   Preview: $147.50

Demonstrates telephone techniques in business situations: planning, placing, and receiving telephone calls. Includes clear communication tips, telephone courtesy, and selling by telephone. Suggested for 4- to 6-hour program.

1513. Telephone Courtesy Pays
Advantage Media   1982   16mm film or super 8mm film or videocassette   color   20 min   instructor's print materials; learner's print materials
Purchase: $495.00   Rental: $150.00   Preview: free

Seeks to instill employees with capabilities of handling a variety of phone calls and reducing their stress while remaining courteous and productive.

1514. Telephone Dynamics
Singer Management Institute   1972   2
audiocassettes   2 hrs   instructor's print materials;
learner's print materials
Purchase: $125.00   Preview: $15.00

Offers basics of telephone courtesy including phrases and techniques for salutation, handling incoming calls and placing calls. Suggested for 3½ hours as group or self-study.

1515. Telephone Know-How: Increasing the Effectiveness of the Manager's Team
AMACOM   2 audiocassettes   60 min ea   learner's
print materials
Purchase: $44.95   Other cost factors: AMA members
$38.25

Addresses ways to handle day-to-day problems and emergencies by telephone. Suggests better habits to ease workload and improve image. Spells out rules and telephone protocol whether information, action, support, or advice is sought.

1516. Telephone Manners
National Educational Media, Inc   1973   16mm film
or super 8mm or videocassette   color   learner's
print materials
Purchase: $320.00   Rental: 5-day $80.00; 3-day
$70.00
Languages: English, French, German, Greek,
Japanese, Norwegian, Portuguese, Spanish

Intended to orient all employees in an organization. Outlines the basic process into practical tips to assure clear communication. Illustrates each point with dramatization. Stresses telephone courtesy as a vital element of both internal and external communications in any organization. Companion film to *Effective Telephone Calling*.

1517. Telephone Techniques for Secretaries and Receptionists
Creative Media   2 audiocassettes
Purchase: $24.50

Shows secretaries and receptionists how to handle almost every phone situation professionally. Features Thom Norman.

"When I'm Calling You...". For complete citation,
see CUSTOMER RELATIONS.

1518. "...Will You Answer True?"
Xicom-Video Arts   1975   16mm film or
videocassette   color   16 min   instructor's print
materials
Purchase: $390.00   Rental: $100.00   Preview:
$35.00

Contains many lessons in general telephone technique and behavior: having relevant information in reach, making notes, watching out for an open phone, not trying to carry out 2 conversations at once, and checking back on important details. An important training instrument for all staff who use the telephone. Special emphasis is given to telephone selling techniques. Companion film to "When I'm Calling You...".

TIME MANAGEMENT

1519. Clues to Executive Time Control
AMACOM   4 audiocassettes   3 hrs   booklet
Purchase: $110.00   Other cost factors: AMA
members $93.50

Dr. Henry Mintzberg reveals how skillful management of time enables successful managers to turn distractions, obligations, interruptions, and pressures to their own personal advantage. He disputes some common myths such as the manager's workday, building good teamwork, and executive mobility.

1520. Do It Now!
Cally Curtis Company   16mm film or
videocassette   color   30 min
Purchase: film $495.00; video $485.00   Rental:
$120.00   Preview: $120.00

Explores what procrastination is and its causes and gives useful techniques to break the habit. Features Dru Scott, Tom Rusk, and Alan Lakein. Time Management Series.

1521. Finding Time
CRM/McGraw-Hill Films   1980   16mm film or
videocassette   color   30 min   instructor's print
materials
Purchase: $560.00   Rental: $95.00   Preview: free

Illustrates common personal adaptations to time scheduling in view of differing perceptions of time. Specific pointers relate to how to manage time for one's self and one's subordinates.

1522. Getting Started
LCA Video/Films   16mm film or
videocassette   color   12 min   instructor's print
materials; learner's print materials
Purchase: $275.00   Rental: $50.00   Preview:
$25.00

Looks at distractions in the workday and, without offering solutions, creates a sense of awareness about efficient use of time. Invites workers to think about their habitual time wasters and challenges them to control them.

1523. Getting to Know Me
LCA Video/Films   16mm film   17 min
instructor's print materials
Purchase: $350.00   Rental: $70.00   Preview:
$35.00

Points out the dangers of overcommitment through portrayal of a manager who needs to reassess his priorities and reorganize his time. Uses humor to contrast how better time management leads to a new and improved work style. Packaged for one-hour workshop.

1524. Ideas for Better Living
Instructional Dynamics, Inc   3 audiocassettes
booklet
Purchase: $34.50

Focuses on the creative use of personal time and how to conquer procrastination in facing overwhelming situations. Explains relaxation techniques such as autonomic relaxation, meditation, and systematic tension reduction.

1525. Mackenzie on Time: How to Save Two Hours a Day
AMACOM   audiocassette   60 min
Purchase: $12.95   Other cost factors: AMA members $11.95

Tells how to recognize and defeat the most common time-wasters and eliminate the climate of crisis management. Discusses how to break the habit of long work hours while increasing productivity.

1526. Make Time Work for You
Audio-Forum   3 audiocassettes   82 min   learner's print materials
Purchase: $34.40

Offers step-by-step course on how to manage time and deal with interruptions and distractions that eat up time and energy.

1527. Management of Time
Resources for Education and Management, Inc   4 filmstrips or slides and audiocassettes or videocassettes or filmstrip cartridges   9–12 min ea instructor's print materials
Purchase: video $280.00 ($85.00 ea); filmstrips $255.00 ($69.00 ea); filmstrip cartridges $340.00 ($85.00 ea); slides $270.00 ($73.00 ea)

Introduces the key elements of good time management. Discusses 2 methods for managing time—breaking down the types of work we do and setting priorities. Points to delegation and training as keys to save time. Shows the importance of avoiding time-wasters by conducting efficient meetings.

1528. Managing Time
AMR International, Inc   9 audiocassettes   learner's print materials
Purchase: $350.00

Shows how to identify major time-wasters and what to do about them, how to control constant interruptions, how to utilize your secretary to increase effectiveness, and how to avoid the trap of reverse delegation. Includes interviews. Presented by Alec Mackenzie.

1529. Managing Time
BNA Communications, Inc   1968   16mm film or videocassette   color   22 min
Purchase: $525.00   Rental: 5-day $150.00; 3-day $105.00   Preview: $35.00
Languages: Arabic, Dutch, English, French, Greek, Portuguese, Spanish, Swedish

Dramatization shows manager's predicament of not having enough time. Peter Drucker offers a practical way to get the most of the time available: a time log. Effective Executive Series, no. 1.

1530. New Time Management
Nightingale-Conant Corporation   6 audiocassettes   2 hrs   learner's print materials
Purchase: $60.00

Reveals the importance of time management and how to clarify priorities, overcome procrastination, handle interruptions, conduct meetings, and delegate.

1531. Perfectly Normal Day
Cally Curtis Company   1976   16mm film or videocassette   color   27 min
Purchase: film $550.00; video $525.00   Rental: $130.00   Preview: $40.00

Helps develop a new attitude toward interruptions and crises and shows how to reduce and manage them. Shows how to set priorities and manage time effectively in the typical day. Features Tom Bosley. Intended for all employee levels. Alan Lakein Time Management Series.

1532. Personal Time Management
Lansford Publishing Company, Inc   4 audiocassettes   instructor's print materials
Purchase: $99.95

Identifies top time-wasters and how to remove them through the use of effective planning. Discusses recognition of priorities which lead to personal control and success through goal setting.

Success Is a State of Mind. For complete citation, *see* STRESS AND STRESS MANAGEMENT.

1533. Take Time to be Successful
Time Management Center   audiocassette
Purchase: $12.95

Offers the basics of good time management presented in summary form for quick learning or review. Useful way to introduce proven time concepts.

1534. Team of Two: Time Management for Managers and Secretaries
Cally Curtis Company   1976   16mm film or videocassette   color   30 min
Purchase: film $550.00; video $525.00   Rental: $130.00   Preview: $40.00

Shows managers and secretaries how to work as a more productive team. Suggests techniques on how to use skills and talents of secretaries and how managers can increase their effectiveness. Alan Lakein Time Management Series.

1535. Tell My Wife I Won't Be Home for Dinner
MTI Teleprograms, Inc   1980   16mm film or videocassette   color   32 min   instructor's print materials
Purchase: film $550.00; video $495.00   Rental: $125.00   Preview: free

Portrays gross time mismanagement. Examines the correlation between time management and effective management procedures through 3 case studies, each demonstrating a variety of common misuses of time. Demonstrates that good management practice is also good time-management practice.

1536. Time Game
National Educational Media, Inc   1975   16mm film or videocassette   color   14 min   instructor's print materials; learner's print materials
Purchase: $420.00   Rental: 5-day $90.00; 3-day $80.00
Languages: English, Japanese, Portuguese, Spanish

Offers basic techniques for managing time effectively. Illustrates time-demanding duties of managers by showing a card game where 4 managers compete for discretionary time. The game plus flashbacks to on-the-job situations show positive principles. Stresses priorities, delegation, and controlling crises.

1537. Time Is Money!
Cally Curtis Company   16mm film or videocassette   color   29 min
Purchase: film $550.00; video $525.00   Rental: $130.00   Preview: $40.00

Points out how being busy with unimportant things is common because such activities are easier and faster. Offers Alan Lakein's time management principles particularly directed at sales personnel. Features Burgess Meredith and Ron Masak. Alan Lakein Time Management Series.

1538. Time—Learn to Master It!
Didactic Systems, Inc   audiocassette   40 min
learner's print materials
Purchase: $15.00

Offers examples from varied business situations. Gives tips in 5 areas of time control. Taped lecture aimed at new supervisors.

1539. Time Management
Lansford Publishing Company, Inc   1981   60 slides and audiocassettes
Purchase: $245.95

Suggests ways to organize the work day for greater productivity. Includes rules for time management, budgeting time, time management by objectives, organizing the work area, internal visitors, external visitors, and meetings and conferences.

1540. Time Management
HBJ Media Systems Corporation   1981   6 slide/audiocassette presentations   instructor's print materials; learner's print materials
Purchase: $1,785.00

Includes principles of time management and procedures for planning, scheduling, executing, and evaluating work efficiently. Intended for those involved in planning and implementing effective work schedules. Suggested for 10–12 hours.

1541. Time Management for Executive Secretaries and Administrative Assistants
Creative Media   3 audiocassettes   learner's print materials
Purchase: $65.00

Presents concepts and techniques for getting more accomplished. Bob Rutherford offers his time management practices and "laws."

1542. Time Management for Managers
Time-Life Video   1980   6 videocassettes   30 min ea   instructor's print materials
Purchase: $3,950.00   Rental: $500.00   Preview: free   Other cost factors: learner's workbooks $19.50

Dramatization shows realistic examples in the business setting. Presents basic principles and distinguishes between goals and activities and how managers should manage rather than how they do. Offers guidelines for making decisions and the use of an action plan. Highlights delegating and how to overcome barriers to do so effectively. Defines the difference between scheduling initiated items and response items and the use of

time blocks. Presents useful techniques for managing interruptions.

1543. Time Management for Secretaries
Training by Design   2 audiocassettes   2½ hrs
learner's print materials
Purchase: $75.00

Promotes "prime time" concept and how to improve the boss's time management. Includes techniques for more effective work scheduling and maximizing time. Self-instructional.

1544. Time Management for Secretaries and Their Managers
AMR International, Inc   10 audiocassettes
learner's print materials
Purchase: $295.00

Acknowledges the importance of the role of secretaries in helping managers achieve their objectives. Emphasizes the importance of planning work and identifying and eliminating time-wasters. Uses dialog and dramatization to show how working together as a team increases productivity and job satisfaction for both secretaries and managers. Features Alec Mackenzie and Billie Sorensen.

1545. Time Management for Supervisors
EFM Films   1979   16mm film or videocassette   color   15 min   instructor's print materials; learner's print materials
Purchase: $395.00   Rental: $90.00   Preview: $40.00

Shows supervisors how to organize themselves and their departments for maximum productivity. Shows proven time management techniques that help them relate their activities to their priorities. Shows the advantages of written daily plans in keeping schedules on target and emphasizes how to schedule work flow to maximize each employee's productivity.

1546. Time Management for Today
Creative Media   6 audiocassettes
Purchase: $65.00

Focuses on conquering procrastination, eliminating time-wasters, organizing work places, and using short cuts in handling paper work. Features Merrill Douglass.

1547. Time Management Videotape
Time Management Center   1982   videocassette
Purchase: $400.00   Other cost factors: study guides $32.00 ea

Uses humor, dramatization, and lecture to show how to reduce paperwork, hold effective meetings, control interruptions, and plan time schedules. Designed for managers and business executives who have discretion over their time but have pressure-packed schedules and tight deadlines. For group or self-study.

1548. Time of Your Life
Cally Curtis Company   1974   16mm film or videocassette   color   29 min
Purchase: film $550.00; video $525.00   Rental: $130.00   Preview: $40.00
Languages: English, Spanish

Based on Alan Lakein's *How to Get Control of Your Time and Your Life*. Outlines 6 simple ideas on how to make more effective use of time. Features James Whitmore. Alan Lakein Time Management Series.

1549. Time Study Methods
Maynard Management Institute   16mm
film   color   19 min
Purchase: $610.00   Rental: $61.00

Shows how time study methods are applied to shop operation. Job is broken into elements and timed, then recorded. Intended for forepersons and shop supervisors.

1550. Time to Think
Roundtable Films, Inc   1975   16mm film or videocassette   color   20 min   learner's print materials
Purchase: $450.00   Rental: $85.00   Preview: $30.00

Identifies problem areas that prevent managers from having time to think, plan, and progress. Provides basic solutions to make time available for a manager without loss of control over his/her responsibilities. Demonstrates that rewards are gained through the proper use of time. Illustrates a pressured, but talented manager who has difficulty organizing his business life so that everything gets completed on time. He is coached in methods of improving the mechanics of his job and the self-discipline required to give himself time to think, plan, and help his company progress.

1551. Time Trap
American Media, Inc   1980   16mm film   color   30 min   instructor's print materials
Purchase: $550.00   Rental: $110.00   Preview: $35.00

Illustrates 15 common time-wasters. Presents 50 time-saving techniques to save 2 hours each day. Dramatized story about a husband and wife who are both professionals in the business world, their problems relating to time management, and how they overcome them. Features Alec Mackenzie.

1552. Total Time Management
AMACOM   1980   6 audiocassettes   learner's print materials
Purchase: $145.00   Other cost factors: AMA members $135.00

Focuses on finding and eliminating personal time-wasters by looking at them against the background of major responsibilities. Step-by-step procedures for creating a time log and a time comparison chart. Shows how to use these 2 devices to relate activities to priorities.

Unorganized Manager. For complete citation, *see* MANAGEMENT.

What Supervisors Can Do about Planning Time. For complete citation, *see* SUPERVISION.

TRADE UNIONS
See LABOR UNIONS

TRAINING AND DEVELOPMENT
See also INSTRUCTION AND INSTRUCTIONAL METHODS; ORIENTATION; TEAM BUILDING

1553. Adapting Training and Development to Changing Values
Development Digest   audiocassette
Purchase: $13.75

Discusses the changing values in society. Provides a frame of reference for developing relevant programs and teaching others about these value changes. Presenter: M. Scott Myers.

1554. Anything Is Possible—With Training
National Audiovisual Center   1970   16mm film   14 min
Purchase: $81.25   Rental: $12.50

Provides examples of successful employee training in a telephone answering service, a boat yard, and a newspaper office. Shows employee training as essential to business success.

1555. Catching On
Roundtable Films, Inc   16mm film   color   20 min
Purchase: $475.00   Rental: $75.00   Preview: $30.00
Languages: English, French

Dramatization intended for entry-level personnel with "new worker anxieties." Illustrates how to learn a job quickly and comprehensively. Useful for orientation and supervisory training.

1556. Coaching for Results
International Film Bureau, Inc   1979   2 16mm films or videocassettes   color   25 min and 14 min   instructor's print materials
Purchase: $900.00 ($450.00 ea)   Rental: $90.00 (5-day $60.00 ea; 3-day $45.00 ea)   Preview: free

Both films use dramatizations to stimulate managers to think about the influence they have on the development of subordinates. *I Owe You* shows the consequences of ignoring staff desire for development. *Received with Interest* follows the first film as an action plan for staff development.

ERIC: It's that Easy. For complete citation, *see* INSTRUCTION AND INSTRUCTIONAL METHODS.

Executive Development and Training Issues—Government and Industry. For complete citation, *see* MANAGEMENT DEVELOPMENT.

Getting Ahead: The Road to Self Development. For complete citation, *see* CAREER PLANNING AND DEVELOPMENT.

Helping Skills for Human Resource Development. For complete citation, *see* COUNSELING.

If You Don't, Nobody Else Will. For complete citation, *see* CAREER PLANNING AND DEVELOPMENT.

1557. Implementing Staff Development
Instructional Dynamics, Inc   audiocassette
instructor's print materials; learner's print materials;
book
Purchase: $59.95

For use in conjunction with Paul Abel's book *The New Practice of Supervision and Staff Development* and David Abbey's *Transactional Analysis in Social Communication*. Offers these as a practical program for understanding and implementing staff development and supervisory techniques. Useful for group or self-study.

1558. Leader's Guide
BNA Communications, Inc   10 cassettes   12 min
ea
Purchase: $100.00 ($10.00 ea)

Deals with important concepts of organizational behavior and sets forth guidelines for developing and training others. Includes motivations, differences, learning, and training. Useful for both trainers and managers. Effective Management Program, no. 4.

1559. Leonard Nadler—An In-Depth Interview with Steve Becker
Learncom, Inc   6 audiocassettes
Purchase: $180.00

Nadler defines human resources development (HRD), makes a distinction between training, education, and development, and then relates it to organization development and change.

1560. Malcolm Knowles—In an In-Depth Interview with Steve Becker
Learncom, Inc   1979   6 audiocassettes   learner's print materials
Purchase: $180.00

Discusses broad issues and concepts in adult education including andragogy vs. pedagogy. Gives specific methods for creating learning climates, designing learning experiences, facilitating learning, and managing human potential. Intended for managers and trainers as well as adult educators.

Management Training. For complete citation, *see* MANAGEMENT.

Non-Traditional Approaches to Human Potential Development. For complete citation, *see* PERSONAL GROWTH.

1561. On-The-Job Training
Singer Management Institute   2 audiocassettes
instructor's print materials; learner's print materials
Purchase: $90.00

Designed to instruct supervisors how to give on-the-job training. Shows supervisors how to teach jobs quickly and thoroughly, cut training costs, and maintain an on-going training program.

1562. On the Right Course
International Film Bureau, Inc   1979   16mm film or videocassette   color   21 min
Purchase: $450.00   Rental: 5-day $60.00; 3-day $45.00   Preview: free

Dramatization shows company helping subsidiary identify participation skills needed by their managers and providing training in those skills. Examines the changes that individual managers may need to make in their ways of managing in order to develop a different approach toward working together. Companion film to *The More We Are Together*. Practical Participation Series.

1563. Pre-Supervisory Training
Resources for Education and Management, Inc   1972   videocassettes or 3 filmstrips or filmstrip cartridges or slides and audiocassettes   11 min ea   instructor's print materials
Purchase: video $245.00 ($95.00 ea); filmstrips $220.00 ($75.00 ea); filmstrip cartridges $255.00 ($85.00 ea); slides $235.00 ($80.00 ea)

Promotes the concept of presupervisory training: training employees in various supervisory skills before they actually assume a supervisory position. Shows the benefits of such training, how to determine the best pay-off areas, and how to use effective presupervisory training techniques. Stresses practice rather than theory. Intended for first and second level supervisors.

Role of Management Education in Management Development. For complete citation, *see* MANAGEMENT DEVELOPMENT.

Setting the Right Climate. For complete citation, *see* TEAM BUILDING.

Supervisor and OJT. For complete citation, *see* SUPERVISION.

Supervisor as a Classroom Instructor. For complete citation, *see* SUPERVISION.

Supervisor's Responsibility for Induction and Job Instruction. For complete citation, *see* ORIENTATION.

1564. Supervisor's Responsibility for Transfer, Promotion, and Training for Responsibility
Continental Film Productions   slides or filmstrip and audiocassette   12 min
Purchase: filmstrip $105.00; slides $125.00

Stresses the importance of the understudy and how initiative can be developed by proper delegation of authority. Supervisor Training Series.

1565. Supervisor's Role in Training New Employees
Bureau of Business Practice   1980   16mm film or videocassette   color   18 min
Purchase: $425.00   Rental: $95.00   Preview: $45.00

Reveals the ways the first few days on the job can vitally affect a new employee's morale and performance. Attendance, attitude, and productivity are 3 patterns developed early. Dramatizations show the necessity of getting new employees off to the right start.

Techniques for Teaching Consultants and the Organizational Aspects of "Psychological Climate". For complete citation, *see* INSTRUCTION AND INSTRUCTIONAL METHODS.

1566. Train the Trainer
Butler Learning Systems 314 slides and audiocassettes instructor's print materials; learner's print materials
Purchase: $2,595.00 plus $55.00 per learner Preview: free

Presents training theory, training methods, and training action. Shows techniques for individualized instructions, group instruction, and self-instruction. Describes the learning process and working with people in a learning situation. Suggested for a 2-day program or 10 2-hour sessions.

1567. Training: A View from the Top
BNA Communications, Inc 1973 16mm film or videocassette color 33 min instructor's print materials
Purchase: $515.00 Rental: 5-day $150.00; 3-day $105.00 Preview: $35.00

Features the views on training held by the top executives of 9 leading organizations. Includes their experiences and approaches to training. Useful for securing support of top management for training programs and to stimulate managerial and supervisory interest in employee training.

Training by Objectives. For complete citation, *see* MANAGEMENT BY OBJECTIVES.

1568. Training Memorandum
National Educational Media, Inc 1973 16mm film or super 8mm or videocassette color 10 min instructor's print materials; learner's print materials
Purchase: $365.00 Rental: 5-day $90.00; 3-day $80.00
Languages: English, French, Japanese, Spanish

Emphasizes the value of training employees and describes practical benefits. Dramatization shows a skeptical supervisor who discovers these benefits. Useful as an introduction to training especially for supervisors and managers who are indifferent or resistant to training.

1569. You Can Surpass Yourself
Ramic Productions 1979 16mm film or super 8mm or videocassette color 28 min instructor's print materials; wallet folders
Purchase: $650.00 Rental: $150.00 Preview: $65.00

Prepares trainers and employees for training and development efforts. Eden Ryl shows how to pinpoint 4 teachability levels: primitive, resistive, adaptive, motivative. Encourages self-examination of one's own styles and possible change.

1570. You'll Soon Get the Hang of It
Xicom-Video Arts 1981 16mm film or videocassette color 24 min instructor's print materials; learner's print materials
Purchase: $625.00 Rental: $120.00 Preview: $40.00

Explores 3 main training situations—manual, clerical, and technical—and demonstrates the major pitfalls. Shows how to organize training to fit the ways people learn and when to use different motivational techniques. Features John Cleese.

TRANSACTIONAL ANALYSIS

1571. I Understand, You Understand, The Dynamics of Transactional Analysis
Creative Media 1975 16mm or super 8mm film or videocassette color 32 min instructor's print materials
Purchase: English $475.00; Spanish $485.00 Rental: $90.00 Preview: $30.00
Languages: English, Spanish

Joe Batten focuses on what Transactional Analysis (TA) is, how it works, and how to apply it. Shows how TA concepts can be used in business and industry to change attitudes, increase motivation and productivity, and bridge communication gaps.

1572. Meet Your Parent, Adult, Child
Salenger Educational Media 16mm film or videocassette color 9 min instructor's print materials; learner's print materials
Purchase: $210.00 Rental: $70.00 Preview: $35.00

Animated film designed primarily as a discussion starter for any group interested in more effective interpersonal relationships. Identifies the 3 ego states revealed through transactional analysis (TA) theory. Intended to help improve interpersonal and intergroup communication.

1573. OK Secretary
Learning Consultants, Inc audiocassette learner's print materials
Purchase: $17.50

Contrasts the qualities of winners and losers in the business world, and how these factors are understood by applying "I'm OK, You're OK." Discusses negative and positive life scripts and the traits of a good adult manager. Recording of a seminar. Features Clay Hardesty. Transactional Analysis Series.

1574. Organizational Transactions
Professional Development, Inc 1976 6 16mm film or videocassettes color 30 min ea instructor's print materials; learner's print materials
Purchase: film $3,900.00 ($650.00 ea); video $2,900.00 ($495.00 ea) Rental: film $795.00 ($195.00 ea); video $750.00 ($175.00 ea)

Explores why people act the way they do in organizational life. Focuses on approaches to developing leadership potential and managerial skills. Offers blueprint for leadership training. Based on transactional analysis (TA), deals with problem solving, competition and conflict, time management, planning and control, and customer transactions.

1575. Practical TA for Managers
American Management Associations 6 audiocassettes workbook
Purchase: $145.00 Other cost factors: AMA members $135.00

Describes concepts, language, and techniques of Transactional Analysis (TA), then applies these to specific business situations. Uses vignettes and exercises to build skills of analysis and changing behavior.

1576. TA for Secretaries
Learning Consultants, Inc   audiocassette
Purchase: $15.00

Introduces Transctionsl Analysis (TA) with examples and suggestions based on real world business situations. Includes a TA self-test and guidelines for evaluating the parent-adult-child scores. Transactional Analysis Series.

1577. TA in the Key of C
Instructional Dynamics, Inc   6 audiocassettes   4 hrs   learner's print materials
Purchase: $54.50

Employs music and song to graphically illustrate Transactional Analysis (TA) concepts and transactions in almost all of their forms. Dr. Warren Welsh uses popular and folk songs to communicate the ideas of TA. For group or self-study. Introductory level.

1578. Transactional Analysis
CRM/McGraw-Hill Films   1975   16mm film or videocassette   color   31 min
Purchase: film $525.00; video $495.00   Rental: $55.00   Preview: free

Uses a combination of animation, diagrams, and live, on-the-job scenes plus an interview with Dru Scott to describe and illustrate how Transactional Analysis (TA) is being used by various firms to increase organizational efficiency and elevate personnel morale. Shows how more valid forms of behavior can be encouraged to improve both human relations and motivation within an organization.

1579. Transactional Analysis: A Tool for More Effective Interpersonal Relationships
Development Digest   audiocassette
Purchase: $13.75

Presents Transactional Analysis (TA) as a method for understanding people's behavior and the ways individuals can learn to act differently. Explores the significance in an organizational context of such TA concepts as stroking, games, and script analysis. Features Dorothy Jongeward.

1580. Transactional Analysis: Better Communication for Organizations
Document Associates   1978   16mm film or videocassette   color   26 min
Purchase: $560.00   Rental: 10-day $110.00; 5-day $80.00

Examines the applicability of Transactional Analysis (TA) for improving communications in organizations. A personnel manager of American Airlines and a ticket counter reservation employee discuss the success of TA in improving customer service. Discusses the growing need for organizations to train personnel in the elements of communication and the advent of TA techniques.

1581. Transactional Analysis in Social and Communications Training (TASC)
Instructional Dynamics, Inc   1973   audiocassette   learner's print materials
Purchase: $49.50

Uses audio and print materials to prompt interaction in groups. Presents introductory Transactional Analysis (TA) principles and elicits personal application of them. Suggested for 8-hour program.

1582. Transactional Analysis Overview
Addison-Wesley Publishing Company, Inc   1972   audiocassette   55 min
Purchase: $15.00

Outlines the dynamics of Transactional Analysis. Can be used as lecture or discussion session. Useful for group or self-study.

1583. What Games Do You Play?
Learning Consultants, Inc   audiocassette   learner's print materials
Purchase: $17.50

"Games" may block communications and the achievement of goals. Discusses games and then goes on to discuss positive factors in business relationships. Recording of a seminar. Features Clay Hardesty. Transactional Analysis Series.

Winning. For complete citation, *see* INTERPERSONAL RELATIONS.

TYPEWRITING
See also SECRETARIAL SKILLS

1584. Basic Typing Skills
HBJ Media Systems Corporation   1981   17 slide/audiocassette presentations (4 audiocassettes)   instructor's print materials; learner's print materials
Purchase: $5,535.00
Languages: English, Spanish

Focuses on basic skills essential for production typing to a typing speed of approximately 35–40 words per minute. Intended to improve or renew typing skills. Suggested for 32–44 hours.

1585. Building Typing Speed and Accuracy
HBJ Media Systems Corporation   1981   3 slide/audiocassette presentations (27 audiocassettes)   instructor's print materials; learner's print materials
Purchase: $3,215.00

Emphasizes improved typing skills with gains measured by increased speed and by a reduction in errors. Exit proficiency is determined individually for each employee whose job performance and productivity depends on typing speed and accuracy. Suggested for 10–12 hours.

1586. Keyboard Mastery
HBJ Media Systems Corporation   1981   21 slide/audiocassette presentations (12 audiocassettes)   instructor's print materials; learner's print materials
Purchase: $6,965.00

Offers an introduction to typing, including typewriter operations and touch typing skills, to meet a typing speed of approximately 20–25 words per minute. Intended for employees with no previous typing experience. Suggested for 34–46 hours.

1587. Production Typing
Reinforcement Learning, Inc   10 audiocassettes
instructor's print materials; learner's print materials
Purchase: $128.00

Designed to meet the specific needs of the entry-level typist. Using audio and printed materials closely together, program gives step-by-step instruction in topics such as centering, punctuation, business letters and forms, outlines and reports, and manuscripts. Emphasizes clarity and simplicity through objectives and graphics. Projects and diagnostic quizzes identify remedial areas.

1588. Reinforcement "500"
Reinforcement Learning, Inc   10 audiocassettes
learner's print materials
Purchase: $128.00

Expands the *Reinforcement of Gregg Symbols and Theory* program to encompass 500 of the words and phrases most frequently used in business correspondence.

1589. Reinforcement Speed Test Tapes
Reinforcement Learning, Inc   10 audiocassettes
Purchase: $128.00

Provides practice dictation and speed development and/or appropriate test drills for evaluating student progress. Sessions graduate in 5-word per minute increments from 45 wam to 140 wam. For group or self-study.

1590. Technical and Statistical Typing
HBJ Media Systems Corporation   1981   16 slide/
audiocassette presentations   instructor's print
materials; learner's print materials
Purchase: $4,760.00

Includes how to prepare typewritten reports, manuscripts, tables, formulas and equations, graphic presentations, and other specialized assignments. Gives instruction in standard formats and procedures. Intended for secretaries, clerk-typists, word processing operators, and others whose duties include technical or statistical typing. Suggested for 30–36 hours.

1591. Typewriter Keyboard Response Program
Reinforcement Learning, Inc   7 audiocassettes
instructor's print materials; learner's print materials
Purchase: $89.50

Assumes zero knowledge on the part of the learner. Helps develop a subconscious memory response to the typewriter keyboard matrix and an automatic motor response for each of the alpha-numeric keys.

1592. Typing Business Correspondence
HBJ Media Systems Corporation   1981   20 slide/
audiocassette presentations   instructor's print
materials; learner's print materials
Purchase: $5,950.00

Shows appropriate styles and formats for business correspondence, including business letters and envelopes, mailing labels, interoffice memos, agendas, and itineraries. Suggested for 36–38 hours.

1593. Typing Financial Statements
HBJ Media Systems Corporation   1981   3 slide/
audiocassette presentations   instructor's print
materials; learner's print materials
Purchase: $895.00

Gives instruction in standard formats and procedures. Includes how to prepare typewritten balance sheets, income statements, and other financial statements; how to assemble auditor's reports; and how to type tax forms. Intended for secretaries, clerk-typists, word processing operators, and others whose duties include typing financial statements. Suggested for 6 hours.

1594. Typing Legal Forms and Documents
HBJ Media Systems Corporation   1981   4 slide/
audiocassette presentations   instructor's print
materials; learner's print materials
Purchase: $1,190.00

Describes how to type contracts, court documents, and other common legal papers. Gives instruction in standard formats and procedures. Intended for legal secretaries, word processing operators, and others whose duties include the typing of legal forms and documents.

1595. Typing Medical Forms and Reports
HBJ Media Systems Corporation   1981   3 slide/
audiocassette presentations   instructor's print
materials; learner's print materials
Purchase: $895.00

Describes how to type insurance claim forms, medical reports, and various kinds of health-care forms. Gives instruction in standard formats and procedures. Intended for personnel assistants, insurance clerks, medical secretaries, and others who deal with medical claims and reports. Suggested for 6–8 hours.

1596. Typing Speed Development
Reinforcement Learning, Inc   10 audiocassettes
instructor's print materials; learner's print materials
Purchase: $73.50

Offers a series of tightly controlled pacing exercises, combining 4 basic speed development techniques.

VALUES
See ETHICS AND VALUES

VISUAL AIDS
See AUDIOVISUAL TECHNIQUES

WAGES
See PAY PRACTICES

WEIGHTS AND MEASURES

1597. Make Mine Metric
Pyramid Films   1975   16mm film or
videocassette   color   13 min
Purchase: $275.00   Rental: $35.00

Offers humorous, reassuring introduction to the metric system that also includes some solid information. Illustrates basic metric units and emphasizes how much simpler calculation will be when all units are multiples of 10.

1598. Meter, Liter, and Gram
Salenger Educational Media 16mm film or videocassette color 13 min instructor's print materials; learner's print materials
Purchase: $295.00 Rental: $80.00 Preview: $35.00

Presents the 3 basic units of the metric system: the meter, the liter, and the gram. Prompts learners to think and visualize metric without converting.

1599. Metric System
Visual Instruction Productions 2 16mm films or super 8mm films or videocassettes color 13 min (16mm); 3½ min (super 8mm)
Purchase: films $400.00 ($200.00 ea); super 8 $70.00 ($35.00 ea) Rental: $65.00 ($35.00 ea) Preview: $25.00 ($15.00 ea)

Introduction to metrication and metric conversion. Covers the history of systems of measurement, metric prefixes and their meanings, comparisons of English and metric measurements, and specific application of metrication. Demonstrates benefits of using decimal calculating and the prefixes for multiples and submultiples.

1600. The Metric System
HBJ Media Systems Corporation 1981 6 slide/audiocassette presentations instructor's print materials; learner's print materials
Purchase: $1,785.00

Gives practical introduction to the units of measurement used in the metric system and skills for performing basic conversions. Intended for any employee who is unfamiliar with this standard international system of weights and measures. Suggested for 10–12 hours.

Ten—The Magic Number. For complete citation, see CHANGE.

1601. Understanding the Metric System
Classroom World Productions audiocassettes learner's print materials
Purchase: $42.50

Covers introduction to the metric system: the meter, the gram, and the liter.

1602. What about Metric?
National Audiovisual Center 1974 70 slides and audiocassette 7 min script
Purchase: $25.50

Discusses the status of the metric system in the US. Provides some guidelines on metric conversion for business and industry. Describes the conversion program of the Beloit Tool Company.

WOMEN
See also EQUAL EMPLOYMENT OPPORTUNITY

Advanced Management Techniques for Women. For complete citation, see MANAGEMENT TECHNIQUES.

Career Awareness for Women. For complete citation, see CAREER PLANNING AND DEVELOPMENT.

Equal Rights for Women. For complete citation, see EQUAL EMPLOYMENT OPPORTUNITY.

1603. 51%
Tylie Jones 16mm film or super 8mm or videocassette color 25 min instructor's print materials
Purchase: $200.00 Rental: $100.00 Preview: $10.00

Presents 3 stories showing aspects of the problems working women still face in business. Intended to help management better understand the upwardly mobile role of women in organizations and to evaluate attitudes toward working women and their goals.

1604. Guilty Madonnas
CRM/McGraw-Hill Films videocassette 51 min
Purchase: $525.00 Rental: $95.00 Preview: free

Explores 3 families' attitudes toward their working mothers and makes the case for day care centers. Shows how organizations face the realities of lowered productivity and absenteeism when working mothers are worried about their children or must take time off to care for them.

1605. Increasing Job Options for Women
National Audiovisual Center 1976 74 slides and audiocassette 10 min script
Purchase: $29.00

Addresses the issue of expanding career opportunities for women and reviews equal employment opportunity regulations against sex discrimination. Shows women working in a variety of nontraditional jobs. Encourages women to consider nontraditional occupations.

1606. I've Got a Woman Boss
Xicom-Video Arts 1977 16mm film or videocassette color 10 min
Purchase: $350.00 Rental: 3-day $100.00 Preview: $35.00

Humorous portrayal of a male manager faced with a woman in management. Raises the issues relevant to dealing with change in general and women in management in particular. Useful for EEO training sessions.

Legal Rights of Women Workers. For complete citation, see EQUAL EMPLOYMENT OPPORTUNITY.

Management Techniques for Women. For complete citation, see MANAGEMENT.

Men Who Are Working with Women in Management. For complete citation, *see* MANAGEMENT.

1607. Moving Mountains
American Federation of Labor and Congress of Industrial Organizations 1981 16mm film color 30 min
Rental: $5.00

Shows women working alongside men in open pit mines, driving mammoth bulldozers and loaders, and working in blasting crews. They talk about why they want to do this work, the men's attitude toward them, and the support they received from their local union president when the company resisted hiring women initially.

Moving Women into the Organization Mainstream for Profit. For complete citation, *see* EQUAL EMPLOYMENT OPPORTUNITY.

Promotion and Transfer. For complete citation, *see* PERSONNEL MANAGEMENT.

Role of the Female in the World of Work. For complete citation, *see* EQUAL EMPLOYMENT OPPORTUNITY.

1608. She's Nobody's Baby: A History of American Women in the 20th Century
MTI Teleprograms, Inc 1981 16mm film or videocassette color 55 min
Purchase: film $750.00; video $550.00 Rental: $24.00 Preview: free

Traces the evolution of American women in this century, incorporating newsreel footage, still photographs, radio and TV footage, cartoons, and music. Intended to increase understanding and improve working relations among men and women.

1609. Space for Women
National Audiovisual Center 1981 16mm film or videocassette color 28 min
Purchase: film $240.00; video $65.00 Preview: $25.00

Focuses on the contributions being made by women in the Space Transportation System (STS) program, better known as the space shuttle. Shows women who work in jobs ranging from electrical engineer to astronaut mission specialist.

Twelve Like You. For complete citation, *see* CAREER PLANNING AND DEVELOPMENT.

1610. Very Enterprising Women
National Audiovisual Center 1980 16mm film or videocassette color 15 min
Purchase: film $130.00; video $55.00 Rental: $25.00

Presents 5 independent businesswomen who have been successful due to their energy, imagination, and hard work. Range is from market research to truck farming.

1611. Why Not a Woman?
National Audiovisual Center 1977 16mm film or videocassette color 26 min

Purchase: 16mm $165.75; video $110.00 Rental: $12.50

Shows women working successfully in nontraditional jobs like welder, carpenter, and mechanic. Explores the attitudes of their male co-workers, supervisors, personnel managers, and teachers. Demonstrates the wide range of job options and training available to girls and women.

1612. Woman as Effective Executive
Learning Consultants, Inc audiocassette learner's print materials
Purchase: $17.50

Deals with woman's breakthrough to management levels. Discusses the qualities of effective executive leadership and how to attain them while overcoming the personal and organizational roadblocks. Recording of a seminar. Features Clay Hardesty. Woman in Management Series.

1613. Woman's Place
Cally Curtis Company 16mm film or videocassette color 25 min
Purchase: film $525.00; video $500.00 Rental: $130.00 Preview: $40.00

Pays tribute to noted women of the past and celebrates that today a woman's place is everyplace. Based on material gathered for *Life* magazine's special report, "Remarkable American Women." Narrated by Julie Harris.

Women and MORe—Winning Techniques for Goal Setting. For complete citation, *see* GOALS AND GOAL SETTING.

1614. Women in Management
Martha Stuart Communications, Inc 1973 16mm film or videocassette or audiocassette color 29 min
Purchase: film $450.00; video $300.00; audio $30.00 Rental: film $65.00/day; video $50.00/day

Group discussion/interview with women executives cuts across race, age, and experience as they talk about the problems of operating in preordained hierarchies and by men's rules. They share what it is like to be a woman manager or to be working with women managers. Points out that success can be achieved without sacrificing values as women. Companion film to *Women in Middle Management.* Are You Listening Series.

1615. Women in Management: Opportunity or Tokenism?
Development Digest audiocassette
Purchase: $13.75

Describes the developmental processes occurring with respect to women in management. Provides understanding of conflicts and challenges in the organizational setting. Proposes a range of optional behaviors as an alternative to the stereotyped roles of female employees. Reviews issues involved in recruiting women for entry-level positions. Features Janice Peters and Jan Margolis.

1616. Women in Management: Threat or Opportunity?
CRM/McGraw-Hill Films 1975 16mm film or videocassette color 30 min

Purchase: $560.00   Rental: $95.00   Preview: free

Through interviews and discussions, shows how the Wayerhaeuser Lumber Company has developed successful methods for resolving dilemmas faced by both male and female employees. Indicates important measures concerned management can take to smooth the transition to nonsexist operation, to eliminate destructive stereotypes and out-dated role concepts, and to help women deal with guilt about conflicts over career goals, aggressiveness, and family responsibilities.

1617. Women in Middle Management

Martha Stuart Communications, Inc   1973   16mm film or videocassette or audiocassette   color   29 min
Purchase: film $450.00; video $300.00; audio $30.00   Rental: film $65.00/day; video $50.00/day

Women who started out at entry-level positions and are now in AT&T middle manager slots share their fears, the difficulty of transition, and how they deal with new experiences. Companion film to *Women in Management.* Are You Listening Series.

Women in the Corporation: On a Par, Not a Pedestal. For complete citation, *see* EQUAL EMPLOYMENT OPPORTUNITY.

1618. Women in the Work Force: A Manager's Role

Applied Management Institute, Inc   1980
audiocassettes
Purchase: $65.00

Records a one-day seminar led by Nicole Schapiro. Focuses on methods that bring out a woman's strengths and how to use them in communicating and managing. Includes career pathing; attitude analysis; corporate politics and fair play; supervision, management, and leadership styles; self-presentation; and communication techniques.

WORD PROCESSING

Distribution and Retention. For complete citation, *see* COMPUTERS.

1619. Generating Documents

Prentice Hall Media   1981   2 filmstrips and 2 audiocassettes   color   program guide
Purchase: $90.00

Demonstrates the ways in which documents and forms of all kinds are generated and transmitted to the word processing operator. Contains 2 modules: "Short and Major Documents and Standard Documents," and "Repetitive Documents and Forms." Word Processing Series.

1620. Introduction to Word Processing

Prentice Hall Media   1981   3 filmstrips and 3 audiocassettes   program guide
Purchase: $135.00

Traces the growth and development of word processing technology and relates it to recent trends in employment and automation. Includes "The Need for Word Processing," "Technical Developments," and "Office Automation." Word Processing Series.

1621. Keyboarding and Editing

Prentice Hall Media   1981   4 filmstrips and 4 audiocassettes   color   program guide
Purchase: $180.00

Describes basic procedures for inputting, storing, correcting, and updating different types of forms and documents including repetitive documents. Consists of 5 modules: "Keyboarding Short Documents," "Keyboarding Major Documents," "Keyboarding Forms," and "Keyboarding Repetitive Documents." Word Processing Series.

1622. Machine Transcription

HBJ Media Systems Corporation   1981   6 slide/audiocassette presentations (6 audiocassettes)   instructor's print materials; learner's print materials
Purchase: $2,885.00

Shows how to operate a transcribing machine. Outlines skills and procedures necessary for the quick and accurate transcription of business letters, interoffice memorandums, and other correspondence from recorded dictation. Suggested for 10–15 hours.

1623. Word Processing

HBJ Media Systems Corporation   1981   16mm film   color   13 min
Purchase: $595.00

Points out the various goals, procedures, and "team concept" behind word processing. Shows how a typical job progresses from its first through final stage. Illustrates various job functions and career paths in the field.

1624. Word Processing

Monad Trainer's Aide   1976   10 16mm films   color   12 min ea
Purchase: $2,750.00 ($275.00 ea)   Rental: $648.00 ($72.00 ea)   Preview: $75.00 ($15.00 ea)

Offers an overview of word processing systems: how they evolved, benefits for top management, role changes in work relationships, the need to use them appropriately, the depth of change they effect, impact on personnel management and training, and how they affect communication patterns. Shows both the benefits and problems posed.

1625. Word Processing Concepts

HBJ Media Systems Corporation   1982   6 slide/audiocassette presentations   instructor's print materials; learner's print materials
Purchase: $500.00

Offers an in-depth orientation to word processing. Shows the relationship of word processing to the "traditional" office; how it benefits a company and its employees; alternative organizational structures; capabilities of word processing equipment; and various job functions and career paths. Suggested for 9–12 hours.

1626. Word Processing: Four Phases

Thompson-Mitchell and Associates   filmstrips and audiocassettes or slides
Purchase: filmstrip $60.00; slides $100.00

Explains input, output, copy processing, and distribution. Also explores the job market for word processing specialists. Word Processing Series.

1627. Word Processing Operations
HBJ Media Systems Corporation   1982   5 slide/
audiocassette presentations   instructor's print
materials; learner's print materials
Purchase: $1,200.00

Shows the basic definitions and procedures that are relevant to
any word processing system. Introduces word processing operations. Demonstrates how to create and revise documents and
how to print, store, and file data. Suggested for 8–10 hours.

Words, Words, Words. For complete citation, *see*
WRITING.

WORK

1628. Cooperage
Centron Films   16mm film   color   17 min
Purchase: $360.00

Documentary captures the pride of workmanship of the Swee-
ney Cooperage and raises silent questions about why this
factory can operate successfully without legions of supervisors
and hordes of quality control specialists. Designed to promote
discussion about pride in one's job.

**1629. Disassemble the Assembly Line to Increase
Production**
Development Digest   audiocassette
Purchase: $13.75

Discusses basic causes of dissatisfaction among assembly line
workers. Proposes changes in our ways of thinking about people
and the work they do which will eliminate injustices imposed by
the assembly line.

**1630. Flexi-Time and Some of Its Consequences: A
Modest Structural Intervention**
Development Digest   audiocassette
Purchase: $13.75

Robert T. Golembiewski and Richard J. Hilles describe a
specific flexible workhours program and some of its effects.
Presents hard data indicators which support the claim of
positive results.

Has Job Enrichment Been Oversold? For complete
citation, *see* JOB SATISFACTION.

1631. Human Resources in the 1980's
Goodmeasure, Inc   1980   slides and
audiocassette   13 min   instructor's print materials
Purchase: $425.00   Rental: $125.00

Graphics show the fundamentals of new approaches to productivity and quality of work life. Presents facts and figures on the
new work force to show managers why new management skills
are essential to raise productivity. P/QWL Series, no. 1.

1632. In White Collar America
Films, Inc   1974   16mm film or
videocassette   color   52 min
Purchase: film $700.00; video $350.00   Rental:
$65.00

Study of the white collar world at a small insurance company in
Atlanta looks at the life styles of workers—in their jobs and at
home. Reflects the questions, joys, and frustrations in their
search for the American dream.

**Interface between Quality of Work Life and Organi-
zational Development.** For complete citation, *see*
ORGANIZATIONAL CHANGE AND
DEVELOPMENT.

1633. Management and the Work Ethic
Creative Universal, Inc   79 slides and
audiocassette
Purchase: $100.00

Explores employee values and management development. Introduces, defines, and discusses 10 indicators: value of work, time
orientation, reliance and dependence, social mobility, saving
and owning, respect for the system, leisure time activity, status
and personal worth, heroes and credos, and family and home.

1634. Nails
National Film Board of Canada   16mm film or
videocassette   color   13 min
Purchase: film $270.00; video $250.00   Rental:
$80.00   Preview: $40.00

Contrasts the solitude of an 18th-century blacksmith working
alone at his forge with the impersonal but highly efficient
machinery of today's computer-controlled mass production.
Raises questions about humanity and work, progress, and the
machine.

1635. One Small Step
Cally Curtis Company   16mm film or
videocassette   color   28 min   instructor's print
materials
Purchase: $550.00   Rental: $130.00   Preview:
$40.00

Provides useful ideas on how managers and employees can
improve their work environments through cooperation. Intended to encourage commitment to pride in work and to treating
people as they want to be treated. Features James Whitmore.

Out of Work. For complete citation, *see*
INTERVIEWING.

1636. Rules of the Game
Journal Films   1980   16mm film or
videocassette   color   19 min
Purchase: film $370.00; video $370.00   Rental:
$40.00   Preview: $40.00

Dramatizes the critical areas of work habits, business etiquette,
and recognition of the power structure. Considers the meaning
of "a day's work for a day's pay," and the responsibilities of
both employer and employee. Suggests a positive approach to
the work ethic and the role each person plays so that everyone
may benefit from improved productivity.

**1637. Where Do You Go from Here? —Installation
and Follow Up of Improvements**
National Audiovisual Center   1973   16mm
film   color   16 min
Purchase: $92.75

Reviews the techniques and procedures discussed in the Army Work Simplification series. Army Work Simplification Series.

1638. Who Does What to What? —The Work Distribution Chart
National Audiovisual Center 1973 16mm film color 11 min
Purchase: $63.75

Demonstrates the work distribution chart as a method of observing at a glance what work is actually going on in an organization.

WORK MEASUREMENT
See PRODUCTIVITY

WRITING
See also COMMUNICATION; LANGUAGE

1639. Basic Report Writing
National Audiovisual Center 1977 16mm film or videocassette color 28 min learner's print materials
Purchase: film $162.50; video $110.25 Rental: $12.50

Shows practical methods for writing better reports. Identifies report writing skills and techniques employees need to aid the decision-making process through 3 types of reports: formal, semi-formal, and informal. You in Public Service Series.

1640. Business Report Series
Edutronics/McGraw-Hill 6 audiocassettes instructor's print materials; learner's print materials
Purchase: $296.50 ($52.50 ea) Other cost factors: additional printed materials available separately

Six audio-tutorial modules offer presentations and practice for deciding on the types and uses of reports, using research sources and techniques, selecting and organizing information, and writing and illustrating reports. Modules may be ordered separately.

1641. Business Writing skills
Resources for Education and Management, Inc 1970 5 videocassettes or slides and audiocassettes or 5 filmstrips or 5 filmstrip cartridges color instructor's print materials
Purchase: video $305.00 ($75.00 ea); filmstrips $280.00 ($64.00 ea); filmstrip cartridges $425.00 ($85.00 ea);slides $295.00 ($67.00 ea) Preview: $20.00 ea

Offers simple techniques for speeding and improving business writing and includes practical exercises. Emphasizes sound organization, clarity, and simplicity. Covers business letter writing, reports, and memos. Recommended for use with Dugan Laird's *Writing for Results.*

Business Writing Skills for Secretaries. For complete citation, *see* SECRETARIAL SKILLS.

1642. Communications Skills for Secretaries
American Management Associations 6 audiocassettes learner's print materials
Purchase: $145.00 Other cost factors: AMA members $135.00; discounts available for bulk orders

Presents proven principles of good letter writing. Emphasizes clear and concise writing. Suggests right psychological approach for special requests or communicating bad news. Includes communications process, letter and memo formats, effective writing style, listening and speaking skills, telephone skills, nonverbals, meeting techniques, presentations, and special secretarial skills.

1643. Effective Writing for Executives
Time-Life Video 1980 6 videocassettes color 30 min ea instructor's print materials; learner's print materials
Purchase: $3,950.00 Rental: $500.00 Preview: free

Offers principles that apply to all business writing. Includes how to define objectives, develop well-organized ideas, use effective language, and edit and condense. For group or self-study. Features Ed Asner.

1644. Feelings—A Way to Better Letter Writing
National Audiovisual Center 1980 16mm film or videocassette color 11 min
Purchase: film $95.00; video $55.00 Rental: $25.00

Uses a humorous approach to present techniques that can help those responsible for correspondence. Urges a letter writing style that is clear, understandable, and to the point.

1645. How to Improve Writing Skills
Singer Management Institute 1981 40 slides and 2 audiocassettes learner's print materials; transparencies
Purchase: $195.00

Designed to help employees learn how to organize and express their ideas, expectations, requirements, and needs in effective writing. Points out the importance of identifying the audience and purpose, using inductive and deductive reasoning, and overcoming writing roadblocks.

1646. Improving Basic Job Skills
Singer Management Institute 1978 7 filmstrips and audiocassette 15 min ea
Purchase: filmstrips $30.00 ea

Intended to sharpen employee skills in basic communications. Separate filmstrip modules cover "Ten Steps to Good Spelling," "Word Parts and Spelling Rules," "Building Spelling Skills," "Spelling Demons," "Writing a Business Letter," "Writing Messages and Directions," and "Filling Out Forms."

1647. Language Skills for Transcription
HBJ Media Systems Corporation 1981 10 audiocassettes instructor's print materials; learner's print materials
Purchase: $2,380.00

Illustrates points of grammar, punctuation, and style essential for accurate transcription. Suggested for 15–20 hours.

1648. Letter Writing at Work
Roundtable Films, Inc   16mm film or videocassette   color   19 min
Purchase: $425.00   Rental: $85.00   Preview: $30.00   Other cost factors: learner's workbook *Modern Business Letter* available separately

Reviews basic letter writing skills for all employees—managers, supervisors, clerical, and technical personnel—who write letters as part of their jobs. Shows how a business letter can be made to fulfill its 2 main functions: as a messenger and as an ambassador.

1649. Now, That's a Report!
Roundtable Films, Inc   16mm film   color   28 min   learner's print materials
Purchase: $475.00   Rental: $85.00   Preview: $30.00

Dramatization is of young executive asked to write a report. Shows how to write more effective reports through an organized 4-step method of investigation, planning, writing, and revision. Explains the purpose, scope, objectives, and essential qualities of a written report.

1650. Power Writing
Learn, Inc   4 audiocassettes   learner's print materials
Purchase: $99.95   Other cost factors: trainer's guide $49.95; classroom learning unit $49.95

Concentrates on developing a system for converting thought into an effective exchange of ideas. Uses writing assignment exercises directly related to job responsibilities. Objective analysis exercises develop skills in analyzing the letters, memos, and reports of others. Competency-based.

1651. Put It in Writing
International Writing Institute, Inc   1972   6 slide sets and 6 audiocassettes   30 min   instructor's print materials; learner's print materials
Purchase: $1,427.50

Emphasizes the importance of clarity, organization, courtesy, and speed. Focuses on building these skills with audiovisual and written exercises. Deals with reports, letters, procedures or memos, and technical writing.

1652. Spelling
Educational Research Associates   8 audiocassettes
Purchase: $133.00   Other cost factors: student syllabus $6.65; teacher's key $3.35; tests and key $3.10

A concentrated, yet detailed, review of spelling primarily through a phonetic approach, rather than a rule approach. Includes audio, kinesthetic, cognitive, and visual stimuli.

Word Power Success Program. For complete citation, *see* LANGUAGE.

1653. Words, Words, Words
Training House, Inc   6 audiocassettes   instructor's print materials; learner's print materials
Purchase: $500.00 (for 10 learners)

Offers exercises to diagnose and build word processing skills. Includes proofreading, typing and layout of handwritten copy, and transcribing and editing dictation. Intended for secretaries and others responsible for written communication. For group or self-study. Suggested as a 24–36 hour program.

1654. Writing Better Letters in Business
Teaching Aids, Inc   10 audiocassettes   learner's print materials
Purchase: $113.00

Presents essential and basic business letter writing skills. Outlines the 4 universal objectives of letters and the 3 requirements of successful letters. Shows basic steps of planning and organizing letters. Stresses the importance of timing letters.

1655. Writing for Results
Time-Life Video   1980   6 videocassettes   color   30 min ea   learner's print materials
Purchase: $3,500.00   Rental: $500.00   Preview: $500.00

Shows how the organization of one's ideas and the use of effective language are critical components in the process of effective writing. Video and print materials are used interactively, paced by the user through drills and exercises after the concepts have been explained and examples shown. Features Ed Asner. Effective Writing for Executives Series, no. 1.

1656. Writing for Work
Time-Life Video   7 videocassettes   color   30 min ea   instructor's print materials
Purchase: $3,950.00   Rental: $500.00   Preview: free

Offers fundamentals of business writing. Introduces tools of writing and how to convey meaning through sentences and paragraphs. Shows how tone and style are important to accomplish a purpose. Intended for first-time supervisors, secretaries, and administrative assistants. Features Cicely Tyson.

1657. Writing Letters that Get Results
Roundtable Films, Inc   16mm film or videocassette   color   28 min
Purchase: $400.00   Rental: $85.00   Preview: $30.00

Discusses and illustrates the principles and techniques of writing effective business letters. Filmed interview with Waldo J. Marra points out that the objectives of letterwriting are to create interest, to present facts and figures, and to stimulate action by making clear the purpose of the letter.

1658. Writing Reports that Work
AMACOM   audiocassettes   learner's print materials
Purchase: $50.00   Other cost factors: AMA members $45.00

Presents important aspects of good report writing including how to select the most effective words, use basic sentence patterns and paragraphs, bridge ideas, write a first draft, edit, proofread, and polish the final draft.

1659. Writing Sense: A Skill-Building Course for Managers
AMACOM   5 audiocassettes   1 hr ea   instructor's print materials; learner's print materials
Purchase: $95.00 per set

Emphasizes word use, sentence structure, and editing. Suggested for a 17-hour program for new and experienced managers. For group or self-study.

1660. Written Communication

National Audiovisual Center   1977   16mm
film   color   28 min   workbook
Purchase: $162.50   Rental: $12.50

Concentrates on organization, style and language in letters, forms, memos, and reports. You in Public Service Series.

List of Represented Producers/Distributors

Addison-Wesley Publishing Company, Inc
Business and Professional Division
Reading, MA 01867
(617) 944-3700

Advance Learning Systems
Central Building
Seattle, WA 98104
(206) 223-1281

Advantage Media
11312 Santa Monica Blvd
Los Angeles, CA 90025
(213) 477-6538

Aerospace Education Foundation
1750 Pennsylvania Avenue, NW
Washington, DC 20006
(202) 637-3300

Affective House
4420 South Columbia
Tulsa, OK 74135
(918) 743-8264

AMACOM
135 West 50th Street
New York, NY 10020
(212) 586-8100

American Educational Films
162 4th Avenue North
Nashville, TN 37219
(615) 242-3330

American Federation of Labor and
Congress of Industrial Organizations
815 16th Street, NW
Washington, DC 20006
(202) 637-5000

American Hospital Association
840 North Lake Shore Drive
Chicago, IL 60611
(312) 280-6000

American Learning Systems, Inc
PO Box 18623
Memphis, TN 38118
(901) 365-3960

American Management Associations
135 West 50th Street
New York, NY 10020
(212) 586-8100

American Media, Inc
1454 30th Street
West Des Moines, IA 50265
(515) 224-0919

American Salesmasters, Inc
7150 East Hampton Avenue
Denver, CO 80224
(303) 758-1818

AMR International, Inc
79 Madison Avenue
New York, NY 10016
(800) 223-6787

A.N.A. Audio Visual Committee
155 East 44th Street
New York, NY 10017
(212) 697-5950

Andragogy Press
PO Box 5690
Austin, TX 78763

Applied Management Institute, Inc
623 Great Jones Street
Fairfield, CA 94533
(707) 422-6822

Applied Management Science, Inc
3740 IDS Tower
Minneapolis, MN 55402
(612) 338-0501

Association for Computer Machinery
111 West 42nd Street
New York, NY 10036
(212) 869-7440

Association for Educational Communications and Technology
1201 16th Street, NW
Washington, DC 20036
(202) 833-4180

Audio-Forum
Room 200
96 Broad Street
Guilford, CT 06437
(203) 453-9794

Barr Films
PO Box 5667
3490 East Foothill Boulevard
Pasadena, CA 91107
(213) 793-6153
(800) 423-4483

BNA Communications, Inc
9417 Decoverly Hall Road
Rockville, MD 20850
(301) 948-0540

Boeing Computer Services Company
PO Box 24346
Mail Stop 9A90
Seattle, WA 98124
(206) 575-7700

Bruno Associates
5811 Santa Catalina Avenue
Garden Grove, CA 92645
(714) 897-8204

Bureau of Business Practice
24 Rope Ferry Road
Waterford, CT 06386
(203) 442-4365
(800) 243-0876

Butler Learning Systems
1325 West Dorothy Lane
Dayton, OH 45409
(513) 298-7462

Cally Curtis Company
1111 North Las Palmas Avenue
Hollywood, CA 90038
(213) 467-1101

Carlocke/Langden, Inc
4122 Main Street
Dallas, TX 75226
(214) 826-9380

Carousel Films, Inc
1501 Broadway
New York, NY 10036
(212) 354-0315

Center for the Management of Professional and Scientific Work
226 West 1060 South
Orem, UT 84057
(801) 224-8522

Centron Films
1621 West 9th
Lawrence, KS 66044
(913) 843-0400

Chamber of Commerce of the United
    States
1615 H Street, NW
Washington, DC 20062
(202) 659-6183

Charles E. Merrill Publishing Company
1300 Alum Creek Drive
Columbus, OH 43216
(614) 258-8441

Classroom World Productions
PO Box 28167
22 Glenwood Avenue
Raleigh, NC 27611
(800) 334-4373

Continental Film Productions
PO Box 526
4220 Amnicola Highway
Chattanooga, TN 37406
(615) 622-1193

Creative Curriculum, Inc
15681 Commerce Lane
Huntington Beach, CA 92649
(714) 898-2658

Creative Media
820 Keosauqua Way
Des Moines, IA 50309
(515) 244-3610

Creative Universal, Inc
21700 Northwestern Highway
Southfield, MI 48075
(313) 557-4100

Creative Venture Films
PO Box 599
Springhouse, PA 19477

CRM/McGraw-Hill Films
PO Box 641
674 Via de la Valle
Del Mar, CA 92014
(619) 453-5000

Dartnell
4660 Ravenswood Avenue
Chicago, IL 60640
(312) 561-4000

Development Digest
PO Box 2337
Valdosta, GA 31601

Development Publications
5605 Lamar Road
Bethesda, MD 20816
(301) 320-4409

Dialogue Systems, Inc
770 Broadway
New York, NY 10003
(212) 475-3900

Didactic Systems, Inc
Box 457
Cranford, NJ 07016
(201) 789-2194

Document Associates
211 East 43rd Street
New York, NY 10017
(212) 682-0730

Drake Beam Morin
277 Park Avenue
New York, NY 10172
(212) 888-2800

Eastman Kodak Company
343 State Street
Rochester, NY 14651
(716) 724-3667

Educational Research Associates
333 Southwest Park
Portland, OR 97205
(503) 228-6345

Educational Resources Foundation
2712 Millwood Avenue, Drawer L
Columbia, SC 29250
(800) 845-8822
(800) 254-0326

Edupac, Inc
231 Norfolk Street
Walpole, MA 02081
(617) 668-7746

Edutronics/McGraw-Hill
PO Box 10003
Overland Park, KS 66210
(800) 255-6324

EFM Films
85 Main Street
Watertown, MA 02172
(800) 225-3215

Employment Training Corporation
300 Central Park West
New York, NY 10024
(212) 595-7682

Exec-U-Service Associates
PO Box 2214
Princeton, NJ 08540
(609) 924-2828

Filmasters, Inc
410 First Avenue
Pittsburgh, PA 15219

Films, Inc
733 Green Bay Road
Wilmette, IL 60091
(312) 256-3200
(800) 323-4222

General Cassette Corporation
Box 6940
1324 North 22nd Avenue
Phoenix, AZ 85005
(602) 269-3111

General Motors Corporation
1700 West Third Avenue
Flint, MI 48502
(313) 762-9867
(800) 521-5850

Goodmeasure, Inc
PO Box 3004
330 Broadway
Cambridge, MA 02139
(617) 492-2714

Guidelines Press
1307 South Killian Drive
Lake Park, FL 33403
(305) 842-9411

Harris International, Ltd
2702 Costabelle Drive
La Jolla, CA 92037
(619) 453-2271

Hartley Film Foundation
Cat Rock Road
Cos Cob, CT 06807
(203) 869-1818

Hass-Haus Productions
2112 Mississippi Street
La Crosse, WI 54601

HBJ Media Systems Corporation
757 Third Avenue
New York, NY 10164
(212) 888-2145

Human Productivity Institute, Inc
1647C Lombard Street
San Francisco, CA 94123
(415) 775-5904

Human Resources Development
20 Guliard Street
Greene, NY 13778

Ibis Media
Box 308
Pleasantville, NY 10570
(914) 747-0177

Idea Development Associates
PO Box 167
Palo Alto, CA 94302
(415) 329-8051

Instructional Dynamics, Inc
666 North Lake Shore Drive
Chicago, IL 60611
(312) 943-1200

International Association of Machinists
    and Aerospace Workers
Machinists Building
1300 Connecticut Avenue
Washington, DC 20036
(202) 857-5200

International Film Bureau, Inc
332 South Michigan Avenue
Chicago, IL 60604
(312) 427-4545

International Training Consultants, Inc
PO Box 3213
Richmond, VA 23235
(804) 320-2415
(804) 794-9429

International Writing Institute, Inc
Hanna Building
Cleveland, OH 44115
(216) 696-4032

Journal Films
930 Pitner Avenue
Evanston, IL 60202
(312) 328-6700

Lansford Publishing Company, Inc
PO Box 8711
1088 Lincoln Avenue
San Jose, CA 95155
(408) 287-3105

LCA Video/Films
1350 Avenue of the Americas
New York, NY 10019
(212) 397-9360

Leadership Catalysts, Inc
903 Edgewood Lane
Cinnaminson, NJ 08077
(609) 786-0695

Learn, Inc
113 Gaither Drive
Mount Laurel, NJ 08054
(609) 234-6100

Learncom, Inc
113 Union Wharf East
Boston, MA 02109
(617) 523-4160

Learning Consultants, Inc
6600 North Lincoln Avenue
Lincolnwood, IL 60645
(312) 677-7116

Learning Dynamics
PO Box 323
Needham, MA 02192
(617) 332-7070

Learning Resources Corporation
PO Box 26240
8517 Production Avenue
San Diego, CA 92126
(714) 578-5900

Lee Boyan and Associates
11813 Crawford Road West
Minnetonka, MN 55343
(612) 938-5904

Management Decision Systems, Inc
108 Old Kings Highway North
Darien, CT 06820
(203) 655-4414

Management Programs
PO Box 72
Glen Ellyn, IL 60137
(312) 469-1719

Management Resources, Inc
155 East 56th Street
New York, NY 10022
(212) 935-4800

Manpower Education Institute
127 East 35th Street
New York, NY 10016
(212) 532-4747

Martha Stuart Communications, Inc
PO Box 246
2 Anthony Street
Hillsdale, NY 12529
(518) 325-3900

Maynard Management Institute
201 South College Street
Charlotte, NC 28244
(704) 376-3584

MBO, Inc
PO Box 10
157 Pontoosic Road
Westfield, MA 01086
(413) 568-1369

Measurable Performance Systems
5501 West North Avenue
Milwaukee, WI 53208
(414) 444-5747

Media Guild
PO Box 881
118 South Acacia
Solana Beach, CA 92075
(714) 755-9191

Monad Trainer's Aide
663 Fifth Avenue
New York, NY 10022
(212) 352-2314
(212) 355-5633

MOR Associates
8022 San Dimas Circle
Buena Park, CA 90622
(714) 995-1244

Motivational Media
6855 Santa Monica Boulevard
Los Angeles, CA 30038
(213) 465-3168

Motivision, Ltd
2 Beechwood Road
Hartsdale, NY 10530
(914) 684-0110

MTI Teleprograms, Inc
3710 Commercial Avenue
Northbrook, IL 60062
(312) 291-9400
(800) 323-5343

National Audiovisual Center
Washington, DC 20409
(301) 763-1896

National Educational Media, Inc
21601 Devonshire Street
Chatsworth, CA 91311
(213) 709-6009

National Film Board of Canada
1251 Avenue of the Americas
New York, NY 10020
(212) 586-5131

National Fire Protection Association
470 Atlantic Avenue
Boston, MA 02210
(617) 482-8755

Nation's Business
Executive Seminar in Sound Division
1615 H Street, NW
Washington, DC 20062

Negotiation Institute, Inc
230 Park Avenue
New York, NY 10169
(212) 986-5557

Nightingale-Conant Corporation
3730 West Devon Avenue
Chicago, IL 60659
(312) 677-3100

NPL, Inc
1926 West Gray
Houston, TX 77019
(713) 527-9300

Organization Development Consultants
522 South Washington Street
Naperville, IL 60540
(312) 420-7673

Organizational Dynamics
16 New England Executive Park
Burlington, MA 01803
(617) 272-8040

PCI
626 Justin Avenue
Glendale, CA 91201
(213) 956-3770

Penton/IPC Education Division
614 Superior Avenue West
Cleveland, OH 44113
(216) 696-0300

Phoenix Films, Inc
468 Park Avenue South
New York, NY 10016
(212) 684-5910

Phoenix-BFA Films and Video, Inc
468 Park Avenue South
New York, NY 10016
(212) 684-5910
(800) 221-1274

Practical Management Associates, Inc
6910 Owensmouth
Canoga Park, CA 91303
(213) 348-9101
(800) 423-5099

Prentice Hall Media
150 White Plains Road
Tarrytown, NY 15091
(914) 631-8300
(800) 431-2266

Prismatron Productions, Inc
155 Buena Vista Avenue
Mill Valley, CA 94941
(415) 383-0449

Professional Development, Inc
2915 Terminal Tower
Cleveland, OH 44113
(216) 781-0169

Professional Resources
PO Box 33197
Raleigh, NC 27606
(919) 833-1121

Pyramid Films
Box 1048
Santa Monica, CA 90406
(213) 828-7577
(800) 421-2304

Q.E.D. Information Sciences, Inc
PO Box 181
141 Linden Street
Wellesley, MA 02181
(617) 237-5656

R. Fischer Olson & Associates, Inc
Woodland Cedar Lane
Ossining, NY 10562
(914) 941-3064

Racism/Sexism Resource Center for
   Educators
1841 Broadway
New York, NY 10023
(212) 757-5339

Ramic Productions
Department 485
4910 Birch Street
Newport Beach, CA 92660
(714) 833-2444
(800) 854-0223

Reinforcement Learning, Inc
PO Box 563
87 Dimmig Road
Upper Saddle River, NJ 07458
(201) 327-8091

Research Media, Inc
4D Midland Avenue
Hicksville, NY 11801

Research Press
PO Box 317720
Champaign, IL 61820
(217) 352-3273

Resources for Education and Management, Inc
544 Medlock Road
Decatur, GA 30030
(404) 373-7743
(404) 373-1956

ROA Films
1696 North Astor Street
Milwaukee, WI 53202
(414) 271-0861
(800) 558-9015

Roundtable Films, Inc
113 North San Vincente Boulevard
Beverly Hills, CA 90211
(213) 657-1402

Salenger Educational Media
1635 12th Street
Santa Monica, CA 90404
(213) 450-1300

Sandy Corporation
16025 Northland Drive
Southfield, MI 48037
(313) 569-4000

Schrello Associates
PO Box 1610
555 East Ocean Boulevard
Long Beach, CA 90801
(213) 437-2234

Schwan-STABILO
6522 Northside Circle, Suite 10
North Fort Myers, FL 33903
(813) 997-1155

Science Research Associates
155 North Wacker Drive
Chicago, IL 60606
(312) 984-2000
(800) 621-0664

Singer Management Institute
1345 Diversey Parkway
Chicago, IL 60614
(312) 525-1500
(800) 621-1900

S&L Communications, Inc
408 West 14th
Austin, TX 78701
(512) 974-6235

Society of Manufacturing Engineers
Technical Division
PO Box 930
Dearborn, MI 48128
(313) 271-1500

Southerby Productions, Inc
PO Box 15403
Long Beach, CA 90815

Spectrum Films
2785 Roosevelt Street
Carlsbad, CA 92008
(714) 729-3552

Tampa Manufacturing Institute
91 Shell Point Building
6300 Flotilla Drive
Holmes Beach, FL 33510
(813) 778-4722

Tape Rental Library
One Cassette Center
Covesville, VA 22931
(804) 293-3705

Teaching Aids, Inc
PO Box 1798
Costa Mesa, CA 92626
(714) 548-5529

Teleometrics International
1755 Woodstead Court
The Woodlands, TX 77380
(713) 367-0060

Thompson-Mitchell and Associates
3384 Peachtree Road, NE
Atlanta, GA 30326
(404) 233-5435

Time Management Center
PO Box 5
3773 Omaha SW
Grandville, MI 49418
(616) 531-1870
(800) 325-8259

Time-Life Video
Time & Life Building
Rockefeller Center
New York, NY 10020
(212) 841-4209
(800) 526-4663

Training by Design
516 Fifth Avenue
New York, NY 10036
(212) 759-5745

Training House, Inc
PO Box 3090
Princeton, NJ 08540
(609) 452-1505

Twentieth Century-Fox Video, Inc
23705 Industrial Park Drive
Farmington Hills, MI 48024
(313) 477-6066

Tylie Jones
10718 Riverside Drive
North Hollywood, CA 91602
(213) 980-7300

University Associates
PO Box 26240
8517 Production Avenue
San Diego, CA 92126
(714) 578-5900
(800) 854-2143

Van De Water Associates, Inc
7914 Jason Avenue
Canoga Park, CA 91304
(213) 883-5992

Vantage Communications, Inc
PO Box 546
Nyack, NY 10960
(914) 358-0147

Video Arts, Inc
3325 Wilshire Boulevard, Suite 700
Los Angeles, CA 90010
(213) 487-0457

Videocenters
1401 Madison Street
Seattle, WA 98104
(206) 323-8583

Visual Instruction Productions
295 West 4th Street
New York, NY 10014
(212) 924-3935

Washington Film Company
122 Willmont Avenue
Cumberland, MD 21502
(301) 724-3100

WMI Corporation
1309 114th Avenue, SE
Bellevue, MA 98004
(206) 455-2323

Xerox Education Publications
245 Long Hill Road
Middletown, CT 06457
(203) 347-7251

Xerox Learning Systems
PO Box 10211
1600 Summer Street
Stanford, CT 06904
(203) 965-8400

Xicom-Video Arts
Sterling Forest
Tuxedo, NY 10987
(212) 989-2676
(800) 431-2395

Producer/Distributor Index

Title Index

ISBN 0-89774-065-3